The Allied Resupply Effort in the
China-Burma-India Theater
During World War II

The Allied Resupply Effort in the China-Burma-India Theater During World War II

LEO J. DAUGHERTY III

McFarland & Company, Inc., Publishers
Jefferson, North Carolina, and London

LIBRARY OF CONGRESS CATALOGUING-IN-PUBLICATION DATA

Daugherty, Leo J.
    The allied resupply effort in the China-Burma-India Theater during World War II / Leo J. Daugherty III.
       p.   cm.
    Includes bibliographical references and index.

    ISBN 978-0-7864-3137-3
    softcover : 50# alkaline paper ∞

    1. World War, 1939–1945 — Transportation — Burma. 2. World War, 1939–1945 — Transportation — China. 3. World War, 1939–1945 — Transportation — India. 4. World War, 1939–1945 — Equipment and supplies — Burma. 5. World War, 1939–1945 — Equipment and supplies — China. 6. World War, 1939–1945 — Equipment and supplies — India. 7. World War, 1939–1945 — Personal narratives. 8. World War, 1939–1945 — Aerial operations. I. Title.
D810.T8D34   2008
940.54'25 — dc22   2007038833

British Library cataloguing data are available

©2008 Leo J. Daugherty III. All rights reserved

No part of this book may be reproduced or transmitted in any form or by any means, electronic or mechanical, including photocopying or recording, or by any information storage and retrieval system, without permission in writing from the publisher.

On the cover: A Curtiss C-46 in flight; T/Sgt Kenneth Quigley with other members of the 187th Composite Chemical Company; the patch of the 4th Combat Cargo Command

Manufactured in the United States of America

McFarland & Company, Inc., Publishers
  Box 611, Jefferson, North Carolina 28640
    www.mcfarlandpub.com

To the pilots, flight crews, maintenance personnel, engineers, quartermasters, and support personnel who fought in the forgotten theater of World War II: Your sacrifices contributed to victory in 1945 and beyond

Acknowledgments

The writing of this book has been one of the most challenging though one of the most invigorating projects this author has ever undertaken. Fortunately, the process was made much easier by the veterans interviewed, the guidance I was graciously given by my advisors at The Ohio State University, the support from my family and friends, and above all by the commitment to tell the story of those daring young men who fought their war in the skies over China-Burma-India (CBI), along the roadways of Iran, China, Burma, and India, and sweated in the maintenance sheds and shops of India and China.

Of those daring young men, without the assistance of Captains David C. Hall and Edward Goodman, Platoon Sergeant Robert Boehm, Corporals Anthony Silva, Jr., Corporal Alexander N. McVean, and Technical Sergeant Kenneth R. Quigley, this project would never have been possible. Secondly, the author would like to thank Mrs. Jan Theis of the Hump Pilots Association for providing the many newsletters and accounts of the air war over Burma and China. Mrs. Theis might recall a phone call from a young Ph.D. student who "wanted to know about the China-Burma-India theater." Later that summer, in 1995, the mailman arrived with about three large bundles of newsletters from the Hump Pilots Association that to this day are an important part of my ever-growing library on CBI. These newsletters have served to foster a love of an important theater of war that has been sadly ignored and in most cases forgotten. Thanks also go out to Major Walter T. Caro, U.S. Army (Ret.), who put the author in touch with T/Sgt Quigley; my aunt and uncle, Johnny and Mary Ann Poslosky, and friend of the family, Vince Taluto, for their assistance in interviewing the late Alexander McVean; to Robert and Terry Boehm, my brother-in-law and sister, for their help in interviewing Platoon Sergeant Robert Boehm; I might add that while interviewing Mr. Boehm, this author could only keep thinking back to the movie *The Mountain Road* about an Army engineer officer sent to China to blow up bridges in order to prevent the Japanese from advancing deeper into China. Sergeant Boehm actually experienced this during the course of the war. Thanks to my parents, Leo and Frances H. Daugherty, and Mary Goodman, for their assistance during the interviews with Captains David Hall and Ed Goodman; and finally, for the assistance and commentary of Corporal Anthony Silva and his wife, Marie, during my visit with him in Spring Hill, Florida.

Thank you to my advisors at Ohio State University, Professor (Colonel) Allan

R. Millett, Ph.D.; Williamson S. Murray, Ph.D.; David Stebbene, Ph.D.; Sam Chu, Ph.D.; Alam Payind, Ph.D.; John F. Guilmartin, Ph.D.; and Michael Hogan, Ph.D. I would also like to thank my advisors at John Carroll University including the late Rev. Donald W. Smythe, S.J.; the late Rev. Howard Kerner, S.J.; William J. Ulrich, Ph.D.; George J. Prpic, Ph.D.; Michael S. Pap, Ph.D.; Wallace J. Kosinski, Ph.D., Marianne Morton, Ph.D.; Kate Howard, Ph.D.; the late Rev. Howard F. Mitzel, S.J.; and Josephine Cerepowicz, Ph.D., and Professor Richard Gildrie at Austin Peay State University; to a very lovely lady and my future wife, Dr. Rhonda Smith, assistant professor of history at Alice Lloyd College; my commanding officers in the Marine Corps Mobilization and Training Unit 7, Colonels Dennis Mroczkowski, Reed Bonadonna, Nicholas E. Reynolds; and Majors Thomas Crecca, Luke Kratky, and Alexander Durr. Without all of you, I could never have been the scholar and historian I am today. To Doris Chang, Ph.D., assistant professor of women's studies, Wichita State University, who constantly reminded me that the writing of this book was more than just an obligation but a necessity given my deep interest in CBI; Chris Ives, Ph.D.; David C. Brown, a long-time friend and mentor from the Breckinridge (later Navy) Library at Marine Corps Base, Quantico, Virginia; to Colonel David H. Gurney, USMC (Ret.), the editor of *Joint Forces Quarterly*, and the members of his very able staff, including Calvin B. Kelley; to several very special friends who have been among my strongest supporters: Mary Lynn Kiacz, M.D.; Bradley M. Welling, M.D., Ph.D.; two very special ladies, Brenda Adkins and Mary French of Ohio State University Hospitals; to my many students at the Ohio State Lima Campus, between 2001 and 2003, who knew of their teacher's deep interest in this theater of operations when he lectured on the war in CBI. I would like to single out a few of them: Susan Chartrand, John Roberts, Derek Dunson, Matt Ream, Ericka Leary, Mary Beth Hartoon, Jessica Biddinger, Melody Kramer, Jamie L. Evans, and Adam J. Rohrbaugh. You and the others made it worth all the effort.

Thanks to the command group and staff at the U.S. Army Accessions Command, including Lieutenant Generals Robert L. Van Antwerp, Benjamin C. Freakley and Dennis D. Cavin; Brigadier General Dennis E. Rogers; Command Sergeants Major Perry L. Roberts and Dennis E. King; Colonels Kevin Shwedo, Paul J. Reoyo, David Glover, Harry C. Hardy, and "Chip" Martin; Lieutenant Colonels Roy S. Brown, Pete Baidon, Daniel P. Dillon, and Michael S. McGurk; Major Terry Love; Captain Andy Peiper; Dr. Susan Canedy, Dr. Steve Anders, Dr. J. Britt McCarley, Carolyn Reynolds, Keli Slusher, Rick Hartline, Joseph Alred, William J. Guillaume, Leslie R. Bulger, Max Padilla, B. J. Hewitt, Trudy Kelly, John Char, Gene Adams, Chris Mack, M.G. Williams, Robert Burns, Robert Jones, Tom Brooks, Bill Copeland, Pat McAndrews, James Larsen, Ben King, Roger Yelverton, Fay Allen, Francine Allen, Mike Swisher, Mary Hall, Gary Lewis, Dr. Alan Phillips, Bonnie Morelen, Agnes Pettyjohn, Delores Mitchell, Major David McCoy, Captain Scott M. Smiley, Rodney White, Romelin Adams, Lee Phillips, SFC's Craig Johnson, Mike Menapace and Mark Mounce; SSG Jodi Carter; Genoa Stanford and Terri Boscia at the U.S. Army Infantry School's Donovan Library, Fort Benning, Georgia.

Contents

Acknowledgments vii

Preface 1

1. "Feeding the Tiger": Background to the War in China-Burma-India, 1941–1945 — 3

2. "Many Mountain Roads": Platoon Sergeant Robert Boehm, U.S. Army Quartermaster Corps — 24

3. Captain Edward M. Goodman, USAAF: "Flying the Aluminum Trail" — 47

4. Captain David C. Hall, U.S. Army Air Forces, and the 4th Combat Cargo Command — 63

5. "A Most Impressive Engineering Achievement in War": Corporal Alexander McVean's War Along the Burma Road, 1944–1945 — 105

6. "A Chemical Company to the Front": Technical Sergeant Kenneth R. Quigley, 1943–1945 — 141

7. "Keep 'em Flying": Corporal Anthony R. Silva, U.S. Army Air Forces, In-Flight & Ground Maintenance Support in China-Burma-India, 1944–1945 — 154

8. "Road Builders and Jungle Warriors": African-American Soldiers and the War in China-Burma-India and the Southwest Pacific Area of Operations, 1941–1945 — 181

9. "The Forgotten Theater of World War II": Reflections of Service in China-Burma-India, 1941–1945 — 198

Appendix 1: Table of Organization of the 516th Quartermaster Truck Regiment, Tehran, Iran, 1942–1944   243

Appendix 2: Observations of Ground Search Party Investigating Wrecks of C-47s #812 and #767   244

Chapter Notes   247

Bibliography   261

Index   267

Preface

Writing this book has been one of the more challenging tasks this author has ever attempted. Initially discouraged from writing on a topic that had, to quote one professor, "minimal military value," I have instead found it to be a theater that had significant military value for it laid the foundation of the United States' ability to conduct large-scale airlift operations in such places as Korea and Vietnam, Kuwait, Bosnia, Iraq and Afghanistan. Indeed, the China-Burma-India theater was the incubator of airlift operations that are today commonplace in the U.S. Armed Forces. The effort put forth in the "forgotten theater" served as the foundation of our victory on the Asian mainland during World War II over Japan. Without the efforts of the men discussed below, Japan's conquest of Southeast Asia (and possibly Southwest Asia) might have gone unchecked.

The experiences of the men covered in this study serve as an excellent cross section of the effort put forth by the United States in the China-Burma-India theater. The CBI theater was not, as Captain David Hall, a pilot who flew C-46 transports over the Himalayas from 1944 to 1945, stated, "the ass end of the war." In fact, as the record indicated, the United States' air and logistical effort in CBI grew in the period after the August 1943 Quadrant Conference in Quebec between the Combined Join Chiefs of Staff, as is evidenced by the fact that all of the men interviewed in the pages that follow entered the CBI theater after 1943.

The Quadrant Conference did not end the opposition to President Roosevelt's policy of keeping Chiang Kai-shek in the war against Japan. As Prime Minister Winston Churchill noted in his postwar history of the Second World War, that while in agreement with the basic strategy to keep Chiang-shek and China in the war, he argued (unsuccessfully) that the "enormous expenditure of manpower and material would not be worthwhile ... [though] ... we [the British Chiefs of Staff] ... never succeeded in deflecting the Americans from their purpose."[1]

Indeed, despite the opposition of the British, who saw the war in CBI as a diversion from the real effort against Nazi Germany on the European continent, and to a lesser degree in the war against Japan in the South and Central

Pacific areas, the American Joint Chiefs of Staff remained "undaunted" in their determination to keep China in the war. As Churchill stated, he and the British Chiefs of Staff were never successful in "deflecting the Americans from their purpose" in the CBI theater.[2] The prime minister emphasized that the main reason the Americans could not be dissuaded from this large undertaking on behalf of Chiang Kai-shek, leader of the Nationalist Chinese, had to do with the very nature of the Americans, who Churchill noted were "obstinate" in the belief that a combined aerial resupply effort coupled with the re-opening of the Burma Road into China would be able to ferry enough aviation fuel and bombs to maintain pressure on the Japanese on the Asian mainland. Churchill believed that the American desire to expand the aerial and overland resupply efforts had more to do with ego than with military practicality. In fact, he noted that for the Americans, "the bigger the Idea, the more wholeheartedly they threw themselves into making it a success." For Churchill and the British chiefs of the Imperial General Staff, the successes (and failures) of the American pilots, crewmen, engineers, quartermasters, and combat troops were due more to the American "can do" attitude than anything else.

The accounts that follow are the stories of the men who carried out the laborious effort to "feed the tiger," facilitating the defeat of Imperial Japan on the Asian mainland. Indeed, for men such as Dave Hall, Ed Goodman, Robert Boehm, Anthony Silva, Alexander McVean, and Kenneth Quigley, the effort in CBI was more than just about national ego or pride; instead, it was more about survival in a harsh, unforgiving environment against an enemy who gave no quarter nor expected any. This is the story about one of the most important theaters of World War II that had been long neglected in the literature of World War II: the China-Burma-India theater. More importantly, this book is about the men who fought, worked, and died in some of the most appalling conditions men have been called to fight in.

Chapter 1

"Feeding the Tiger": Background to the War in China-Burma-India, 1941–1945

The China-Burma-India (CBI) theater was undoubtedly the most politicized of all the wartime theaters during World War II. It was a theater of operations that received what little was left in the way of logistical support and manpower only after the other major theater commanders had received theirs. While CBI was the recipient of U.S. Lend-Lease aid before and after the U.S. entrance into the war on 7 December 1941, it remained the one theater of operations that bedeviled the war planners in Washington, D.C., and in London insofar as logistical requirements and manpower needs were concerned almost to the very end of the war in Southeast Asia. While Generalissimo Chiang Kai-shek's Nationalist troops battled the Japanese in neighboring China (all the while preparing to renew his battle with the Chinese Communists after the war), British and Imperial troops conducted a fighting retreat from Singapore along the Malay Peninsula up through Thailand and Burma to the very borders of India from December 1941 until their expulsion in May 1942.

Indeed, as Japanese forces poised for their thrust into India, the Allies regrouped and prepared for the long road back into Burma and re-establishment of the supply line into China along the Burma-Ledo Road, severed by the Japanese advance in April 1942.[1] The Allied effort, primarily led by the United States and Great Britain, focused its main efforts during the final two years of the war in China and Burma with the reinforcement (and evacuation) of Chiang's beleaguered forces and supplying the air efforts of Colonel (later Major General) Claire L. Chennault's American Volunteer Group or AVG.[2]

"A Hell of a Beating": The Loss of Burma, 1941–1943

Burma's importance to the Allied war effort centered upon its geographic location between China and India. Prior to the entrance of the United States into World War II in December 1941, China and Japan had been at war for nearly four and one-half years with Chinese forces, commanded by Chiang Kai-shek, being gradually pushed into the southwestern portion of China centered around Kunming. Japan's attack on Pearl Harbor, welcomed by Chiang, as it now promised a massive infusion of aid from Washington to his beleaguered forces, also brought with it a Japanese invasion of the Malay Peninsula. Over a period of six months British and Imperial troops conducted a rearguard action that culminated in the loss of Rangoon and Mandalay in April 1942. Myitkyina fell on 8 May 1942 and forced the remnants of the British and Indian Army to retreat into India. Both U.S. and British officials believed India was next on Japan's list of conquests. With the bases in Burma lost and the vital Burma-Ledo Road cut at Myitkyina both British and Chinese forces retreated into neighboring India along with its commanders, including Lieutenant General Joseph W. "Vinegar Joe" Stilwell, who had only been recently appointed in January 1942 by General George C. Marshall to take over direction of the American war effort in China. Upon his arrival in China, General Stilwell presided over the retreat of his forces into India where, after a harrowing retreat through the Burmese jungle, the acerbic general remarked, "We got a hell of a beating. It was as humiliating as hell. We ought to find out why it happened and go back!"[3]

"A Vital and Necessary Theater": Allied Strategy in China and Southeast Asia, 1941–1942

Regrouping in India, the Allies set about the task of re-organizing, training, and re-equipping for what would be the long road back to Rangoon, deemed by Allied logisticians to be the best port able to handle the immense tonnage required by Chiang's Nationalist forces. For its part, the Japanese military leadership could not agree on its next move. After taking Burma and the Malay Peninsula, the Japanese High Command repeated the mistake it committed in the Southwest Pacific, and that was its failure to act swiftly to destroy the Allied armies in the field. The Japanese Army's failure to act ultimately doomed Japan after its easy conquests of 1941 and 1942 as it could not agree on its next move with the naval hierarchy. This operational pause gave Allied planners the time to re-organize their forces in India and organize the massive airlift that began in the summer of 1942. In fact, by the time the Japanese launched their drive toward India starting in late 1943, the Allies had rebounded from their earlier setbacks and had started on the long road back to Mandalay via the Himalayas.

The Japanese weren't the only ones, however, that remained indecisive. The Allies, oftentimes at odds between themselves, could not agree on a unified strategy on how to best defeat the Japanese in CBI. While a Joint Allied Military Council recommended the construction of both the Ledo and Imphal Roads on 13 January 1942, it was not until after the Cairo Conference in April 1943 and later the Trident conference in Washington, D.C. (12–25 May 1943), that Allied planners began to formulate definitive plans to re-take Burma and increase the amount of material flowing to both Chiang Kai-shek and General Chennault. In fact, it was at the Trident conference that the Allies decided to: (1) initiate a series of minor land operations as a first step toward opening the Burma Road (closed by the Japanese seizure of northern Burma), and (2) increase the air routes and tonnage flying over the Himalayas to supply Generalissimo Chiang Kai-shek's Nationalist Army fighting the Japanese.[4] At the subsequent follow-on Quadrant conference in Quebec, Allied war planners reorganized the command arrangements in China-Burma-India with the creation of the Southeast Asia Command (SEAC) under the command of Admiral Lord Louis Mountbatten and the appointment of Lieutenant General Joseph W. Stilwell as his deputy supreme commander. Lieutenant General Stilwell, who had arrived in the CBI theater in February 1942, was already Chiang Kai-shek's chief of staff and had been involved at the time in a massive reorganization and re-training of the Chinese Army. Stilwell's appointment as Mountbatten's deputy in late 1943 later led to friction (and his relief) between himself and Chennault as to how best to defeat the Japanese in both Burma and China. Whereas both Chiang and Major General Claire Lee Chennault, who had been appointed commanding general of the Fourteenth Air Force and had been the generalissimo's air advisor, favored a strategy through airpower, Stilwell remained committed to a strategy of re-taking northern Burma with his re-organized and re-trained Chinese divisions, in order to re-open the Burma Road as well as tie down as many Japanese troops as possible in China in order to prevent their use elsewhere in Asia or the Pacific Ocean area.[5] The debate between Chennault and Stilwell as to the best strategy in "feeding the tiger," or the resupply of China and re-taking of northern Burma, ultimately brought hundreds of thousands of U.S. servicemen (and women) to air bases in India, Burma, and China.

The debate between Chennault and Stilwell was not the only hindrance in the efforts to re-supply China. A much larger debate between the United States, Great Britain, and China over the best overall strategy to defeat Japan on the Asian mainland likewise forced a delay at first, and later a cancellation of several major offensives aimed at driving the Japanese out of Burma in mid–1944 that might have led to a faster re-opening of the supply lines (land and air) going into China. Indeed, both Prime Minister Churchill and the chief of the British Imperial General Staff, Lord Alan Brooke, saw the idea of a major land offensive aimed at re-opening the old Ledo Road and construction of the Burma Road as a waste of time and effort. Prime Minister Churchill, in fact, wrote:

> I disliked intensely the prospect of a large scale campaign in Northern Burma. One could not choose a worse place for fighting the Japanese. Making a road from Ledo to China was also an immense, laborious task, unlikely to be finished

> until the need for it had passed. Even if it were done in time to replenish the Chinese armies while they were still engaged, it would make little difference in their fighting capacity. The need to strengthen the American air bases in China would also, in our view, diminish as Allied advances in the Pacific and from Australia gained us airfields closer to Japan. On both counts therefore we argued that the enormous expenditure of man-power and material would not be worth while. But we never succeeded in deflecting the Americans from their purpose.[6]

Churchill added that the British.

> of course wanted to recapture Burma, but we did not want to have to do it by land advances from slender communications and across the most forbidden fighting country imaginable. The south of Burma, with its port of Rangoon, was far more valuable than the north. But all of it was remote side-tracked and entangled there.[7]

Field Marshal Alan Brooke, not one who minced his words, commented on the original command arrangements in CBI in his diary as being "wild and half-baked and catering for only one area of action namely the Western Pacific, one enemy Japan, and no central control."[8] Indeed, the chief of the Imperial General Staff remained steadfast in his opposition to "schemes," as he labeled them, that promised very little return during the entire war. In fact, in their first meetings to discuss the limited offensives proposed for Northern Burma at the Trident Conference, Brooke wrote that he and the other British chiefs of staff disagreed with the strategy outlined by General George C. Marshall and the other American chiefs of staff over the conduct of the war in Burma and China. By the time this third inter-allied meeting ended, the British field marshal wrote that "what is not a very simple problem had become a tangled mass of confusion," as the British and Americans argued as to how to best keep Chiang Kai-shek in the war. Indeed, Brooke admitted that this was, in fact, the situation facing Allied planners in late 1941 as, "The whole problem seemed to hinge on the necessity of keeping Chiang Kai-shek in the war."[9]

In his first official meetings with President Franklin D. Roosevelt and the American Joint Chiefs of Staff after the attack on Pearl Harbor at the Arcadia Conference (24 December 1941–14 January 1942), Prime Minister Churchill and his military advisors agreed, much to the consternation of Brooke, on the necessity of keeping Chiang in the war though they differed on the means and methods to be used to accomplish that objective. Churchill's thoughts, outlined in a letter to British major general Sir Hastings Ismay, chief of staff to the minister of defense, eventually became official allied policy concerning the re-supply efforts to China for the next three years. In the letter to General Ismay, dated 7 January 1942, the prime minister wrote, "The supply lines to China via Burma must be kept open and fought for with the utmost energy."[10] Churchill disagreed, however, with FDR's belief that China could be useful in Japan's overall defeat, though he admitted later that it was "necessary to defer to [the] American view" insofar as the strategy to be followed in what eventually became the China-Burma-India theater of operations.[11]

It is important to stress the fact that American strategy in China and Burma remained committed to its pre-war objectives of keeping Lend-Lease flowing to Chiang's (and Wavell's) forces in China and Burma, which Washington had hoped would translate into keeping the Chinese forces in the field against the Japanese. In fact, the task of Brigadier General John Magruder, head of the military mission sent to Chungking (seat of the Nationalist Chinese government), was to:

- Advise and assist in all phases of aircraft production, transport, and maintenance.
- Advise and assist in the training, use and maintenance of weapons and equipment.
- When requested, assist the Department of State and other agencies in carrying out the Lend-Lease Act pertaining to China.
- Help obtain prompt and coordinated administrative action to ensure the orderly flow of war material to Chinese forces.
- Explore port, road, and railroad facilities with a view to establishing and maintaining an adequate line of communications.[12]

Shortly after the United States' entry into World War II, however, Washington delayed in sending some 500 airplanes promised China pending a review by the War Department of the immediate needs of both the U.S. Army Air Forces (USAAF) and the Royal Air Force (RAF). The War Department did allow the transfer of some availability of 100 of the latest P-40B fighters destined for the RAF in Burma, then under the command of Air Vice Marshal Sir Robert Brooke-Popham to Brigadier General Claire Lee Chennault's American Volunteer Group (AVG) and the U.S. military with the promise that Britain would receive a similar number of the newer P-40E models then in production. In addition to his agreement to transfer the P-40s to Chennault, Brooke-Popham agreed to rearm the aircraft and offered the use of RAF airfields in Burma to train Chinese pilots and crews as well as logistical support for the AVG.

Even before the war, discussions between Washington and London on China and Southeast Asia pointed to the differences that existed insofar as Anglo-American strategy was concerned on the defense of the vital natural resources located there (oil, tin, and rubber). In fact, as early as October 1941, the Americans and British, fearing future moves by the Japanese toward Burma and Southeast Asia, discussed at one point forming the AVG into an Anglo-American organization. Indeed, as time went by, the whole question over China's survival likewise grew in importance since Washington and London now saw the Sino-Japanese conflict, which had been ongoing since 1937, as a large holding action capable of delaying the Japanese from using those same troops now in China elsewhere throughout the Pacific. Despite the various attempts by military planners in Washington to make China a major wartime theater, the attack on Pearl Harbor and Germany's declaration of war on the United States several days later (11 December 1941) changed the strategic formula as American war planners focused on a Germany First strategy, in accordance with the implementation of Rainbow 5 or "Plan D."[13] With the emphasis now shifted away from the Pacific to Europe, the China-Burma-India theater slipped into virtual obscurity, only peripherally discussed at the subsequent wartime conferences until Japan resumed its offensive toward India in late 1943.

While American and British war planners settled on a Germany First strategy, Chiang Kai-shek, on the other hand, not surprisingly believed that China and Asia should be the Allied focal point. On the very day the Japanese attacked Pearl Harbor, he called a meeting of Allied representatives in Chungking to discuss the creation of a council which he would chair to direct the war in that theater. Besides calling for severing Japan's lines of supply and communications through a strategic bombing campaign, the Chinese leader proposed that he now be given control and priority over all lend-lease equipment. The generalissimo rightly thought Britain would try to "preempt the lend-lease arms that were piling up in Burma on consignment to China ... [and] wanted American leadership of the war council to keep the British from taking his goods."[14]

Chiang's Asia first strategy was quickly set aside at the first major interallied conference. During the Arcadia meetings in December 1941–January 1942, President Roosevelt and Prime Minister Churchill reaffirmed the Germany First strategy though both acknowledged the necessity of defending Burma and supplying Chiang's beleaguered forces. They agreed, moreover, that CBI was to remain a solely defensive front until the defeat of Germany. Despite the low priority assigned to China, Roosevelt believed it crucial not to permit China to either pull out of the war (as Chiang himself threatened several times) or side with the Japanese. He likewise advocated that China be given great power status and permitted to direct the war in China from Chungking (later Kunming) instead of granting General Sir Archibald Wavell, the governor-general in India, overall command. Roosevelt also believed the British and French hold over Asian colonies would not survive the war, and thus a strong China would be needed as a policeman to arrest any Soviet moves into the region. Churchill, who was in no mood to discuss the dissolution of the British empire or Britain's postwar position in Asia, including India, informed Roosevelt, in effect, that what went on in the British colonies was none of his business.

Despite these differences between Churchill and FDR, the Allied leaders nonetheless formulated a strategy that was purely defensive and would continue supporting China against Japan as well as holding the line against further advances into Burma and India. As both the president and prime minister saw it, China's strategic and operational importance was as a base to defend Burma, India, and the Malaya-Java barrier and possibly as a jumping off point for the re-taking of Indochina. In order to reduce the friction between Chiang and the British (whom Chiang believed imperialistic), the U.S. War Department would take responsibility for China while the British would take charge of the Burma theater. The separation of responsibility for the Burma and China theaters, however, disrupted the regular logistic channels, and eventually led to problems of command and control in CBI that threatened the conduct of the war against Japan on the Asian mainland. In fact, the divergence in how to best defeat Japan in Southeast Asia nearly derailed the subsequent supply effort to China. Only through the intervention of President Roosevelt and General Marshall was CBI kept on the table at the Allied conferences from 1942 until the end of the war. In fact, the center of the debate focused not on China staying in the war against Japan but on how to best supply her forces, either through a massive air effort or the re-taking of northern Burma and re-establishment of a land route into China. It was at this point that questions over how to supply Chinese, American, and British forces fighting in Burma while at the same time maintaining Chiang's forces in the field arose. For General George C. Marshall, the chairman of the Joint Chiefs of Staff, and the War Department as a whole, the problem centered not on the need to supply CBI but on how to do it with the limited assets available during the first fourteen months after Pearl Harbor.

"By Land or Air"

As long as Britain controlled Burma and the vital Burma Road which ran from Mandalay to Lashio and into China, the Allies could supply both China and Chennault. During the Arcadia conference, Churchill had, in fact, been pressured by Roosevelt to focus British efforts at defending the only land routes to China, much to the disgust of General Sir Alan Brooke and the other members of the Imperial General Staff, who considered it a waste of valuable war materiel better used elsewhere (i.e., in the war against Germany). Nonetheless, throughout early 1942, British, Commonwealth, and Chinese forces waged a ferocious rear-guard action after losing Rangoon in order to protect both the Burma Road and the Yenangyaung oilfields and prevent the Chinese from being cut off in the northeastern Shan states.

Loss of the Burma Road and the vital rail and road networks into China would force the Americans to undertake an aerial resupply effort over the Himalayas in northern Burma. Stilwell proposed that a new truck route running through northern Burma, from Ledo to Myitkyina, be constructed after the area was cleared of Japanese by a three-pronged Allied offensive. The British and Chinese saw the idea as both time-consuming and wasteful. The British proposed instead to launch a new offensive in order to recapture the port of Rangoon and reopen the old Burma Road from Lashio to Kunming. To meet the short-term needs of Chiang's Nationalist forces and Chennault's Fourteenth Air Force, the British and Chinese suggested a massive airlift. The Combined

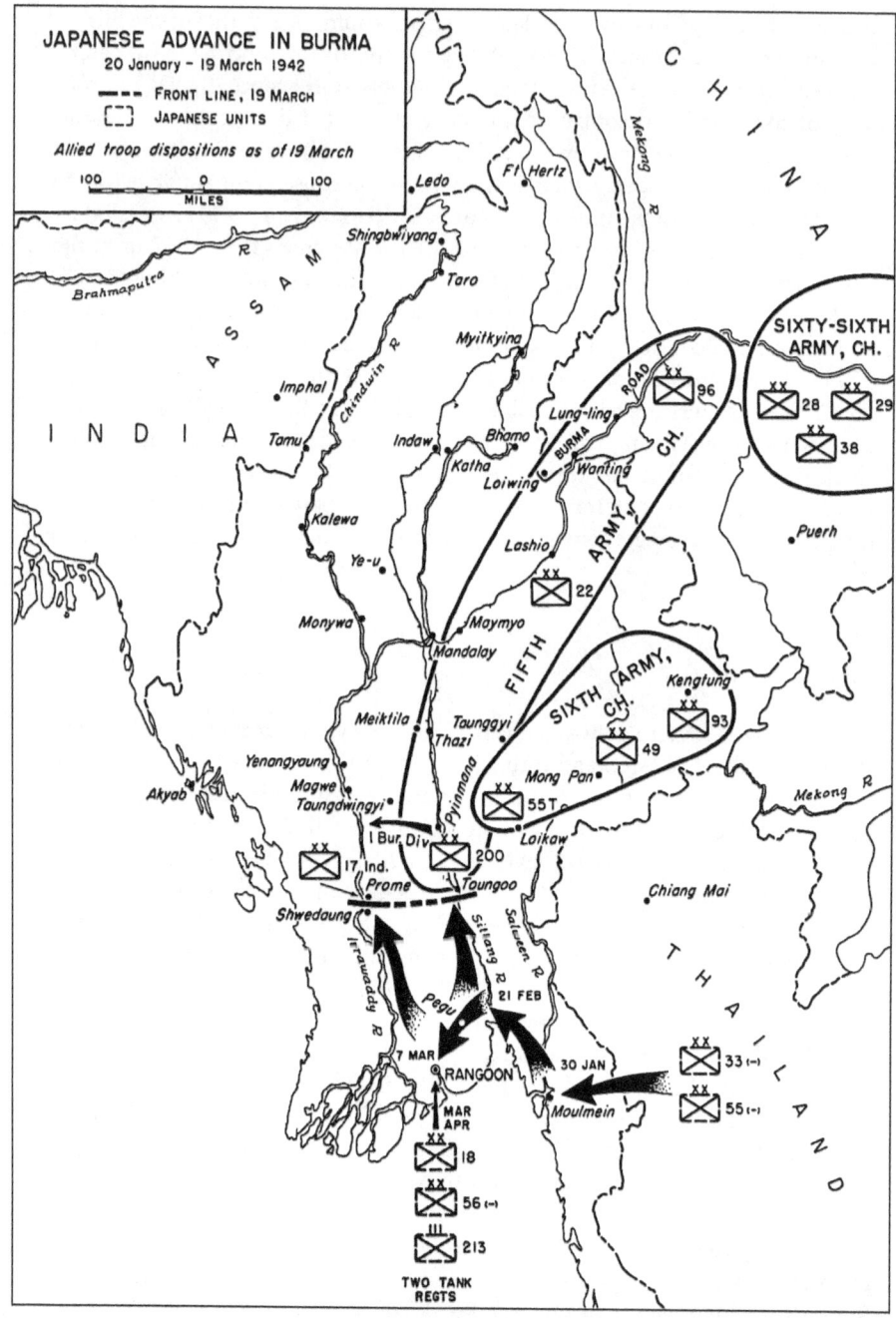

Map 1. The Japanese Drive from Rangoon to Myitkyina, January–May 1942 (Romanus and Sunderland, *Stilwell's Mission to China*, p. 83).

Chiefs reached a compromise: the Americans would undertake the airlift even as the Allied (British, Commonwealth, and Chinese) forces launched a series of offensives to retake Myitkyina, opening the way to build a new land route to China.

In fact, even before the U.S. involvement in the war getting lend-lease to China was a major concern to the War Department. Prior to the fall of Rangoon in March 1942, ships carrying lend-lease supplies would dock and unload there and then be trucked by way of the Lashio Road. The new Burma Road was to stretch from Ledo, India, through Fort Hertz and Myitkyina to Lung-Ling in China. Chiang optimistically believed it would take only five months to build the road while Washington estimated two and half years. Support for such a construction project nonetheless came quickly from Marshall and presidential adviser Lauchlin Currie. Currie, in fact, told Roosevelt that building such a road under American auspices would eliminate many of the problems between Chiang and the British, permitting lend-lease to flow relatively uninterrupted to Chinese forces. But as Chiang and the War Plans Division in Washington, D.C., hammered out planning for the road, Allied planners organized an interim air route from India to China by way of Sadiya, India, and Kunming over a rough and forbidding stretch of terrain over the Himalayan Mountains soon to be simply known as "the Hump."

The Chinese foreign minister, T.V. Soong, estimated that 100 C-47 Skytrains or Dakotas could fly 12,000 tons of supplies into China every month. Despite Roosevelt's concern that the unarmed transports would be easy prey for Japanese pilots, Soong assured him that "the supply route to China via India can be maintained by air even though there should be further setbacks in Rangoon." Though Soong promised air support (as did Wavell from the RAF) many transports flew missions under a constant threat of attacks and with little or no fighter support. While British planes did, in fact, fly cover for the transports, this support was both spotty and determined by British requirements once Lieutenant General William Slim's 14th Army resumed offensive operations in Burma in early 1944 and not airlifting supplies to Chiang Kai-shek's forces.

Added to the problem of British fighter cover was the simple fact that much of the fighter cover from the RAF came from squadrons based in India. It was not until 1944 when Merrill's Marauders retook the Japanese airbase in Burma at Myitkyina and the elimination of the enemy air threat to the transports flying the Hump that the RAF could provide adequate fighter support to the unarmed transports. Thus, it became the task of Lieutenant General Stilwell to not only serve as Chiang's chief of staff (and of all U.S. personnel and lend-lease in China) and "set up the airline to China," but also to lay the groundwork for construction of the Burma Road. Despite the renewed emphasis on building a land route, logistical and engineering problems as well as the drain of manpower and materiel to other theaters delayed construction, and thus forced the War Department to resupply the Allies with a massive airlift. Over time, the airlift established a vital link with Chiang's forces in China and set the stage for the re-conquest of Burma in 1944.

China-Burma-India, 1942–1944: The Defensive Phase

Despite the delays in the construction of a road into China and the ever-present shortages of men and aircraft, due to more pressing concerns in the Mediterranean and European theaters of operation, the U.S. Army Air Forces (USAAF) inaugurated Project 7A which called for the requisition of 25 American Airways DC-3 passenger planes and their conversion to the military configured C-47 transports for the Assam-Burma-China Ferry Command (later the Air Transport Command or ATC). The mission of the Assam-Burma-China Ferry Command, established on orders from FDR on 21 March 1942, and organized by Brigadier General Earl L. Naiden with the day-to-day operations directed by Colonels Edward Alexander and Thomas Hardin respectively, was to deliver equipment and supplies to British, American and Chinese forces as well perform humanitarian flights in the evacuation of refugees and wounded Allied soldiers from the battlefield.[15] During its three years in operation, the Air Transport Command (including the Assam-Burma-China Ferry Command) delivered 736,374 tons of supplies into China. Tragically, however, while the pilots and crews of the ATC set new records in aerial delivery, it nevertheless lost some 468 transports, in fact, "as many planes as the Fourteenth Air Force lost during three years of combat."[16]

Despite Washington's desire to placate Chiang, operations in the Mediterranean, Pacific, and European theaters of operation proved to be a constant drain on transport for the ferry command. American strategy in China thus became hostage to the operational tempos in North Africa, Italy, and later Northwest Europe with regards to both men and material originally slated for CBI. Chiang, on the other hand, insisted that by August 1942 "the monthly aerial support should by 5,000 tons," a figure that was impossible given the fact that it took 85 days from embarkation in the United States to reach ports at Calcutta and Karachi some 12,000 miles away and then overland to points in Assam prior to their transshipment over the Hump which took a further eight weeks to be distributed throughout the air bases in China. In fact, by August 1942, the airlift fell far short of its promise to adequately supply Chiang's (and Chennault's) forces with tonnage over the Himalayas totaling 2,200 tons with the average monthly total slowly approaching 800 tons, a far cry from the generalissimo's nearly impossible request for 5,000 tons.[17] In fact, Chiang's request for a monthly total of 5,000 tons came just as the Allies were putting the final touches on the plans for the invasion of North Africa (Operation Gymnast, renamed later as Operation Torch), as well as the initial build-up for Operation

Sledgehammer, the invasion of northwest France. Indeed, throughout 1942 and into 1943, troop and support problems plagued Stilwell's plans to re-organize and re-train thirty good Chinese divisions (known as the Y-Plan) in order to re-take Northern Burma, due in large part to the inter-service and inter–Allied squabbling that took place among the members of the American, British, Dutch, Australian Supreme Command (ABDACOM) over the best strategy to defeat Japan on the Asian mainland. This inter-allied squabbling about who got what of the trickle of supplies flowing into CBI strained the already tenuous alliance between the Americans and British as well as between the British and Chinese forces in Burma to the near-breaking point.

From the outset of the war in CBI, the British and Chinese fought over the lend-lease assistance coming to India. In fact, after the organization of the Assam-Burma-China Ferry Command, the British sought to have the airlift "placed at its disposal and under the air officer commander in chief (India)." In fact, Marshall, who overrode the objections of both Stilwell and Chennault, personally reassured Field Marshal Sir John Dill, the British liaison in Washington, that the Tenth Air Force would be turned over to British forces in India when necessary. Stilwell, already suspicious of the lackluster British efforts in Burma and all the while attempting to placate Chiang's demands, drew up his own plans for a limited air and ground offensive that would keep the pressure on the Japanese and the Chinese fighting.

The center of Stilwell's plans during the summer of 1942 was an air campaign designed to support a series of limited ground offensives in China and northern Burma. While Chennault's Fourteenth Air Force was to assist Chiang's forces inside China, the Tenth U.S. Air Force, flying from bases in India, was to "bomb strategic targets in Burma and China" when they could be supported there. The India Air Task Force, activated in October 1942, supplemented the India-based Assam-Burma-China Ferry Command. Leading the airlift, after a major command re-arrangement of the Tenth Air Force was Brigadier General Francis M. Brady. General Brady's task was to "receive and train crews for combat and transport operations," flying back and forth into China. Working alongside Brady's command was the Air Service Command, commanded by Colonel Robert C. Oliver.[18] The Air Service Command, based throughout northern India (Agra, Allahabad, Chakulia, Bangalore, Dinjan, and Chabua), and at Kunming, China, served as a maintenance and supply echelon for the Tenth Air Force. Directing the entire air re-supply effort was Major General Raymond A. Wheeler's Service of Supply (SOS). Despite its dependence on a 12,000-mile, four-month-long odyssey by ship from ports in New York and Los Angeles to Karachi through India's vast interior to Assam, and over an antiquated rail and road network, the SOS performed nothing short of a miracle in getting supplies to Stilwell and British Field Marshal Sir Harold Alexander, general in chief of the India-Burma theater (to 1943).[19]

Flying the "Aluminum Trail": The Airlift to China, 1942–1944

Missions across the Hump and into Burma were long and dangerous. The Hump portion of the flight into Kunming, China, averaged over 600 miles from either Assam or New Delhi. It began on leaving Myitkyina (before its fall in April 1942) where pilots with oxygen masks flew at 17,000–20,000 feet. According to Captain Edward Goodman, who flew in a converted B-24, the transports carried little or no armament. Even the machine guns found in the rear or turrets of the converted B-24s were removed to make room for bladder bags for aviation fuel or cargo. "The old slow transports not designed for such conditions, flew without aids to navigation or arms against [the] Japanese pursuit" planes.[20]

Pilots flew from 13 to 14 hours a day, in operations that continued round the clock, seven days a week, and in all types of weather. The only down time was during the monsoon from May to October when only limited flight operations took place. The C-46s, C-47s, and later C-87s carried everything from 500-pound bombs, 50-gallon drums of 100-octane aviation fuel, small arms ammunition, and whatever else Chiang or Stilwell required. Loaded at night by British, American or native Indian or Chinese coolies, the tightly-packed "gooney birds" flew off runways made of steel mats or concrete and crushed gravel on flights that took anywhere from 5 to 8.8 hours to complete.

When flying through the monsoon and all night, pilots relied heavily upon AI or actual instrument flying. To assist the pilots flying in such bad conditions Chinese and American technicians based at Kunming or Luliang operated beacon radars in order to guide the aircraft flying in on instruments to these remote Chinese bases as well onto the fog-shrouded Indian air installations upon their return from their flights. In time, pilots simply came to know the approaches and landing sites (as well as the dangers) by heart.

The majority of problems encountered in navigating the Hump, however, were due to the weather. Lieutenant General William H. Tunner, who later assumed command of airlift operations into China, wrote:

> Looking back at the Hump weather on a year-round basis, it's easy to see that it was no real picnic at any time of the year. The combination of weather and terrain would have made the Hump airlift a difficult one even if the route had been over the middle of the United States.[21]

As Captain Goodman stated, pilots, in fact, dubbed the Hump the "aluminum trail," because of the 3,000 aircraft that went down over the four years the Army Air Forces ran the supply line over the Himalayas; 85 percent of the aircraft were lost due to the weather.[22] Goodman likewise recalled that on two particular nights "the airwaves were filled with Mayday [distress] calls" with the result being the loss of some 60 to 65 aircraft.[23] Despite the use of the radar beacons and instrument flying, Goodman stated that the "primitive radio signals from the Chinese bases couldn't pierce the frequent thunderstorms [there]." Instead, the veteran pilot added, "we flew by the seat of our pants and came to know the approaches and landing sites by heart and flew by memory" into Kunming and Luliang.

Besides flying into Kunming and Luliang, the Air Transport Command (comprising the 1st, 2nd, 3rd, and 4th Combat Cargo Groups) later supported the advance by the British toward Rangoon, ferrying and inserting into Burma radar teams, commando teams, including Brigadier Orde Wingate's famed long-range penetration group known as the Chindits, as well as supplying the famed U.S. long-range penetration force known as Merrill's Marauders. Toward the middle of 1944, the ATC likewise began to ferry into Northern Burma and Southwest China Chinese soldiers belonging to the Y-Plan from bases in India. Captain David C. Hall, a C-46 pilot assigned to the 4th Combat Cargo Group, recalled that on several occasions GHQ assigned his squadron the task of transporting Chinese soldiers from bases in India and Burma into China.[24] In fact, by 1944, the bulk of the ATC's efforts were directed toward supporting Slim's advance toward Rangoon down the Irrawaddy River valley as well as supporting Chennualt's Fourteenth Air Force as well as the XX Bomber Group sent to China in order to bomb the Japanese mainland and bases in Formosa (Taiwan). Despite the renewed emphasis on the CBI after the Trident (May 1943) and Quadrant (August 1943) conferences the European theater of operations continued to claim the bulk of supplies coming from American and British factories. Lieutenant General Slim wrote that at times it seemed that the air effort was not enough to sustain his forces in the field:

> There were, of course, some anxious moments; we had some over air supply. The American and British transport aircraft were proving too few to meet our increasing demands.... This difficulty was met by Admiral [Lord Louis] Mountbatten obtaining the permission of the Combined Chiefs of Staff to borrow aircraft from the Hump. Twenty-five Commandos [C-46s] were lent for three weeks, thus enabling Dakotas to be sent to [Orde] Wingate's force [the Chindits] to tide over the peak demand.[25]

Slim emphasized the fact that what made flying the Hump all the more successful was the flexibility of the Combat Cargo Groups to respond to operational requirements. Indeed, during Slim's advance down the Irrawaddy River (January–June 1945) American C-46s kept British forces resupplied from the air by flying round-the-clock sorties during the Battle for Kohima Ridge until relief came in after two weeks of extremely bitter fighting. Indeed, during the campaign for Kohima Ridge, C-46 crews braved heavy Japanese anti-aircraft fire by dropping bundles of supplies that included ammunition, water, and food to the beleaguered British and Indian forces. Once over the target area, the C-46s and C-47s would fly toward an open field while kickers, primarily from African American quartermaster units, quite literally kicked the supplies out of the cargo doors onto the ground where British soldiers anxiously awaited, many times under deadly fire, to retrieve the valuable cargo.[26] It might be added that the lessons and techniques learned during the Battle for Burma (1944–1945) were later applied by American pilots and crews during the American re-supply efforts of Chiang's forces during the Chinese Civil War (1945–49), and during the First Indochina War (1947–1954) when American-hired transport crews employed a similar method of resupply to the French paratroopers who had been surrounded by the Viet Minh in March–April 1954 at Dien Bien Phu.

"Allies of a Different Kind": Inter-Allied Relations and the War in CBI, 1943–1945

Despite the hazards encountered by the pilots and crews over the Hump, the tempo of the war in CBI began to quicken as inter–Allied staff planning after the Trident and Quadrant conferences began to make preparations for a series of limited offensives aimed at securing northern Burma and the reconquest of Rangoon. Indeed, as Allied planners laid out the logistical foundation and air support for Operation Overlord or the invasion of Northwest France, and as tempo of the war in the Central and Southwest Pacific areas likewise increased, they discovered that both Stilwell's and Mountbatten's theaters had become even more dependent on the ever-dwindling pool of aircraft and men even as Chiang's demands increased. Indeed, even before the Trident conference was held the Joint Chiefs of Staff put forth a more aggressive plan (Anakim) to launch a series of limited offensives designed to re-open the Ledo Road into China. General Marshall's motivation for backing such an operation met with serious resistance from both the British and the Chinese. For their part, the British maintained the position that any operation to open the Burma Road was a waste of resources that the allies could employ better elsewhere [i.e., in the Mediterranean]. The Chinese, on the other hand, agreed to participate in such a ground offensive in Burma only if Britain would provide an adequate force of naval and air support. When Field Marshal Wavell informed Generalissimo Chiang Kai-shek that Britain could provide only a "limited amount of naval and air support," the Chinese declined to participate.[27]

At the Casablanca Conference (January 1943), Roosevelt and Churchill discussed a wide range of issues and problems confronting the Allies in the third full year of the war. The president, aware that both the American public and Joint Chiefs of Staff (particularly Admiral Ernest J. King, USN) wanted an expanded effort in both the Pacific Ocean area and on the Asian mainland, nonetheless sided with Churchill's desire to first secure the Mediterranean bases and prepare for the eventual invasion of Northwestern Europe (Bolero), and to appease Soviet leader Josef Stalin's call for a second front to relieve pressure from the German force on the Eastern Front. Although both leaders were able to fend off any suggestions for a major offensive in Burma, General Marshall and Admiral Ernest J. King were able to convince President Roosevelt to approve a limited offensive in Burma for late 1943. To alleviate British fears that any offensive in Burma would require additional British lend-lease, Roosevelt and Marshall pledged that any supplies used in such an offensive would be replaced immediately from American stockpiles.

General Marshall's desire for even a limited offensive was twofold. His first goal was to reopen the line of communications to China in order to secure bases for operations against the Japanese home islands and Formosa (Operation Matterhorn). The second and more important reason for a limited offensive was to re-assure Chiang Kai-shek of America's continued support in his war with the Japanese armies in China. Despite Roosevelt's approval for a limited Burma offensive both Marshall and King stressed, in a message to Stilwell, that priority must go toward rebuilding the Chinese army into a credible offensive force. China, however, despite its relative importance to the U.S. Joint Chiefs, was to get only enough logistical support to prevent its collapse. As events turned out, it was Chennault's Fourteenth Air Force and not Stilwell's half-starved and ill-equipped Chinese and American forces that received the greatest amount of Hump tonnage. In fact, Chennault's personal lobbying campaign against Stilwell's desire for a ground offensive finally turned the tables insofar as FDR's decision to support the idea of an air campaign to drive Japan from the Asian mainland. General Marshall, while supportive of President Roosevelt's position, nonetheless remained skeptical of Chennault's claim that air power alone could drive Japan from China. Indeed, both FDR and Marshall thought air power a "quick fix" alternative to Stilwell's plan to refit 30 Chinese divisions. Despite this change of priorities in CBI, the impact of Anakim on the Service of Supply and Air Transport Command was immediate as an already strained system became even more hard-pressed to keep up with even the limited demands of the theater commanders in CBI (Stilwell, Mountbatten, Chennault, and Major General Raymond A Wheeler, who had assumed command of the SOS in mid–1942).[28]

During the Trident conference in the spring of 1943, Roosevelt, Churchill, and the Combined Chiefs of Staff sought to finalize agreements made at Casablanca the previous winter, particularly in regard to Anakim. As mentioned above, both Chennault and Stilwell, the latter representing Chiang Kai-shek, presented their plans on how to best defeat Japan in China. After a lengthy presentation by Chennault on the efficacy of airpower, Stilwell discounted the effects of airpower to stem the Japanese Army's ability to maintain the offensive in China and warned Roosevelt that the latter still had the ability to march whenever and wherever they wanted. Until his dismissal in October 1944, Stilwell maintained his belief that a reformed Chinese Army of some 120 divisions, and not airpower, would be the only way to defeat the Japanese on the Asian mainland.[29]

The British, on the other hand, believed any offensive in Burma would divert manpower and logistics just when the war with Germany was entering its most crucial phase. In fact, both Churchill and the British chiefs of staff advocated bypassing Burma as the Americans were, in fact, doing throughout the Southwest and Central Pacific areas. The British favored, instead, a limited amphibious campaign (Dracula) to retake Rangoon, the Andaman Islands, the northern tip of Sumatra, and the reoccupation of Singapore. The British likewise believed that it was impossible to airlift sufficient supplies over the Hump in order to sustain even a limited offensive in Burma given other priorities.[30]

From Quadrant to War's End in CBI, 1943–1945

Any offensive to retake Burma or to assist Chennault in his proposed air campaign against Japan would require flying increased tonnage over the Hump. Major General Chennault based his requirements on 150 B-17 bombers; 32 B-24, B-25, and B-26 medium bombers; air and ground personnel; and 2,500–3,000 tons of supplies not only to protect the air routes to China but to strike the Japanese all along the Chinese and Burmese coasts.[31] Despite Stilwell's opinion that airpower alone could not defeat the enemy, General Marshall ordered the CBI commander in chief to give the Fourteenth Air Force commander a firm allocation of 1,500 tons a month regardless of Chiang's needs. Stilwell complied and informed the JCS that Chennault would receive an additional 1,000 tons per month. Chinese forces would still get their monthly allocation of 2,500 tons, providing that in bad weather Chennault would share equally with everyone else no matter what it did to air operations. Chennault saw Stilwell's plan as undercutting his efforts to launch the air campaign against Japan. He not only insisted on priority in Hump tonnage but that he get enough to fly and fight.

Aggravating Stilwell's command problems with Chiang and Chennault was the constant interference by the president in this theater of operations. Roosevelt oftentimes circumvented the normal chain of command in Washington — General Marshall and the JCS — in order to conduct the war in the same ad hoc way his pre-war policy on China had been conducted. While Roosevelt's aim was to assure Chiang that China was a full partner, his meddling frequently sent confusing signals that ultimately hampered the war effort in CBI (and elsewhere). Moreover, his personal relationship with Chennault, which went back to 1937, hindered Stilwell's attempts to reform the Chinese Army and make it an effective fighting force. Roosevelt's personal diplomacy, in fact, not only prevented Chiang from reforming his government but also drove a wedge between the U.S. and Mao Zedong and the Communists with whom the United States would have to deal with after the war. Roosevelt's insistence that Chennault receive a guaranteed monthly minimum not only reduced the ability of Stilwell to accumulate the requisite supplies he needed but also forced a revision of the planned offensive into northern Burma. In short, the decision to maintain the pressure on the Japanese via an air offensive also impeded an effective Chinese effort against the enemy in both Burma and China.

Despite the War Department's pronouncements on the bravery and fortitude of the Chinese soldiers, inter–Allied squabbling and British mistrust of Chiang's pro–Indian nationalism (which was, in fact, the main reason for Wavell's vehement dislike for Stilwell's 30-Division Plan, as it would bring hundreds of thousands of Chinese troops into contact with Indian nationals) drastically slowed down Stilwell's efforts to re-organize and re-train an effective Chinese Army. Inter-Allied friction over Hump priorities, strategy, and operations likewise scuttled plans to resume the offensive in CBI in 1943. Only after the appointment of Lord Louis Mountbatten as SEAC commander in chief did the Allies resume plans for a major operation against the Japanese in Burma and China. In the end, it was Trident and not Quadrant that set in motion the plans that called for the reconquest of Burma and the opening of the Burma Road in late 1944. Quadrant, however, confirmed the Allied goals and objectives in Burma and greatly expanded the air effort to supply Chiang Kai-shek, this despite the objections of Prime Minister Churchill and his advisors over a planned offensive to recapture northern Burma and increase the tonnage to the Chinese leader's forces.

Cooperation at Last: Trident to Quadrant

The immediate result of the Trident conference was increased Hump tonnage reaching both Chennault and Stilwell's respective forces in China. Chiang's approval of the Trident decisions meant that training and equipping of the Y-Force (the 30 re-fitted Chinese divisions) could go forward and the tactical plans for Burma updated. Decisions reached in Washington, D.C., by Roosevelt, Churchill, and the Combined Chiefs of Staff on a series of limited offensives into Burma set in motion plans for Slim's reconquest of Burma and the opening of the Burma-Ledo Road in February 1945. Trident also gave more emphasis to Chennault's plan for an air campaign instead of Stilwell's proposed ground offensive into northern Burma. President Roosevelt's backing of Chennault's plan not only diverted resources from road construction to airfield construction in India but essentially took the wind out of Stilwell's plan to keep the pressure on the Japanese in China itself. With the increase of Hump tonnage from 4,000 to 10,000 per month came the expansion and reinforcement of Wheeler's SOS. After Trident, General Wheeler's first task was to get SEAC's permission to build several airfields to enlarge the air effort in both Burma and China. Wavell readily agreed and flew to Assam to survey construction of four main bases: Chabua, Mohanbari, Sookerating and Jorhat. The British commander gave Wheeler's engineers licenses to requisition material for the airfields from British and Indian stocks of lend-lease after which, of course, Mountbatten rushed trucks, steel matting, and gravel crushers and rollers to Assam to complete the airfields in time for the planned spring offensives.

Despite the deep Anglo-American differences as to how to proceed in CBI, the theater began to experience a steady influx of men and material by mid-1943. Acting on Marshall's request for added aircraft for the Assam-Burma-China ferry, the War Department rushed 30 C-46 transports to Wheeler's Service of Supply. In order not to strip the planes from the stockpiles accumulating for Operation Sledgehammer, the U.S. Army Air Forces initiated Project 7-A, and requisitioned the necessary aircraft from three civilian airlines: American Airlines, Trans World and Northwest Airlines.[32] Recognizing that Roosevelt's air campaign could not be launched without more men and equipment, General Marshall ordered the diversion of more men and equipment from both the United States and Great Britain to CBI in order to bolster both Chennault's and Stilwell's respective campaigns. Indeed, by mid-1943, the theater was receiving a quarter of all supplies coming off assembly lines in the United States. Also, as evidenced by the assignment of the 4th Combat Cargo Group from its base in Louisville, Kentucky, as well as the diversion of men and material from the Persian Corridor, as well as the appointment of air maintenance and Army combat engineers to CBI, both the air and ground effort did, in fact, capture the attention of the JCS and the CCS at both Trident and later Quadrant conferences. This attention was later translated into concrete action in order to bolster Chiang's campaign against the Japanese.

"A China-Burma-India Theater Is Formed," 1943–1945

By mid-summer 1943, in fact, the Air Transport Command had three more transportation groups and four airway detachments assigned to the theater, with more personnel arriving monthly. Whereas before 1943 each transport had one crew they now had, after the summer of 1943, two crews, that in turn translated into around the clock air operations. In fact, by August 1943, the JCS had assigned 46 extra crews to the CBI theater and thus alleviated shortages in parts and personnel in the event of losses. Despite the assignment of additional manpower and aircraft to CBI, however, it became clear after the summer of 1943 that the lofty goal of 10,000 tons per month flowing into China could not be reached without the construction of additional airfields and maintenance facilities in Assam, and their being fully staffed by qualified maintenance personnel.

Indeed, the conferees in Quebec, where Quadrant was held, agreed to increase the amount of aid flowing to Chiang and Chennault. In light of past conferences, such as Cairo and later Trident, Quadrant was, in effect, the open-

Lieutenant General Albert C. Wedemeyer, who succeeded Lieutenant General Joseph W. Stilwell as commanding general, China Theater during World War II (1944–1945) (Leo J. Daugherty III Collection).

ing of the floodgate to increased aid going over the Hump from bases in India. Here, Allied leaders agreed to:

1. An increase in the amount of air cargo being flown to China by the Air Transport Command (ATC) to 20,000 tons a month by mid–1944.
2. (Construction) of a road from India to China (the Ledo Road) with an initial (January 1945) capacity of 30,000 tons per month.

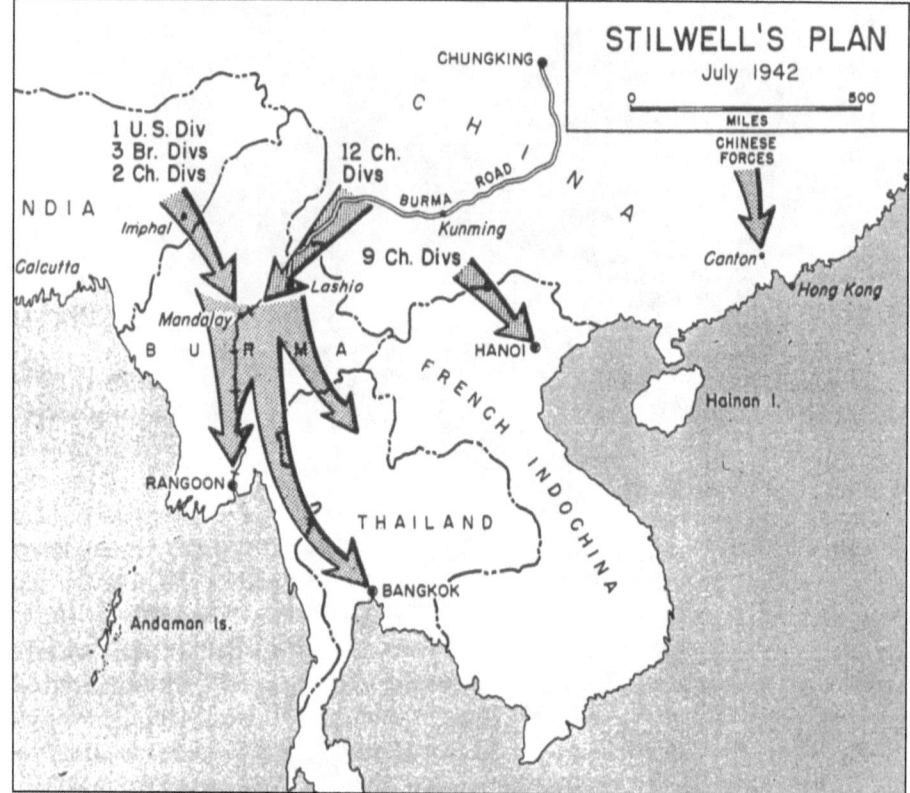

Map 2. Stilwell's planned offensive in Northern Burma and construction of the Burma Road after Quadrant conference in July 1942 (Romanus and Sunderland, *Stilwell's Mission to China*, p. 83).

3. (Construction) of a gasoline pipeline from Assam via Fort Hertz in northernmost Burma to Kunming (China).
4. (Construction of a) thin-walled 6-inch pipeline from Calcutta to Assam Province to supply the Air Transport Command located airfields there.
5. (Construction) of a thin-walled 6-inch pipeline to China.
6. (Establishment of) an American-operated barge line on the Bramaputra River to bring supplies forward from the great port of Calcutta to the Allied bases in Assam.
7. Improvement of the Bengal and Assam Railway.[33]

Indeed, after the Quadrant conference (14–24 August 1943), the Combined Chiefs of Staff finally agreed, if somewhat reluctantly, upon a limited series of offensives designed not only to re-take northern Burma but to "improve the air route and opening ... [of an] ... overland communications route with China." In fact, it was the Quadrant conference that ended two years of intense and oftentimes bitter inter–Allied bickering on how to best defeat the Japanese on the Asian mainland and expel them from Burma and the Malay peninsula. With the addition of the pilots and planes from Project 7-A, tonnage over the Hump increased significantly. By the end of 1944, in fact, transports had ferried into China by way of the Himalayas over 23,000 tons in a single month. Indeed, by the end of the war in Asia on 1 September 1945, "air freight reached a greater volume by far than ever went over the Burma Road."[34] In fact,

> These greatly accelerated operations over the India-China route were made possible by doubling the number of transports in service in the India-China division, by greater efficiency in maintenance and repair, loading and unloading of cargo to reduce the length of time planes spent on the ground and by an increase in the number of airfields in the area. The accrued benefits of pilot-training programs also were noticeable.[35]

Among the more important lessons of the China-Burma-India strategic airlift were those applied later to supplying U.S. and allied troops in Korea and Vietnam, as well as in the Persian Gulf in 1990. In fact, as Tom Barnard wrote, "Besides helping to defeat Japan, the Hump operation was the proving ground for mass strategic airlift, for ... [it was here, in China-Burma-India that] ... the AAF demonstrated conclusively that a vast quantity of cargo could be delivered by air, even under the most unfavorable circumstances, if only the men who controlled the aircraft, the terminals, and the needed material were willing to pay the price in money and men." Indeed, despite the inter–Allied squabbling that took place over how to best defeat Japan on the Asian mainland, at Trident and later at Quadrant, the JCS and CCS set in motion the plans that revolutionized the supply of war for decades to come. Decisions made in Quebec in August 1943, in fact, brought to the CBI theater men such as Captains Edward Goodman and David C. Hall, Staff Sergeant Robert Boehm, Corporals Anthony R. Silva and Alexander McVean, and Technical Sergeant Kenneth R. Quigley, whose accounts of service in CBI as the build-up began in mid–1943 are found in this study on the Allied effort to feed the tiger in its war against Japan.

Chapter 2

"Many Mountain Roads": Platoon Sergeant Robert Boehm, U.S. Army Quartermaster Corps

During the China-Burma-India campaign many of the American troops sent there included aviators, aircraft maintenance, quartermaster, engineer, and combat troops. Included in this group of U.S. soldiers sent to the CBI Theater in the spring of 1945 was Platoon Sergeant Robert Boehm, U.S. Army Quartermaster Corps. Born and raised in Cleveland, Ohio, Sergeant Boehm entered the Army on May 8, 1942, and after basic training at Camp Claiborne, Louisiana, went first to Fort Dix, New Jersey, where he shortly thereafter embarked for overseas via New York Harbor. The transport carrying Boehm and his fellow soldiers was accompanied by four destroyers, although, as the Army sergeant remembered, the number of escort vessels gradually diminished as the ship headed into the South Atlantic. Boehm recalled that while aboard ship the main concern was the threat posed by the German U-boats which "were sinking a ship a day."

Arriving off the coast of Brazil, the transport then headed for Rio De Janeiro, Brazil, where the ship took on fresh supplies. Assigned to the 1st Platoon, 3949th Quartermaster Truck Company, Boehm, who was by this time a platoon sergeant, was ordered to oversee a force of some one hundred soldiers tasked to load the ship prior to pulling anchor and heading southeast. From there, the ship rounded the Cape of Good Hope in South Africa and headed northeast toward the Persian Gulf with the destination being Iran. Here, Boehm spent the next two and half years assisting in the shipping of lend-lease goods to the Red Army via the Persian Corridor in northern Iran.

"A Very Small Regiment"

Prior to his embarkation overseas Sergeant Boehm recalled that the 3949th Quartermaster Truck Company he was assigned to was unusually small for a typical quartermaster unit in the Army. Boehm stated that when he joined the unit, called a regiment, it was in utter confusion as to who was in charge or what its mission was to be. Indeed, as the ship headed on a southeast course, Boehm and his fellow soldiers began to wonder where the Army had assigned them. Boehm recalled:

> When we went overseas, we were a very small regiment, 118 men with 4 officers 122 people ... and we were unattached ... our CO was a major, you know 122 people, and our commanding officer was a major ... we were pretty heavily ranked.... But after he turned his jeep over and broke his back, well, first they put him in a big cast and sent him home. Well then we got a Captain Gray who came to us. He was an insurance salesperson, and he was just putting in his time in. That is what he was doing. He didn't know who we were or what we were doing. He was the CO of our company. We ended up doing every crappy job that nobody else wanted to do.

Boehm added that once they arrived in Iran, they were properly identified by the Army as the 3949th Q.M. Truck Company and assigned to the area near Tehran. Sergeant Boehm recalled that upon arrival in Iran the "British were pretty much in charge of the southern half of the country while the Russians controlled the area from Tehran to the Caspian Sea."[1] Boehm stated that upon landing the first sergeant "must have had it out for me," as he was once again placed in charge of a special detail, this one assigned to guard duty at a large military headquarters. At the headquarters, in downtown Tehran, Boehm met up with a regular U.S. Army colonel who informed the sergeant that he could use his office as a headquarters and that "he didn't have a problem with us using it." After setting up the guard details, Boehm began to look around this headquarters. Inside the headquarters, Boehm recalled, he came upon a large wall map with a large arrow drawn on it. Army personnel working there informed Boehm that this was a situation map detailing the ongoing German drive toward the oilfields of the Caspian Sea near Baku. Boehm said that the arrow "pivoted westward toward the Middle East" and seem to indicate that the Germans were heading for the Suez Canal.[2] Boehm added that the map showed two giant arrows coming together in a pincer against British forces fighting in North Africa.

"Supplying the Bear": The Persian Corridor, 1942–1945

Once in Iran, Boehm and his fellow soldiers set about the task of shipping U.S. Lend-Lease equipment to the Red Army.[3] With his original regiment of approximately 118 enlisted men and 4 officers, and assigned to the U.S. Persian Gulf Command's Motor Transport Service or MTS that was organized from Army quartermaster personnel at Camp Lee, Virginia, in October 1942, Sergeant Boehm and his fellow soldiers of the 3949th Quartermaster Company spent the next two and a half years (1942–1945) transporting U.S. equipment to the Russians with their 2½-ton tractors, 7-ton semitrailers, and 10-ton trucks.⁴ While formed as a supplement to British and Russian truck operations and in conjunction with the Iranian State Railroad, the MTS eventually picked up the slack caused by the failures of the other two operations (i.e., the British and Russians). Indeed, the MTS proved to be a lifesaver, as it hauled from 1942 to 1944 a total of 619,000 long tons and operated over 100 million truck miles in all types of weather and over rough and largely unpaved roads.⁵ In fact:

> After a slow beginning in early 1943 and hampered by delayed receipt of troops and equipment, the Persian Gulf Command went on to meet and exceed assigned goals for port discharge and rail and highway movements, which constituted the theater's main mission. Setting up the Motor Transport Serve was more time-consuming than planners estimated, but its contributions were substantial. By October 1943, Soviet aid through the corridor exceeded the monthly goal of 200,000 long tons.⁶

Indeed, as Sergeant Boehm vividly remembered, this aid was critical as the German drive toward Stalingrad at the time seemed unstoppable. When the Germans stalled on the Volga, it became apparent to all that the Wehrmacht's Caspian plan had failed. Nonetheless, the effort went forward to assist the Russians throughout the summer of 1943 and into 1944. Boehm said "It was just a matter of us supplying through the Persian Corridor, supplying whatever they [e.g., the Russians wanted] up to this time during the Battle of Stalingrad then going on. So

Sergeant Robert Boehm (right) and a friend outside their barracks in Tehran, Iran, during the summer of 1943 (Robert Boehm Collection).

A member of the U.S. Army's 3949th Quartermaster Truck Company poses for a photograph in front of the company office in Tehran, Iran, in mid–1943 (Robert Boehm Collection).

we were running everything you could think of, you know, 2½ ton trucks loaded with a jeep inside and a machine-gun on the jeep and appropriate ammunition [stored] on both sides of the jeep and in the back of these trucks, some medical supplies, some food, and things like that."[7] Boehm said that these convoys operated twenty-four hours a day, seven days a week with American and Persian drivers sitting behind the wheels of the trucks. Boehm proudly asserted that "we taught Persians how to drive." In fact, as the official record illustrates, the U.S. Army established a school for interpreters in order to teach the Persians how to drive, as well as deploying U.S. personnel to maintain roads, and prioritize and coordinate construction programs all along the main supply route on which motor transport operations would be conducted."[8] Indeed, in its three years of existence, the U.S. Army hired more than 9,275 Iranians in order to

Platoon Sergeant Robert Boehm (left) and a soldier of the 3949th Quartermaster Truck Company at their base in Tehran, Iran, in mid–1943 (Robert Boehm Collection).

build and maintain roads, repair vehicles, and act as drivers. Of the 7,500 drivers trained by the MTS, approximately 3,155 of them worked directly with Army Quartermaster personnel in Iran at any given time.[9] As for teaching the Iranians to drive, Boehm stated that this proved to be difficult since many of them "didn't know a gear shift from a camel. We taught those guys [i.e., the Iranians] how to drive and of course there were a lot of Russians there too."

Besides the lack of decent native drivers, the road conditions in Iran were far from perfect. These conditions coupled with the many sandstorms resulted in the deadlining of many trucks that had to be cannibalized, due to a shortage of spare parts to keep the truck convoys flowing north. Nonetheless, of the trucks used by the U.S. Army in the Persian Corridor,

> certain types of Internationals, Studebakers, and Mack diesels, none of them specifically designed for the peculiar conditions of the Corridor operation, bore the chief burden of the load. It was reported that, all factors considered, the Studebaker 6 × 4 tractor with 7-ton trailer and the 2½-ton cargo trucks gave good service. It was stated that these vehicles could cover 50,000 miles before repair became uneconomical. Generally, the basic chassis developed only a few serious faults: the cabs, fenders, hood, dust skirts, on hood side panels, hood tops, transmission cover plates, radiator cores, storage battery supports, fan belts, and distributor caps.
>
> Studebaker 1-ton trailer mortality was high, largely as a result of the abuse when operated empty. Tarpaulins required frequent repair. The Mack diesel 10-ton 6 × 4 cargo trucks were considered well adapted to MTS needs. They were good for 100,000 miles before repairs became uneconomical. Parts consumption was low and failures infrequent but their bodies were too small and were structurally weak. Mack weaknesses were in the radiator cowl, starter switches, series parallel switches, flexible fuel lines, fuses, and air cleaners.
>
> Most diesel road failures were caused by clogged fuel lines. On the basis of experience in MTS, it was felt that the ideal truck would have been a 6 × 4 tractor trailer with air brakes and a 150-horsepower engine, ten forward speeds, a maximum speed of forty-five miles per hour, power to carry its net load of fifteen tons up 15-percent grades, and stamina enough to operate 100,000 miles over mountainous roads. The trailer would have had a dual axle with air brakes and a van type of body 28 feet long, 7 feet high, and 8 feet wide. But there was no time, in setting up the MTS, to design and produce the perfect truck for the job. It was a supplementary service with a limited life to live and it made the best of available equipment.[10]

During the critical fighting around Stalingrad (September 1942–February 1943), Sergeant Boehm said, the Americans stepped up the supply effort as the tempo and pace of operations increased significantly before and after this crucial battle. Boehm remembered that the trucks were tactically arranged to meet this growing demand. The truck convoys, organized from the Motor Transport Service's 516th and 517th Quartermaster Truck Regiments, and broken down into what were called serials and made up of about 60 trucks, proved easy to form into convoys as each regiment consisted of three battalions each (see Appendix #1). Meanwhile, the MTS's 26th Quartermaster Truck Regiment, which consisted of a single battalion, was likewise formed into a serial and like-

Platoon Sergeant Boehm and a comrade pose in a Willys jeep somewhere in China in the spring of 1945 (Robert Boehm Collection).

wise proved to be up to the job insofar as the relief effort was concerned. While there were an average of about 3 convoys a day heading north toward Russia the intensity of the fighting in Russia prompted U.S. Army officials to step up the pace of re-supply to an average of 6 convoys or 360 trucks per day. Boehm added that this not only included the standard Army GMC 5-ton and 2.5-ton trucks but also big diesel trucks driven mostly by the Americans. Boehm stated that the Russians drove the smaller 1.5-ton trucks. The big equipment was handled by the Americans. As for the port operations, Boehm recalled that "they were unloading these ships like you couldn't believe." Loading would take place on the docks as the trucks were brought close to the ships and lined up. Prior to this, each truck fueled up and had its air pressure in each tire checked in order to prevent a blowout or accident once they headed north as the route was both difficult and deadly due to the mountainous nature of the terrain in northern Iran. Boehm added that the turn around for each truck was normally two days with a day given for rest and a change of crews.

Allies of a Different Kind

As for relations with the British, Boehm stated that for the most part they (i.e., the British) remained quite aloof though some befriended their American cousins. In fact, Boehm became friends with a Welshman named Michael Fonakey. Sergeant Boehm said with amusement that for the most part he could hardly understand Fonakey, due to the fact that "he [Fonakey] had quite a thick brogue." Except for Fonakey, Boehm added that unless you drank with them in the pubs or went to some of their affairs or drank in their canteens, they remained pretty much aloof of their American cousins. Indeed, "for the most part, while we were buddies we never could get very close to them."[11]

As for the Russians, Boehm recalled that they remained cool, and were very cautious toward the American soldiers. Boehm said that for the most part he avoided most Russian soldiers unless he found a Russian soldier "with a bit more brass on his uniform or with one or two stripes before he would attempt to either offer him a single or pack of cigarettes." The American sergeant said that for the most part, however, the Russians did not want to be seen fraternizing with the American soldiers.

In sum, despite the coolness toward their American allies, the Soviets were nonetheless grateful for the equipment transferred to them through Lend-Lease. From its beginnings in late 1942 through its peak in July 1944, the Motor Transport Service operated some 3,430 trucks and tractors along with 2,779 trailers carrying over 90 percent of the supplies into Russia. By the time operations officially ceased on 31 December 1945, the Persian Gulf Command managed to demonstrate "how rail, port, and motor transport operations could be successfully conducted in semi-developed area" under wartime conditions.[12]

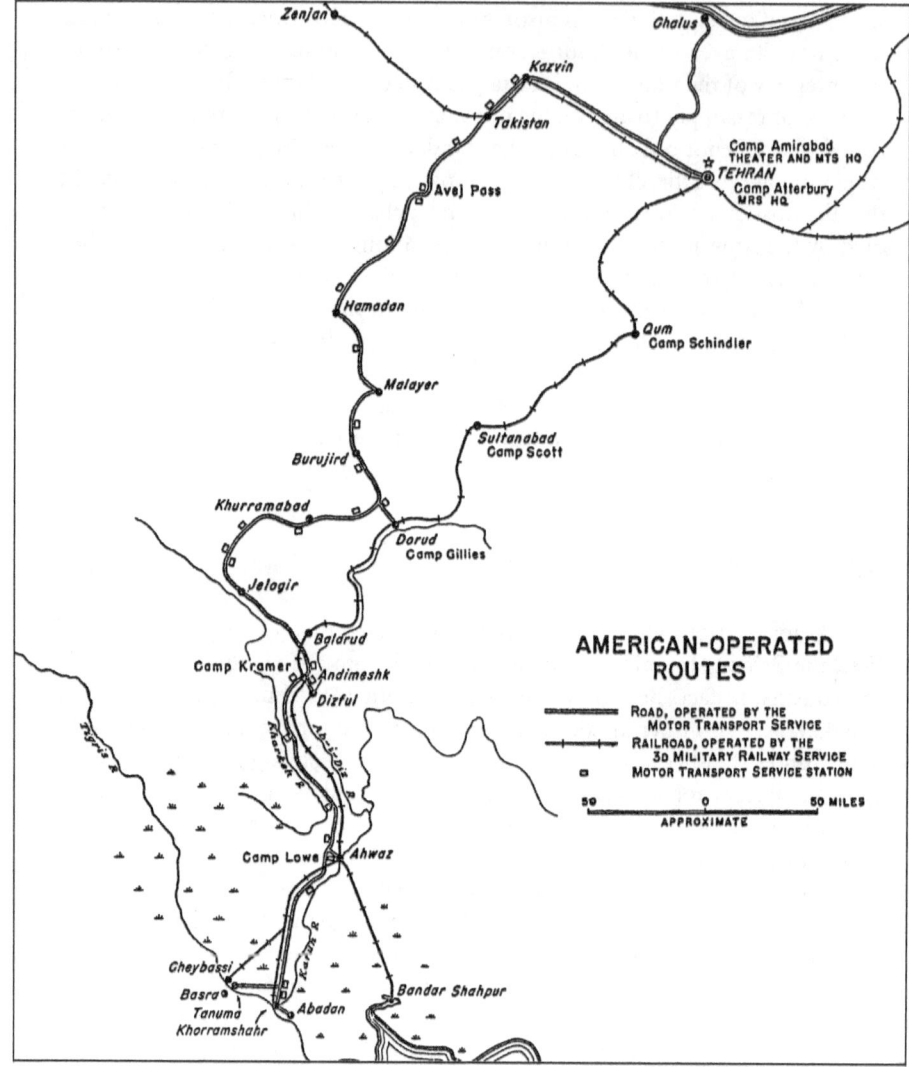

Map 3. The Persian Corridor during World War II (Motter, *The Persian Corridor and Aid to Russia*, p. 314).

To the China-Burma-India Theater: Winter 1944–Summer 1945

Sergeant Boehm and his fellow soldiers remained in Iran until the winter of 1944. By this time, Boehm recalled, the war in Europe was "winding down, and that is when we got the call" to transfer to the Pacific. "We had already

Sergeant Boehm (fourth from left) and fellow GIs take a break while running supplies northward to the Russians along the Persian Corridor during World War II (Robert Boehm Collection).

spent a considerable bit of time over there, and we thought we were going to be sent home as the war with Japan was also winding down. So we went down to Bombay," Boehm remembered. After arriving in Bombay the Army issued Boehm and his men "new equipment, all trucks, new jeeps, new everything, including field kitchens as well with new orders directing them to proceed by train eastward." Sergeant Boehm recalled that the most memorable event of this part of the journey was when they boarded a train which he said was unusual in that the tailgate of the first car would fall down on the train and you could drive across them." Boehm stated that the cars resembled something

> like our gondola cars used in hauling coal. They were open on the sides and they had the ends that could fall down, and you could drive from the end of the train all the way up to the coal tender. All these trucks and vehicles, all these personnel carriers and weapons carriers and jeeps and all that stuff we drove onto the train and went overland from Bombay to Calcutta, where we got off the train and started to drive to Assam to Nepal and from there into Burma.[13]

As Sergeant Boehm and his comrades discovered, the CBI Theater was far different from what they had experienced up to now. In fact, of all the theaters during the Second World War, the China-Burma-India Theater or CBI proved to be the most militarily and politically challenging during World War II to achieve unity of effort and inter-service cooperation.[14] Also, CBI proved to a major test of the durability of the alliance between the United States, Great Britain, and China with the greatest challenge being, of course, the command relationship between the three powers. Lord Alan Brooke, chief of the British

Imperial General Staff, in fact, called the command arrangements in CBI "half baked ... a wild scheme with no central control."[15] Part of the confusion in the command arrangements was due to the suddenness of the British and Chinese collapse in Burma. With the fall of Rangoon in April 1942, the Japanese managed to cut the only port funneling critical lend-lease supplies to the Chiang Kai-shek's Nationalist forces. As British, Chinese, and Commonwealth forces fought a rearguard action against the Japanese to the borders of India, both the American and British chiefs of staff concluded that the re-supply of Chiang's armies was necessary in order to tie down hundreds of thousands of Japanese troops that could possibly be used to reinforce its Pacific conquests in the Solomons, New Guinea, and the Marianas. Hence, the Combined Chiefs of Staffs organized the Assam-Burma Ferry Command as well as laid the groundwork for an eventual retaking of Northern Burma and the re-creation of a land route into China. Despite the heroic efforts by the pilots and crews who flew in the unarmed transports over the Hump or Himalayan Mountains, in all types of weather, they were nonetheless limited as to the tonnage of supplies that they could bring into China.[16] Thus, the Combined Chiefs of Staff agreed at the first three major wartime conferences, at Casablanca (January 1943), the Trident Conference at Washington (May 1943), and at the Quadrant Conference in Quebec (August 1943), that the Allies would launch a major offensive in northern Burma in order to reestablish and secure both the air and land routes leading into China. Under the direction of Major General W. E. R. Scovell, who took command of the Service of Supply (SOS), China, Burma, India, in November 1943, an SOS Transportation Service was established at New Delhi on 1 January 1944, and placed under the command of Brigadier General Thomas B. Wilson. Meanwhile, Allied planners drew up plans to re-take Burma and secure the land route into China. As the planning for a series of limited offensives commenced, the Allies concluded that for the time being, the main effort would be toward strengthening the air supply routes going into China. Indeed, over time, intra-service and inter-Allied squabbling as to who or what mode of transport should have priority almost derailed the plans laid out at the early conferences for the reconquest of Burma. Only through the insistence of Chiang Kai-shek and Lieutenant General Stilwell did the Allies decide to stay the course and rebuild the Burma-Ledo Road. Despite the opposition voiced by Major General Chennault, Lieutenant Stilwell and his successor, General Albert C. Wedemeyer, saw the re-opening of the Burma Road as a means of increasing the tonnage of supplies flowing to Chiang's Nationalist Chinese forces that had trickled over the Hump during the early days of the airlift.[17]

From his own vantage point, Boehm agreed with General Stilwell's contention that the Burma-Ledo Road was vital to the Allied war effort in CBI. In fact, the Army sergeant took issue with the contention that the Hump pilots flew in the major portion of supplies going to Chiang Kai-shek's Nationalist Chinese forces.[18] Sergeant Boehm emphasized that the overland routes used by the Quartermaster units were "critical to the war in China-Burma-India," as the Japanese had overrun Rangoon and had cut Chiang's overland supply routes after the fall of Myitkyina. Boehm added that this supply route had been a vital link in the Burma-Ledo Road prior to its fall in May 1942. Hence, the "Allies had to have an overland supply route to supply the Chinese." In order to correct this situation, the Combined Chiefs of Staff (CCS) decided to construct "a road from Ledo in Assam to the old Burma Road located on the China-Burma border" in order to supply Chiang's forces whom were on the offensive against the Japanese. Also, with the tempo of the air offensive against the Japanese in China, on Formosa (Taiwan), and the Japanese home islands, the CCS likewise wanted to increase the flow of supplies going to Brigadier (later Major General) General Claire L. Chennault's 14th Air Force. Thus, as early as October 1942, the United States Army began the arduous task of expanding the ports of Karachi, Bombay, and Calcutta in order to accommodate the ships carrying war materiel for Chinese, American, and British forces fighting the Japanese in Burma and China. With the establishment of the Service of Supply (SOS) and the creation of the Assam-Burma Ferry Command under the command of Brigadier General (later Lieutenant General) Raymond A. Wheeler, the U.S. Army undertook the difficult though not impossible mission of resupplying Chiang's forces as well as Chennault's growing air forces.[19] In fact, for the next two years (1942–1944), the Assam-Burma Ferry Command, as well as the Combat Cargo Command, began a massive though woefully inadequate logistical airlift from bases in India to Kunming, China over the Himalayas or Hump, as it was known to the American pilots. Flying the durable and dependable though unarmed Curtiss C-46 Dakotas or the Curtiss C-47s, the American pilots braved enemy fighters and treacherous flying conditions to bring what supplies they could to Chiang's forces. During the summer of 1942 and throughout the next year and one-half, Wheeler's SOS concentrated "on supporting the Tenth Air Force and the nascent Chinese Army in India."[20]

After a two year campaign to prevent the Japanese from penetrating into India after the fall of Burma the Allies, including Slim's 14th Army, Major General Orde Wingate's Chindits, and elements of the 5307th Composite Unit or Merrill's Marauders launched a series of counterattacks designed to retake northern Burma that included the vital air and land base at Myitkyina. In March 1944, Brigadier General Frank D. Merrill's 5307th Composite Unit began a six-month-long drive to retake the vital link in the Ledo Road at Myitkyina. After some of the most bitter fighting of the war in CBI, Myitkyina fell to a combined American and Chinese force in August 1944. On 18 January 1945, the U.S. Army's 5332nd Brigade seized the ridge located at Loi-kang that overlooked the Burma Road and moved artillery into position to prevent an enemy counterattack. Several days later, on 24 January, U.S. Army Brigadier General Robert M. Cannon promised that the Burma Road would soon be open to American and Chinese supply convoys.[21] By the time of Boehm's arrival in the theater, the Burma-Ledo Road was in full operation. With the arrival of some 2,000 U.S. Army 2½-ton and 5,000 lend-lease trucks, rushed to the CBI Theater by Lieutenant General Brehon B. Somervell, commanding general of the Army Service Forces (ASF), logistical support to the Chinese Armed Forces increased significantly and, in effect, assisted in turning the tide in favor of the Allies once the Stilwell Road[22] had been completed in January 1945.[23] With the invasions of Iwo Jima in February 1945 and Okinawa in April 1945, the Japanese began to withdraw significant numbers of troops from China in order to protect the home islands. The Japanese redeployment allowed Chinese troops to re-occupy the evacuated territory though it did not mean, however, the end of the war in China. In fact, the Japanese still had significant numbers of troops in China as well as throughout Southeast Asia. With the threat of Japan greatly diminished Chiang turned his attention toward his old nemesis: the Communists under Mao Zedong. In the middle of this internal conflict between the two rival Chinese warlords were the American troops and pilots sent to China to help her defeat the Japanese. As Boehm recalled, American troops oftentimes found themselves the target of both the retreating Japanese and the many warlords who began to target American supply convoys in order to feed and arm their private armies.

In fact, as Boehm recalled, there were times the that Japanese were "the least of his worries" as the Chinese couldn't be "trusted worth a shit" due in large part to the pilferage of supplies and food that the Americans were bringing into Kunming, the main hub of the Chinese resistance in Southwestern China. Boehm, in fact, reiterated that the Chinese "stole, they stole everything from me. In fact, one day, I was ready to run toward them with my Tommy gun[24] as they began taking food from the back one of my vehicles." Boehm added, "[One time] a buddy and I were on official business ... at Chin-ning, about thirty miles east of Kunming, and were only gone for a short time. We went down to a place where it was cool to eat, a Chinese kitchen where, if one presented himself in uniform, they had rice bread and eggs and that sort of thing." Boehm said, "While we were gone and came back you could tell somebody had gone through our trucks and saw a squadron of guys [i.e., Chinese soldiers], and thought that it had to be them [that took the supplies], so the corporal who had been standing guard and I took the Tommy Gun and headed toward them in the trenches. They knew what we were there for and they gave us back what they had stolen."[25]

As for contact with British forces, Boehm stated that during his time in Northern Burma and southwestern China he and his men had very little contact with the British Fourteenth Army. By this time, in fact, the 14th Army, under Lieutenant General William Slim, had driven the Japanese out of northern Burma and down the Irrawaddy toward Rangoon. Indeed, Sergeant Boehm recalled that most of the soldiers and airmen there were Americans. In fact, even as far west as Calcutta it was an American effort. It was in Calcutta that

Boehm saw for the first time what soon became the massive American air effort toward the relief of China via the tortuous route known as the Hump. "Calcutta," Boehm remembered, "was where the flyboys[26] would take off over the Hump into Kunming, drop off their supplies and return home. This was a milk run for them. They were supplying whatever their airplanes could carry. And the trucks ran all of the essential supplies into China."

The Army sergeant stated that trucks were, in fact, vital to the supply effort, as the rail head stopped at a town east of Kunming and that was as far as the railroad went. Boehm said this presented a problem as "all of this brand new equipment being carried by the railroads, including these huge Pratt-Whitney radial engines, that were being put on the American bombers," had to be taken off the trains. Boehm recalled that this in and of itself was a problem as they were big and bulky. Added to this was the complication that they had to be unloaded in a driving rain into a morass of mud. The motors had large hooks with propellers attached and as the cranes lifted them from the flatbeds they were placed in all of this mud. Boehm said that this "was atrocious and shows you the amount of goddamn waste that went on there during the war."

"A Small Town Called Hanoi"

One of the more interesting missions that he and his fellow soldiers embarked on while in China was when his unit was instructed to re-supply a stranded Chinese infantry regiment that had been cut off by a large Japanese force. This mission would bring Boehm and his unit northwest of Hanoi in the Red River Valley in what was then French Indochina (Vietnam):

> Assigned to run a supply mission to Chinese forces in Southeastern China near the town of Poseh, whatever it was, and I looked on a map and we were very close to Hanoi, and we made an emergency run to one of the Chinese units in desperate need of ammunition and medical supplies. There were thirteen of us fellas involved [in the resupply effort] and we went down there. In one truck was myself and another sergeant and a corporal, a kid from Baltimore, and we became separated from the main convoy. And I became concerned because there was no real place where you could stop or where you felt you were safe because the road was never on high ground but on low ground where if the enemy were any place around you, you didn't have a good advantage place and lay-up and feel secure.[27]

Boehm said that his small convoy eventually came back together and had managed to make its way into an unknown small town, about two blocks in length, with no modern conveniences of any kind. The big man there had a mill, and he befriended us, and took us in and eventually and fed all us fellas with chicken, sweet and sour pork, greens, and some wine that tasted like oranges." Before this, however, Boehm, who was, "hungry as hell," recalled that he and a corporal and had gone into this store and saw some potatoes that got all brown when baked under charcoal. Not realizing that he had stumbled into a mortuary, Boehm "took them and I offered the guy [the store owner] some money. But this guy was having a fit, waving his arms and didn't want to take it [the money]. Well, later, on I discovered that this guy was a mortician and that when guys are dead they are buried with two potatoes in order that they have some food when they enter into the next world." Looking around Boehm then realized that he was inside a mortuary as there were firecrackers and other supplies and now could see why the owner was making such a fuss over the two potatoes he had taken. Laughing, Boehm said, "I then realized that the reason for his anger was that someone would be denied his two potatoes to take into the next world!" This was, Sergeant Boehm added, "quite humorous." Having returned to the convoy, Sergeant Boehm said that all of the people of the village were around his jeep. So he decided to win over their "hearts and minds" and took some dynamite and lit it and tossed into a nearby river. After doing this three times, a school of dead fish came to surface which the people, who were smiling in approval, quickly gathered up.[28]

As for the relief of the Chinese unit, Boehm recalled that they came upon only dead Japanese. At times, in fact, Boehm indicated that the Japanese were the least of their concerns as it appeared that the Chinese warlords were the ones killing and robbing more Americans than the enemy. Boehm remembered one incident prior to entering China when a convoy that he was traveling in came upon a large number of dead American GIs lying along the banks of the Irrawaddy River killed, as it was discovered later, not by the Japanese but "by the armies of a local Chinese warlord." Boehm said that the warlord's forces "killed every goddamn one of them [American soldiers]. There were dog tags and money belts laying around. I am sure that the Japanese did not do this. It was this Chinese warlord that did it." Boehm recounted another such incident when "we had more than one of our convoys shot up by the warlords. When one of our trucks became separated from the rest of the people they [the Chinese bandits] would come up from over a hill forcing the Chinese driver to pull his emergency brake and pull off to the side of the road and run. Because if he didn't they [the bandits] would kill him too." Boehm added, "Once they killed all of the occupants of the vehicle they then ripped open the sides of the truck and took everything inside. They then took off once the job was completed."

Despite the problems with the marauding armies of the warlords and lack of enthusiasm on the part of the Chinese in fighting the Japanese, Boehm reiterated the point that Chiang was the man. Boehm recalled one instance when his convoy rolled into Kunming and he had managed to get close up to Major General Claire Lee Chennault, the commanding general of the 14th U.S. Army Air Forces, and Generalissimo Chiang Kai-shek, both of whom had been at the airfield that day. Boehm recalled that while at the airfield a plane came in with a load of male and female lieutenants who had been on passes in Calcutta and had overrun the runway and crash landed into a group of adobe huts and had gone tail up, blocking the rest of the runway. Boehm stated that at the time his convoy had a tank retriever and that a master sergeant had come up to him and asked if could he borrow it in order to wrap a line around the tail of the plane and pull it off the runway. Realizing the gravity of the situation Boehm said that it wouldn't be a problem and ordered the crew of the retriever to assist the master sergeant and his crew in the removal of the plane. As for Chiang and Chennault, Boehm said, "We had heard about them ... the Flying Tigers and all this stuff. By that time, both men were world figures," though, as Boehm added, "at the time Chennault was on the outs with the Army and thus was not viewed favorably by the Army. But," as Boehm said, "you have to consider the times and at the time I looked at him as doing his thing in a great cause." Boehm had similar sentiments for Chiang Kai-shek who, despite his obvious flaws, "was our man, and just waiting to do his thing again once the war ended."

"A Very Rugged Country": China, Spring-Summer 1945

Boehm described the roads and people he and his fellow drivers encountered as they crossed over into China as "quite an experience." He said, "It's funny when you cross over a mountain and come out into the next valley, and that is how all of China is, a very rugged country. Every time you go into a valley, and come into a village, the people had large bags of charcoal. All these guys would be carrying these big goddamn bags of charcoal, and everybody would have elphantitis or some skin disease and have a limb limp. You go into the next village, and everyone's teeth would be black and rotting off. You go into the next village and everybody's teeth would be red and their eyes would be burnt because they chewed a lot of betel nuts. So every time you crossed the mountain you would experience something different."

Boehm said that one of the most distinguishing similarities among most outlying Chinese villages was the preponderance of opium. Boehm said that "you could always smell the sweet scent of opium burning. I will never forget that smell for as long as I live. Also, do you know that for as long as we were in China, I never knew of one GI that ever smoked opium. Yes, they rolled their own cigarettes but never did I see any of them put any opium in the wrappers. You see, opium is a like a little dough ball that is put into a pipe with a long stem, and they took the pipe and inhaled some and then passed the pipe around as they sat in a circle until everyone was, well, high, you know!"[29]

Convoy Movements on the Burma-Ledo Road

Most of the truck convoys ferrying supplies into China were based at Kanchrapara, near Calcutta where, prior to departure, a convoy received as many trucks as it could handle. Vehicles were then delivered to Makum Junction, between Chaua and Ledo, and it was from here that drivers such as Boehm took over the vehicles. The drivers then drove to Margherita, near Ledo, bivouacked there overnight and the next morning crossed the initial point at Ledo. If a unit was destined for China, it was normally staged at Kanchrapara; near Calcutta the allocations officer dispatched it by rail to Siliguri or Bongaigon in Assam, and then by road to Chabua onto Margherita, where the vehicles of the convoy "were inspected and repaired" prior to their movement into China.

From Margherita, the truck convoys headed into China where the drivers found way stations at regular intervals. By June 1945, there were nine of these way stations established along the Ledo Road where drivers could have their vehicles serviced or, they could obtain a meal and find bathing facilities. In order to protect the convoys, military policemen regularly patrolled the road from the some thirty stations that had been established to provide security for the drivers from marauding Chinese bandits. "Ordnance and maintenance detachments manned twenty-two repair points along the road in order to keep the convoys moving."[30]

Depending on driver fatigue and the availability of fuel, the journey from Ledo to Kunming normally took ten days. While road conditions and the availability of fuel oftentimes determined the length of the journey into China, the health of the drivers remained at the center of a successful delivery. Indeed, as Army Service Force officials discovered, "increasingly numbers of men with dust pneumonia, cysts, fatigue, and kidney ailments began to appear at sick call." Bouncing up and down on the unsurfaced roads, Army truck drivers who spent prolonged hours before the wheel of a Studebaker or Mack truck in both Persia and along the Burma-Ledo Road complained of having "pounded their ... kidneys ... to jelly."[31] In fact, at one point during the campaign, these problems became so acute that quartermaster companies were forced to remove many men from their duties for great lengths of time.[32] Accidents and local attacks by bands of Chinese bandits also hindered convoy operations. "For the first five months of 1945, 10 percent of the vehicles dispatched were either lost by accident en route or delayed along the way."

As for the equipment they used, Boehm said that they drove "International semis, with the cab over the engine, and we had some 2½-ton trucks and jeeps." Sergeant Boehm recalled that while in China, "I did a lot of jeep driving, you know. I think a little too much." Boehm recalled a rather humorous incident when his first sergeant became curious as to the letters he had been receiving from home. "Indeed," Boehm continued,

> our First Sergeant really had it out for me. You know how fellas used to pass letters around? Well, Gracie[33] sent me some photos and we were living in the noncom tent and he [the first sergeant] was kind of curious about my mail and he had seen my pictures. So he wanted to read my mail. So I said to him, "Hey,

Sergeant, you are not going to read my mail." From then on, I bet I was the only guy in my company who rode what they called the point more than anybody in a jeep loaded with enough goddamn dynamite to blow myself and the convoy up with![34]

**Vehicle and Cargo Deliveries
to China and Burma by Months (1945)**

Month	Conroys	Vehicles	Trailers	Gross Weight*	Vehicle and Trailer Weight*	CHINA Cargo Weight*	BURMA Cargo Weight*
Total	433	25,783	6,539	146,948	108,886	38,062	161,986
February	22	1,333	609	5,231	4,120	1,111	27,087
March	22	1,152	745	6,788	5,279	1,509	34,579
April	38	2,342	1,185	15,447	11,249	4,198	31,797
May	78	4,682	1,103	28,080	19,645	8,435	28,357
June	82	4,901	964	27,962	20,977	6,985	14,923
July	75	4,745	828	23,370	17,470	5,900	16,085
August	51	2,652	647	15,866	11,582	4,284	5,046
September	53	3,060	508	18,599	14,291	4,308	4,112
October	12	916	50	5,605	4,273	1,332	....

*Short Tons

Relations with the Chinese

As for the Chinese, Boehm recalled that the ones that he had contact with he liked. Boehm specifically remembered his interpreter, Hoang, whom he and his fellow soldiers named "Frankie." Boehm stated that Hoang spoke fluent English and was a little guy, "but I got along with him very well." Boehm admitted that it was Frankie who taught him something about how Chinese society was structured. Boehm stated that shortly after meeting Frankie, "I soon discovered that there was some different castes among the Chinese where 'don't you tell me as I am better bred than you are.'" Boehm recalled that he discovered this caste system shortly after "we had stopped for a break, so I told Hoang to go down the line with me and had come across two guys really going after each other with one guy, in fact, armed with a knife, you know, and Frankie didn't know what to do. He started hollering and I pulled my .45 caliber pistol and cocked it, and put it up against the guy's leg who was the aggressor. And his eyes got real big and he backed off." Boehm then asked Frankie what was this all about. "The interpreter replied, 'Well the guy comes from a better class and how could he ask him to check the water?'" Boehm added, "I said to tell him [the aggressive one] that I told you to tell him to do so. So that ended all that." Boehm admitted that he was quite surprised at this because he thought everyone was a peasant in China. "But I guess they did have their different levels of strata over there."[35]

Boehm stated that the primary assignment was to supply the U.S. Air Forces in China. He remembered that the bulk of his supplies went to Chennault and the other Allied air forces in the area, "primarily Chinese as I didn't really see any British forces up there." Boehm said that in addition to the resupply effort, many of the Chinese saw the American convoys as a means of conveyance away from the battle area. Boehm said that while on the same trip to the village where he had become separated from the rest of the convoy he had been tasked to purchase a large truckload of sugar from a local merchant for the company back in Kunming. He said that the first sergeant had given him a small ditty bag full of Chinese $100 bills and he was instructed not to let anyone know that had such a large amount of cash. Sergeant Boehm stated that after the sugar had been loaded the corporal with whom they had been traveling came running to him and said, "Sarge you had better get back there" as apparently many of the people wanted to board the truck on top of the sugar. Sergeant Boehm later discovered that the people had gotten the word of a major Japanese force approaching the village and they wanted to flee. Boehm said, "We couldn't take everybody but agreed to take an American-trained Chinese pilot and his wife, who was eight months pregnant. So, I never saw any Japanese there. As I later discovered, somehow, word had gotten out that the Americans had a large amount of money. Well, they just wouldn't leave. So we had to take our sidearms, .45 caliber pistols and M1 carbines, and fire a few rounds over their head in order to get them to leave." Boehm added, "It was at this point that we decided we had better get the hell out of there."

Despite this incident, however, Boehm said that the Chinese people, outside of the Chinese soldiers, could be quite gracious. Sergeant Boehm recalled a time when his column came into a village high in the mountains and they had gotten word that a Chinese armored column was approaching. "Well, we had been ordered to stay with our vehicles and avoid any contact with them. Nevertheless, some of our guys had to leave their vehicles and go into the village below for something." Boehm said that when they got into the village, these Americans were really roughed up by the Chinese troops, so badly, in fact, that many of them had to be hospitalized for a long time as they had been "beaten pretty bad." Yet in the same village the people were, Boehm recalled, "very friendly, very gracious." He specifically remembered that the women living there had very small feet as their feet were tied [bound] into what they called 'Lotus feet.'"

"Marauders and Roadbuilders"

Boehm recalled that his convoy came into frequent contact with American soldiers who had identified themselves as Merrill's Marauders. Sergeant Boehm quite candidly admitted that the Marauders "were over built." He added

"Let me tell you, that one time one of our guys came across a bunch of Merrill's Marauders who were walking along one of the convoys with their rifles and packs and their dog faces. So I stopped in my jeep to offer them a ride. Well, you know I couldn't take many of them so I asked them where they were going, and they replied to 'so and so,' so I asked, 'do you guys want to hop in one of the trucks?'" Boehm said that they were quite grateful and they said, "'Gee thanks, Sarge,' so the truck pulled over and picked them up." After arriving at their destination the sergeant asked the truck driver where the Marauders were. The driver replied that once the GIs got into the back of the truck they had put their feet up against some "clover packs," with canisters containing 3-inch shells. Not knowing what they had their feet up against, one of the Marauders asked the driver what it was that the trucks were carrying. The driver replied, "High explosives." Boehm said that with that, "they, the Marauders, decided that riding perhaps wasn't such a good idea and exited the vehicles and walked the rest of the way." Boehm said that by this time the ranks of the Marauders had been depleted, due in large part to the hard fighting at Bhamo and Myitkyina, and the soldiers that his convoy encountered were the remnants of the original group formed in 1943 by Brigadier General Frank D. Merrill.[36]

Sergeant Boehm recalled the devastation he encountered when his convoy entered Bhamo after its re-capture by elements of the Chinese 38th Division and the U.S. 475th Infantry Regiment on 15 December 1944:

> When I drove up to Bhamo, I could not believe it, you could not hardly drive because there were bomb craters everywhere. You just had to drive between everything. and they had a couple of gendarmes but they were not military clothed but had white cuffs (on their sleeves) much like European or Asian policemen. And they were out there directing traffic ... what traffic there was ... was very little, perhaps very few rickshaws and bicycles and trucks. But when we got to Bhamo there were metal buildings up there. You could not put your hand on a building without covering up a bullet hole. That place was shot to shreds.... It was just shot to shreds. And there was ammunition ... there were some live, some duds, all kinds of ordnance you wouldn't believe what a shamble. I think that the people, the graves registration people, had gone through until we got there but the people who pick up the ordnance, they hadn't come through yet. They picked up all the brass ... they then stacked the brass like cordwood and stuff like this, you know ... and that stuff hadn't been done. In some cases there were some [shell] cases still laying around.... You didn't know if there were any live cases still lying around. It was quite a mess.[37]

As for the support of the Chinese in the construction and repair of the Burma-Ledo Road, Sergeant Boehm said, "I was utterly amazed. The first time we came to the foothills of the Himalayas I stopped at the bottom and looked up and all I could see were these Chinese in blue denim jackets and trousers. They all had these jackets and straw hats and they had all come to the edge of the road and they looked down over and as far as I could see all I could see are these goddamn Chinese with those hats on as far as the eyes could see. Also I could see what these guys were doing. They were all on the road and they all

Wrecked Japanese Type 95 Chi Ha tanks stand as mute testimony to the bitter fighting for Bhamo and northern Burma in late 1944 as General Stilwell's combined force of American and Chinese soldiers cleared the area of the veteran Japanese 18th Division (Alexander McVean Collection).

had hammers. Some guys were hauling stones and some guys had big stone crushers, like a roller. These guys were making big [stones] into little ones. When they got there, these coolies, ... there were tons of them, and they didn't have rollers!"[38]

One particularly intriguing incident that caught Sergeant Boehm's interest even more was what he saw while observing the construction of an airfield near Kunming:

> I saw ... I don't even know where in the hell but it was where we saw here the B-29s [SuperFortress] had to come in there. They [the Chinese peasants] had to make this runway and I stopped there and was utterly amazed. I said to this corporal, "Look at this." These guys had the biggest earth rollers I had ever seen. And they had these long ropes. Christ, they must have had several hundred people pulling these big ropes and they put big rocks on the bottom with small ones on top and then poured gravel on top. These big rollers must have been 18–20 feet high and they had four big ropes with people pulling them like ants with this stone crusher making this runway for the B-29s to land on. It was absolutely amazing. I wish had taken a picture of it.[39]

Boehm said that watching both the construction of the Burma Road and the airfield were the most amazing things he had even seen. He added that despite having only a short amount of time watching the coolies build the road, it was the fact that they took big rocks and turned them into small ones. It was, as Boehm recalled, "like a production line." He also said that watching the construction of the airfield was "an awesome sight to see. All those people had one thing in mind: build that airfield." The Army sergeant said that he observed this throughout the mountains where he and his convoy traveled. "The Chinese were," Boehm said, "just doing their thing." In contrast, Boehm stated that in the flat areas, the American combat engineers had their graders and stuff like that, and were able to push the gravel around as well as having tar and pitch in order to bind the road together.

Sergeant Boehm recounted a rather humorous incident that occurred about one hundred miles west of Kunming when he and his driver came upon a truck speeding toward them with U.S. Navy markings. After letting it pass by, the two soldiers realized that they were hundreds of miles from any large body of water. Turning to his driver, Boehm, joking, said, "What in the hell are they doing out there? Maybe they're running away from the war, who knows!"[40]

Boehm said that disease was pretty rampant in China. Throughout his stay in China Boehm took note of the unsanitary conditions in many of the villages he came across. He specifically noted that the two most common diseases he and his comrades encountered were amebic dysentery and malaria. He recalled one instance when "a Chinese lady had fixed them all a chicken dinner and one of his drivers got dysentery so bad that they thought he wouldn't make it." Sergeant Boehm said that the driver fortunately overcame it, although, he added, unlike today, "they had no drugs to cure such illnesses at this time as penicillin or sulfa had only recently been discovered."

The End of the War and Home: June 1945

The end of the war in Europe came with little fanfare as the American troops in the Far East were still fighting the remnants of a dying Japanese empire. For Boehm, however, the war ended on one hot day in June 1945 when after a long supply run he remembered pulling into a camp made up of tents where they were staying and noticed that his commanding officer, Captain Gray, was waiting for him. Approaching Boehm, Captain Gray hollered, "Sergeant Boehm.... Good news. You're going home." Boehm said that this "was June 6." After that, Boehm said, "we then went down to Camp Shapiro, outside of Calcutta. That was where the staging area was located and waited for transportation home."

Boehm said that "it seemed like we were there an eternity waiting for transportation. We finally shipped out of Calcutta in September 1945. Actually, we left out of there on an Army transport, the USS *General Sherman*. It was supposed to have been made into a tanker. But it was somebody's brainchild that they could put racks into them. These were our sleeping accommodations.

On board, we took some of the flyboys and stopped off along the west coast of Australia before heading past Tasmania. We then went up to Okinawa. where we picked up a bunch of guys waiting to go home. While on board, somebody gave us an alert that we were being followed by a two-man submarine. There were a lot of alerts though I didn't see any Japanese submarines. They sounded general quarters and everyone was running around aboard ship with their helmets and they fired depth charges. Having gone through the war you just hoped that everything was all right. We then went to Hawaii. After we left Hawaii, you could turn on the running lights. I finally got home September 17, 1945, got furlough, and finally got separated from the Army on November 4, 1945."[41]

Postscript

Re-united with his wife, Grace, in September 1945, with whom he had spent only eleven months prior to shipping overseas, Bob celebrated his first wedding anniversary together with her in November 1946. Returning home to Cleveland after three years in the Army, Platoon Sergeant Robert Boehm became a printer and pursued his hobbies of golf and bowling, and raised two daughters and three sons. Looking back on his time in Iran, India, and China, Sergeant Boehm admitted that it was an interesting time. More important, however, is the fact that he saw a part of World War II that was exotic though dangerous, and in the course of those three years had an opportunity to meet people whom he still can remember in a theater of operations that was not — at least in his opinion as well as that of the other young Americans who served there — a backwash. Indeed, Boehm concluded "that had it not been for the war, I would've never seen these countries, except maybe in a book or magazine."

Chapter 3

Captain Edward M. Goodman, USAAF: "Flying the Aluminum Trail"

Missions over the Himalayas, or the Hump, were both long and dangerous. Indeed, the Hump portion of the Assam-Burma Ferry Command's route into China averaged over 600 miles from bases located either in Assam or New Delhi. Colonel Ralph S. Marshall, USAF, in fact, stated that flying unarmed transports over the Hump was "like no other flying experience before or after this tour of duty."[1] One of these pilots who experienced flying this route was Captain Edward M. "Goodie" Goodman, USAAF, who flew unarmed B-24s and C-87s over the Himalayas from the spring of 1943 until his return to the United States in November 1944 after 82 successful missions. In fact, after his arrival in India in the spring of 1943, Captain Goodman was the first pilot to have flown the B-24 and C-87s during the airlift into China.[2] As Goodman said, "I wouldn't have missed it for anything, but I don't think I'd want to do it again."[3]

An experienced pilot, Captain Edward M. Goodman flew "over jungles and rivers and above uncharted mountain peaks" onto dirt and grass airfields in China, oftentimes dodging Japanese planes, and under all kinds of weather conditions in order to keep Chiang Kai-shek's Nationalist armies and Claire Chennault's Flying Tigers in action. Keeping nearly 1 million Japanese tied down on the continent of Asia as U.S. and Allied troops began the long, arduous island-hopping campaigns in the Central and Southwest Pacific Ocean areas, the pilots and crews of the Assam-Burma Ferry Command maintained the supply lines into China and in so doing, contributed greatly to the Allied victory in September 1945.

Early Career, 1921–1943

Born in 1921, in Brooklyn, New York, Goodman spent his youth building plane models and dreaming of the day when he would solo in an airplane.

While attending college in Brooklyn, Goodman realized his dream of flying and took advantage of President Franklin D. Roosevelt's program to train college students as pilots in order that the United States Army would have a pool of trained aviators should the United States enter war in Europe or in the Pacific. Goodman, in fact, soloed at Roosevelt Air Field, Mineola, located on Long Island, New York, in September 1939 in a twin-winged Stearman Kaydet, "a fine plane," the native New Yorker later recalled, "one that was used for crop dusting."[4] Shortly thereafter, Goodman was flying in air shows and, in fact, won a flying competition judged by a little known Army aviation officer named Jimmy Doolittle.

Even as Goodman flew in air shows the Wehrmacht and Luftwaffe overran Western Europe and launched a savage air war against the British Isles in the summer of 1940. Much to the opposition of his parents, Goodman, eager to enlist in the war against Nazi Germany, dropped out of college and volunteered for the Royal Canadian Air Force in the late summer of 1940. He remained in Canada until he returned home in the summer of 1941 where he took a job training U.S. Army Air Corps cadets. When the United States entered World War II after the German declaration of war on 11 December 1941, Goodman enlisted in the U.S. Army Air Force. Already a seasoned pilot, Army officials assigned Goodman to train newly-appointed U.S. Army Air Corps cadets in flying Stearman PT-17s at Douglas, Georgia. Already a veteran, Goodman recalled that at that time "we already had a trained cadre of 3,000 pilots, aged 19 to 22," and that "they could be turned into military pilots in 90 days."[5]

Goodman's next assignment was as a co-pilot in a Martin B-26 medium bomber known as Martin Marauders or as "flying coffins" by the pilots who flew them due to the fact that "so many guys were killed training on them." One such crashed, in fact, nearly killing then–Second Lieutenant Goodman and his pilot, 1st Lieutenant Carl Triest, when the B-26 they were flying crashed into a cornfield near McCool, Indiana, approximately ten miles from Gary, Indiana, on 7 August 1942. Lieutenant Triest, who had managed to circle the cornfield three times before landing the plane under a heavy overcast sky and in poor visibility, was unable to reach the airport at McCool about a quarter mile away from where the plane came down. As the plane rolled through the cornfield, a utility pole sheared its right wing off while both its engines and landing gear came off their moorings.

While Triest emerged from the plane, shaken though uninjured, he discovered that his co-pilot, Goodman, had suffered a fractured right arm, numerous lacerations and bruises, and shock. Before both men were taken to a nearby hospital by a local resident. Goodman, who realized that the bombsight was still in the plane, jumped out of the vehicle which had already begun to move and began to shout, "My God, the bombsight! The bombsight!" He then ran toward the plane and removed the valuable piece of equipment. Placing the bombsight in a hospital vault, the second lieutenant remained in the hospital for several days until he was able to resume his journey. Later, Army Air Force officials launched an investigation but were unable to determine the cause of the near-fatal crash.⁶

After further training in the United States, the Army assigned Goodman and his crew to ferrying B-25s and B-26s into the North African theater of operations. Because he had experience flying at night, the Army re-assigned Goodman to the Assam-Burma Ferry Command which had been ferrying supplies over the Himalayas. Assigned to the U.S. air base at Tezpur, in Assam, India, Goodman's job was to

> pilot a small plane loaded with 500-pound bombs, strapped to 50-gallon drums of 100-octane aviation fuel, on a chancy 3½ to 4½ hour trip. He took off from an airstrip surfaced with steel mats, flew over jungle and rivers and above uncharted mountain peaks and landed on a grass airstrip in China.⁷

Flying unarmed transports (i.e., converted B-24 medium bombers), with the recently activated Assam-Burma-China Ferry Command, Goodman soon discovered that Japanese fighters would be the least of his worries as he and his crew braved monsoons, snowstorms, ice, and dense fog over the so-called "Aluminum Trail" or "Rock Pile" known as the Himalayan Mountains.

Liberators Over the Hump

The B-24 Liberator was perhaps one of the best medium-range bombers flown by Allied pilots during World War II. Indeed, thanks to pilots such as Ed Goodman and Captain Elmer H. Haynes, who flew B-24s over the Hump, the planes were oftentimes labeled "Chennault's Secret Weapon." In fact, like the dependable C-46s and C-47s, the B-24s were ideal for the conditions encountered in Burma and China.⁸ For Haynes, who originally had been assigned to fly the B-17 Flying Fortresses, the B-24 was "more difficult to handle from a physical perspective. It was heavier then the Flying Fortresses, and required more exertion to operate the dual rudders and aileron controls. But its Davis wing allowed the aircraft to cruise at a much higher speed than the B-17." Haynes also noted that the B-24 had much better "visibility than that of a Fortress, due in large part to the Liberator's "shoulder mounted wings, which gave the pilot excellent observation from the cockpit under and around the plane ... [while] ... its tricycle landing gear afforded better frontal vision when taxiing, since it sat level on the ground."⁹ Furthermore, as Captain Goodman added, "the B-24 could carry 2½ times more cargo than either the C-46 or C-47."¹⁰

In order for the B-24 to fly the long distances back and forth from bases in Assam to airfields in China, Liberator crews installed an extra gasoline tank in the bomb bay which gave the plane "enough fuel to keep it airborne for long distances — often more than 16 hours at a stretch." In fact, the B-24 was spe-

A Martin B-26 Marauder, known by the pilots who flew the Hump as a "flying coffin" due to its tendency to crash or catch fire (Edward M. Goodman Collection).

cially modified to carry more fuel to increase the range of the aircraft as well as its fuel-carrying capacity. The basic B-24 sent initially to CBI could carry 2,814 gallons of fuel. Eventually, in addition to the standard fuel tanks, mechanics attached two additional "non-metallic 400-gallon tanks" to the forward half of the bomb bay in order to increase the range of the aircraft. Two more 400-gallon tanks were fitted in the rear end of the bomb bay as well as a 102-gallon tank fitted in the bombardier's compartment. Finally, "three specially contoured metal tanks were fitted in the space above the bomb bay. These three deck tanks provided an additional 334 gallons of gasoline that could be airlifted into China. The addition of the extra tanks gave the B-24 a carrying capacity of 4,500 gallons when fully loaded.[11]

Despite its extra fuel tank and the position of its wing, the B-24 required longer airstrips than the B-17. In fact, the plane's long takeoff runs, higher landing speeds, and tricycle wheels allowed the aircraft to roll for miles before it finally braked to a stop. Prior to the B-24 becoming fully operational, tests conducted on the dry Utah lake beds indicated that a B-24 had to roll five miles before coming to a complete stop.[12] Haynes likewise wrote that in flying the B-24, pilots had to angle the plane and fly "with its nose slightly below the level position" over the Hump in order to prevent the ship from angling "tail down" and thereby increasing the drag on the aircraft which caused the plane's engines to work harder and slower. This condition also caused the B-24 to burn more fuel in order to compensate for the loss of air speed.[13]

One last problem which proved fatal in some instances was that with the addition of so many fuel tanks the plane was, in effect, a flying bomb. Normal operating procedures called for bomb bay doors to be cracked in order that gasoline fumes could escape. One spark could set off a chain explosion. Normally, this occurred when the electric flaps were retracted during takeoff or, as in some cases by a spark thrown from a radio transmitter, a bolt of lightning from a thunderstorm or if enemy fire struck a B-24. In order to reduce the chances of an explosion occurring, flight engineers developed a system that greatly prevented fumes from developing inside half-empty fuel tanks by injecting inert gases into the tanks as they were being emptied. Also, all planes carried a 30-foot long, 1.25 inch defueler hose that crews used after every flight to reduce the fumes present inside the bomb bay compartments after every delivery.[14]

Despite the dangers, the B-24s and later the Liberator Express or C-87 and C-109s nevertheless filled a much-needed gap when it came to carrying supplies to China and, in fact, throughout the Pacific theaters of operation:

> As early as July 1941 the Ferrying Command, in the absence of long-range transports, had begun using stripped-down B-24 bombers in its North Atlantic Service. The B-24 was unusually well-suited for transport work after most of its armament had been removed and its bomb-bay section rigged to accommodate passengers and cargo. With fuel tanks, the plane was estimated to have a maximum range of 4,000 miles.... Stripped of all combat equipment and armor plate, the Liberator could carry 7,500–8,000 pounds of payload with full fuel tanks. In addition to its long range and powerful lift, the Liberator alone among major aircraft then in production or planned for early production had one prime characteristic of true cargo aircraft — its fuselage stood low to the ground, and so it could be easily loaded.[15]

It is important to note that although the two follow-on designs — the LB-30 (a modified Liberator) and the C-87 could carry heavier payloads they did not have the range of the B-24.[16] The LB-30 entered service in June 1942 while both the C-87 and C-109 later came on line and proved to be well-suited to the rugged flying conditions encountered by Goodman and his fellow B-24 pilots over the Hump. It is also important to note that the ATC converted over 200 B-24s into tankers, despite the fact that they proved more highly flammable than the standard C-47s or C-46s. As for basing, Goodman noted that while he flew in China-Burma-India, there were two squadrons of B-24s based at Tezgaon, Jorhat, and Tezpur.[17]

Navigating the Hump

Colonel Ralph S. Marshall, who flew B-24s from India to China with the 493rd Bomb Squadron, 7th Bomb Group, 10th Air Force, recalled that "flying the Hump was like no other flying experience, before or after this tour of duty."[18] Colonel Marshall stated that the minimum flight level was 12,000 feet and, in keeping with the rule of thumb "East Odd, West Even, we would be assigned to 13, 15, or 17,000 feet on the eastbound run to China. Usually it was an instrument flight all the way, but occasionally we would break out on top or between cloud build-ups or layers."[19] Both Marshall and Goodman remembered that flight conditions over the Hump varied from mission to mission, oftentimes for the worse. Goodman recalled that crews were often forced to fly below the clouds, causing many planes to crash into the sides of the Himalayas.

Besides snow and ice, thunderstorms likewise plagued air operations. Goodman recalled one such storm when his plane emerged from the clouds and was hit "by a buildup of static electricity ... [that] ... traveled from the tip of one wing to the other, and exploded off the wing tip in a ball of blue light."[20] Colonel Marshall recalled,

> The first few trips ... [over the Hump] ... weren't too bad, but about the fourth trip we ran into an updraft that lifted us 1,200 feet per minute, gear down. Much of the time the air was quite turbulent, at times requiring the combined efforts of the pilot AND the co-pilot to keep the ship under control. Other times it was very smooth and this updraft was like stepping on an up elevator with no way to stop it or get off. Rough or smooth the uplift eventually slackened off, and about the time you collected your bearings we started DOWN. Now it was back to seven degree flaps and, at times, up to full take-off power, and still reading 1000 to 1500 feet per minute DOWN. Talk about a helpless feeling—especially when thinking about the mountains below and, at times, seeing we were below our assigned altitude. Then came the next updraft which was quite welcome this time. This roller coaster ride repeated itself over each ridge, and we soon learned to take advantage of the first updraft because we knew what was coming next.[21]

When flying over the Himalayas pilots became veterans very fast. Goodman said, "Inexperienced crews survived by pure luck. If a plane was hit or crashed, its cargo exploded."[22] Crews had to react fast to the changing nature of the flying conditions, which varied from mission to mission. While many crews survived some, unfortunately, did not. Captain Haynes recalled that while traversing over the Hump one time he could see "scattered along the mountainsides, and in the jungle, ... the wreckage of American, British, and Japanese aircraft—pitiful victims to the harsh weather and fierce air battles."[23] Marshall recalled one such flight:

> One crew reported a downdraft that put them below the clouds as well as the mountain ranges just ahead. He saw the terrain just in time to make a 90 degree turn to the right and climb back to altitude. A number of crews were never heard from, and it was speculated they may have been forced below the mountain tops and never saw what they hit.[24]

Indeed, as Captain Haynes noted, many times, B-24s (and other cargo-carrying aircraft) oftentimes hit condors which could, as in Haynes' case, be just as fatal as if his craft were hit by lighting. In fact, in one such incidence, as they were flying over the Hump during one mission, there was a large thud that jolted the plane on its right side. One of the crew members in the waist of the plane radioed the pilot and said that they had just hit a large flying bird as he had seen a ball of feathers immediately after the jolt. This fact was confirmed by the guide pilot who said that this was not an uncommon event, for even at this altitude condors had been observed. As it turned out, Haynes' B-24 was so severely damaged by the bird that he was forced to land his plane at the first available airstrip until ground crew repaired the damaged portion of the right wing. Haynes later wrote that upon landing, "I inspected the right wing of the aircraft. The condor had made quite a dent — about a foot deep and two feet long in the leading edge of the wing. The crumpled metal was covered with blood and feathers. It seemed incredible that a bird, even the size of a condor, could have caused this much damage."[25]

Captain Edward M. "Goodie" Goodman, USAAF (Edward M. Goodman Collection).

As for emergency landings while over the Hump there were, as all three pilots noted, very few places to land, as the terrain below was dense jungle, inhabited by headhunters and Japanese soldiers. Marshall commented that "there was never the possibility of a forced landing, due to the dense jungle along most of the route. Airmen who were forced to bail out, and survived, told of a jungle that was so tall and dense, it was totally dark on the ground. The soft and velvety appearance of the jungle from the air was very deceptive." Goodman remembered that there was one crew that did manage to bail out over Lhasa, Tibet. "The monks brought them out to us after the snows thawed in the spring." Haynes noted that pilots and crew maintained a "constant chatter" about the "rugged countryside below." Haynes said that "besides jungles, swamps, wild rushing rivers, and deep canyons, the territory was inhabited by tribes of headhunters and cannibals."[26] Indeed, if in fact the pilot and crew survived the crash each on wore his leather flying jacket a "blood chit" sewn on the back with a message, written in Chinese that read, "I am an American pilot in the service of China," and promised to reward anyone who got the wearer back to his base. Goodman stated that many downed pilots and crewmen were returned by local residents or rescued by search and rescue teams or missionaries who had lived among the natives and would assist downed pilots and crewmen in reaching Allied lines. This was the case of one such Hump pilot whose plane was forced down into the Burmese jungles:

> On 29 March 1944, Chuck Allison and crew parachuted into the Salween River Valley. Only minutes after Allison reached the ground, a native gave him a typewritten letter written by Eugene Morse [a missionary] assuring the Americans the Lisus, local tribesmen, would assist the downed crew. Guided by the Lisus, flyers made an arduous 4-day trek northward along the Salween to Morse mission at Latsa, roughly 70 miles east and north of Ft. Hertz. Allison, and Robert A. Engels, Edward A Salay and Rocco J. Commaratto remained with the Morse family about 2 months before Robert and Eugene, with many carriers, led the Americans over mtns. to Ft. Hertz, N. Burma.[27]

In addition to the blood chit, pilots and crews carried .45 caliber pistols in shoulder holsters or M1 carbines for self-defense if the need arose. Captain Haynes recalled that the Army Air Force had established two emergency fields in case a plane could not make it all the way to Kunming. The first one, Myitkyina, was approximately 150 miles east of Chabua; it had been carved out of a mountainside and was put into use shortly after its recapture in August 1944. The other one, hacked out of the dense jungle, was located at Yunnanyi, approximately 185 miles from Chengkung. As Haynes wrote, "Neither of these fields had anything to offer except the basic needs for survival and minimum repair service. However, they were lifesavers to countless planes and their crews."[28]

After 1943, missions over the Hump occurred around the clock, seven days a week, in good and in bad weather. The only exception to this was during the monsoon. Colonel Marshall noted that the time of day mattered very little as most pilots flew on instruments. However, instruments could not overcome the sleet, ice, and torrential rains that accompanied most flights to and from China. Marshall, in fact, stated that the flights themselves varied from being "very smooth to very turbulent." When faced with strong winds B-24 pilots had to use extra fuel and were forced to "drop the gear and add additional power just to keep the engine cylinder head temperatures within range."[29]

Despite the B-24's sturdy construction, engines did, in fact, fail, oftentimes when forced to climb to a higher altitude. Colonel Marshall recalled an incident where an engine fell off 20 minutes into his takeoff from Chengkung:

> During the "gas haul" period a number of aircraft had an engine failure during the long and laborious climb to altitude. Our instruction manual said the B-24 was designed to carry about 6000 pounds of bombs, with a maximum gross weight of about 58,000 pounds. Our gas load of over 10,000 pounds increased the gross weight to approximately 72,000 pounds. With this excess weight there was little choice in what to do when an engine was lost. Bomb bay tanks were salvoed, hopefully where the resultant damage would be minimal.... I, fortunately, had only one occasion to lose an engine about 20 minutes after take off. A crew member looking out the right waist window said a lot of oil was streaming out behind No. 3 engine. All of No. 3 instruments were normal except for a slight reduction in oil pressure and a slight increase in cylinder head temperature. I asked Mac (our navigator) for a heading and ETA[30] back to base. In the meantime No. 3 oil pressure started fluctuating and I told the co-pilot to feather No. 3 and set the

flaps to seven degrees; the engineer to start the electric hydraulic pump on No. 3 engine, and keep his hand on the salvo handle; and to the rest of the crew to buckle up tight. I explained our situation to the crew and it was agreed to take the tanks as far as was practical. We could always salvo them and make a "normal" three-engine landing. In an emergency, it was not necessary to open the bomb-bay doors, as the heavy tanks would tear right through the doors when released. The ADF[31] was tuned to the base homing beacon, and I was able to maneuver the aircraft so that with the ADF needle pointing straight ahead, the compass was aligned with the runway heading. We were lined up with the runway but had no idea how far away we were. We were still in the clouds but the air was smooth with no rain. I was able to keep the rate of descent to 500 feet per minute and all the time hoping we would break out of the clouds before passing over the runway. There was no way we could go around for another approach without dropping the tanks, and I already decided to drop them if we didn't see the ground at 500 feet. All this time visions went through my head of the plane trying to land with his tanks a few days before [that plane's left tire blew out, lost its left wing and cartwheeled on the runway before exploding into a ball of flames].[32]

On this particular mission, Marshall and his crew were lucky, for just as they were about to drop the fuel tanks on the runway a B-24 was taking off down the runway. Frantically, Marshall radioed the pilot that he was about to drop his fuel tanks due to a faulty engine. At the last minute, the B-24 on the ground veered off the runway as Marshall's stricken aircraft touched down on the runway, with the nose of the airplane pointed "up" in order to create the maximum air drag, and Marshall then cut the engines as the B-24 rolled to a complete stop with the brakes literally smoking. Watching all of this was the rescue squad that had stood ready on the far end of the runway to assist if necessary. Fortunately, Marshall's plane was one of the luckier ones with the only damage being worn brakes and a faulty engine.

As for visibility and weather conditions in general, there were days when the pilots traversing the Hump could see for about a mile without any restrictions. Besides the weather, both Haynes and Marshall wrote that one of the most unsettling things while flying over the Himalayas was to "discover another plane approaching nose on, right at our assigned altitude." This often necessitated an abrupt mid-air turn that caused anything not fastened down to scatter throughout the plane. Indeed, in flying in all types of weather in what became a "crowded sky," as well as suffering equipment failures (such as the radio compasses), all three B-24 pilots agreed that besides "the Man upstairs," the next most important person aboard their plane was the navigator. Goodman recalled that for two consecutive nights in 1944, an estimated 60 to 65 aircraft crashed, and that "the airwaves were filled with Mayday calls" from downed pilots. Haynes added that one of the most severe problems encountered in traversing over the Hump was icing. The B-24 pilot stated that 'icing and the sudden wind shifts over the mountains can easily blow an aircraft off course and into a mountainside.... There was no easy way to escape icing except to keep climbing and hope to get above the cloud cover. If the ice buildup was too rapid, the plane gradually slowed because of the increased weight and drag. A flight crew's only salvation in this situation was to bail out before the ship stalled. But parachuting into the jungles or mountains was also usually fatal."[33] Besides turbulence and icing, however, "becoming lost and running out of gas were the two great dangers in Hump-flying."[34]

Flying with 500-lb bombs with high octane fuel in 55-gallon drums or bladder bags could prove to be deadly. Marshall wrote:

> Gas missions were always flown with the bomb-bay doors open about four inches. This was due to the many fuel lines, pumps, valves and connections in the bomb bay, creating the possibility of a fuel leak somewhere. The air blasting through this opening hopefully kept any leak from becoming an explosive mixture. We felt some of the aircraft that were never heard from probably blew up, unless it hit a peak first. I don't believe they had "explosion proof" electric switches at that time so that all of the dozens of equipment switches in the bomb bay were capable of making a slight spark when turned off or on. Of course, it goes without saying, smoking was not permitted in the plane at any time on the ground or in the air.[35]

As for the safety concerns of both the pilots and crewmen aboard the planes, Goodman stated, "When you're 20 or 21, you think you're indestructible ... and we had a mission we believed in. We were the good guys and they [the Japanese] were the bad guys. But anybody who flew missions like that and tells you they were never scared is not telling the truth."[36]

Missions Over the Himalayas

As for the missions themselves, the men aboard the B-24s readily agreed that they were not milk runs. They were, in fact, dangerous affairs from the start to the finish of the mission. While few Japanese planes rose to challenge the unarmed (in the case of Goodman) to the slightly armed (as in the case of both Marshall and Haynes) B-24s, the planes often bore the marks of enemy small arms fire as they flew over Burma or China. In fact, as Colonel Marshall recalled, each flight was unlike the one before that as pilots encountered a different set of problems and concerns during each flight:

> Several of our China missions were to an air strip at Luichow, about three hours' flying time further east than Kunming (about seven hours from Tezgoan). Our first trip to Luichow was instrument weather for all but the last 15 minutes of the flight. We hit our checkpoints going over the Hump and checked in at Kunming as we passed. It was another three hours to Luichow with no radio beacon or radio transmitter to home in on. Our usual procedure was for the first plane that finds the base to land, while gas was being unloaded, to transmit a signal that others could home in on. This particular day we were the first to arrive in the area. As we approached our estimated time of arrival, we broke out on top of a cloud deck at about 5,000 feet, with no breaks to be seen in the undercast. In a few minutes I asked Mac, our navigator, to tell when the time was up. When he said "Now" I racked it up and, what do you know, there was

a break in the clouds below with the Luichow airstrip right in the center. We all yelled "BINGO," and, needless to say, made a hasty descent through the break and landed. All heaved a big sigh of relief, as the tension drained out. We sent the proper signal for other planes to go home in on and they began landing in quick order. During our last couple of trips into Luichow, several aircraft experienced some random small arms ground fire, as evidenced by small holes in the fuselage, wings or tail section. As far as I know we didn't lose any planes or sustain any personnel injuries, but we knew someone down there didn't like us. We didn't know it till later, but the Japanese supposedly had the base surrounded and were only about ten miles away. We were also told (later) that many 1,000 pound bombs had been buried in the runway, ready to be detonated as soon as the base was evacuated, and there we were landing our potential "Molotov Cocktail" on those bombs.[37]

Indeed, the navigational tools carried aboard the B-24s (and C-46s and C-47s) saved many lives as well as the precious cargo they carried. Captain Haynes wrote that after flying over the Hump for nearly four hours, "we crossed the last range of mountains and Kunming Lake came into view. It would be a landmark for our base at Chengkung. With the radar equipment we carried on board, this lake could be picked up on our scope at high altitude and long distances—thus giving us a very valuable navigational aid"[38] (Map #1). As for landing, Haynes recalled:

> The single runway at Chengkung ran north and south. It was 6,000 feet long and was constructed of crushed rock. The airstrip was laid out in a large valley with high mountains to the east and south. There was also a small range on the west side, between the runway and Kunming Lake. The north end of the strip opened up into the valley and was free of obstacles.[39]

Once on the ground, the B-24 crews, ground maintenance and Chinese coolies hurriedly unloaded the aircraft of their valuable cargo or, as in the case of Colonel Marshall's squadron, began to pump the fuel either into 55-gallon drums or sometimes directly into the 14th Air Force's B-25s and P-40s that were parked on the runway. Marshall wrote that they had to be careful as to not drain all the fuel out of the B-24 "so we would have enough fuel to go home on." He added, "Those coolies would take it all if we didn't watch."[40]

Once on the ground, the ground crews and Chinese coolies unloaded the aircraft while a truck or jeep took the just-arrived flight crew to the Operations building or tent. Here, the squadron intelligence officer de-briefed the crew before it could get a hot meal, shower, and possibly sleep or rest before the return trip. Sometimes, if they could not fly back to their bases that same day, the pilots would throw a "Jing Bow Juice" or booze party and talk about their "adventures" in flying over the Hump or Burma. Despite the relaxed atmosphere, however, each pilot realized that this could be his last flight. Speaking for all of the pilots and crews that traversed the Hump, Haynes summed it up best when he wrote, "the continual thought of survival was uppermost in the minds of us all. We still had plenty of combat hours to put in, and the mis-

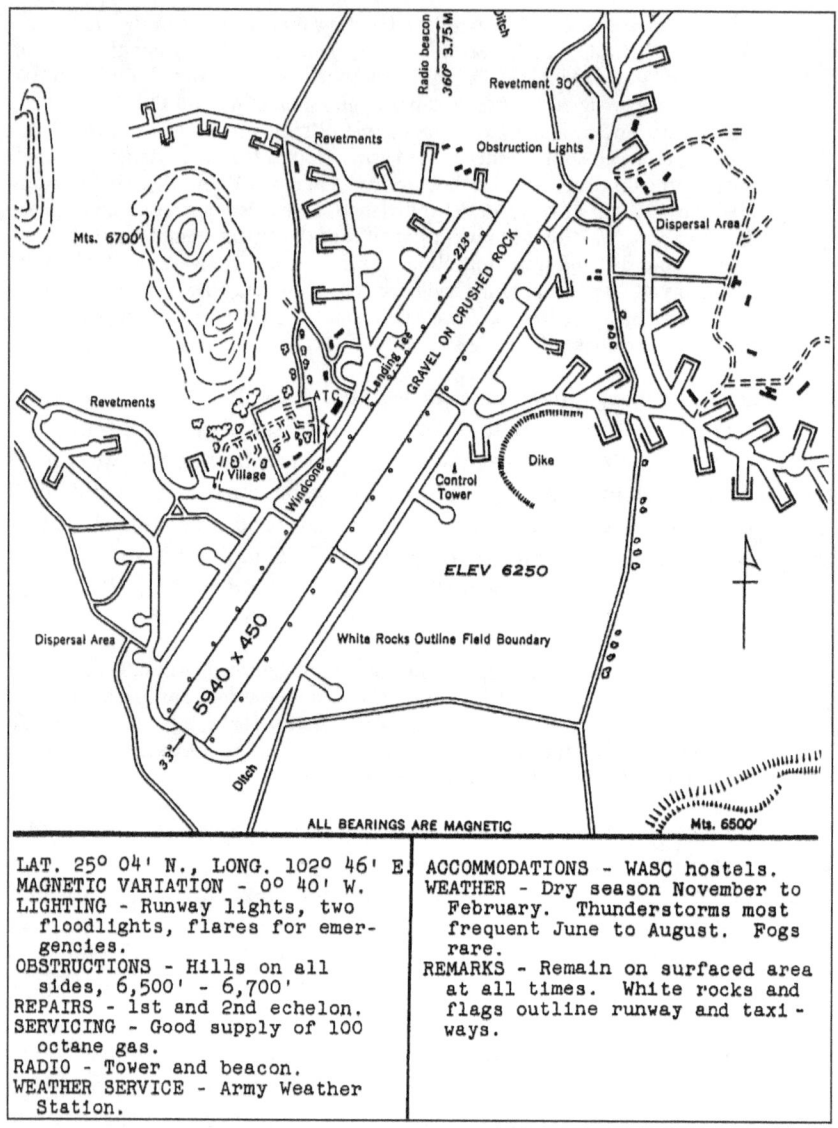

Map 4. Chengkung (Ch'eng-Kung-hsien), China (Hump Pilots Association).

sions were becoming more and more dangerous with every air strike." In fact, the veteran pilot concluded that there was no doubt in his mind that every pilot who flew the Hump had a hard time falling asleep due to the fact that he might have had a "premonition of disaster" entering his thoughts as he lay there thinking of friends who had gone before him and had died attempting to shuttle supplies to China[41] (Map #5).

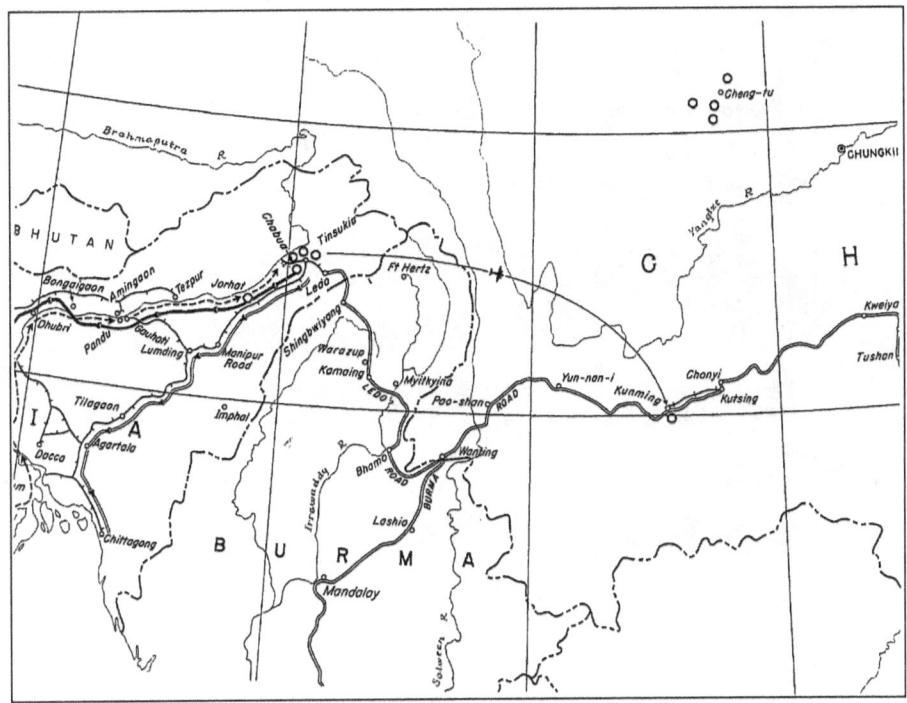

Map 5. "The Aluminum Trail," India-China October 1943–October 1944 (Romanus and Sunderland, *Stilwell's Command Problems*, Insert pp. 36–37).

"A Bunch of Crazy Kids"

As Ed Goodman stated, flying the Hump required good flying skills, attention to detail, steel nerves and, a bit of luck. In fact, Goodman emphasized that there was no room for error when flying over the Himalayas. One mistake could cost seven lives as well as an airplane and its precious cargo.[42] Nevertheless, as both Haynes and Goodman concluded, it was a mission that had to be undertaken. Despite this, however, flying over the tortuous Himalayas was a job for young men. Ed Goodman said, "With a war like that, you had to have a bunch of crazy kids that didn't care" about the dangers in flying over the mountain ranges.[43]

As for the "crazy kids" who flew B-24s over the Himalayas, their record remained unparalleled in the annals of aerial re-supply. Major General Claire Lee Chennault, in fact, praised the 308th Bomb Group, Haynes' squadron, when he wrote, "The 308th was unique among heavy bomb groups. It was entirely self-supporting across the Hump, and operated from tactical bases from 500 to 900 miles. After the war, when Army Air Force Headquarters in Washington tallied the bombing accuracy of every heavy bomb group in action, I was aston-

The "blood chit" worn by all U.S. pilots and crewmen on the back of their flight jackets while aboard their aircraft. Written in fifteen languages, the inscription reads, "I am an American pilot in the service of China. You will be rewarded for returning me to my own lines" (David C. Hall Collection).

ished to find that the 308th led them all." Indeed, the former commanding general of the Fourteenth Air Force praised the efficiency and versatility of the B-24 when he wrote, "The Liberators did many things their designers never intended. They skip-bombed ships from mast height, strafed at low level, ferreted out enemy radar stations, mined rivers and harbors, flew transport missions, and on one occasion, functioned as fighters."[44] In short, besides the venerable C-47s and C-46s, the B-24 was perhaps one of the most reliable aircraft used in the China-Burma-India theater during World War II.

Postwar and Beyond

Captain Goodman remained in CBI for the remainder of the war and continued to fly both the B-24 and later C-87 transports until his transfer back to the United States for a stateside assignment prior to the end of the war. He returned home upon the cessation of hostilities and remained in the Air Force Reserve as a pilot for several years. He turned down several offers to fly for commercial airlines as he believed it would be "too tame" after surviving and flying over the Hump. Goodman eventually entered the food brokerage business in Cleveland, Ohio, until his retirement in 2001. Sadly, Captain Goodman passed away in August 2006. Survived by his wife, Mary, Captain Ed Goodman was laid to rest with full military honors, a fitting tribute for a true hero of a forgotten theater. During his career as a pilot, he flew five different aircraft, that included the Stearman Kaydet, the Martin B-26, Mitchell B-25, the B-24 Liberator, and the C-87 transport. For his services in CBI, the Army awarded Goodman the Distinguished Flying Cross and Air Medal, both with oak leaf clusters; a presidential citation as well as the China War Memorial from the Nationalist Government on Taiwan. Proud of his service in CBI to the end, Goodman's desire to fly was rivaled only by his tenacity and courage while flying the Hump.

Captain Elmer E. "Bud" Haynes remained in the Army Air Force until the end of the war, upon which he was discharged. He later became a pilot and education officer with the Missouri Air National Guard at Lambert Field, where he served with the 131st Aircraft Control Squadron. He also flew chartered flights throughout the United States. Later re-locating to Roanoke, Virginia, Haynes served for five years in the U. S. Air Force Reserves as well flying for a private company near Hopewell Field, Virginia. Haynes retired in 1982 and has spent his golden years in Roanoke, playing golf and still recalling when he flew the Hump in his B-24.

Captain (later Colonel) Ralph Marshall remained in the Air Force at the end of the war. After serving in a variety of assignments that included service as a project engineer in the development of a pilot optical viewfinder for reconnaissance aircraft during the Korean War, and later as the Air Force representative to the Army Corps of Engineers Research and Development Lab at Fort Belvoir, Virginia, where he monitored the progress of many developmental projects specifically requested by the Air Force. He returned to Korea to assume command of the 67th Reconnaissance Technical Squadron based out of Kimpo Airfield with the 5th Air Force. At the end of the Korean War, Marshall returned to the United States where he served at the Wright Patterson Air Force Base, and later at the Air Research and Development Command located first in Baltimore, Maryland, and then to Andrews Air Force Base, Maryland. Promoted to colonel, Marshall became chief of the Air Force's Reconnaissance Branch until his transfer to the Satellite Test Center in Sunnyvale, California, where he served as the field director for several satellite programs until his retirement after twenty-three years' service in October 1964. He later entered real estate development and pursued his other hobbies along with his wife, Mary. Despite the many dangers in flying B-24s filled with combustible fuel over the Hump Marshall, like the other B-24 pilots, remained proud of his service in CBI.

Along with the immense pride of having served in the forgotten theater, the men and women who served in CBI during World War II were, in fact, survivors. Flying unarmed or barely armed airplanes, oftentimes overloaded with dangerous or combustible cargo, in weather that grounded most planes in the European or Mediterranean theaters of operation, the pilots and crews who flew the Hump were among the best flyers and crewmen ever to serve in the U.S. Army Air Forces. Despite being a crazy bunch of kids, as Ed Goodman stated, they were, and still are today, the true heroes of a war on the Asian mainland that history has by and large forgotten. Nevertheless, the airlift and subsequent ground operations by Allied forces remains as one of the more important components of Japan's ultimate defeat on the Asian mainland. Also, it was in CBI that Army and Air Force leaders had a unique opportunity to test new ideas that allowed them to write the manual on future airlift operations in later wars on the Asian mainland (Korea, Vietnam), and during Desert Shield–Desert Storm in 1990–1991. Those "daring young men in their flying machines" who flew the "Aluminum Trail" were, indeed, pioneers of a revolutionary new concept of aerial re-supply that enabled the ground forces of Britain, China, and the United States to maintain the offensive even while being resupplied by air in the midst of battle.

Chapter 4

Captain David C. Hall, U.S. Army Air Forces, and the 4th Combat Cargo Command

With the evacuation of Burma in April 1942, the Allies were faced with the prospect that the Japanese might succeed in cutting off supplies to both Chiang Kai-shek's Nationalist Chinese forces and Major General Claire L. Chennault's American Volunteer Group (AVG) known as the Flying Tigers.[1] In fact, the Japanese plan was to "capture the Imphal Plain and move into India to cut the supply lines that carried the material for the Air Transport Command's (ATC) 'Hump' airlift over the Himalayan Mountains into China."[2] After the fall of Mandalay, Myitkyina, and later Loiwing in May 1942, the Japanese Army managed to block the land route to China from India. The question now arose among allied planners in New Delhi and Washington on how to not only defend India but to supply Chiang's and Chennault's forces and thereby maintain pressure on the Japanese. To supply China by air, the War Department activated the first aerial re-supply outfit — the Assam-Burma-China Ferry Command — on 21 March 1942 and placed it under the overall command of the Tenth Air Force, commanded by Major General Lewis H. Brereton.[3] The Assam-Burma-China Ferry Command, led by Brigadier General Raymond A. Wheeler, was to "do whatever was necessary to rush equipment and supplies through to [Lieutenant General Joseph W.] Stilwell."[4] Along with twenty-five transports, primarily converted DC-3s from Pan American Airways, flown from bases in Karachi, Dum Dum, and Chittagong, General Wheeler's Ferry Command dropped supplies to both the retreating Allied soldiers and thousands of refugees fleeing the advancing Japanese.[5] Flying countless numbers of sorties, American and British pilots evacuated hundreds of wounded British, Indian and Chinese soldiers, as well as civilian refugees. No sooner would a pilot return home from a supply run delivering ammunition and fuel than he would take off again, this time to pick up these helpless victims of what had become a full-fledged retreat. Indeed, "When after the fall of Mandalay it became obvious that Myitkyina and Loiwing were also doomed, Army pilots began to ignore the normal load limits.

Planes built to carry twenty-four passengers often took off with more than seventy. Some of the civilian pilots vigorously opposed the practice at first, but after seeing military pilots flying incredible loads without mishaps, they too revised their estimate of the capabilities of the planes and joined wholeheartedly in the effort. In the process the DC-3 and its Army equivalent, the C-47, established a lasting reputation for dependability and durability under the most adverse flying conditions."[6]

As for the importance of the establishment of an uninterrupted supply route into China, both the Joint Chiefs of Staff and Combined Chiefs of Staff agreed (with some pressure from Chiang Kai-shek) that the supplying of Chinese forces was vital to the allied war effort in the war against Japan. This importance can be seen in the establishment of an air supply route into China via India. Indeed, even before Lieutenant General Stilwell arrived in the theater, the Tenth Air Force and the Assam-Burma-China Ferry Command had established a healthy reputation as being a reliable component of the efforts to keep China in the war. Stilwell himself noted in his diary on 9 February 1942, "Events are forcing all concerned to see the vital importance of Burma. We must get the airline going at once, and also build the back-country roads."[7]

For the next two years, the Assam-Burma-Ferry Command, flying unarmed transports, braved enemy fighters and the treacherous Himalayan Mountains. The Himalayas, or Hump, shortly thereafter gained the reputation by the American pilots, including Captain Edward M. Goodman, who flew unarmed B-24s and C-87s with the 97th Transport Squadron, 28th Group, as the "Aluminum Trail," due to the many planes that littered the mountainsides after having crashed due to poor visibility or enemy fighter activity.[8] Over time, the Allied forces, primarily British, Commonwealth (Indian and Gurkhas), as well as Australian and New Zealand forces, as well as Chinese and a small though growing number of American forces, took to the offensive in the spring and summer of 1944, the air effort to assist the British 14th Army, as well as Orde Wingate's long-range penetration force known as Chindits increased significantly.

Despite the overall Allied emphasis placed on the defeat of Nazi Germany by President Franklin D. Roosevelt and British Prime Minister Winston Churchill at the Cairo Conference in January 1943, the Combined Chiefs of Staff, as well as both General Stilwell and Admiral Lord Louis Mountbatten, commander, Southeast Asia Command (SEAC), planned a series of limited offensives aimed at driving the Japanese out of northern Burma in order to link up with the old Ledo Road and continue the extension of the road into China, as far east as Kunming, in order to supply Chennault's 14th Air Force and Chiang Kai-shek's Nationalist forces. After the fall of Myitkyina to American and Chinese forces under the command of Brigadier General Frank D. Merrill in August 1944, the British 14th Army, under the command of Lieutenant General William J. Slim began a combined offensive aimed at the defeat and destruction of the Japanese Army and the liberation of southern Burma, including the vital port of Rangoon. Assisting the British in this effort was the newly-established 4th Cargo Command, which was stationed at bases in Tezpur, Jorhat and Chittagong in Assam, India. After its arrival in Sylhet on 1 December 1944, the 4th Cargo Command, flying Curtiss C-46 transports, was directed "to support the British as they fought their way toward Mandalay and eventually to Rangoon."[9] Indeed, after the Japanese had been expelled from northern Burma, the Army Air Forces re-designated all three Combat Cargo Groups as Troop Carrier Groups. Also, with a change in priorities being the operational status came the switch in aircraft from the C-47s to the Curtiss C-46, which was larger and could carry a much larger payload.[10]

One of the pilots assigned to the 4th Cargo Command and who flew the much larger C-46 was Captain David C. Hall, from Girard, Ohio, who, along with his co-pilot, First Lieutenant Richard "Pop" Reynolds, and crew chief, Staff Sergeant Baldwin, flew in support of the British 14th Army and the re-supply of China. Captain Hall likewise flew countless numbers of resupply sorties into Kunming, China, in support of Chiang Kai-shek's Nationalist Chinese forces. Captain Hall likewise flew missions in support of the British drive toward Rangoon and in the transport of Chinese soldiers and officers from Burma to Chanyi, in order to block a Japanese drive toward Kweilin and Luichow. In one of the most impressive displays of airlift capability, the pilots of the Air Transport Command (ATC) flew, in Operation Grubworm on 5 December 1944, "logged over thirty-six trips" and transported "2700 Chinese officers and men and all their equipment back to their homeland" in order to meet this Japanese threat.[11] Such was the enormity of the Allied effort that only five days later, in a similar aerial re-supply effort that commenced on 10 December and lasted to 31 December 1944, pilots and crews of the ATCs 3rd Combat Cargo Group transported, in Operation Jackrabbit, two Chinese divisions, or approximately 25,491 Chinese and American soldiers, 1596 horses and mules, 42 jeeps, 48 75mm howitzers, 48 4.2-inch mortars, 48 A/T guns and miscellaneous supplies. In fact, in less than twenty-one days, the pilots of 3rd Combat Cargo Group flew over 1,351 sorties in support of the Chinese.[12] In support of the 3rd Combat Cargo Command's efforts were the pilots and crew of the 4th Combat Cargo Group of which Captain Hall, who participated in the final operations of Operation Grubworm, had flown aviation gasoline, tires, and ammunition into Kunming, Luliang and elsewhere in China.

On the Road to China-Burma-India: 1942–1943

While still a high school senior in June 1942, Hall passed the Air Force's rigid entrance examination in Cleveland, Ohio, and entered the Army Air Corps as one of the youngest aviation cadets (he was 18) that October. After induction, the Army sent Hall to flight school at San Antonio, Texas, where he soon learned to fly "a number of aircraft with speed that astonished his instructors."[13] After his arrival at San Antonio, the Army subjected Captain Hall and the other prospective Army aviators to a series of classification tests in order to determine their suitability as pilots, navigators or bombardiers. As Hall recounted:

> I was classified as a pilot. I had a letter ... from the commanding general to my mother and dad that read, "I'll be glad to tell you that your son, well, we hope that he will be a pilot." [I was in] classification school for two and a half months; we went from there to primary school in Stanford, Texas. I had never been in an airplane in my life before I went into the service. I spent two and a half months in Stanford, Texas, [I] went through the primary, went to Enid, Oklahoma, and went through basic, advanced. I'll never forget this, my instructor said, "I've seen a lot of dumb cadets, and you're about the dumbest I've ever seen, but you can fly." And of course, he was trying to wash you out. I went from Enid, Oklahoma, to Frederick, Oklahoma, graduated from twin engine advanced, in the class of 43H in August of 1943.[14]

Captain Hall recalled that in those days flight training was broken into two parts with basic flight school centered upon single-engine aircraft fighters or bombers while advanced school focused on twin-engine aircraft such as transports. Still an aviation cadet, Hall reported to twin engine flying school, where he flew C-9s and C-17s, twin-engine Beechcraft. While at advanced school in Frederick, Oklahoma, the Army commissioned Hall a second lieutenant. He then went to Dodge City, Kansas, assigned to the U.S. Army Air Corps' medium bomber school located there that trained future B-26 pilots. Here, Hall learned to fly the twin-engine B-26s and bombers. In spite of the fact that the B-26 proved to be a difficult and dangerous aircraft to handle, Hall remembered, "I went through that school like a breeze. I had no problem flying airplanes. I had a lot of fun flying B-26s."[15] In fact, Hall stated that the B-26, referred to as Martin Marauders, had the ominous reputation among the pilots as "flying coffins," due to the fact that "so many guys were killed in training."[16] Successfully completing the B-26 course in Dodge City, Hall, who was by now a second lieutenant (and still only eighteen years old!), reported first to B-26 school, then located in Shreveport, Louisiana. Hall stated that "while most of the fellas who attended B-26 school received orders for Tampa, Florida, prior to shipping over to the European Theater of Operations ... for some God unknown reason to me, Lieutenant David C. Hall received orders for Pierre, South Dakota," where he towed targets for aerial gunnery practice for the B-17s and B-24s during the winter of 1943.[17] Hall recalled that there were a couple of close calls when tracer rounds or, as he said, "these red things" sailed by the cockpit of his B-26. He said that he immediately radioed the pilot of one plane and said, "Hey, you guys, you're supposed to shoot at the targets ... not me." Despite the fact that at times it was monotonous flying the tow targets, Hall said "we were having a good time."

Captain Hall continued to train the B-17 and B-24 pilots until the spring

Second Lieutenant David C. Hall, USAAF, stands on the wing of his AT-6 Trainer at Enid, Oklahoma (David C. Hall Collection).

of 1944 when he received orders to transfer to a Combat Cargo outfit in Syracuse, New York. Hall remembered that it was quite "a disaster" when he and his comrades saw their new airplane — the C-47 transport airplane. Not as sleek as the B-26, Hall said the C-47 "was cumbersome, bulky, had tricycle landing gear ... and [was] slow!" The young pilot recalled that during his first flight in it he "checked out in it at 4 hours and 50 minutes." For Hall and the other pilots this was to be the aircraft they would fight the Second World War in as the Army assigned them to the newly-constituted Fourth Cargo Combat Group,[18] where he became assigned to the group's 14th Squadron. After practicing para-drops and short field landings in and around Syracuse, the squadron left for its new home near Louisville, Kentucky, where they prepared to go overseas. After their arrival in Louisville, the 4th Combat Cargo Group shortly thereafter exchanged their C-47s for the Curtiss C-46 Commando transport, which was both faster and could carry more cargo than the former.[19] Indeed, Hall stated that while the C-46 was "considerably faster and larger" than the C-47, the latter was nonetheless a "beautiful plane" to fly. Hall admitted that the "C-46, on the other hand, was big and clumsy, and had been designed to tow gliders." Hall added that the C-46 had a limited range unless it had extra fuel tanks attached, a factor that prevented its use in the South Pacific. After becoming familiar with the C-46 Hall and the rest of the 14th Squadron remained briefly in Louisville until they received orders on November 11, 1944, to proceed overseas.

While in Louisville, Hall said he flew quite a bit, attempting to learn the intricacies of the C-46. Also, being a first lieutenant, Hall had both more money and a bit more freedom than most of the second lieutenants; thus, he said, "I could take off when I wanted" once liberty call sounded. Hall said that "he flew by day and saw Louisville by night.... I had a great time in Louisville, Kentucky." In memory of this great time in the Bluegrass State, he renamed his airplane the "Shack Rat." Hall said that this was the name his crew gave him because "I liked shacking up with all the girls. 'Shack Rat'—that was the name of my plane. I didn't miss too many nice girls and was thus given the name 'The Shack Rat,' because I was shacking up with the girls in Louisville. This was ... due to the fact that I was 19 and single." Indeed, before departing wartime Louisville, the pilots and crews lived up to their reputation as the area had, as Hall amusingly stated, "fast horses and slow women," or in his case, "Fast Horses and Fast Women!" When not chasing women or betting on the ponies, Hall's squadron practiced every day on the missions they would soon encounter in China-Burma-India: towing gliders and dropping supplies. Prior to leaving Louisville, the Army promoted Hall, who by this time had flown B-26s, C-47s, and other Army aircraft, to First Lieutenant which was, as the native Ohioan admitted, quite an achievement given the fact that "I was only nineteen years old." In fact, however, Hall was not the only "youngster in the group, as the majority of the pilots were in their early twenties. Hall said that the oldest man in the squadron was First Lieutenant Richard "Pop" Reynolds, his co-pilot and flight officer, who was 27 years old, and was the man responsible for most of the day-to-day administrative matters and operational concerns (such as the all-too-critical combat loading process). Hall admitted that "I didn't pay too much attention to detail. It was, in fact, 'Pop' who had the more important of jobs as the flight officer, for it was his responsibility to insure that the cargo was properly loaded and stored evenly in the front and back of the aircraft." Captain Hall emphasized that the flight officer was perhaps the most important of all the crew as it was he who performed the most critical functions aboard the aircraft. Hall recalled that while in India, their C-46s were oftentimes "overloaded and very often crashed due in large part to their being 'front or back heavy.'"[20] Indeed, Captain Hall added, "without a doubt, First Lieutenant Reynolds was *the* most important person aboard my plane who insured the success of the flight or mission" [Hall's emphasis].

Captain Hall stated that on November 11, 1944, the group (100 aircraft) received their orders marked "'POE'—Point of Embarkation," and headed first for Fort Wayne, Indiana, where they picked up newer aircraft (C-46 Curtiss Commandos), and then proceeded southeast to West Palm Beach, Florida, along the old Spanish Main of Puerto Rico to Ascension Field or British Guyana to Natal. After a brief stopover in Natal, Hall and his crew took off at 2:00 A.M. and flew across the South Atlantic heading first for Ascension Island and then on to the Gold Coast of Africa. Flying across the continent to Nigeria the 14th Cargo Squadron proceeded northeast to Khartoum to Aden, Saudi Arabia and

Captain David C. Hall looks out of the pilot's window of the "Shack Rat," his C-46 Curtiss Commando at Dum Dum, India in 1944 (David C. Hall Collection).

First Lieutenant Richard "Pop" Reynolds relaxes between missions at his base in Chittagong, India (David C. Hall Collection).

finally to Karachi. Of the original 100 airplanes that started the journey at Fort Wayne, 92 made it safely to Karachi. Captain Hall specifically remembered that in Aden two C-46s crashed and killed both pilots and co-pilots. Ordered to carry their crew members onto India, Hall stated that the stunned crewmen refused to board his airplane and told him "they were not getting on another airplane."[21] Lieutenant Colonel Stuart D. Baird, the commanding officer of the 4th Cargo Command Group, understood their concerns and ordered the men to wait in Saudi Arabia where a transport eventually picked them up and transported them to Karachi. Once in India, the crew members of the doomed ships then boarded a train which took them to Syhlet, India, where they linked up with the 14th Cargo Squadron. After refueling and re-fitting in Karachi, the 14th Combat Cargo Squadron flew onto Sylhet located in the eastern end of India, a journey of some 1600 miles. Arriving in Sylhet on November 30, 1944, Captain Hall recalled the flight there took approximately three hours and thirty-five minutes to navigate. Attached to the British 10th Army, the 14th Cargo Squadron then flew to Argatala and on to its permanent base at Chittagong along the coast. Here, the pilots and crews of the 14th Squadron (and indeed, the entire 4th Cargo Command) supplied the British 10th Army by paradrop in its campaign against the Japanese in Burma and later during its drive toward Rangoon.[22]

The Campaign in Burma, 1942–1944

In order to understand the complexity of the re-supply efforts in CBI, it is necessary to understand the competing strategies that existed between the two rival American commanders in the China-Burma-India theater: Lieutenant General Joseph W. Stilwell and Major General Claire Lee Chennault. Indeed, even as Captain Hall trained in the United States for a yet unknown mission, both the Combined Chiefs of Staff and U.S. Joint Chiefs of Staff (headed by General George C. Marshall) began deliberations as to the feasibility of re-taking northern Burma in order to restore the land route from India into China. Prime Minister Winston S. Churchill wrote that this goal was high on the priority list of the U.S. Joint Chiefs of Staff at both the Casablanca conference (January 1943), and later at the Trident conference in Washington, D.C., in May 1943, where the Allied leader decided to not only "build U.S. Army Air Forces in the China-Burma-India area ... [but to] increase the flow of supplies" going to the Chinese armed forces and General Claire Lee Chennault's Fourteenth Air Force. Known officially as the Anakim plan, the first "steps toward opening the Burma Road" had been undertaken by the Allied leaders.[23]

Prior to the opening of the Burma Road, however, both Generalissimo Chiang Kai-shek (through Lieutenant General Joseph W. Stilwell) and Major General Chennault began to press for increased tonnage over the Hump, the sole Allied lifeline into China. Prior to Hall's arrival in China-Burma-India, the cargo brought over the Hump by the Assam-Burma Ferry Command (later the Air Transport Command or ATC, "was barely enough to keep Chennault's 14th Air Force marginally operational and provide some aid to Chinese forces."[24] In fact, throughout 1942 and 1943, General Stilwell labored to rebuild and retrain the remnants of the Nationalist Chinese Army that had fled into India after the retreat from Burma while the British 14th Army, under the command of Lieutenant General William S. Slim, prepared to resume offensive operations against the Japanese 18th Army in northern Burma. Meanwhile, the airmen and planes under General Chennault continued their offensive against the Japanese in both China and Burma.

It was at this point that inter–Allied and inter-service rivalries threatened to further disrupt what was already a major dispute over the allocation of supplies, aircraft, and manpower. As Chiang Kai-shek pressed President Roosevelt for increased tonnage for his forces, both Chennault and Stilwell competed for what little material support was left for their respective missions. Added to this was Lord Louis Mountbatten's desire to initiate operations to clear the Japanese not only from the northern half but from the whole of Burma as far south as the port of Rangoon. Indeed, in a subsequent meeting between Roosevelt, Chennault, and Stilwell, both theater commanders argued for increased tonnage and acceptance of their respective plans to defeat the Japanese in China and Burma.[25]

Stilwell, on the other hand, had hoped to reform the Chinese Army and use it to clear northern Burma of the Japanese before funneling more supplies by way of a land route to Chennault's Fourteenth Air Force in China.[26] Stilwell confidentially admitted that in order to clear northern and, in fact, all of Burma, as well as to open the Burma-Ledo Road, "a combined land and seaborne operation was necessary."[27] Chennault, however, disagreed, and instead lobbied President Roosevelt directly for not only an increase in the tonnage (up from the 2,000 tons to 3,500 tons per month) being sent his forces in China but also permission to "attack military objectives in Japanese-held China; destroy the Japanese Air Force when it tried to defend them; then bomb the Japanese home islands after the Japanese Air Force had been destroyed."[28] Chennault argued that the amount of freight carried over the Himalayas was "very small" though he promised both Generals George C. Marshall and Henry A. "Hap" Arnold that with his air force he would "accomplish the downfall of the Japanese Air Force ... probably within one year at the outside." The veteran fighter pilot argued that in order to achieve this objective, "the aerial supply line over the Hump should be built up."[29] Indeed, General Arnold later admitted that Chennault had requested from FDR that an additional two hundred aircraft be supplied to him in order that he could achieve air superiority in China. Finally, at the core of the dispute between Chennault and Stilwell was that Chennault disliked the fact that Stilwell had ordered him to make the defense of the Hump his primary mission. Stilwell, in fact, recommended in a radio message to General Marshall that the tonnage over the Hump should be increased to about 10,000 tons per month, and that 2 fighter groups, 1 medium bomber group, and 50 transports should be sent at once to the China-Burma-India theater for just such a purpose.[30] In arguing his case for increased tonnage and allocations in a White House meeting with President Roosevelt, Chennault insisted that "if we received 10,000 tons of supplies monthly my planes would sink and severely damage more than a million tons of shipping." Upon hearing this Roosevelt supposedly banged his fist on the desk and said, "If you can sink a million tons ... we'll break their backs."[31] For his part, Stilwell informed FDR that as he saw it, his primary mission in China was to "increase the effectiveness of the Chinese Army in order that the Chinese (and the British) "be held to their commitments for the retaking of Burma."[32] Stilwell's goal was to begin the reconquest of Burma as soon as possible with the very Chinese forces known as the Yoke or Y force that he had re-organized and re-trained in India. General Stilwell believed that once this force was equipped and properly trained, "it was to strike down the [old] Burma Road into Burma from the east, to effect a junction with the Yoke or Y force striking from India."[33]

At the time of the conference between the two rival American commanders-in-chief in the CBI the fact remained that the Japanese held practically all of Burma with the exceptions being the northern and western mountains. Irrespective of whose plan was finally adopted the fact remained that any campaign to alleviate China's tenuous supply line depended on the British plans for the re-taking of Burma, and the British were themselves encountering similar inter-service rivalry and policies.[34] Indeed, with the increased tempo of operations on both land and in the air in both the Mediterranean and Pacific claiming more and more logistical support, as well as the diversion of supplies to meet the needs of the impending invasion of the continent which was tentatively set for the spring or early summer of 1944, CBI took a back seat to both Allied war planning and priority insofar as critical war supplies were concerned. The war in Burma and the air supply campaign over the Hump to China nevertheless became the focus of three mid-war conferences held in 1943. These conferences included Trident, held in Washington, D.C., from May 12 to May 25; Quadrant, held in Quebec from August 14 to August 24; and Sextant, held in Cairo and Tehran from November 22 to December 7. Here, President Roosevelt, Prime Minister Churchill, and Generalissimo Chiang Kai-Shek laid out plans for the re-taking of northern Burma, the doubling of tonnage being airlifted into China, and the reopening and construction in some parts of the Burma-Ledo Road.

While Trident dealt more with the European and Mediterranean theaters of operation, the participants did agree that a series of minor land operations were to take place in order to re-open the Burma Road as well as increase "the capacity of the air routes into China."[35] During the subsequent Quadrant meet-

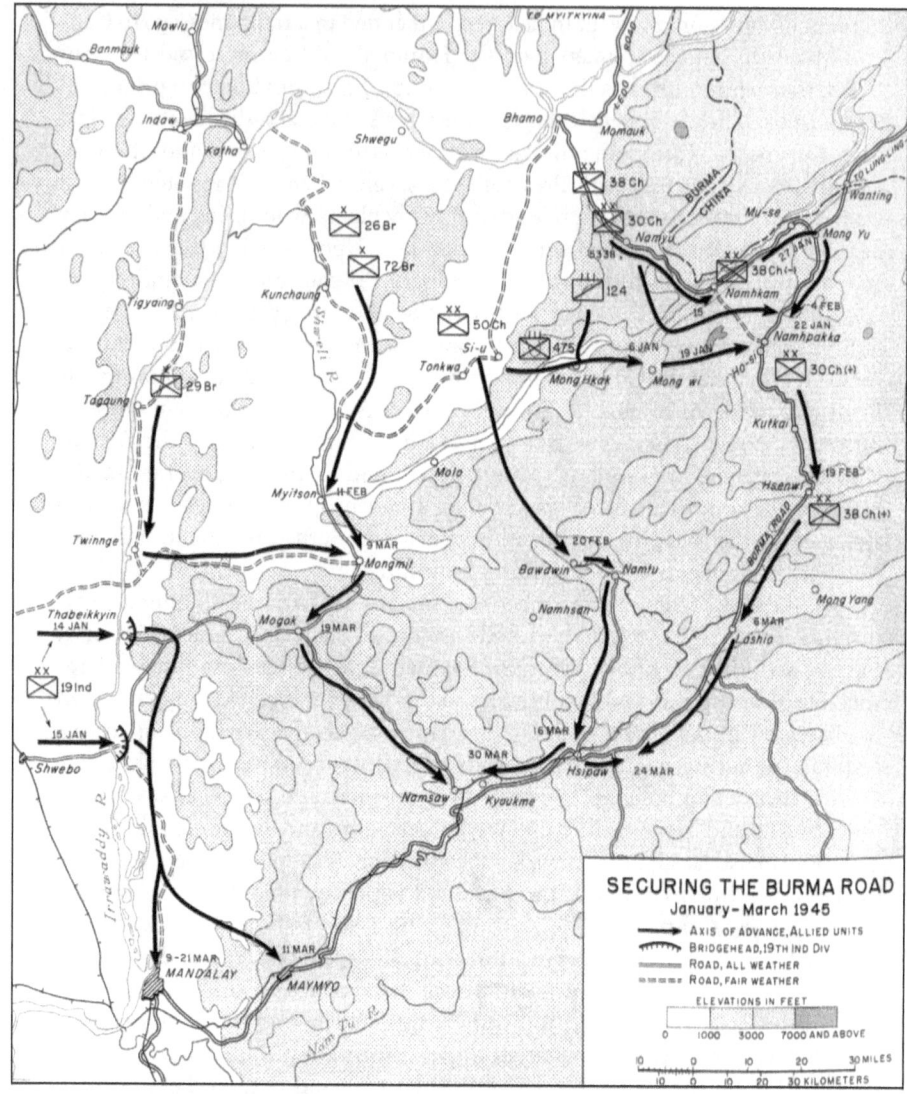

Map 6. Securing the Burma Road, January–March 1945 (Source: Romanus and Sunderland, *Time Runs Out in CBI*, p. 183).

ing in Quebec, President Roosevelt and Prime Minister Churchill agreed to the reorganization of the command arrangements in CBI with the appointment of Admiral Lord Louis Mountbatten as supreme commander, Southeast Asia Command (SEAC), and Lieutenant General Stilwell as the deputy supreme commander. In turn the Combined Chiefs of Staff authorized Admiral Mountbatten to initiate a series of limited offensives in North Burma sometime in February

1944 as "a prerequisite for improving the air route and opening of overland communications with China." At the Sextant Conference, held partly in Cairo and Tehran, the Allied chiefs, in order to secure more landing craft for the planned spring invasion of Northwestern Europe and the follow-on operation for Southern France dubbed "Anvil," scaled back the amphibious phases of Mountbatten's planned offensives toward Rangoon (Culverin) and likewise pushed back the timetable for the re-taking of North Burma.[36] With the bulk of logistical support going to General Dwight D. Eisenhower's forces preparing for Operation Overlord, Admiral Mountbatten later stated that the lack of adequate logistical support "condemned our strategy [in South-East Asia] to being planned against a background of perpetual uncertainty about the higher policy."[37] The SEAC commander nonetheless proposed a series of seven minor operations designed to tie down as many Japanese as possible until a concerted offensive could be launched against the main body of Japanese forces in North Burma. These included:

a. A seaborne operation to capture the Adaman Islands (Operation Buccaneer).
b. An advance with one corps along the Arakan coast and the Mayu Peninsula, leading eventually to the capture of Akyab.
c. An advance with one corps on the central front across the Chindwin River.
d. An advance by Stilwell's three divisions on the northern front.
e. An advance by the Chinese forces in Yunnan (known as the Y force) to Bhamo and Lashio, to secure the Chinese end of the Ledo Road.
f. Operations in support of (d) and (e) by Brigadier Orde Wingate's long-range penetration forces (Chindits).
g. Airborne operations to capture Indaw, on the railway from Mandalay to Myitkyina (Operation Tarzan).[38]

Upon his assumption of command of SEAC the British Chiefs of Staff directed Admiral Mountbatten to "engage the Japanese as closely and continuously as possible in order by attrition to consume and wear down the enemy's forces, especially his air forces, thus making our superiority tell and forcing the enemy to divert his forces from the Pacific theatre — and secondly, but of equal consequence, to maintain and broaden our contacts with China, both by the air route and by establishing direct contact through Northern Burma *inter alia* by suitably organized air-supplied ground forces of the greatest possible strength."[39] The British Chiefs of Staff, in fact, directed Mountbatten to execute the plan advanced by his predecessor, General Sir Claude Auchinlek, the previous September that called for "an advance on the central front to a line Indaw-Katha with three divisions supplied by twenty-three squadrons of transport aircraft and supported by a complementary and diversionary advance by the Chinese troops from Yunnan."[40] The success or failure of this offensive depended not only upon cooperation from Chiang Kai-shek and General Stilwell, but also upon the availability of sufficient transport aircraft which, one might add, Mountbatten did not possess. Nine days after his arrival in the CBI Theater, Admiral Mountbatten met with Chiang Kai-shek in order to seek his cooperation in the undertaking of this offensive operation.

For his part, the generalissimo demanded that in return for his cooperation in allowing Y force to participate in this offensive, the British demonstrate "their seriousness in the carrying out their part of the operation." Having received assurances from both the British Chiefs of Staff and Prime Minister Churchill of the Allied (i.e., British and American) commitment to just such an undertaking, Mountbatten then "hinted" to Chiang that he could assure the generalissimo that such "assistance was forthcoming." Thus, assured that the Allies "meant business" in the carrying out of a series of land operations against the Japanese in Burma, Chiang gave the "go ahead" for planning to commence for such an operation.

Indeed, Prime Minister's Churchill's assurance of support in the carrying out of Culverin, and the execution of a series of amphibious forays against Sumatra and Malaya, was, in fact, bolstered by a letter sent by President Roosevelt on February 24, 1944, to the prime minister assuring Churchill of the availability of air transport assets to carry out offensive operations called for in Anakim. Roosevelt, in fact, after assuring Prime Minister Churchill of the continued importance in keeping China in the war against Japan, wrote:

> It is mandatory therefore that we make every effort to increase the flow of supplies into China. This can only be done by increasing the air tonnage or by opening a road through Burma. Our occupation of Myitkyina will enable us immediately to increase the airlift to China by providing an intermediate air transport base as well as by increasing the protection of the air route. General Stilwell is confident that his Chinese-American forces can seize Myitkyina by the end of the dry season and once there, can hold it, provided Mountbatten's IV Corps from Imphal secures the Shwebo-Monywa area. I realize this imposes a most difficult task, but I feel that with your energetic encouragement Mountbatten's commanders are capable of overcoming the many difficulties involved.[41]

While FDR stressed the importance of the carrying Anakim out and the threats posed by the Japanese toward India his letter nonetheless questioned the feasibility and value of the series of amphibious operations proposed by the British Chiefs of Staff in Operation Culverin:

> I fail to see how an operation against Sumatra and Malaya, requiring tremendous resources and forces, can possibly be mounted until after the conclusion of the war in Europe. Lucrative as a successful Culverin might be, there appears much more to be gained by employing all the resources we now have available in an all-out drive into upper Burma so that we can build up our air strength in China and insure the essential support for our westward advance to the Formosa-China-Luzon area. I most urgently hope, therefore, that you back to the maximum, a vigorous and immediate campaign in upper Burma.[42]

In his reply to President Roosevelt, Churchill expressed his doubts as to the success of such an offensive in North Burma, given not only the presence of the Japanese 18th Army but also the nature of the terrain, of which the prime minister wrote, "one could not choose a worse place for fighting the Japanese." The prime minister likewise dismissed the need for the building of the Burma-Ledo Road, citing that it would "too laborious a task" and was unlikely that it would be finished "until the need for it had passed." Churchill admitted that the purpose of the Burma Road was to assist Stilwell's efforts in bolstering the fighting abilities of the Chinese forces. The British prime minister candidly admitted, however, that "it would make little difference to their [i.e., the Chinese] fighting capacity." Finally, Churchill dismissed the value of an air campaign launched from Chinese soil in assisting the Allied advances in the Pacific. In a direct reference to his proposed amphibious forays against the Japanese in Malaya and Sumatra, the British prime minister emphasized that it would be a waste in both "man-power and material" that could be better used elsewhere in "containing and neutralizing the Japanese" in Burma in much the same manner that General Douglas MacArthur's Southwest Pacific forces had done in New Guinea and the Solomons.[43]

Planning for increased assistance to China as well as British forces preparing to retake Burma involved two major concerns. The first was the provision of the necessary transports for the Air Transport Command. With the Mediterranean and soon-to-be European theaters of operation placing an ever-increasing demand on resources, the China-Burma-India Theater was at the bottom of the list insofar as priority shipments were concerned. Directly related to the first problem was the assignment of personnel to fly the planes and to keep them flying. With the increased tempo of the air war over Germany in preparation for the invasion of Northwestern Europe in the spring or summer of 1944, Major General Lewis H. Brereton's Tenth Air Force remained hard-pressed to find pilots and ground crews to keep the Assam-Burma Ferry in operation. As early as May 28, 1942, General Brereton, in fact, wrote in his diary, "It was absolutely essential that the air transport link to China be maintained at top capacity, and if air operations were to be conducted from China, aviation gas would have to be moved by transport plane."[44]

Despite the British prime minister's objections to the launching of a land offensive from India into North Burma by Stilwell's Y Force, which began in December 1943, he nonetheless instructed Mountbatten to fully cooperate with the American and Chinese forces. Hence, on January 19, 1944, the British XVth Corps, commanded by Lieutenant General Sir Phillip Christinson, launched its offensive down the Arakan coastline where it immediately met stiff resistance from the Japanese 15th Army (see Map #2). On February 5, 1944, Lieutenant General Christinson's offensive was temporarily halted as the British forces sought to counter a determined Japanese counter-offensive along the Arakan coastline aimed at taking the port of Chittagong.[45] Cut off and surrounded by elements of the Japanese 15th Army, the British 5th Division "grouped into perimeters, stood their ground, and fought it out." As Prime Minister Churchill recounted, what saved the 5th Division was the airlift by C-47s and C-46s that brought in supplies such as food, water, and ammunition, as well as a counterattack by the British 26th Division "which had been brought in from reserve" that broke up the Japanese counterattack and forced them to retreat into the Burmese jungle, though not before leaving some 5,000 dead littered across the battlefield.[46]

In keeping with the planned offensive operations to harass the Japanese rear areas as well as cut off their communications, Brigadier Orde Wingate's 16th long-range penetration group or Chindits marched into North Burma on 5 February 1944 in order to draw attention away from Lieutenant General Stilwell's main offensive against the Japanese 18th Army. During the offensive, the Chindits marched over some 450 miles through one of the thickest jungles and over mountain ranges, supplied solely from the air. Prime Minister Churchill noted that the bulk of Wingate's force was flown into Burma at a landing strip code-named Broadway. Here, 250 transports belonging to the Air Commando Group flew in a combined British-Gurkha force from the 77th and 11th Brigades whereupon after landing they set out to cut the railway lines north of Indaw.

The airstrip, cut out of the dense jungle by the Chindits and Gurkhas, was barely able to sustain the gliders and Dakotas of the Air Transport Command. Indeed, the enormity of the airlift was impressive, given the fact that between March 6–11, 1944, the planes and gliders of the ATC flew in 7,500 men while losing only a small number of gliders and 143 men in the process. Unfortunately, a later casualty was the commanding officer of the Chindits, the brilliant though eccentric Wingate, whose C-47 crashed into a nearby hillside on 24 March, killing him and all aboard the aircraft.[47]

Despite the death of Wingate the British offensive continued to press against the Japanese 18th Army which had, in the meantime, launched its long-awaited and much expected offensive aimed at taking Imphal. As Prime Minister Churchill later recounted, the key to both stopping this offensive and to continued success by Lieutenant General Geoffrey Scoones' IVth Corps in blunting the Japanese at Imphal was the transport aircraft supplied by the Americans. During the fighting at Imphal to Kohima, in fact, Lord Mountbatten requested the use of approximately one hundred American transports, diverted from the Hump traffic in order to win the battle. Among the pilots flying ammunition and other supplies to the British forces was the 14th Cargo Squadron, to which Captain Hall and his crew were attached.[48] Indeed, Hall recalled that shortly after his group flew into India word had filtered down that FDR had promised Stilwell more logistical support for his planned offensive. The airlift over Burma now entered its most crucial stage as the tempo of the war there was about to intensify.

"Confusion Beyond Imagination": In Support of the British in Burma, January 1944–May 1945

A month prior to Hall's arrival in India, the Air Transport Command had managed to airlift some 24,715 short tons of supplies to China and 12,224 tons inside India.[49] With the British and Chinese preparing a series of minor offensives the 4th Combat Cargo Squadron arrived in Chittagong, Captain Hall said, "the fun was about to start!" Hall recalled that his squadron arrived in CBI long before Lord Mountbatten took over command of SEAC. Prior to their permanent assignment to the British, Captain Hall said, "We were on detached service. Flying out of Dum Dum, near Calcutta, we flew Australian mutton to the British at Jorhat way up in the northeastern portion of India. We would pick this mutton up in Calcutta and by the time we got to Jorhat, the mutton began to defrost!" Hall said that is why to this day he cannot stand the smell of mutton! Hall emphasized that the planes of the 14th Squadron spent the majority of their time flying in support of the British, who were stationed in Jorhat as well as all along the northern frontiers of India near the Burma border. Hall recalled that the British, primarily Orde Wingate's Chindits, were then fighting to re-take Myitkyina while Stilwell's forces were fighting from the Imphal Valley." We were supplying the troops from Sylhet and we used to conduct paradrops all the way from the Imphal Valley until we took over Myitkyina. Then all of a sudden, for some reason or another, we were moved to Chittagong."[50]

Captain Hall recalled that the most remarkable aspect of the 4th Combat Cargo Command was its ability to move on such short notice. While the 4th Combat Cargo Command carried essentially the same logistics that is where the similarities ended as the 4th was much different from the 1st, 2nd, and 3rd Combat Cargo Command Groups. The 4th Combat Cargo Group was the first group to "come overseas, carrying all of its personnel and equipment by air from the US." Indeed, in its first month of operation pilots and crews of the 4th Combat Cargo Group hauled 9,500 tons of material up front, doubled the figure in the second month and, by March 1944, transported some 27,500 tons of supplies. Within the six months of operation in CBI, in fact, the 4th Combat Cargo Group doubled the tonnage carried by the other three combat cargo groups as well as carrying more tonnage per square mile than "could be moved to the front by trucks in a month."[51]

What made the 4th Combat Cargo Group all the more unique was the fact that unlike the other more stationary combat cargo groups, it could move almost at a moment's notice to another location and resume flying within a short period of time. This latter fact must not have been lost on Mountbatten as the British Army resumed its offensive that January. Indeed, the

> difference between the 4th Cargo and older cargo outfits is the difference between a horse and buggy and a motor car. At present, each cargo squadron has an air-

drome squadron to keep house for it, but it does not depend on these ground personnel to a crippling extent. The Combat Cargo squadrons can move out to new permanent stations on very short notice, leaving the airdrome squadrons behind. They've already done so. When the outfit moved from Agartala to Chittagong, it transported everything without missing a flight. One month before that, they were told at 2300 one night to leave Sylhet; they were out of there at 0500 the next day.[52]

Like the other three combat cargo groups, however, the 4th Combat Cargo Group normally flew an average of 17 sorties a day for each of its four squadrons who in turn flew anywhere from 12 to 18 hours a day, with each squadron averaging four sorties carrying approximately 30,000 pounds a day, seven days a week.[53] Carrying everything from drinking water to ammunition, mules, aviation fuel, gasoline, jeeps, and mutton, the pilots of the 4th Combat Command, flying sorties in unarmed transports, and oftentimes without the benefit of fighter support, kept Lord Mountbatten's British forces well-supplied from the air. One of the most notable and perhaps daring re-supply efforts occurred when the pilots of the 4th Combat Cargo responded to a call from the British 14th Army when their advance was halted before the Meiktila River due to a

Staff Sergeant Baldwin, from Toledo, Ohio, looks on from the front of the the "Shack Rat," amidst the 55-gallon oil drums that contained aviation fuel for Major General Claire Lee Chennault's 14th Air Force. Note that the gasoline barrels are lashed to the deck of the C-46s by chains due to turbulence (David C. Hall Collection).

bombed out bridge. Braving the darkness and the chance of meeting enemy fighters, the pilots of the 4th Combat Cargo nonetheless were able to fly the Bailey Bridge out to the British who quickly assembled it and laid it across the river. When dawn arrived, soldiers of the 14th British Army were able to cross the river and continue their advance.[54] Hall said that most of the drops were by parachute, due in large part to the fact that there were very few airfields as the British proceeded down the Irrawaddy toward Rangoon. Hall said that "this is why we paradropped a lot of supplies as there were very few airfields able to accommodate us or our planes."[55]

Captain Hall stated that the primary mission of the 4th Combat Cargo Command was to supply the British 10th Army by paradrop "on the run down to Rangoon." Upon its arrival in Chittagong on February 2, 1944, the pilots of the 4th Combat Cargo group flew in not only ammunition but also food and other supplies that an army would use. "We'd fly the supplies to them, either dropping them or, if the British would stake out a field, we'd go in there and land."[56] Hall stated that when the squadron operated in northwestern Burma near the border with India they oftentimes transported Orde Wingate's Chin-

A Chinese work gang loads a C-46 from the 4th Cargo Command based in Chittagong, India, with 55-gallon drums of aviation fuel. Notice the ramps being used to slide the fuel drums into the cargo area of the airplane from the 2½ ton truck used to carry the fuel to the flight line (David C. Hall Collection).

dits or later Merrill's Marauders in and out of Burma.[57] Hall added that the bulk of supplies they dropped to the British came from American lend-lease stocks:

> They all came from America. They'd lease to you. They brought them all into Chittagong, which is a port. This even irritated me at that time, but we were supplying everything to the British. Except the beer, which was American. In fact, we used to scrounge some of the American beer that was supposed to go to the British. After every supply run a few cases would come up "missing" each week. Anyway, basically all American supplies were lend-lease. We were picking them up there at the port of Chittagong. As the British Army kept moving down the Irrawaddy River, either to Salween, different towns, we'd move also. They were going into Mandalay, places like that I recall.[58]

Hall emphasized that the pace of flight operations was furious once the British offensive commenced in January 1944. Hall said, "We would fly anywhere from 14 or 15 hours a day. In fact, I remember in Chittagong, in a matter of one month, we had more traffic in and out of Chittagong than in any other airport in the world, I think. We were going basically seven days a week almost 18 hours a day, with these 90 some planes just going in and out. Like I said, in my log book, it shows that I recorded something like 14 to 15 hours a day up in the air, getting ready, flying time. I built up a lot of twin engine time"[59] (see Diagram #1). From their base in Chittagong, Hall stated, his crew would fly an average of four paradrops a day, primarily to Prome or Pegu, or an average of thirteen hours and fifty-five minutes a day that started somewhere between 4:30 or 5 in the morning and ended around 9 P.M. every evening, back and forth between Chittagong and such bases as Mandalay, Shwebo, Magwe, or Meiktila.[60] The veteran pilot remembered that perhaps the longest

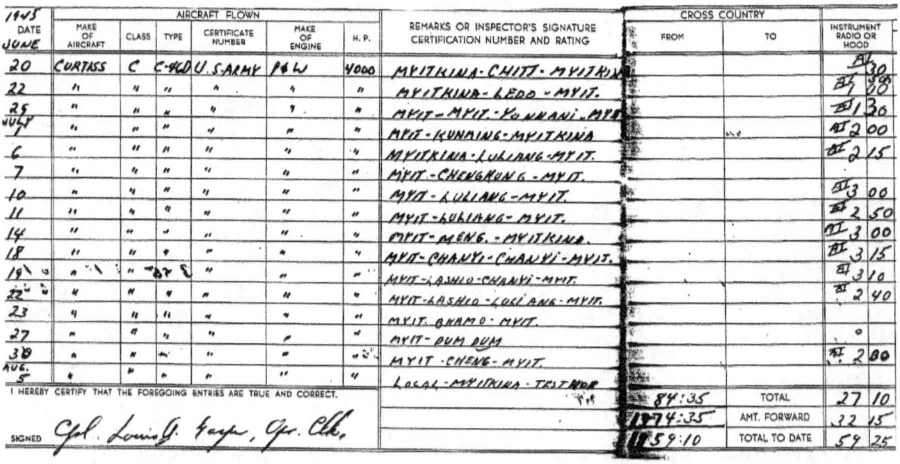

1945 DATE JUNE	AIRCRAFT FLOWN: MAKE OF AIRCRAFT	CLASS	TYPE	CERTIFICATE NUMBER	MAKE OF ENGINE	H. P.	REMARKS OR INSPECTOR'S SIGNATURE CERTIFICATION NUMBER AND RATING	CROSS COUNTRY: FROM	TO	INSTRUMENT RADIO OR HOOD
20	CURTISS	C	C-46D	U.S. ARMY	P&W	4000	MYITKINA-CHITT.-MYITKINA			AI 30
22	"	"	"	"	"	"	MYITKINA-LEDO-MYIT.			AI 1 00
25	"	"	"	"	"	"	MYIT-MYIT.-YUNNANI-MYIT			AI 1 30
JULY 1	"	"	"	"	"	"	MYIT-KUNMING-MYITKINA			AI 2 00
6	"	"	"	"	"	"	MYITKINA-LULIANG-MYIT.			AI 2 15
7	"	"	"	"	"	"	MYIT-CHENGKUNG-MYIT.			
10	"	"	"	"	"	"	MYIT-LULIANG-MYIT.			AI 3 00
11	"	"	"	"	"	"	MYIT-LULIANG-MYIT.			AI 2 50
14	"	"	"	"	"	"	MYIT-MENG.-MYITKINA.			AI 3 00
18	"	"	"	"	"	"	MYIT-CHANYI-CHANYI-MYIT.			AI 3 15
19	"	"	"	"	"	"	MYIT-LASHIO-CHANYI-MYIT.			AI 3 10
22	"	"	"	"	"	"	MYIT-LASHIO-LULIANG-MYIT.			AI 2 40
23	"	"	"	"	"	"	MYIT. BHAMO-MYIT.			
27	"	"	"	"	"	"	MYIT-DUM DUM			
30	"	"	"	"	"	"	MYIT.-CHENG-MYIT.			AI 2 00
AUG. 5	"	"	"	"	"	"	LOCAL-MYITKINA-TEST HOP			
								84:35	TOTAL	27 10
								1774:35	AMT. FORWARD	32 15
								1859:10	TOTAL TO DATE	59 25

I HEREBY CERTIFY THAT THE FOREGOING ENTRIES ARE TRUE AND CORRECT.

SIGNED Cpl. Louis J. Gaye, Opr. Clk.

Diagram #1. A page from the log book of Captain David C. Hall for 20 June 1945 (David C. Hall Collection).

day was when he and his crew flew fifteen straight hours. Hall added that "by this time we just kept following the British advance down the Irrawaddy." Hall recounted that by this time—late May 1945—they were making three trips a day, flying to Prome and Pegu. Indeed, the pace of operations was so great that "operations never ceased, even while on the move." Indeed, "during the last two weeks of February and early in March, the group went on a round-the-clock flying schedule. Co-pilots, radio operators, and crew chiefs were conscripted from B-24, B-25, and P-47 groups to relieve the strain of the 24-hour operations."[61]

The patch of the 4th Combat Cargo Command in China-Burma-India during World War II (David C. Hall Collection).

The 4th Combat Cargo Group's semi-official history provided an excellent glimpse of the group's pace of operations after the fall of Meiktila which became "a 24-hours-a-day operation for both the men and machines of the squadrons."

> The British, joined by the Indian 17th Division, struck south, and the armored columns raced down the all-weather road from Mandalay towards Rangoon. The first resistance was at Pyawbe, 27 miles down river. The enemy lost 3,500 men and many guns in the retreat. Finally, in a three-day battle the Japanese were completely driven out of the area.
> Following this battle the 5th Indian Division took the lead, and in 16 days drove on south 180 miles toward Pegu. Pegu was an important rail and communications center. Here, once again, the Japanese dug in for a fierce fight. In the meantime, supplies were still being flown to units west of Mandalay where a mop up operation was going on. C-47s from the 12th Combat Cargo Squadron and C-46s from the 4th Group supplied these units. The units now turned south and advanced down the Burma Railroad to Satthwa. At this town the forces split. One column moved toward the southeast, and then east to join the Rangoon-Mandalay Railroad at Pyinmana; the other continued south toward Prome. This division resulted in three columns of advancing British-Indian fighting units. All three of the spearheads were solely supplied by air—the 4th Combat Cargo Group doing the lion's share.[62]

In fact, the furious pace of operations can be seen in the tonnage carried by the 4th Combat Cargo Group during the months of March–April 1945. Indeed, in March 1945, the four squadrons of the 3rd Combat Cargo transported over 26,522 tons of supplies while the next month they carried 26,055 tons, only 467 tons less than in the previous month.[63]

Also, while flying in support of the British 10th Army, Hall recounted that it was about this time "we started supplying Merrill's Marauders, who would have us drop stuff off to them." Flying from bases at Chittagong and Sylhet the pilots and crews of the 4th Cargo Command supported Merrill's Marauders as

Captain David C. Hall barters with the locals in Kunming, China, while his aircraft is unloaded (David C. Hall Collection).

they penetrated into Burma in order to clear the area of the Japanese and allow the engineers to begin construction of the Burma Road in November 1944. Captain Hall said, "I remember specifically flying this group of Merrill's Marauders, as well as small combat teams that set up small radar sets into fields at Mogaung."[64] Hall stated that he vividly remembered one such operation when they received a "desperate call from a group of Merrill Marauders who had been working along a road near Mandalay. We got an urgent call to pick some of these guys up. Apparently, some other outfit had flown them [the Marauders] in, and the Japanese were still pretty damn active around Meiktila. Nevertheless, we went in and picked some of them up and dropped them off [back at their base camp]."

Besides the ever-present threat posed by Japanese fighters Hall stated that the greatest enemy was the monsoon that occurred from the end of March to the beginning of October. Hall recounted that it was during the monsoon season that he normally logged quite a bit of instrument flying time. One last problem that oftentimes hampered normal flight operations was the fact that many of the planes were overloaded. While the Dakotas or C-47s could carry only about 14 or 14.5 tons the C-46 could carry approximately 16 to 16.5 tons of supplies. Hall remembered that in either case the planes were often "notoriously overloaded." Unlike the C-47, however, the C-46 normally had no problem in carrying the overload as it compensated with more horsepower.

Hall said that the greatest threat posed by the enemy was his use of high altitude radar. This is why "we always flew in at low level, in order to avoid detection." In fact, Hall stated that most of the time "we flew along a pre-arranged flight plan and thus could avoid enemy radar flying so low." This in and of itself caused a slight problem as it oftentimes was not a matter of navigation but of simply time and distance. While supplying the British south toward Mandalay and Prome, Hall said that they would look for landmarks, such as the Irrawaddy or Chindwin rivers. He amusingly recalled that on one such flight, "a buzzard crashed into the windshield of my cockpit, shattering the glass everywhere." Hall said that this incident forced his command to ground him and "Pop" in New Delhi until the plane could be repaired.

As for fighter support, Hall said that the British could never be relied upon as "sometimes we would see them, sometimes we wouldn't see them." The only time that Hall said he saw a large number of British fighters was when Lord Louis Mountbatten made an inspection trip to the front. Hall recalled that during this instance he had just happened to glance up at the sky, "and it was as dark as black birds with Hawker Hurricane fighter planes, Spitfires.... I then turned to 'Pop' [Reynolds] and asked, 'What the hell is going on?' When the plane landed ... who comes floating in? Lord Louis Mountbatten! Lord Louis was reviewing the troops ... [and] when he left, the fighter planes left and we didn't see any more for a week after that." After Mountbatten left, Hall said, "I turned to Pop Reynolds and said, 'Well, this is why in the hell the British [planes] are out today!'"[65] Shortly after this incident with Mountbatten, the 4th Combat Cargo Group was re-assigned to fly supplies to Major General Claire L. Chennault's 14th Air Force as well as to Chiang Kai-shek's Nationalist armies.

As part of the air strategy formulated in 1942 by General Brereton and reinforced at the Trident Conference in Washington, D.C., in May 1943, the main effort of the Allied air forces in India was placed on supplying Chennault's 14th Air Force and Chiang Kai-shek's forces. As the tempo of the ground offensive to re-take Burma (Anakim) increased in late 1943 and early 1944, the air transport command shifted some of its efforts in supporting Lieutenant General Slim's offensive aimed at re-capturing Myitkyina, Mandalay, and finally Rangoon in order to open a land route into China. Along with this shift in priorities, so too did the fighter support Captain Hall and the 4th Combat Cargo Group were supposed to receive from the Royal Air Force. Hall said that his outfit rarely experienced fighter support despite the fact that the British agreed to provide protection for the unarmed transports flying the Hump into Kunming and Burma. General Brereton wrote as early as May 1942 that this fighter support was to "provide air defense for the air transport terminals in Assam."[66] In order to achieve the goal set out by both Lieutenant General Brereton and later Major General Raymond Wheeler in shifting the bases of the heavy bombers to Kunming where they would then join in with Chennault's bombing campaign against the Japanese home islands, American officials determined that fighter support was critical to the success of this objective. The first part of this strategy was to accumulate the necessary fuel and ammunition in China. Then, after the necessary air forces were in place, "it was hoped this plan would increase American operations considerably and give the Chinese morale an immediate boost."

Perhaps the finest tribute to the efforts of the pilots and crew of the 4th Combat Cargo Command came from Lieutenant General (later Field Marshal) William J. Slim, who wrote after the war that without the efforts of the pilots and crews of the Air Transport Command there would have been "no victory":

> We had proved right in our reliance on the air forces, British and American, first to gain control of the air, and then to supply, transport, and support us. The campaign had been an air one as well as a land one. Without the victory of the air forces there could have been no victory for the army, and, when it came, shares of the soldier and the airman were so intermingled that it was a joint victory. Air supply and close support by fighters and bombers had been carried out with precision and effect in full view of the army.[67]

Slim added:

> The air forces, British and American, were magnificent. The transport planes that remained to us flew incredible hours. They identified themselves completely with the army. It was as much a point of honor with them as with the soldiers that, not only the troops, but the thousands of tons of supplies and gear required, should get through in time.[68]

Supplying the Tiger: The China Airlift, 1944–1945

From January to June 1945, the C-46s and C-47s of the 4th Combat Cargo Group hauled supplies, troops, and equipment to the troops of the British 14th Army. In one of the most audacious missions, the squadrons of the 4th Combat Cargo Group participated in the initial assaults on Rangoon when on May 2, 1945, C-46s "appeared over Rangoon and dropped hundreds of 15th Corps paratroopers south of the city at Elephant Point."[69] In June 1945, after the British re-took Rangoon (the Japanese had, in fact, abandoned it prior to the arrival of the British), the 4th Combat Cargo Command was re-assigned to the Air Transport Command and supported both General Chennault's 14th Air Force as well as the Chinese Nationalist forces fighting the Japanese. For the pilots and crews of the C-46s, this meant flying over the ever-dangerous Himalayas. As mentioned above, Captain Eddie Goodman stated this route earned the reputation as the "Aluminum Trail," as the steep mountainsides were littered with the skeletons of C-47s and B-24s that had crashed into its sides.[70] Hall stated that when the 4th Combat Cargo Group took over the air ferry route from Chittagong to Kunming, there was one peak, known as the Baker Jig Yunnanyi that stood out as it was about 15,200 feet and had on its side the wreckage of some 52 or 53 C-47s. Hall stated that at best, the Dakotas, or C-47s, could climb anywhere from 13,500 to 13,800 feet and just barely make it past the Hump [Map #7]. Because the C-46 had two R2800 engines and put out some 2,000 horsepower it could better maneuver above the Baker Jig Yunnanyi even when loaded with a cargo bay filled with 55-gallon drums of high octane fuel.[71] Hall emphasized the fact that the C-46 Commando was easier to maneuver on the return trip as it could climb to some 20,000–21,000 feet.[72] Captain Hall stressed the fact that unlike the C-47, "the C-46 could get over it [the Hump] if we had to!"[73] "Fortunately," Hall said, "we had the C-46, which was powerful enough to climb over the highest peaks."

In rating the C-46 and C-47, Hall added:

> The C-47 you could fly; it was one of the easiest planes. It was very forgiving. If you made a mistake it would forgive you. It was a slow wing bird. The C-46 wasn't quite that forgiving as the C-47. The C-46 had larger engines, [it was a]

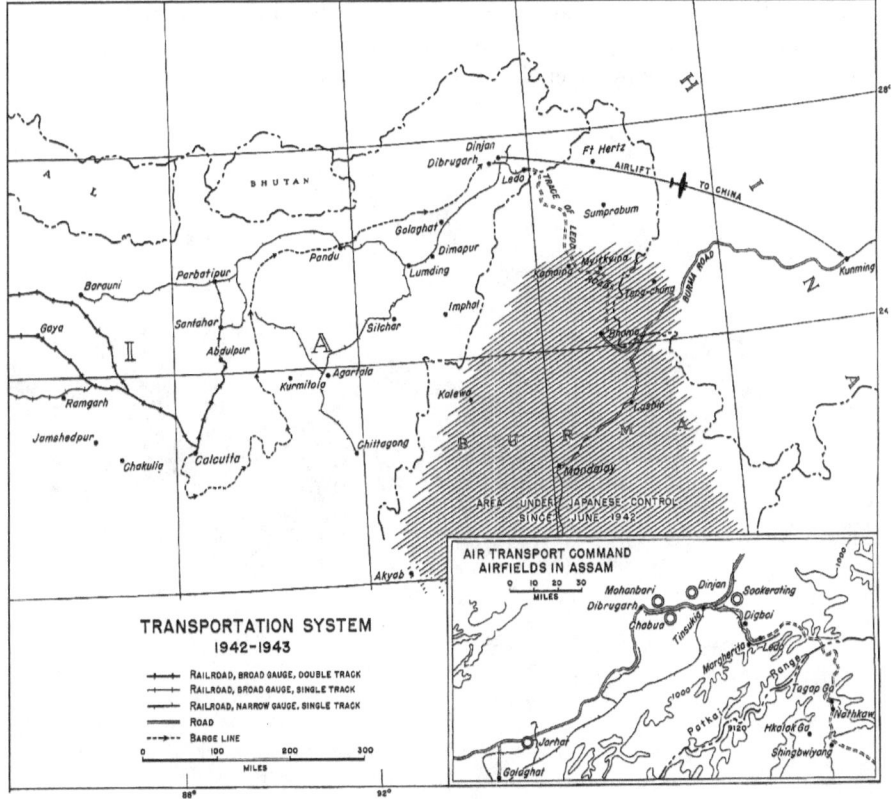

The transportation system in China-Burma-India during World War II (Romanus and Sunderland, *Stilwell's Mission to China*, p. 114).

faster plane, 15 miles of hydraulic fuel lines. It wasn't quite as forgiving as the C-47 was. I only had maybe 100 hours on the C-47, 1600 hours on the C-46. All of my combat time. The B-26 wasn't forgiving at all. You made a mistake, ah, it wasn't forgiving at all. You couldn't make a mistake in that, very few mistakes. The C-47, I could teach you know, and good instrumentship. The C-46, because a lot of our flying was on instruments. The C-46 was a good instrument plane, but not as well as the C-47. They have a lot of C-47s still flying today, right?[74]

Hall, in fact, was somewhat critical of the C-46, adding that it constantly leaked hydraulic fluid, "so if we could get forty to fifty planes a day into the air we were doing ... good!"[75]

Once Myitkyina fell to the Allies, Hall recounted that the 4th Combat Cargo Group occupied the former Japanese airfield and took over the route into Kunming, which was "nothing like flying from the original route used by the veteran Hump pilots." Hall added, however, that "this was no fun," as here "you had the Baker Jig Yunnanyi." Hall stated that the original Hump pilots (1942–43) flew the route that started in Jorhat (India) and ended in Kunming, Li-liang, or Chen-kung, which was where Chennault's American Volunteer Group (AVG) or Flying Tigers had flown out of and, where the 14th Air Force

Captain David C. Hall stands in front of a restored C-46 Commando at Castle Air Force Base in September 1983 (David C. Hall Collection).

was stationed. Hall admitted that "once we made it past Baker Jig [Yunnanyi], you were pretty well home safe" insofar as flying into Kunming.

In keeping with Lord Mountbatten's strategic directive that there would be no pause in flight or land operations during the monsoon, American and British pilots flew around the clock, seven days a week with no respite. In fact, the further down the Irrawaddy toward Rangoon the British moved so too did the length of the re-supply flights. There were continued protests from both Lieutenant General Albert C. Wedemeyer and Major General George E. Stratemeyer, commanding general of the XX Air Force, that the British were siphoning off their allotments of Hump tonnage. General Marshall, in a letter to Prime Minister Churchill, delivered through the chief British liaison officer in Washington, D.C., Field Marshal Henry Wilson, informed Churchill that contrary to the opinions of his two theater commanders in China (Wedemeyer and Stratemeyer), the U.S. Joint Chiefs of Staff had no intention "to remove U.S. air resources from Burma prior to the fall of Rangoon, or June 1, whichever date is earlier." Marshall added, "It is our purpose to leave with Mountbatten all that he requires to secure Rangoon this dry season, but [we] reserve the right to transfer U.S. air resources to China if Mountbatten is not successful in his attempt to capture Rangoon before the monsoon."[76] Hall stated that this is how "we lost a lot of our planes." Hall said, "The tempo of operations was such that if we could get fifty airplanes a day into the sky we were lucky!" The C-46 pilot admitted that by far the monsoon was the most dangerous time to fly. Hall recounted:

> Once we moved into Myitkyina, flying up to China, basically because of the weather. We didn't worry about the Japanese, they were around. One time we went to pick up Merrill's Marauders some place up in Burma, and I said let's get the hell out of here and I got out. I just dumped the load on the ground. I don't know where the guy was that was supposed to go back with us, but I wasn't waiting on him. We got out, and of course, they caught some of the guys on the ground, the Japanese did. I mean, the Japanese planes came in. Anyway, we lost most of our pilots and crews from the weather flying in the monsoons. At that time they did not have the radio navigation and the radar that you have today. Anyway, we flew to China, and of course, back to Myitkyina.[77]

Hall said that the 4th Combat Cargo Group maintained this routine until after V-J Day in September 1945. In fact, the veteran Hump pilot stated, "Even after V-J we were flying this same schedule until we were ordered home."

Allies of a Kind: Relations with the British Army

One of the most important tools in maneuvering over peaks such as Baker Jig Yunnanyi, Hall stated, was the radio link between Jorhat and Kunming, although "sometimes it worked and sometimes it didn't." Hall blamed most of the problems associated with the maintenance of the radio link as they flew over the Hump on the Chinese operators, who he said "were worse than the British insofar as dependability was concerned." As for the British loaders, Hall said, "Our job was get the supplies into China ... if the weather was too bad ... the British crews refused to load the airplanes or as was mostly the case, they would overload them." Hall said that this oftentimes was a major problem as the British normally loaded the planes at night which meant "that all we did was get up, fuel up, and take off."[78] He stated that "Pop" Reynolds would normally check the manifest before takeoff. If they didn't, Hall added that the pilots and crews would not realize that they were overloaded until they were airborne.

Hall recalled one such instance that stuck in his mind that occurred near Chittagong. After hearing that the monsoon was about to set in, Hall remembered he hurriedly jumped into his seat in the cockpit and turned to "Pop" and said, "Crank this goddamned thing up, we're getting out of here." As the C-46 rolled down the runway "Pop" turned to him and said, "Dave, we were seriously overloaded." With his plane now airborne and flying over the Bay of Bengal, Hall yelled, "'Pop' ... get your ass back there and get rid of some of that weight." The Army Air Force captain said that "from that point on I listened to Pop whenever he recommended something."[79]

Hall likewise criticized the British custom of stopping for tea, even if it was in the middle of the action. He said that prior to a late afternoon drop, about 4 P.M., "everything just stopped. I looked around and the British were having tea. Here we were bustin' our asses 12 or 14 hours a day and we would fly onto a British base and everyone was in the officers' mess or elsewhere having tea. What the hell is this! But, I guess that is how they operated." Hall frankly admitted that for the most part, "we hated the British. And what irritated us even more was the fact that they were supposed to but rarely provided us with fighter support."[80]

Hall said that sometimes there were serious misunderstanding between the two allies. Hall specifically recounted one instance when after landing at Prome, a British general pulled up in a jeep and "his aide [a captain] came out looking out for the captain of the aircraft (me). All I had on was a T-shirt, hat, and a .45 caliber strapped on. That's how we dressed while flying. I was just getting the plane ready for takeoff as we wanted to get the hell out of there because we had three or four more runs to finish. This aide, however, said, 'I have General So and So who has to get back to Chittagong.' I said that is fine but I don't have any more parachutes. I told him that I have three parachutes to pick up three American communicators (a staff sergeant and two sergeants) who had been working with the British. Our orders were, once we finished dropping off our supplies, to haul them back to base. So you see I have only three parachutes for them. They are for these three GI's." Hall said that the British captain was quite persistent, however, and said rather pointedly, "'Listen, I have General So and So' and, I said, 'General So and So doesn't mean shit to me. He is welcome to come along as I am going back empty [to Chittagong].'

You see, we had bucket seats that pulled out once the plane was empty. So I told him that he can sit in any one of them, but he cannot have a parachute. I said if he wants to ride back he can but without a parachute." The aide continued to insist that "this is *General So and So*." Hall replied, "I don't care who the hell he is. My orders are to pick up these three GI's and I have only three chutes." Hall recalled that the British aide curtly said, "We'll, you'll hear from us." As the exchange between Hall and the British officer was going on, the three Americans that Hall had been ordered to pick up climbed onto the airplane. Hall then turned to "Pop" and said, "Crank this thing up. Let's get the hell out of here."

Hall continued:

"As the plane began to taxi down the runway the jeep with the British general came up and blew its horn and signaled us to stop." Hall said that both the British general and his aide then climbed aboard the plane. Once on board the British aide then came up front to the cockpit and Hall, who by now had grown quite exasperated over this whole affair, pointedly told the British captain that the chutes were for the Americans. He then told the British officer, "'If you want a ride, get your ass back there and sit down on one of the bucket seats.' Now, you have to understand that in the meantime, we had received reports that there were bandits [Japanese fighters] in the area and I didn't want to get caught in the open and get shot down. I wanted to get the hell outta there! Anyway, we took off and headed back to Chittagong. Once in Chittagong, the next day, Colonel Baird [the 4th Combat Cargo Group's commander] called me and 'Pop' in to his office and said, 'Dave, you know you guys got us into a lot of trouble. You know that was *General So and So*. He said that you were very impolite to him the other day. He is probably going to report us to authorities in New Delhi and tell them that some smart ass American captain was disrespectful to him and that will be the end of our careers.'" Hall then said to Colonel Baird, "Look Colonel, we had reports of bandits in the area and we wanted to drop our load and get the hell outta there."[81] Hall said that he left the tent with a mild reprimand from the colonel to "behave himself and to try and be more accommodating to our 'allies.'"

The Living Conditions in the Field

Hall stated that while in Chittagong or Myitkyina he and his crew members lived either in grass huts or in tents that the British leased to the United States for thousands of dollars. These quarters, which were made of bamboo, leaked when it rained, and while better than living in tents, had both little green snakes known as "creeks" and other insects that would get into the boots or bedding. Hall said that each morning "you had to shake out your shoes as these little green snakes would fall out that had crawled up into them during the night." Hall added that overall, "it was just poor facilities. Very crude and very limited facilities. That's why we would want to fly to the places where we could get there and then get back" to Chittagong where they at least had a roof over their heads.[82] Despite the crudeness of the quarters Hall said that he and the other American pilots improvised and made them as habitable as possible. He added that while in India, "Everyone had a pet monkey and a local native boy known as a *bashaboy* to take care of his place. We paid the *bashaboy* a couple of rupees a month and he would sweep and do our laundry and stuff like that."

Hall recalled that insofar as recreation was concerned, "We used to be allowed to go down to the ocean and go swimming or something like that. We had picked up some motorcycles from the British. You know, we would kind of pick them up here and there, and we would go into town and ride the motorcycles. Until one of the British commanders said they were short of motorbikes and so we had to give them all back. But that was some of our recreation. I don't play cards, I never did. That was quite an avocation of a lot of them, but I didn't get into that. I used to watch them play poker, but I really didn't have a lot of time for recreation, but we used to have some. That's when we were overseas."[83]

As for food, Hall indicated that because they were assigned to a British base they normally ate British rations which the Americans thought to be very bland. As mentioned earlier, Hall had an aversion to mutton though he liked the British beer. He recalled one incident when entire 14th Combat Cargo Squadron was forced to stand down due to the fact that everybody in the squadron came down with dysentery and diarrhea due to eating mutton and the improper handling of food by the natives. As a result, Colonel Baird ordered the Americans to set up their own kitchen and prepare their own food. The Americans also ate K and C rations. "You couldn't eat their [British] food." Hall said that in order to supply their mess pilots, on return flights the pilots flew into Calcutta or Dum Dum where they normally picked up several cases of food a week that would be prepared by U.S. Army cooks assigned to the 4th Combat Cargo Command. As for the beer, Hall said that during their time in CBI, they had no refrigeration to speak of, and because the British normally drank their beer warm the American pilots would strap a few cases of beer into a cargo net, and take it up during a flight over the Hump and hang it outside the cargo bay for a few minutes in order for the beer to chill. Upon landing the pilots and crew enjoyed a cold one once the mission was over.

Captain Hall emphasized that contrary to the popular belief that normally portrayed pilots and ground crew as being undisciplined and unmilitary, such was not the case in CBI. In fact, Hall said, the opposite was true while they were in Chittagong. "We had very strict military discipline. That's why I am here today, because there was none of the stuff you see in the movies. We had very strict military discipline; they were not overbearing ... but you'd obey your orders, and there was a purpose for the discipline. That's why we did it."[84] Hall

Captain David C. Hall stands outside his grass shack in Jorhat, India. These huts were built by the British and leased to the Americans during World War II (David C. Hall Collection).

added, however, that many times conditions and the nature of the mission in CBI did not allow for proper military etiquette to be adhered to. Hall recalled one such instance when he and "Pop" dined at a British officers' mess in Jorhat. After landing, he remembered, he and his co-pilot walked into the mess in their normal flight uniforms, unshaven and dusty, and proceeded to eat their meal as the other officers, mostly British or Indian, and all in their in proper mess uniforms, stared at what they believed was the Americans' rather unkempt appearance. Hall said that he and "Pop" quickly ate their meal as they sensed that they were not wanted in the mess.[85]

Part of the emphasis on military discipline, Hall stated, was the fact that "we were a team," and part of this team depended on maintaining a good officer-enlisted relationship." He said that in CBI, "We had a very close relationship. They might have been across the street, they didn't live in the same tent as we did, but we ate in the same mess hall, they were with us day in and day out. We had a very close relationship with our enlisted personnel. I mean, we have the ground crews and the mechanics, who repaired the planes. They are the ones that kept us flying. So, we had a good, close relationship."

Like most pilots, Hall said that he had an excellent crew. "You see, I was the youngest guy in the outfit, and my co-pilot, was the oldest guy in the outfit. 'Pop' Reynolds, he was 27 years old. I was 19, and he was an old man. He was my co-pilot, very meticulous. [I normally had him] check the weights, and the manifest and check the weights to make sure you weren't overweight, overloaded. He did that very religiously; that's why I'm here today. I had a good co-pilot, a good crew chief, [Staff Sergeant] Baldwin from Toledo. I had a good radio operator, and I had a good crew. I told them, 'your asses are up here as high as mine. If we fall and you screw up, you're going to fall just as far as I am.'"[86]

Hall said that the normal flying day began at 0430 with the daily briefing and then "we would start flying, and flying to wherever. Paradropping food to the troops, bailey bridging, combat cargo. Whatever they loaded the plane up with the night before, that's what we delivered." Captain Hall added, "We didn't necessarily know what we were carrying before the drop." Finally, and with some pride, Hall stated that in almost three years of flying that included service over the Hump, he never crashed or damaged any of the aircraft he had been assigned to. Hall emphasized that throughout his entire stay in Chittagong, the British essentially ran the entire operation, from setting the flight plan to loading the planes as well as filling out the manifests. "In effect," Hall said, "the British ran the entire show in CBI."

At the end of every mission was, of course, the de-briefing by the 4th Combat Cargo Squadron's intelligence officer. Hall said that these sessions took place after the planes had ended their last mission for the night or on the next day. They normally lasted anywhere from fifteen minutes to three hours depending on the questions and types of information the intelligence officer was looking for.[87]

While the discipline was very strict, the uniform code was very casual. Hall said his normal flying uniform consisted of a T-shirt, khaki trousers, a cap that had his bars on it, a flight jacket and shoulder holster with a .45 caliber pistol in it. He said that "this was usually the uniform. We didn't care. We were working. We weren't dressed up in a uniform, or a flying suit, that particular day when we met Lord Louis [Mountbatten]. I know I had my khakis on, and a T-shirt, and of course, my cap with my captain's bars on it."[88]

Feeding the Tiger: The China Air Lift, June–August 1945

Even meeting the modest goal of 4,000 tons a month set in mid–1942 by Generals Arnold and Stilwell proved to be difficult at best (see Chart #1). Hampered not only by a lack of planes and personnel, the pilots and their brave crews, who were flying approximately 100 hours week, oftentimes fell victim to flying fatigue as they braved the high mountain peaks and heavy cloud cover of the Himalayas. With the introduction of round-the-clock operations in October 1943 the rate of accidents significantly increased from the previous six-month period (June–December 1942) or roughly 25 per month to 38 major accidents on the Hump. After a month-long safety standdown, and a renewed emphasis by the ATC's high command, the number of accidents dipped to 28 the following month (December 1943). In fact, the ATC's commanders took this increased percentage in accidents very seriously. General C. R. Smith, who had been attached to the Air Transport Command's headquarters and was on an inspection trip to CBI, reported to his superiors in Washington, D.C., that the air effort was taking a heavy toll on the men and airplanes on the Hump route:

> We are paying for it in men and airplanes. The kids here are flying over their head — at night and in daytime and they bust them up for reasons that sometimes seem silly. They are not silly, however, for we are asking boys to do what would be most difficult for men to accomplish; with the experience level here we are going to pay dearly for the tonnage moved across the Hump ... [yet] ... there is nothing else to do.[89]

Captain David C. Hall poses in his typical flight gear in front of the "Shack Rat" in Dum Dum, India, prior to the start of another mission over the Hump (David C. Hall Collection).

Added to the stresses placed on the pilots by the terrain and long flying hours was the constant fear of enemy fighters. As both Captains Hall and Goodman recalled, that fear was a constant reminder that they were unarmed and oftentimes alone once airborne as Allied fighter support could never be guaranteed. In order to boost the morale of his own crew and to possibly ward off any

The crew of the "Shack Rat" pose next to their airplane at Dum Dum, India (Left to right) Staff Sergeant Baldwin, Captain David C. Hall, and First Lieutenant Richard "Pop" Reynolds.

potential enemy fighters, Captain Goodman instructed his crew chief to place broomstick handles painted black in the empty gunports of his B-24 to give it the appearance of being armed.[90]

Chart #1
Gross Tonnage Hauled by the Air Transport Command Over the Himalayas, December 1942–July 1943[91]

Month / Year	Tonnage Delivered
December 1942	1,227
January 1943	1,263
February 1943	2,855
March 1943	2,278
April 1943	1,910
May 1943	2,334
June 1943	2,382
July 1943	3,451

As the pace of offensive operations increased after Sextant and Quadrant in mid to late 1943, so did the tonnage going into China. After December 1943, the amount of tonnage, in fact, "exceeded all commitments," and with that so too did the morale of the Hump pilots and other Air Transport Command personnel. Indeed, during the last six months of 1944, the actual tonnage flown by the C-47s, B-24s, and C-46s "exceeded the planned accomplishments, month by month," but it was what had, in fact, been envisioned at the three mid-war conferences in 1943 (see Chart #2).

Chart #2
Hump Tonnage, August–December 1944[92]

1944	Proposed Deliveries in Tons	Actual Deliveries in Tons
August	13,000	23,675
September	14,000	22,314
October	20,500	24,715
November	27,500	34,914
December	31,000	31,935

The increased tonnage airlifted into China was due, in large part, to the number of aircraft involved in the supply operation. In June 1944, the average number of aircraft involved was 108; in December the number doubled to 249. Sorties by aircraft into China went from 3,702 in June to 7,612 in December.[93] With the increase in the number of aircraft involved in the airlift there was the problem of congestion in the form of stacking at bases in Kunming "where much gasoline and time was wasted in bad weather by planes stacked up over the airport, awaiting their turn to let down through the overcast." As Captain Hall indicated, when the 4th Combat Cargo Group took over the air supply mission into China, there were more air bases in China that could accommodate the overflow. Hall specifically stated that the pilots of the 14th Squadron oftentimes flew into nearby Luliang and not Kunming. This gave the pilots of the ATC a second all-weather alternate (Chanyi was the second) to Kunming. Also assisting the pilots of these transports was a beacon that was placed near the airfield that the radio operator could home in on and permit the navigator to set the course even if bad weather or fog covered the airport (see Map #8).

As more and more accessible airfields were built, more pilots added, and more ordnance and supplies assigned to the CBI theater now that the war in Europe was nearing its bloody climax, the "ATC was able to aid XX Bomber Command while increasing [at the same time one might add] its deliveries to Chennault's heavily reinforced command from 7,439 tons in January, and only 4,988 in March, to 12,448 tons in June, 16,985 in November; and 14,688 in

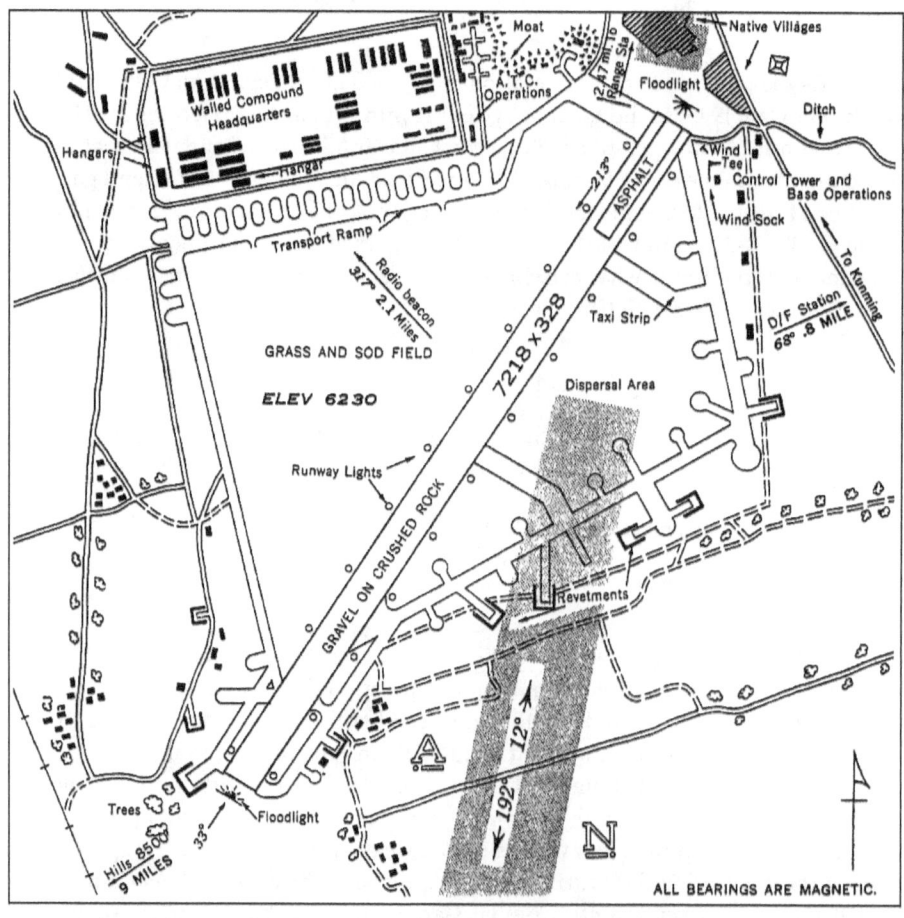

Map #8. Kunming, China, and surrounding area (Hump Pilots Association).

December [1944]."[94] Unfortunately, due to inaccurate record keeping, the statistics maintained by the Air Transport Command differ slightly with those of the 14th Air Force. What can be discerned from the official figures kept by the ATC, however, is the fact that there was a significant increase in tonnage going to the various commands in 1944 in CBI (see Chart #3).

Chart 3
Actual Tonnage Flown by Air
Transport Command Over the Himalayas, 1944[2]

Month	Total	14th AF	XX BC	Other U.S.	Chinese
January	13,399	7.601	.....	1,177	4,621
February	12,920	7,017	383	1,640	3,880
March	9,587	4,379	3,603	940	665
April	11,555	6,757	1,693	1,772	1,333
May	11,383	6,231	1, 532	1,826	1,794
June	15,845	12,537	350	1,033	1,925
July	18,975	13,213	1,070	2, 664	2,028
August	23,676	13,871	3,055	3,919	2,831
September	22,315	13,245	3,452	2,686	2,932
October	24,715	13,014	7,037	2,557	2,107
November	34,914	14,476	7, 881	9,018	3,539
December	31,935	12,805	4,348	13,188	1,594

Supporting Chiang Kai-shek's Nationalist Armies

After Operation Elephant Point and the retaking of Rangoon, the ATC re-assigned the 3rd and 4th Combat Cargo Groups to Myitkyina, where they were to spend the remainder of the war ferrying Chinese troops and equipment into China. Indeed, the stage had been set for this new assignment as early as November 29, 1944, when Lieutenant General Albert C. Wedemeyer[95] and Chiang Kai-shek informed both the Combined Chiefs of Staff and Lord Mountbatten that "a large part of the Chinese troops fighting with the Allied forces in Burma were needed in China." Reluctant to lose the Chinese troops though ordered by the CCS to transfer them back to Chiang's control, Mountbatten ordered the Chinese 14th and 22d Divisions re-assigned to Wedemeyer's forces then fighting off a major Japanese offensive in Southwestern China. The transfer, code-named Operation Grubworm, which involved not only the 14th and 22nd Divisions but also elements of the Chinese Sixth Army Headquarters, one heavy mortar company, one signal company, and two portable surgical hospitals, was placed under the direction of the Tenth Air Force which was then engaged in re-supply efforts for Slim's 14th Army and its advance down the Irrawaddy River. Eventually, Operation Grubworm "was carried out from five airfields in Burma- Myitkyina North, Sahmaw, Warazup, Nansim, and Myitkyina-South, as well as from Ledo in Assam." As the official history stated, "the whole operation[96] was completed in a surprisingly short time: the first of the heavily-laden transports rose from the Burma fields and headed toward China on the morning of 5 December 1944, and the last of the transports emptied its cargo on Chinese runways on 5 January 1945 — exactly a month after the beginning of the operation." Indeed, "From June through late September (1945) thousands of Chinese and American soldiers and their equipment, were flown to China. Tons of materials and thousands of gallons of gasoline were flown on a twenty-four-hour-per-day around-the-clock schedule. There were no more off-altitude and ground-hugging flights like the OSS trips and other trips into combat areas. Day and night, ignoring the terrible weather, the C-46s (and C-47s) made the trips back and forth over the mountains, averaging two round trips per day for each airplane."[98] Hall added that what made the trips across the Hump all the more easy was the fact that the C-47 was a beautiful instrument plane.

The pilots and crews of the 4th Combat Cargo Command were released from the North Burma Air Task Force in early June 1945 and placed directly under the ATC. Eventually, Hall's squadron became involved in the transporting of Chinese soldiers, many of whom.

> were flown directly to the fighting lines at Nanning. The normal loading procedure of the Chinese was to divide them into planeloads consistent with the type of aircraft in which they were be transported in, with every attempt to keep the rations, equipment, and ammunition intact with the proper unit. While the ground crew loaded the passengers into the plane, the pilot of the aircraft determined the load he would carry and directed the placement of the cargo within the plane. Since the Chinese equipment depended upon the use of hundreds of draft animals, specially trained personnel were needed to load the animals aboard the planes.[99]

Staff Sergeant James H. Cortright, who served with the 3rd Combat Cargo, Command recalled that there were reasons for the stowing of the Chinese soldiers' weapons before they boarded the plane:

> While loading the Chinese, we stowed their rifles in the rear compartment in the belly of the plane. Getting those rifles in that compartment took some doing. There was a great amount of arm waving, pointing, bowing, and nodding before this task was complete. I finally learned that the reason for stowing the rifles in the rear compartment was because the Communist movement was strengthening and that there was concern that they would try and take over the planes. I also learned that stowing the rifles in the rear compartment didn't mean much because most of them (the Chinese) had some type of handgun concealed someplace on their person.[100]

Staff Sergeant Cortright added,

> The learning process continued during which I learned that the load "klunk" made by a burlap bag when it was more or less dropped on the cargo compartment floor was because it contained hand grenades. Yes, they did carry hand grenades in a burlap bag. (So much for the Chinese mentality.) I can vouch for this because I personally, very carefully I might add, checked it out.[101]

Captain Hall recounted that on one such mission, he picked up a group of sixty Chinese soldiers with orders to fly them into Kunming. Once aboard, he said, "I usually bolted the door to my cockpit and kept my .45 handy in order to prevent the plane from being hijacked or commandeered by the Chinese." Once airborne he said that he and "Pop" heard a scuffle taking place in the cargo bay though he still refused to open the hatch of the cockpit until the plane safely landed. After the plane touched down in Kunming, he said that he counted two fewer passengers than had been on the original manifest. He added, "I didn't bother to ask where the other two were." Hall remembered that after the fall of Rangoon to the British, he and his crew started "hauling gasoline, basically 100 octane, 95–100 octane gasoline ... [not only to the Nationalists but also to] the Communists" in China (see Chart #4). He stated that while the Japanese still posed the greater threat by now it appeared even to them that "the handwriting was on the wall as V-E (Victory in Europe) had been declared."

Chart #4
Airlift to China
Hump Tonnage to China and in India, 1944–1945

Year and Month	To China	Intra-India
1944 October	24,715*	12,224
November	34,914	15,553
December	31,935	16,249
1945 January	44,099	17,112
February	40,677	17,118
March	46,545	19,424
April	44,254	19,589
May	46,394	15,015
June	55,387	14,269[102]

*Short Tons

As for supplying the Communist forces, Hall said that he wondered "what in the hell we were giving the Communists gasoline. They didn't even have any airplanes. You see, however, the war by this time was almost over. In fact, as late as 2 October 1945, we were flying supplies to them and the Nationalists."[103] Hall added, "I was flying almost up until the time I went home in November 1945."

As for direct contacts with the natives, Hall said that "we had very little with the Chinese. We were flying up into China, and basically they unloaded the plane and we would barter with them. But we had very little personal contact. The contact with the Chinese was the same with the Burmese. Other than a few trips down to the Mogaung Ruby Mines trying to negotiate. You know, we stayed away from the natives, primarily because of health reasons."

The End of the War and Home: October–November 1945

The end of the war on 1 September 1945 did not mean an end to flying. In fact, Captain Hall said the 4th Combat Cargo Command continued to fly even after the Japanese surrender and "continued to lose airplanes" due in large part to the weather, which was "to me ... absolutely ridiculous. Well, you do what you are told to do, right?" Realizing that every pilot lost was one less that would go home, Hall decided to take matters into his own hands and went to see the flight surgeon about having the men in his squadron grounded in order to prevent their exposure to any more hazardous duty. After the latter refused to ground the entire squadron, Hall took it upon himself to stand the squadron down, which brought him into direct contact with the new group commander.[104] Hall said by this time the 4th Combat Cargo Group was still flying gasoline, mortars, ammunition and other ordnance to Chiang Kai-shek and the Communists and he said that we had lost two planes to the monsoons. Finally, he said, "What the hell is this, the war is over. And while everybody had had enough points to go home, you had to wait for the assignment to go home. So anyway, I went to see this flight surgeon who, as it turned out, had no personality whatsoever, and refused my request to stand the crew down, and we were ordered to resume flying by the squadron's commanding officer."

Eventually as the U.S. military began to redeploy its personnel for demobilization in CBI, Hall and his crew received their long awaited orders home in mid–October 1945. Impatient to get home and not wanting to return via the more traditional way aboard a crowded troop ship, Hall said, "we were going to fly back. So, a bunch of us got in this plane in Myitkyina and we took it to Calcutta. Then from Calcutta we went to Bombay. Stayed there a few days, goofing off. Then we went to Karachi. When we landed in Karachi, the British military was waiting for us." Unknown to Hall and the other Americans inside the C-46, "the United States Army had transferred the C-46s and C-47 in the CBI theater to the British military who in turn gave them to the Chinese National Air Force, and they were supposed to take it to China."[105]

Shortly after landing, Hall said that several jeeps came racing onto the tarmac filled with British military policemen. Getting out of their jeeps, one British military policeman shouted, "Who's in charge of this plane?" One of the American passengers said, "I don't know, that guy over there said his name was Captain David C. Hall." Hall replied, "Yes, we're taking this [plane] home. Because we are going to go from Karachi to Abadan, then the Middle East, then back through Europe, and were just going to monkey around flying." Hall said that the British were not moved by his story, and instead told him, "You can't take this plane. You should have left it in Myitkyina and this now belongs to the British, and then assigned to the Chinese." In vain, the American captain countered the British policeman's argument and said, "Wait a minute. This airplane is mine. I got it when it was brand new from Fort Wayne, Indiana. They would see that it was assigned to me." Finally, however, the American said, "You could see we were getting no place with them." Hall then turned to the British military policeman and said, "Well, what do we do?" The British policeman then said, "We will get you on a troop ship." Hall added, "So, big deal, they got us a stateroom, on a troop ship, from Karachi. Nineteen days I had to spend on the water and get back to New York City. I came back to New York on November 11, 1945. From there I was assigned 100 enlisted men. Then I had to take this bunch back to Louisville, Kentucky."[106]

"Kept On Doing It Month After Month"

Still not sure what he was going to do insofar as re-enlistment was concerned, Hall said that he made his decision after he had been told by one of his superior officers, Ed Hatch, that he would not promote Hall, who thus decided that he would leave the military. Regretfully, Hall added that he was slightly disappointed in that "while I never really cared for the military, I did enjoy it."[107] After remaining in Louisville for a short time, Captain Hall returned home to Youngstown and entered Youngstown State University, where he received his degree in 1950 in civil engineering. Hall remained in the Air Force Reserve and said that between classes he would go to the Youngstown Air Base, "jump in an airplane and buzz around." Shortly after the outbreak of the Korean War on 25 June 1950, Hall said that he received a letter from "some Air Force Brigadier General" who noticed that Hall had a considerable amount of twin engine time and went on to say in the letter, "We need your services again, and if you will sign these papers and return to us, you will automatically go in as a Major in the United States Air Force, and we will leave you on flight pay." Hall said that he said, Phhh ... and threw it [the letter] ... away." About a month later, Hall said that he received another letter from the same Air Force brigadier general. In the letter, "it reminded me of all the money they spent teaching me to fly, and my record, and I had served for the United States Air Force, and reminded me how much they had done for me. If I did not sign to be reenlisted or come back again, I would lose all my rights and privileges of an officer of the United States Air Force."[108] Hall said that this time, however, he seriously considered the offer and "was tempted to put bull crap on it and send it back, but I did not sign it or send it back, and that was on May 19, 1951, and I never heard from them since. So I gave up all my rights and privileges of a commissioned officer in the United States Air Force. I thought I did enough for them.... Maybe they [the Air Force] could have forced me [to come back on active duty] ... I didn't spend a lot of time dwelling on it, and I never heard from them since. Anyway, I enjoyed it; it was great."

After graduation from college, Hall became a civil engineer and settled down in Girard, Ohio. He shortly thereafter married his wife, Amy, and together they raised two daughters and a son. An avid pilot and traveler, Dave and his wife frequently traveled around the United States and Western Europe (and yes, he even visited the United Kingdom in later years!). Despite being retired, Dave still does some consulting work and is immensely proud of his wartime experiences in Burma and China, the "Shack Rat," and his marvelous crew — particularly his late friend and co-pilot, Richard "Pop" Reynolds.

There was one final tribute to Captain David C. Hall and the pilots and crews of the Air Transport Command who braved enemy fighters, the monsoons, and the rugged peaks of the Himalayas. In his postwar memoirs the former commanding officer of the 14th Army, Field Marshal William J. Slim, wrote:

> Although we moved great tonnage and many thousands of troops by air, the largest number of transport aircraft we ever had was much less than would elsewhere have been considered the minimum required. It was quite easy theoretically to demonstrate that what we were doing was impossible to continue over any length of time. Yet the skill, courage, and devotion of the airmen, British and American, both in the air and on the ground, combined with the hard work and organizing ability of the soldiers, not only did it, but kept on doing it month after month.[109]

For Captain David C. Hall, and Flight Lieutenant Richard "Pop" Reynolds, SSgt Baldwin, and the rest of the "Shack Rat's" crew and ground maintenance personnel, their devotion and commitment to their mission was plainly evident as they did keep "on doing it month after month," in some of the most appalling weather and under some of the most adverse conditions imaginable. For a young man of 19, the China-Burma-India theater was exotic. In fact, service in CBI was one of the high points in Hall's life and career. While at times CBI seemed more like "Confusion Beyond Imagination" insofar as the politics and war were concerned, the war on the Asian mainland tested the youthful vigor and endurance of a whole generation of young Americans like Captain Hall. Placed into a theater that had little if any glory as well as more challenges than those experienced in either the European or Pacific theater of operations, the men of the Air Transport Command, and more specifically, the 4th Combat Cargo Group responded with what Prime Minister Churchill and Field Marshal Slim said was the "*American Can Do*" spirit, and made the airlift into Burma and China "a stunning success."[110]

Chapter 5

"A Most Impressive Engineering Achievement in War": Corporal Alexander McVean's War Along the Burma Road, 1944–1945

From the start of re-supply operations in the China-Burma-India theater, American and British planners wrestled with a logistical system spread out over thousands of miles and reliant upon an industrial base some 12,000 miles away. In fact, both China's and Burma's immense distances and logistical requirements proved to be the cause of many diplomatic crises and remained a constant irritant between the Allies (United States, Britain, and Nationalist China) until nearly the end of the war. Despite the organization of the Assam-Burma-China Ferry in March 1942, the task of organizing the theater's resources proved to be an impossible one. This in turn contributed to the marginalization of CBI's overall strategic importance as it became apparent that victory over Japan would come in both the Central and Southwest Pacific theaters and not on the Asian mainland as originally conceived by President Franklin D. Roosevelt and Prime Minister Winston S. Churchill.[1] Though it might be added that by the beginning of 1945, CBI became the focus of a large-scale Allied effort as both the American Joint Chiefs of Staff (JCS) and Combined Chiefs of Staff (CCS) saw China as a front containing Japanese troops that could be used elsewhere (notably on Iwo Jima, in the Ryukus, i.e., Okinawa, and in the Japanese home islands) in the Pacific Area of Operations.

Indeed, as the airlift began, it became apparent to all that the airlift could bring in only so much by air to China. The rest, the CCS chiefs reasoned, would have to come into northern Burma and China via a land route. Despite this reasoning, U.S. Army and British Army combat engineers nevertheless spent the first two years of the war in CBI (1942–43) building airfields, revetments, hangars, and port enhancements in order to accommodate the massive air and sea supply effort being expended on behalf of both Chiang Kai-shek's Nationalist forces and Major General Claire Lee Chennault's Fourteenth Air Force. Indeed, British and American planners had decided early on that a land route into China was to be built. As a result, "late in 1942, when the Allies had completed plans for a campaign to recapture northern Burma, the engineers were given the primary mission of building ground communications to support a campaign in Burma and to make possible the sending of large quantities of supplies overland to China."[2] After the Japanese had been driven out of northern Burma, in lieu of a two-pronged offensive designed to begin the long march down the Irrawaddy River to Rangoon and the seizure of Myitkyina, thus securing the air routes used by the Air Transport Command over the Himalayas, "American engineers were to help the Chinese improve the world-famous Burma Road linking China with northeastern Burma, and later were to take sole charge of constructing the Ledo Road from northeastern India across northern Burma to a junction with the Burma Road."[3]

Besides the re-supply of Chennault's Fourteenth Air Force and Chiang's armies, the CCS had another motive for improving and expanding the old Burma Road with that of a connection starting in Ledo: a strategic bombing campaign directed against the Japanese home islands and Formosa (Taiwan). The combat engineering units sent to CBI after the Quadrant conference held in Quebec in August 1943 had as their main tasks the construction of a series of airfields to accommodate the massive B-29 Superfortress bombers that had started to roll off the assembly lines in American aviation plants. The B-29, with its impressive payload of bombs and longer range, was the ideal plane to carry out Chennault's cherished objective of a major bombing campaign against the Japanese home islands. The American combat engineers sent to CBI were, in fact, "the first to build airfields overseas large enough for the big bombers." With the decision taken at Quadrant to initiate a series of limited offensives in northern Burma, the engineers were likewise "called upon to link eastern India and southwestern China with the most extensive military pipeline system ever constructed—to supply, in fact, an airlift to China, facilitate combat [operations] in Burma, and American units in China."[4]

It was at this juncture of the war in CBI that a difference of opinion emerged between American and British planners over to how best accomplish this goal. While the American Joint Chiefs of Staff saw an opportunity to supply Chiang and Chennault with an increased amount of tonnage by both air and land, the British desired to reconquer all of Burma in order to re-open the port of Rangoon. The differences that arose with this plan at Quadrant and later Sextant (22 November–7 December 1943) held in both Cairo, Egypt, and Tehran, Iran, came into the open as British Field Marshal Alan Brooke noted in his diary that, "All they [American planners] want is north Burma and the air routes and pipe lines and Ledo Road into China. They now practically have got all of these, and the rest of Burma is of small interest to them."[5] In spite of the differences voiced by the Allied leaders at Quadrant and later Sextant on what military strategy to pursue in regard to China, planning nonetheless commenced for the construction of the pipeline and connection of a road leading into the Burma Road to Kunming. The decisions taken at both wartime conferences concerning Burma set the stage for the dispatching of Corporal Alexander McVean and his fellow combat engineers, known unofficially as the second group of Merrill's Marauders, to CBI during the summer of 1944.

A Yank in Burma: Corporal Alexander McVean, June–December 1943

Alexander McVean entered the Army in June of 1943 and underwent basic combat training at Fort Sutton, North Carolina, located near Charlotte. McVean recalled that relations with the locals were oftentimes terse as the soldiers were "damn yankees." The Army corporal added, however, "they [the locals] still invited them in for Sunday dinner if they were on liberty." McVean stated that due to the wartime emergency, there were no barracks per se, and instead, the men slept in tents throughout their basic and advanced training. After McVean completed basic training at Fort Sutton, the Army assigned him to the combat engineers. The Army corporal recalled that while undergoing advanced training at Fort Leonard Wood, Missouri, he received a heavy amount of basic infantry training, learning the use of flamethrowers, heavy machine guns, as well as infiltration tactics, demolitions and hand-to-hand combat. McVean likened the intensity of this training to Ranger-like training of today.[6] Specifically, he recalled one Sunday morning during advanced individual training when the drill sergeants came into the tents where he and his fellow soldiers were sound asleep and awakened them about 4 A.M. and ordered them outside to dig foxholes after which they stood in place as Sherman tanks crossed over the hastily dug fighting holes. McVean stressed that this type of training, which included a heavy dose of cross-training, particularly in both infantry and non-infantry skills, was "an important part of their overall training" while at Fort Leonard Wood. McVean added that "I fired everything they had ... .50 caliber machine guns, flame-throwers, etc." Unknown to McVean at the time was the fact that the Army Ground Forces had placed increased emphasis on infantry training, due in large part to the lessons learned in North Africa and Sicily. Indeed, the training McVean and his comrades received at Fort Leonard Wood was part of a program called "unit conversion," designed by Army planners to meet the needs of the service at the time. This unit conversion took on added meaning with engineer units, the type to which McVean had been assigned, due to the fact that combat engineers oftentimes preceded the infantry's advance in clearing minefields and other obstacles that impeded the advance. In fact, units designated as combat engineers received a considerable amount of infantry training until the end of the war. While the skills the AGF taught proved to be extremely useful to U.S. soldiers during World War II, post–World War II studies, however, pointed to the fact that such "reorganizations were wasteful," due in large part to the failure of the Army Ground Forces to make full use of specialist training.[7] Interestingly, however, McVean stated that the infantry skills he received at advanced individual training proved invaluable in the jungles of Burma as they cleared the way for the construction of the Ledo Road.[8]

After completing training at Fort Leonard Wood, McVean and the other soldiers in his unit boarded trains for Newport News, Virginia, still not sure where it was exactly they were headed. After boarding a ship, the troop transport headed southeast into the Caribbean Sea and passed through the Panama Canal. After a long voyage across the Pacific Ocean, the transport which McVean was on pulled in to port at Calcutta, India. From there they boarded trains into the heart of India where, near the border of India and Burma, the Americans boarded a ferry on the Ganges River and crossed over to the opposite shore. After they assembled all of their duffel bags, rifles and other equipment, they then "walked ... and walked," McVean stated, "into Burma."[9] On their backs and shoulders the soldiers carried the normal combat load which included an M1 Garand rifle, gas mask, two barracks (duffel) bags, ammunition belt and spare ammo. With this load strapped to their backs, McVean recalled, he and his comrades set out for Burma. Shortly after their arrival in Burma in late December 1943, Corporal McVean and the other combat engineers began to clear a trail in what became their assigned section of the Ledo Road.

Initially, McVean said, "we had very little to do with the British though we did meet up with quite a few Chinese soldiers." Asked about his impressions of the Chinese soldier, McVean said that they were "tough ... hard fellows." McVean added that the only Chinese word that he remembered was "scheeschee," which meant "thank you."[10] McVean stated that on several occasions he witnessed firefights between the Nationalist and Chinese Communist troops. McVean added that this became a common occurrence as the Americans marched further into Burma. McVean admitted, "I had never heard of any actual fighting between the Chinese and Japanese, basically." McVean said that while in the jungle, he saw some strange things, such as one memorable incident when "we saw, in fact, some guy come riding by on a big white horse. He almost got killed. Turned out he was a Chinese general. Imagine that, right in the middle of the jungle ... on a white horse." Another unusual sight was the appearance of a large hospital ship right in the middle of a river located, McVean said, "in the middle of nowhere."[11] Corporal McVean recalled the day he and his platoon came upon some Japanese underground bunkers, "some occupied ... some of them not occupied. If they were occupied ... well, we killed them with our rifles or flame-throwers. We couldn't take prisoners. What are you

Corporal McVean (far right) walks away after cleaning his mess kit while working on the Ledo Road (Alexander McVean Collection).

going to do with them?" McVean stated that the "Japanese were good fighters. Happy to commit suicide. But they were the worst people ... they would go to villages, rape all the women ... and shove bamboo up through them." McVean added that he and his fellow combat engineers came upon things like that "all the time." The combat engineer likewise recalled that many of the villages they came upon had very few young women in them due to the fact that "the Japanese took a lot of Chinese and Burmese women and turned them into prostitutes or sex slaves."[12]

McVean recalled that he and his fellow combat engineers began their war in Burma along the northernmost end of the Irrawaddy River Valley during the fight for Myitkyina. McVean acknowledged that the fighting for the airfield at Myitkyina continued even as work began on the Burma Road. Following close behind Merrill's Marauders, McVean stated that operations in Burma, which were normally patrol-sized operations, usually covered about a mile a day as the construction workers began to clear the area with machetes. As for supplies, McVean said they "were primarily supplied by air," normally with K-Rations, C-Rations, and sometimes 10-in-1 rations (given to the Air Force, "which were ... the best"), and "once in a while ... a case of Blatz beer and for each of us a carton of cigarettes!"

Contrary to popular myth, and unlike Merrill's Marauders, who were withdrawn from the battlefield after Myitkyina had been captured, McVean stated that "we ... the engineers ... just kept going and going toward China." He added that as they made their way to the Chinese border, "our contact with the Nationalist Chinese forces" increased. In fact, McVean added, as they began to construct the road Chinese troops, normally on the squad level, oftentimes accompanied their American allies and provided flank security against remnants of the 18th Imperial Japanese Army that were still offering resistance to Lieutenant General Stilwell's forces in northern Burma. McVean said that contrary to popular belief at the time, the Chinese were "good fighters ... at least the ones I saw ... which were many!"[13]

Construction of the Ledo Road: May 1943–December 1944

Even as the Japanese drove the remnants of Stilwell's battered Chinese forces across the Burmese frontier into India, Allied leaders busied themselves with plans to retake northern Burma in order to re-connect the severed supply lines running to Kunming, Chengtu, and other strategic airfields in China. In order to carry out Major General Chennault's planned aerial offensive against Japanese forces in China, Formosa, and the Japanese home islands; to accommodate the new B-29 Superfortresses rolling off the assembly lines destined for the XX Air Force, whose ultimate mission was the strategic bombing campaign of Japan; and to assist Chiang's Nationalist Chinese forces in their land campaign against the Japanese Army, the Combined Chiefs agreed at the Quadrant Conference in August 1943 that the Ledo Road would have to be reopened in order to truck and pipe in much needed aviation gasoline, bombs, and other supplies. The primary goal thus became the retaking of Myitkyina and the establishment of an air base that would shorten the route of C-47s and C-46s

"We Were Soldiers Once..." Corporal Alexander McVean (standing, center) poses with comrades in the winter of 1944 during a pause in the construction of the Ledo Road (Alexander McVean Collection).

flying over the Hump. Also, as the Tenth Air Force's massive airlift campaign over the Himalayas picked up in intensity by way of the Assam-Burma-China Ferry Command, Allied leaders admitted that the C-46s and C-47s could not bring into China the quantity of fuel necessary to sustain a massive bomber campaign by the B-29s. Lieutenant William C. King, a U.S. Army engineer assigned to the 1875th Engineer Aviation Battalion, later wrote:

> The distance from the B-29 bases in India to Tokyo was approximately 3,800 miles or twice the range of the B-29s. The southern part of Honshu Island, Japan, was at the limit of the B-29's range when flying from the Chengtu bases; Tokyo was about 200 miles further. The B-29s flew fully loaded from the Indian bases to the Chengtu bases. There they refueled, flew to Japanese cities such as Osaka, dropped their bombs, returned to Chengtu for refueling and then flew back to India.
>
> From India to Chengtu the planes had to fly over the "Hump," a massive arm of the Himalayan Mountains, characterized by peaks as high as 20,000 feet, unpredictable jet streams, great storms, and often severely limited visibility. Until the Japanese were driven out of Myitkyina, Burma, their fighter planes forced the B-29s to take a more northerly route, significantly increasing these hazards. The greatest problem was flying fuel into the Chengtu base. It took six to eight B-29s converted as fuel tankers to deliver enough fuel to Chengtu for one B-29 to make a single bombing run over Japan.[14]

As was the case with King's "assignment to the 1875th Engineer Aviation Battalion and its assignment to build B-29 bases in India," McVean's (and King's) attachment to the Combat Engineers was the direct result of the "deployment of the B-29s (to India) and the campaigns in northern Burma."[15] Army engineers likewise engaged in other building projects during the war in China-Burma-India. These included two major pipelines supplying oil and gasoline to the B-29 bases around Calcutta, and the other from the Budge-Budge oil terminal of the Burma-Shell Co., about sixteen miles below Calcutta, to a tank farm in Tinsukia in upper Assam. The gasoline coming across this pipeline was then loaded onto awaiting B-29s, C-47s and C-46s that flew the precious fuel and lubricants into China over the Hump.[16] The pipelines to the air base and bases in Assam proved to be short-term solutions to a larger problem which was the increase in the amount of tonnage going to Chiang's and Chennault's forces in China, as well as to British and Commonwealth forces fighting in northern Burma after January 1944. Finally, after much inter–Allied disagreement as to who was to do what in regards to helping Chiang and the liberation of northern Burma, the Combined Chiefs agreed to a limited course of action to help alleviate the supply problems in CBI. The agreed upon solution was the construction of a road leading into the Burma Road that ran directly into Kunming. In time, this road would be known as the Ledo Road.

In fact, both Prime Minister Churchill and the Chief of the Imperial General Staff, Field Marshal Alan Brooke, saw the building of a road leading into China as a "wild and half-baked" scheme that would have little effect on the outcome of the war in Burma. Both British leaders nevertheless agreed to the

A U.S. Army combat engineer poses with a Kachin guerrilla in Burma in mid–1944. Trained by the Office of Strategic Services (OSS), the forerunner to the Central Intelligence Agency in World War II, the Kachins acted as scouts and rescued downed American flyers in the Burmese jungle (Alexander McVean Collection).

building of a road across northern Burma in order to reconnect with the Burma Road as soon as available resources permitted.[17] Prime Minister Churchill later wrote:

> The Americans had established a bomber force in China which was doing good work against the enemy's sea communications between the mainland and the Philippines. They wanted to extend this effort by basing long-range aircraft in China to attack Japan itself. The Burma Road was cut, and they were carrying all supplies for them and the Chinese armies by air over the southern spurs of the Himalayas which they called "the Hump."
>
> This was a stupendous task. I had always advocated air aid to China and the improvement of the air route and protection of the airfields but I hoped this might be done by forces essentially airborne and air-sustained on the Wingate model, but on a larger scale. The wish of the Americans to succor China, not only by an ever-increasing airlift, but also by land, led to heavy demands upon Britain and the Indian Empire. They pressed as a matter of urgency and importance the making of a motor road from their great air starting point at Ledo through five hundred miles of jungle and mountains into Chinese territory. Only one narrow-gauge single-line railway ran through Assam to Ledo. It was already in constant use for many other needs, including the supply of troops who held the frontier positions; but in order to build the road to China, the Americans wanted us to reconquer Northern Burma first and quickly.[18]

The prime minister added, "on both counts ... we [the British] argued that the enormous expenditure of man-power and material would not be worth while."[19] Despite the misgivings of the British Chiefs of Staff, the Combined Chiefs of Staff authorized the construction of the Ledo Road into Burma as a means of increasing the tonnage flowing into China in order to help both Chiang and Chennault in their fight against the Japanese.

Actual construction of the Ledo Road, in fact, began in the fall of 1942 as engineers and coolies began to hack out a path across the dense jungle path. The road itself "utilized delivery by rail of supplies from the port of Calcutta to Ledo in the northeastern tip of India, then by truck convoy from there south, largely along existing jungle tracks, to the eastern portion of the Burma Road, and on to Kunming, China."[20] The lack of resources and manpower, coupled with the pressing demands of the other theaters of operation during the war, placed CBI at the bottom of a long list of recipients of manpower and material assistance. Indeed, by the end of 1942, U.S. Army engineers had completed only 15 miles of the Ledo Road.[21]

With the arrival of the 45th Engineers in India in September 1943, however, the tempo of construction on the Ledo Road increased significantly. As coolies and soldiers hacked and blasted their way through the almost impenetrable jungle the bulldozers and graders of the 45th Engineers moved mounds of dirt and spread tons of gravel southward through the jungles and defiles of northwestern Burma. In spite of the 23 inches of rain that fell in October 1943 alone, the engineers continued to work toward Ledo. With the presence of two general service regiments, three aviation battalions (including King's 1875th

"A Most Impressive Engineering Achievement in War"

Corporal McVean (left) and another combat engineer enjoy a Lucky Strike with a Chinese coolie while sitting on a makeshift bridge in Burma (Alexander McVean Collection).

Aviation Battalion), and one engineer maintenance company, altogether there were now 5,250 engineers alone assigned to the Ledo Road project.[22] Also in October 1943, the engineers received a new commanding officer, Colonel Lewis A. Pick, who, upon his arrival on 17 October 1943, called a meeting of his staff in order to counter what he saw as a defeatist attitude toward the building of the Ledo Road. Colonel Pick "bluntly" informed them that in spite of "too much mud, too much rain, too much malaria ... we're forgetting this defeatist spirit. The Ledo Road is going to be built — mud, rain, and malaria be damned."[23]

The seriousness Colonel Pick attached to the construction of the road can be seen in the re-institution of an around-the-clock schedule first introduced by Brigadier General John C. Arrowsmith in August-September 1942. Also, Colonel Pick had lights constructed along the construction routes in order to provide proper lighting. The colonel also told engineers to place flares in buckets full of oil to illuminate the work at night. In sum, Colonel Pick made it clear that "work would have to go on without interruption."[24] Stressing the urgency and need for a road into China, General Stilwell paid a surprise visit to Colonel Pick's headquarters on November 1, 1943, where the general "impressed upon Pick the urgent importance due to the tactical plan of having a jeep trail open to Shingbwiyang by the first of the year." Colonel Pick respectfully

A pontoon bridge is nearly completed as U.S. Army engineers make their final inspections to insure that the bridge is secured tightly to its mooring (Alexander McVean Collection).

reminded the general of the difficulties in maintaining a narrow track in the swampy jungle, though he added, "but I'll build you a military highway to handle truck traffic."[25] Colonel Pick assured General Stilwell that the road would be completed by 1 January 1944. In mid–November 1943, the race was on to keep good on Pick's promise to Stilwell with elements of the 330th Engineers and Chinese 10th Engineers picking up the pace of construction of the 54-mile stretch of road to Shingbwiyang.

With the arrival of the 849th and 1883rd Aviation Battalions and its grading and leveling equipment, as well as the 823rd engineers, who maintained the completed sections of the road while the 479th Maintenance Company repaired equipment, Pick's engineers opened an advance roadhead at Mile 70 by the end of October. By 30 November the engineers of the 330th "had pushed its lead bulldozer twenty-two miles beyond that point."[26] With the arrival of Lieutenant Colonel William J. Green on 3 December 1943, as well as clear weather, progress on the road increased dramatically. In fact, by early December, engineers of the 330th averaged a mile a day while the units in the rear maintained the steady pace from their positions. Indeed, the reasons cited for the rapid progress of the road construction include (1) around-the-clock operations, (2) the trickling forward of new equipment, and (3) Pick's insistence on constant supervision of construction and maintenance by all commanders and on giving junior officers a detailed insight into the planning behind each phase of the work.[27] Despite the lack of spare parts, a perennial problem in CBI, the maintenance crews, mainly through ingenuity and persistence, kept the equipment running as the pace of construction increased rapidly. In fact, the progress on the road can be seen in the diary kept by Lieutenant King:

> **February 1943:** Thirty-eight miles of road [i.e., the Ledo Road] have been constructed, reaching the India-Burma border at the summit of Pangsua Pass (Elevation: 4,500 feet) in the rugged Patkai range.
> **October 1943:** At General Stilwell's urging, a highly qualified officer, Colonel Lewis A. Pick, assumes command of constructing the Ledo Road.
> **November 1943:** Road construction reaches mile 50. The village of Shingbwiyang (mile 103) is captured from the Japanese. Construction of the airport there begins.
> **December 1943:** Road construction reaches Shingbwiyang.[28]

Indeed, with the arrival of the 1905th Engineer Aviation Battalion, Pick quickly ordered them to assist the other combat engineers in the completion of the Ledo Road. By 23 December 1943, Green's men had pushed completion to eleven miles from Shingbwiyang. In order to meet Pick's promised 1 January 1944 deadline, Lieutenant Colonel Green split the 330th Engineers into two grading parties. Shortly before noon on 27 December, the advanced grading party of engineers "connected their traces 3 miles north of the town." Ahead of schedule by five days, Colonel Pick radioed word to General Stilwell's headquarters in New Delhi "that the 117-mile road from Ledo to Shingbwiyang was open."29 Sitting at the head of a convoy of jeeps and 5-ton trucks, Colonel Pick led his men along the entire stretch of the highway that started at Ledo and arrived at Shing-bwiyang. While there was still some grading and leveling to do the Ledo Road had been completed ahead of schedule, meeting Stilwell's deadline. More important, however, was the construction of a fuel pipeline alongside the Ledo Road. Under the command of Colonel Kenneth McIsaac, who arrived in theater along with four other petroleum engineers in November 1943, and through the utilization of a company from the 330th and from the recently-arrived 209th Combat Engineer Battalion, the engineers laid a pipeline starting from the factory at Digboi toward Ledo, a distance of some fourteen miles to the south. Through perseverance and good weather, the engineers laid approximately 1.2 miles of pipeline a day. While the mountainous countryside proved to slow the work down to about a half mile a day, Colonel McIsaac's engineers were able to catch up to the main body of Pick's men at Mile 60 of the road project.30

As Corporal McVean noted, the engineers, who trained as infantrymen, "oftentimes found themselves fighting and building" at the same time. Such was the case on 16 October as the Ledo Road project commenced. As the engineers bulldozed and graded the vast tracks of jungle into a passable hard-surface road, General Stilwell simultaneously launched his long-awaited offensive to re-take northern Burma. Meeting strong enemy resistance fourteen days into their offensive aimed at retaking Myitkyina, some 140 miles away, the Chinese troops began their long campaign at Shingbwiyang toward the Tarung River, some twenty miles southward. After securing the Tarung River, the Chinese troops began the long fight toward the vital airfield at Myitkyina. Myitkyina, it might be added, "was the main operational base for the Japanese holding northern Burma. Astride the route planned for the Ledo Road, it was a key rail terminus. Near the outskirts of the town was a vitally important airfield."31

Indeed, the significance of Myitkyina was not lost on the Japanese high command, as the Chinese soldiers shortly discovered. Upon leaving Shingbwiyang, Chinese troops, many of whom expected only light resistance, met the full force of the Japanese 18th Division guarding the approaches to northern Burma. In fact, on 30 October, the Chinese 112th Regiment of the 38th Division met a large force of the 18th Division on the west bank of the Tarung River and, in what was supposed to be "quiet forward displacement" soon found themselves engaged in what became a "seesaw battle." In a battle that lasted nearly a month and half, elements of the 18th Division unsuccessfully attempted to cut off and destroy piecemeal the 112th Regiment by laying siege to their encampment. Aided by elements of 114th Regiment, the Chinese soldiers of the 38th Chinese Division withstood repeated counterattacks by the Japanese. Indeed, by early January 1944, the Japanese troops that had originally laid siege to the Chinese forces on the Tarung River had been "wiped out."32 Indeed, as McVean noted, the victory by the Chinese troops of the 38th Division demonstrated that when well-trained, equipped and led, Chinese troops could and did fight. The victory by Chinese forces at Yupang Ga was, as the official Nationalist Chinese history of the campaign noted, "the first of our [Chinese] victories in Northern Burma," this despite the fact that the Japanese troops displayed a ferocity not yet seen in the Burma theater.[33] As 1944 began, the Chinese 38th Division, joined by the newly-formed 22nd Division, continued its southerly advance toward Myitkyina, and slowly rooted out and destroyed the Japanese forces that attempted to block its advance toward the vital airfield.

Nevertheless, Lieutenant Colonel William E. Hicks, the executive officer of the 330th Engineers, concerned for the safety of his engineers, in a letter addressed to Colonel Pick, complained that there was little if any coordination or liaison between the advance parties of engineers and combat troops on the front lines. By December 30, 1943, however, the battle between the Chinese troops and Japanese reached its climax. By that time, the Chinese had successfully defeated the large Japanese force at Yupbang Ga which insured their hold on the Tarung River line and gave them an excellent jumping off point for the march on Myitkyina. In a footnote to the battle, Lieutenant General Stilwell praised the soldiers of the 38th Division when he wrote in his diary, "The Chinese soldier is doing his stuff, as I knew he would if he had half a chance."[34]

By late 1943, Allied leaders were prepared to begin the long march back into northern Burma. This was in line with the agreement at the Quadrant Conference that priority would be given to improving the air route and opening of overland communications with China. The urgency which President Franklin D. Roosevelt placed on increasing the flow of aid to both Chiang and Chennault by both an aerial and overland route was further emphasized in his letter to Prime Minister Churchill on January 29, 1944:

> Operations of the Air Transport line from India into China and operations in Burma have, from the outset, been embarrassed by a lack of vigorous management of the lines of communication. Efforts on the part of the civilian management for improvement have produced disappointing results which are now directly and adversely affecting the support of U.S. Air Forces in China at a critical moment. Up to the present time, steps leading to military control have been fruitless except for the acceptance of American railway battalions on Bengal-Assam Railroad. These troops are now progressively taking over portions of that line. This, however, has not prevented a breakdown elsewhere on the line of communication which has put three of our China Air Ferry fields in Assam out of action because of a lack of aviation gasoline. Congestion begins in Calcutta itself where many vessels are seriously delayed through lack of effective coordinating control over the activities of the port and on the barge lines leading therefrom.
>
> I feel that only your personal intervention will secure the prompt adoption of those forceful measures which are essential to success in handling the port of Calcutta, railway and barge lines leading from that port into Assam. I urge that all of the lines of communication, from Calcutta inclusive, into Assam be placed at once under full military control and that officers of outstanding competence who will tolerate neither failure nor delay be assigned to this work. The

United States stands ready to assist in furnishing expert personnel should you desire this. *I am sure Mountbatten would agree that the situation is serious.* [Roosevelt's emphasis] Roosevelt[35]

In a follow-up letter, Roosevelt explained to Churchill that as a result of the agreement at the Sextant Conference in Tehran, Iran (22 November–7 December 1943), concerning the bombing of the Japanese home islands from bases in China by the new B-29 Superfortresses, "A necessary part of this project is the fighter protection required" for the large bombers.[36]

While work progressed steadily along the Ledo Road and the amount of tonnage airlifted into China to Chiang's armies and Chennault's Fourteenth Air Force increased with every passing day, work on the Burma Road remained at a snail's pace. In fact, due in large part to the presence of a sizable Japanese force still in northern Burma and its hold on Myitkyina, as well as to a lack of funds to complete even the western end of the road east of the Mekong River, Chinese indifference and mismanagement also prevented any significant effort from being placed on repairing and extending the Burma Road.

Fighting and Building Along the Ledo Road: December 1943 to March 1944

By late 1943, however, work on the B-29 fields in China was well underway while in India, the Service of Supply underwent a complete reorganization—all a part of Mountbatten's realignment of the command arrangements in the China-Burma-India theater. In fact, "by early 1944 Army combat engineers were making progress in providing the logistics base for the impending Allied offensives" in northern Burma. The emphasis on the various construction projects can be further seen in the number of U.S. Army personnel to assigned to CBI. Of the 100,000 American troops in CBI, 11,000 of these were engineers, with another 5,000 en route from bases in the United States. As for the projects they were assigned to, the engineers, for instance, were tasked to build or maintain some forty-five airfields in India and twenty-five in China. Nearly 90 percent of the troops were working on the Ledo Road and the pipelines in Base Section 3. In regard to the amount of supplies, in 1942 and early 1943 the engineers had been confined to utilizing lend-lease equipment borrowed from Chinese or British stocks or, in the case of Base Section 3, manufacturers in India. Base Section 3, which had been tasked with the construction of airfields in India and the building of the Ledo Road, had approximately 80,000 tons of supplies in hand by the start of 1944. As for spare parts, this remained one of the most serious shortages in CBI as "nearly half the machinery in Pick's command was deadlined because of the lack of spare parts."[37] Dependence on Indian manufacturers and other local sources likewise was limited due in large part to India's low level of industrialization and the lack of adequate facilities to alleviate the bottlenecks at various Indian ports. Finally, sabotage by the Indian National Congress (aimed primarily at the British) as well as the activities of black marketers who tapped into the long fuel lines and siphoned off the precious fuel, remained a constant source of worry to American (and British) military planners, so much so that troops were diverted from guarding the Ledo Road and the associated pipeline to prevent serious damage to the extensive supply network being constructed.[38]

Once work began on the Burma Road, the threat came primarily from the large Japanese forces in the area and the hostile terrain. After the Chinese victory at Yupbang Ga, Stilwell re-directed his thrust southward toward the Tanai River which flowed northwest for about 50 miles through the Hukawng Valley to within ten miles of Shingbwiyang and then northward to the Tarung River. Hoping to capitalize on the Chinese victory at Yupbang Ga, Lieutenant General Stilwell had hoped to envelop and destroy the remaining elements of the Japanese forces in the Hukawng Valley. Stilwell believed that "if this plan of the campaign could be carried out successfully, the Japanese would be trapped and destroyed in the Hukawng Valley. After that, the march on Myitkyina would be virtually unopposed."[39]

As for the terrain, Corporal McVean stated that the most memorable part of his time in Burma was the jungle! Indeed, one of the most prominent features of the jungle in Burma was the canopy that oftentimes blocked the sunlight from penetrating the tree tops, making it seem like evening—all day! On the ground was the thick brush that the Americans and native laborers were forced to hack out—at first with machetes and later with machines (and animals—most notably elephants). During the monsoon, the rains turned the ground into a thick, soupy mud that prevented almost anything from moving over the improvised trails. Even when the dry season was present, the men were forced to negotiate around hairpin turns, steep crevices and mountains that proved to be very formidable. Indeed, American combat engineers oftentimes spent hours clearing the recently constructed roads of falling rocks and mudslides. In fact, the terrain was such that the advanced construction units oftentimes were forced to rely almost solely on aerial resupply for almost everything including food, water, ammunition, and medical supplies. When not raining, the hot, unrelenting sun and humidity, as well as the mosquitoes and leeches which, as McVean noted, "were quite a nuisance," proved as formidable as did the Japanese army. Wracked by malaria, dysentery, the heat, humidity, and monsoons, as well as disease carrying insects and blood-sucking leeches, the combat engineers nonetheless labored on to meet General Stilwell's deadline of 1 January 1944.[40] Besides the ever-presence of disease-carrying insects, there were other dangers. Lieutenant King noted that while working on one section of the Ledo Road past Shingbwiyang, his battalion lost three men: one due to a tumor, another to cerebral malaria, and one by falling debris from blasting while clearing the right of way.[41] McVean added that contrary to popular myth

A U.S. Army truck convoy carrying supplies forward crosses over a pontoon bridge built by Corporal McVean's battalion during the British advance down the Irrawaddy River toward Rangoon in the winter of 1945 (Alexander McVean Collection).

that work ceased during the monsoon, the opposite was, in fact, true, as work "slowed but it did not stop" during the monsoon. McVean stated that the C-47s and C-46s would drop supplies to him and his comrades as they advanced. Corporal McVean recalled that the engineers on the ground oftentimes labeled the Hump pilots who flew under the command of the Air Transport Command or ATC "Allergic to Combat," as they took off at the first sighting of a Japanese plane. McVean admitted, however, that he knew that this was not the case as the planes were not armed and were sitting ducks to any Japanese pilot that might be in the area. "They had a job to do and they did it good."[42] Indeed, in direct support of the engineers on the ground, pilots of the ATC flew in over 100 five-ton trucks, more than 200 smaller trucks, 11 road scrapers, each weighing some 25,000 pounds, and 50 jeeps. Some of the vehicles were cut into sections and reassembled on the China side of the run.[43]

As for relations with the natives in India, Burma, and later China, Corporal McVean stated that while the natives, many of whom were farmers, were polite, they tended to ignore or avoid direct contact with the Americans unless necessary. On the other hand, American soldiers generally avoided Indian and Chinese women due to the fact that many carried sexually transmitted or other debilitating diseases. American troops likewise avoided eating native foods or vegetables as these were carriers of dysentery or other gastro-intestinal diseases. In short, the Americans were to "smile, wave hello, and move on" as there was a war to fight.

Most of the contact McVean had while in India with the native population occurred in Calcutta and Bombay. The corporal recalled that these cities were "a sea of humanity," filled with peoples of all classes and socio-economic groups. In Bombay, for instance, McVean said, they came upon the poor, wealthy doctors and lawyers and also the "untouchables" with whom nobody talked or dealt with. McVean also recalled the squalor that existed in Bombay, as well as hawks and vultures that waited patiently outside the dwellings for the garbage to be disposed of.

As the Chinese troops prepared to resume the offensive, Stilwell detached two companies of the 330th Engineers to "clear trails through the ten miles of jungle between Shingbwiyang and the Tarung so that the [Chinese] infantrymen could move forward more easily." Because of the constant threat of Japanese troops, both the Chinese and 330th put out patrols on the flanks of the engineers as they graded and widened a 12-mile-long dry weather road leading eastward from Shingbwiyang to the Tarung. Stilwell had hoped that the new road would be able to supply the Chinese as they advanced southward.[44] With the objective of enveloping the Japanese in the Hukawng Valley, the Chinese resumed the offensive on 13 January when a regimental combat team (RCT) crossed the Tarung where it soon encountered stiff enemy resistance from the main body of Japanese forces in the area. Another Chinese RCT crossed the Tanai farther south and met heavy resistance as well. Fighting hard, the Chinese managed to push the enemy forces eastward beyond the confluence of the Tarung and Tanai Rivers. Meeting stronger than expected enemy resistance, the attack failed to roll up and envelop the Japanese flanks. Elsewhere, however, the Chinese met with success as they pushed the Japanese beyond their original positions along the south bank of the Tanai River. With enemy resistance

Two Chinese soldiers pose after the battle of Bhamo in January 1945. Note the pock marks from the bullets expended during the fighting for this vital town in Burma. These two soldiers belonged to the Y Force trained in India by Lieutenant General Joseph W. Stilwell (Robert Boehm Collection).

stiffening all along the front Colonel Pick ordered a pause in the work on the Ledo Road until Chinese forces removed the enemy threat from their flanks. While the Chinese troops fought it out with the stubborn enemy, Pick's engineers graded and widened the existing stretches of road already built. Meanwhile, Colonel Rothwell H. Brown's Chinese tank group, on orders from General Stilwell, moved down an oxcart trail in support of the Chinese forces engaged in the attack on Mogaung. In turn, Colonel Brown directed Pick's engineers to "improve and hold open this 'combat trail' as it was henceforth unusually called." Already having been rejected as unsuitable for military traffic, Pick's engineers nevertheless set out to make this oxcart trail passable.

Within one month, the men of the 1st Battalion, 330th Combat Engineers "worked long and hard" to make the trail passable for military vehicles. Joined shortly thereafter by elements of the 76th Light Pontoon Company and Company A of the 1883rd Aviation Battalion, the 1st Battalion of the 330th Combat Engineers were able to construct a 470-foot pneumatic pontoon bridge across the Tarung. In fact, the progress on the Ledo Road was encouraging as Pick's engineers dodged Japanese artillery in order to construct a dry-weather transport strip at Taihpa Ga south of the Taini River.[45]

As McVean noted, besides their main responsibility to build roads and airstrips, the combat engineers were, above all else, infantrymen. This latter fact was highlighted during the first week of March 1944 when Pick, now a brigadier general, assigned a number of the engineers of the 330th to fight as infantrymen as American and Chinese forces advanced on the Japanese controlled hamlet of Walawbum, twenty-two miles southeast of Taihpa Ga. General Pick likewise ordered his engineers to provide front-line engineering support as the Chinese and a force of Americans. In fact:

> At the beginning of the month [March 1944], at Taihpa Ga, the 71st and the 77th Light Pontoon Companies built a 470-foot pontoon bridge across the Tanai over which Brown's Chinese tankers and infantrymen passed and then moved down the combat trail. Ten bulldozer operators from the 330th General Service Regiment volunteered to support Brown's forces with their machines. On 3 March they went into action with the tankers at a point thirteen miles southeast of Taihpa Ga. The engineers' mission was to hew a trail through the jungle to the southeast and help get the tanks across numerous streams so that they could make a surprise assault on the Japanese at the hamlet of Walawbum, twenty-two miles southeast of Taihpa Ga. Three of the engineers were wounded the first night. Three were subsequently awarded the Silver Star, and the entire group was commended, as Stilwell put it, "for resolute conduct under very difficult terrain conditions and while frequently in contact with enemy opposition."[46]

On March 5, 1944, troops of the Chinese Army's 66th Regiment attacked the Japanese forces located west of Maingkwan and cut off their retreat. After nearly ten days of furious fighting, the 38th Division captured Makaw and Lashuka, "and wiped out all the enemy on the north bank of the Tanai River."

Despite having cleared the Japanese from the surrounding area, American guards were posted as flank security in order to prevent Japanese infiltrators from attacking the combat engineers as they worked on the Ledo Road. Here, an American platoon sergeant sits on a railing with his M-1 Garand rifle at the ready (Alexander McVean Collection).

Meanwhile, the Chinese 22nd Division launched an assault on Maingkwan and captured it by 5 March. As Chinese forces attacked Maingkwan, a new force appeared on the battlefield in the form of an American-manned regimental combat team, known officially as the 5307th Composite Unit (Provisional), commanded by Brigadier General Frank D. Merrill. Dubbed later as Merrill's Marauders, the American long-range penetration group attacked Walawbum on 4 March though they were forced back eight miles until support arrived from the Chinese 113th Regiment. The next day, 5 March, after bitter fighting, the 113th Regiment, along with elements of the 38th Division and Merrill's force, forced the Japanese in and around Walawbum to retreat. After repeated attacks, the Chinese and American troops entered Walawbum on 9 March after having severely mauled the Japanese forces there.[47]

As the fighting intensified in the effort to recapture Myitkyina so too did construction on the Ledo Road. Assigned to assist in this mammoth effort were quartermaster and maintenance units as well newly-activated aviation engineer and regular combat engineer battalions. In fact, of the 15,000 American troops assigned to connect the Ledo Road, which was to run some 271 miles and link up with the old Burma Road to Kunming, over 60 percent were African American soldiers.[48] Indeed, "the first two American Army units assigned to the new route were the 45th Engineer General Service Regiment and the 823d Engineer Aviation Battalion, both of them Negro units that had previously worked on airfields in Assam and elsewhere in India as the first American engineer units in the theater."[49] Under the command of then–Colonel John Arrowsmith, both the 45th and 823rd began work on the Ledo Road starting on 15 December 1942. Pushing through the Patkai Mountains to Shingbwiyang, and surrounded by some 103 miles of dense jungle, steep grades, hairpin turns and sheer drops, some estimated to be at least as much as 200 feet, the men of the 45th and 823rd Engineers moved some 100,000 cubic feet of earth with bulldozers, graders and dump trucks despite the fact that the Japanese sniped at and harassed these Americans. In response to these attacks, Colonel Arrowsmith routinely sent out patrols made up of African American troops to protect and oftentimes preempt Japanese attacks against the combat engineers as they labored on. On 1 April 1943, intelligence reported that the enemy had planned to launch an all-out attack on the 45th Engineers as they proceeded ahead toward Myitkyina. While Negro troops were trained to build roads and bridges, as well as drive trucks and other vehicles, official War Department policies restricted their use as combat troops due to pre-war prejudices and policies.[50] In Burma, however, they were considered to be soldiers first, as Colonel Arrowsmith routinely ordered patrols to stand guard and ward off any attack. Within a few days of this latest incident, when no attack surfaced, headquarters recalled the patrols and the men pressed ahead to meet Brigadier General Pick's deadline of 1 January 1944.[51]

Construction of the Ledo Road occurred in three distinct phases. The first phase, according to Lieutenant King, was to "open a trace that combat troops could use in dry weather and for supplying them. The second phase was to widen the road and install the necessary bridges, culverts and gravel so heavy two-way traffic could travel on it in both wet and dry weather."[52] King said this was the normal procedure as the engineers inched their way past Shingbwaying towards linking up with the Burma Road. The lieutenant noted that the assignment of his outfit, Company A, was to carve a road out of a twenty-five-mile stretch of land located over the Pangsau Pass, down the road past Shingbwiying and Tingkawk-Sakan to mile point 170. As King later wrote, "When we arrived it was a 20-foot-wide dirt road with many river fords. When we left it was straighter, 33 feet, heavily graveled, and with many new bridges and culverts. In straightening one two-mile section of the road, Company A moved 26,260 yards of dirt."[53]

As the link up with Shingbwiyang continued ahead of schedule, the original two engineer units were joined by "other units necessary to road operations: three light pontoon companies, including two Negro units of this type, to bridge the swift mountain rivers and operate ferries; the 45th Quartermaster Regiment, whose trucks hauled surfacing materials and, later, supplies; and additional engineer units."[54] In fact, on 27 December 1943, three days ahead of schedule, the lead bulldozer from the 45th Engineers reached Shingbwiyang. Indeed, throughout the construction of the Ledo and later Burma Roads, African American units distinguished themselves with one of the most impressive records of accomplishment in the annals of military engineering as they labored under the hot sun, the torrential rains of the monsoon, the numerous

A U.S. Army supply convoy races across a completed pontoon bridge in northern Burma in early 1945 (Alexander McVean Collection).

"A Most Impressive Engineering Achievement in War"

U.S. Army combat engineers look as a bulldozer pushes away mounds of dirt and brush as the arduous job of clearing out the dense Burmese jungle on what will be a portion of the Ledo Road begins (Alexander McVean Collection).

malaria-infested swamps and rivers, and the oftentimes difficult terrain to carve out a highway from the Burma jungle.[55] Later on, Quartermaster and Transportation Corps units made up primarily of both white and African American troops convoyed supplies to forward bases and into China itself once the link up occurred after the fall of Myitkyina to Chinese troops and Merrill's Marauders in August 1944. McVean stated that the Negro units he encountered in Burma were segregated from the white soldiers while in bivouac. McVean added that "there were no problems in working alongside African American troops while carving out the Ledo and Burma Roads, as we were all doing the same thing."

A Turning Point in CBI: August 1944–January 1945

After the fall of Myitkyina on 3 August 1944 to the combined American and Chinese forces "a turning point had been reached in the long struggle to help China."[56] McVean stated that "the pace of construction of the Ledo-Burma Road picked up considerably," as did the threat from the retreating Japanese.[57] McVean noted that as they passed beyond Myitkyina his outfit began to construct "many pontoons" across what seemed to him to be an endless trail of rivers and swamps. In fact, Lieutenant King's battalion, assigned a section of the road past Mogaung near Kadaw, had the task of building a road between two rivers in what was essentially uncharted territory. Relying on aerial maps of the area, King's platoon, at the head of the convoy, and riding in M3 Half-tracks, ¼-ton trucks, and jeeps armed with .50 caliber machine guns, rode into the valley buttoned up, ready to deal with any enemy sniper that might decide to take pot shots at the passing Americans. As King later wrote, the trip in and of itself was a harrowing experience. King's platoon, ordered to move south past Myitkyina and 90 miles farther to a point approximately 15 miles north of Bhamo with the entire battalion not too far behind, shortly thereafter encountered an enemy force well dug in. King wrote that due to the fact that they were the lead element his platoon

> carried our small arms, had ample ammunition, and were assigned the battalion half-track, an armored truck with wheels in front and steel tracks in the rear instead of wheels. It was equipped with a .50-caliber machine gun on a swivel mount. We followed an unimproved dirt road south of Mogaung, then drove up over a range of high, steep hills. At the crest the roads were soaked from recent rains and were covered with a thick clay. The road bed sloped down away from the uphill side. In India and Burma all traffic followed the English practice of driving on the left. But when driving in these conditions around blind right-hand curves, we did not dare drive on the outside for fear of skidding off the road and down the mountainside. So we went around those curves hugging and honking our horns. Fortunately, we met no oncoming traffic and arrived safely in Myitkyina. There we crossed the wide Irrawaddy River by ferry and camped for the night on the far side.[58]

After arrival at their portion of the road between the Irrawaddy and the Bhamo, the lead elements of King's company began to scout out an area for a suitable camp in territory that could only be described as an excellent site for an ambush. With this in mind, King recalled that his platoon

> continued on along the trace for a mile or two and came to a small, tree-cover round hill right in the middle of the valley and completely blocking the road which led around it. I stopped the convoy, climbed the hill, and saw the road leading straight ahead for about one-half mile, then curving into a thick woods, a perfect point for a Japanese sniper. I had the platoon position themselves on the hill, and got in my command car with the half-track following behind, buttoned up and ready to fire. One of my corporals was driving the car, the windshield was down, and I had a fully loaded M-1 rifle at the ready. We proceeded slowly down the road. If there was sniper there he could get in one shot with his bolt action rifle. Before he could fire a second shot, my M-1 semi-automatic could fire all six of its rounds, and the .50-caliber machine gun could blow the whole tree away. We might have a casualty, but the sniper would be obliterated. I was more concerned about a Japanese patrol being in ambush on the left side of the road where the ground sloped up and provided ample cover. As we passed the tree with the vantage point looking straight back along the road, I looked up. There was the sniper's platform, some 15 feet above the ground, and pointing straight down the road.[59]

"A Most Impressive Engineering Achievement in War" 131

Lieutenant King's company eventually settled in along the right bank of the second river and bivouacked at the site of a former Japanese camp that came complete with trenches and foxholes. In time, this former enemy camp became the permanent home of King's company until the end of the war in September 1945. For the next several months, both King's company and McVean's battalion struggled to complete the final links from Ledo to the Burma Roads. Indeed, even as Company A as well as McVean's battalion sweated and fought off remnants of the Japanese Army in northern Burma, the British began their long drive toward evicting the Japanese from all of Burma proper.

As the fighting continued so too did the construction along the Burma Road. As both Lieutenant King and Corporal McVean noted, one of the biggest fears among the engineers was the Japanese soldier's preference to die rather than surrender. As a result, King's men, as well as the other units assigned to build the Burma Road, were required to be on constant alert even as they labored to complete the section of the highway assigned to them. Patrols fanned out along the perimeters of the engineers, equipped with rifles and other small arms to deal with the still defiant enemy. By late 1944, however, the tempo of construction increased considerably. By January 1945, King's battalion was ready to build the last of the links into China from Burma. In fact, the 1st Battalion's official history illustrated this latter point:

> All the companies bent to the tasks of widening the trail into a road, improving, grades, blind curves and mud holes that were really swamps. Thousands of feet of culvert were installed.
>
> "A" Company installed three Bailey Bridges, 170 ft, and two 70 fts. All in all, we had moved several thousand yards of earth, straightened and widened dozens of curves, and drained it all.
>
> Traffic, when we first arrived, was a mere handful of vehicles. Occasionally, a lone truck would pass. Then the road became passable — temporary bridges and fords had been built ... a Chinese armored division passed through on its way to Bhamo. Bhamo fell. Chinese and Indian troops, pontoons, bridges, food and other supplies moved on to the fighting forces behind Namkhan.
>
> At Christmas time [December 1944] we hosted units of the Mars Task Force, the successor to Merrill's Marauders which had played such a key role in the fighting in North Burma and at Myitkyina. Merrill's Marauders had experienced such high losses from combat, disease, and exhaustion that the remnants of the unit had been withdrawn and the unit had been reconstituted. The Mars Task Force was marching on to the front.
>
> "A" Company, in January, continued their work on the stretch of road that really needed speed control. They hauled 3,500 cubic yards of gravel to their road and moved some 4,000 cubic yards of dirt to eliminate the tortuous hairpin turns in their area.[60]

As Lieutenant King pointed out, the Burma-Ledo Road, even absent the Japanese threat, was still was not entirely safe as the nature of the terrain as well as the twists and turns of the road demanded strict adherence to speed limits and constant vigilance. King correctly stated that "being a convoy driver was difficult and dangerous." The lieutenant wrote:

> In the dry weather, the vehicle would kick up huge clouds of dust that obscured vision and covered the windshields. To see the truck ahead — which was essential to avoid collisions— a driver had two choices. He could tailgate the vehicle ahead, risking a collision if that truck slowed or stopped suddenly. Or he could lag far behind where the dust thinned out, greatly stretching the convoy. The latter action had the added problem that dust on the windshield blinded a driver when driving from bright sunlight into deep jungle shade. Sunlight reflecting off the dusty windshield prevented the driver from seeing anything in the dark shadows ahead. In addition, the gravel road developed corduroy-like bumps with heavy travel. On curves, these had the same effect as ice — greatly reducing friction. At significant speeds this could cause a vehicle to spin and go over the side of the road. In mountainous country this often resulted in the loss of the driver, truck and contents. Drivers wanted open cabs so they would have a chance to jump clear if the truck had left the road.
>
> In the rainy season the roads got muddy, causing similar problems with spattered windshields and slick roads. Inexperienced drivers frequently tried to keep a truck's speed under control going down steep mountain slopes by using only the brakes. This would cause the brake lining to overheat and catch fire, incinerating the entire vehicle. Fortunately the drivers did not have to drive the empty trucks back to Ledo. The trucks were left in China for use of Chiang Kai-shek's army and the drivers flew back over the Hump to Ledo shortly to join another convoy.[61]

The steep inclines were not the only terrain feature dreaded by the drivers and engineers as they traversed and snaked their way through the same towns and mile markers that had up until only recently been the scene of heavy fighting between Allied and Japanese troops. Huge cuts and overpasses cut into the sides of mountains, in fact, dominated the routes selected for the Burma-Ledo Road and often caused "constant trouble" for the engineers and truck drivers.[62] In fact, as one observer noted, "It was often a mess, impassable to wheeled traffic," as rocks, some weighing as much as fifteen tons "washed out by the rains and tumbled across the road, sinking into the mud and water." Thus, the engineers were oftentimes forced to blast their way forward and clear the rubble "before the bulldozers could edge them off the road into the rivers" and valleys below or be carried way and used as fill.[63] Also, the dump trucks, graders, and bulldozers served as magnets for Japanese gunners and airplanes that happened overhead or from their jungle hideouts. Indeed, in spite of the fact that the engineers became dependent on the truck drivers and heavy equipment operators the saying in CBI was, "Get 'em in and then get 'em out quick before some damn Jap sees them and bombs the hell outta' the place."[64]

Despite the hardships, harsh terrain, and lack of equipment, the combat engineers, by the end of January 1945, had removed the last cubic feet of dirt and had graded the last layer of gravel, as well as having laid the last pontoon or Bailey bridge over Burma's many rivers and streams. Indeed, by January

1945, the building of the Burma-Ledo Roads had become one of the largest engineering projects ever undertaken by U.S. Army engineers. Far from a "half-baked" idea, the Ledo-Burma Road became a reality as the last Japanese forces were cleared from northern Burma at Lashio and engineers began the last phase of construction that would link Ledo with Kunming.

The Stilwell Road Becomes a Reality: February–August 1945

As the Ledo Road entered its last phase of construction, Corporal McVean and his fellow combat engineers labored on, clearing jungle, grading, and laying gravel. To the south, Lieutenant General William Slim's 14th Army continued its relentless offensive against the Japanese in southern Burma. Meanwhile, on 19 October 1944, General George C. Marshall, chairman of the Joint Chiefs of Staff, recalled the main architect of the Burma Road, Lieutenant General Joseph Stilwell, to the United States after repeated clashes with Generalissimo Chiang Kai-shek. Also, despite the heroic efforts of the combat engineers, troops (American, British, and Chinese), and ATC pilots, the war soon by-passed the need for the Burma Road. As predicted by both Lord Alan Brooke and Prime Minister Churchill, the pace and direction of the war in the Pacific negated any value of the need for a land route into China.[65] In fact, by mid-1944, as American B-29s, based on the islands of Saipan, Guam, and Tinian, blasted and incinerated Japanese cities on a daily basis, and U.S. Marines and soldiers fought their way from island to island, in the Marianas, the Palaus, the Northern Solomons, the Bonin Islands (Iwo Jima), the Ryukus (Okinawa), and the Philippines with the ultimate objective being the Japanese home islands, the need for Chinese air bases had become obsolescent. With the cancellation of Operation Matterhorn (the air campaign aimed against Japan from bases in China by B-29s of the XX Air Force) in April 1945, the main focus of the U.S. Army's effort in the China Theater was to supply Chiang's forces in its renewed campaign against the Japanese Kwangtung Army.

Despite the road's apparent obsolescence, the Army combat engineers continued to fix and refine vast stretches of the Burma Road until finally, on 12 January 1945, they completed the last stretch of the road as Brigadier General Pick organized the first convoy to roll from Ledo to Kunming over the entire span of the recently completed road. Lieutenant King wrote that on this day there was great fanfare as the first convoy rolled out from Ledo with General Pick riding in the lead jeep. Indeed, General Pick had his own plans for a first convoy. After the convoy assembled at Mile 0 in Ledo, General Pick shouted to his convoy commanders, "Line 'em up, [Colonel DeWitt T.] Mullet." After uttering these words, 113 engines, which had been idling for an hour began to rev up. Led by two military policemen in white helmets and white gloves, the trucks and weapons carriers rolled out of Ledo and headed for Kunming. On the sides of the canvas-covered trucks were huge banners that read, "FIRST CONVOY LEDO ROAD. PICK'S PIKE-LIFELINE TO CHINA."⁶⁶ Indeed, prior to the road's completion General Pick

> had assembled at Ledo a caravan of "jeeps, weapons carriers, ambulances, [and] heavy cargo trucks"—113 vehicles in all—loaded with enough artillery and ammunition to equip two Chinese batteries and one weapons company. The drivers had been selected from all the engineer units which had worked on the road [including the African American units]. Among the civilian passengers were 65 radio, magazine, and newspaper correspondents. At Ledo, the convoy passed in review before [Major] General [Daniel I.] Sultan. On 12 January, Pick led the procession out of the city. Three days later it reached Myitkyina, where it was forced to halt because the Japanese were still in control of the area around Namhkam, seventy miles east of Bhamo. While waiting, Pick received news that the Myitkyina-Teng-chung Road was open. He gave it a frosty reception. On the 23d the convoy resumed its forward movement. When it reached Namhkam three days later, it had to halt again because of the fighting near Mong Yu. The next day, the Chinese drove the Japanese from the city. Company B of the 236th Combat [Engineer] Battalion rushed to connect the Ledo and Burma Roads; at the same time, the 71st Light Pontoon Company hastily put a 450-foot pontoon bridge across the Shweli at Wanting on the Chinese border. On the 28th Pick's convoy left Namhkam and soon covered the 40 miles to Wanting, where T.V. Soong, the Chinese Minister of Foreign Affairs, welcomed the Americans in a brief ceremony. On 4 February the caravan reached Kunming.⁶⁷

It is important to note that General Pick's column was not the first convoy to reach Kunming. In fact, as Pick's column made its way eastward, a three-truck convoy that consisted of two trucks and an 11-ton wrecker, led by 1st Lieutenant Hugh A. Pock, met up with the engineers under the command of Lieutenant Colonel Robert F. Seedlock near Myitkyina where they then proceeded eastward over a one-lane, unsurfaced jungle track that had been recently bulldozed out by Seedlock's engineers into China where they arrived in Kunming two days later on 22 January. When news of Lieutenant Pock's convoy entering Kunming reached officials at Southeast Asia Command and China Theater, they immediately sent word over the wires to Washington, D.C., and London that "the blockade of China was broken."⁶⁸ In a letter to Lieutenant General Daniel J. Sultan, General Stilwell's deputy commander, General George C. Marshall praised both the American and Chinese engineers and soldiers who labored to complete the road on time. In his letter, Marshall avoided mentioning the bitter opposition to the road by Lord Mountbatten and the British Chiefs of Staff and instead emphasized the contributions made by the Combined Allied Forces in building the Ledo Road:

> I send you my personal congratulations on the American part of the enterprise, particularly the engineers and other service troops who labored so prodigiously against extraordinarily difficult conditions to provide the connecting links and to insure the forwarding of the necessary supplies and material to maintain the troops and make possible the construction work. Great credit is due General Stilwell for his vision in conceiving the project of the Ledo Road and fighting

"I wonder who put him up to that." The starting point of the Ledo Road was renamed the Stilwell Road, in honor of Lieutenant General Joseph W. Stilwell, by Generalissimo Chiang Kai-shek (Alexander McVean Collection).

grit in carrying it forward towards completion. The combined Allied Forces have made possible what I think will be a great milestone in the history of the Far East.[69]

Even as the first column rolled into Kunming amidst the flag-waving and cheers of both Chinese and American officials who saw the convoy as a sign that China's land route with the outside world had been restored, the combat engineers, as McVean stated, nonetheless "kept going ... pushing further into China ... beyond Kunming."[70] In fact, the work along the Burma Road had really just begun as the engineers continued to "improve the Ledo Road" and make it an all weather road as well as extend a 4-inch aviation and gasoline fuel line to Kunming.[71]

As for the Nationalist Chinese leadership, with the war coming to an end, there was the realization that as the U.S. Army demobilized and sent its soldiers home, they would have to assume the responsibilities of supplying their forces in the field now that the Japanese Army had been defeated and civil war with the Communists now seemed all but inevitable. In an attempt to keep the supplies coming over the Himalayas and Ledo Road with American pilots and drivers continuing to shoulder the burden, T.V. Soong, the Nationalist Chinese ambassador to the United States, appealed to General George C. Marshall to continue the operation of the pipeline laid by Lieutenant King and Corporal McVean for three more months, "in order that there would be sufficient fuel oils and gas for the Chinese re-deployment requirements in western China."[72] General Marshall, in a letter to Lieutenant General Thomas T. Handy, commanding general of the Army Ground Forces, dated 27 September 1945, wrote that General Wedemeyer already had some 1200 to 1400 troops involved in operations along the pipeline, and that in spite of the fact that the majority of the men were "high point men," the rapid pace of demobilization was such that he could not justify (nor guarantee) their continued presence in China (as well as in Burma and India) for more than two months at the latest. General Marshall, in fact, later informed Ambassador Soong that even a two months' presence of U.S. forces could not be guaranteed. The chairman of the Joint Chiefs hinted to Soong the possibility of having the Chinese assume the responsibilities of supplying their own troops with gasoline and other equipment when he wrote of the presence of "so many Chinese troops at the ports of Haiphong (in Indochina) and Canton." Indeed, for Marshall, U.S. involvement along the Burma-Ledo Road was coming to an end.[73]

As for the 1875th Aviation Engineer Regiment, Lieutenant King wrote that "rumors started flying madly as to the next assignments for the U.S. forces in India and Burma." King noted that for his outfit, the rumor mill had them being sent to the island of Hainan, off the southeast coast of China, to build more air bases in order to bomb both Taiwan and the Japanese home islands.[74] As fate would have it, the Army ordered Captain King to Ledo where he supervised the maintenance of the Burma Road until ordered home in February 1946.

While historians have debated the contribution of the engineering efforts and usefulness of the Burma Road, there is no doubt that this was, as Churchill noted, a "significant undertaking" by the United States. Far from being a "half-baked" idea, as Lord Alan Brooke called the building of the Ledo Road, this vital road network was, in fact, vital to the war effort in CBI (see Map #9). While

"A Most Impressive Engineering Achievement in War" 137

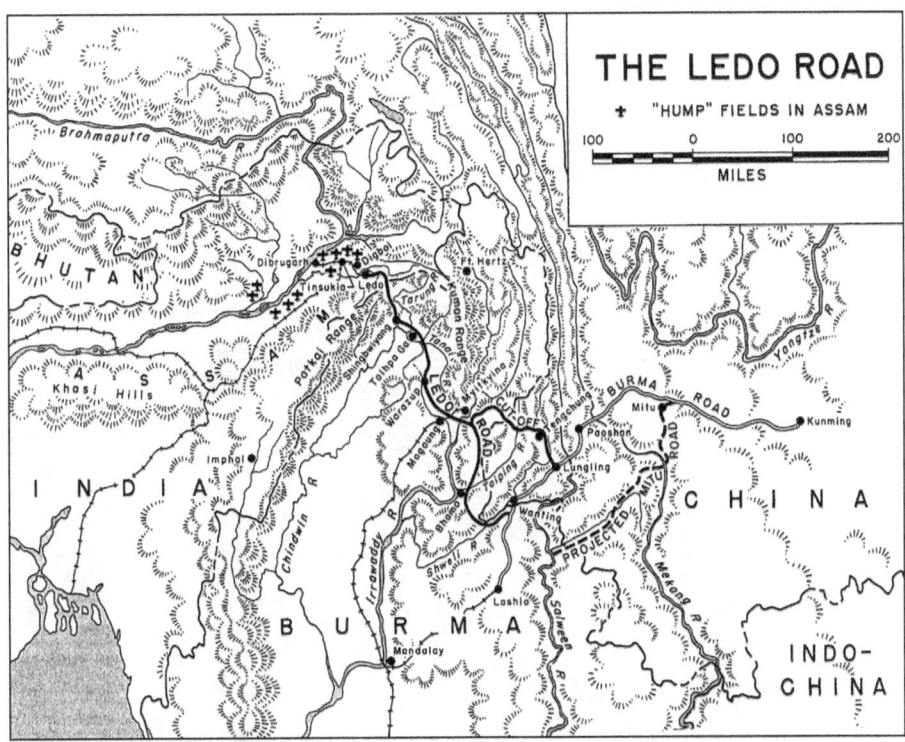

Map 9. The Ledo Road (Dod, *Corps of Engineers: The War Against Japan*, p. 474).

its completion came too late in the war to play a significant role in the defeat of Japan, the Burma Road's strategic impact, as well as its utility lay in its conception and undertaking. With too few men, very little material, and the oftentimes bitter and acrimonious squabbling that took place between the United States and Great Britain, as well as the arguments that took place between Chiang Kai-shek, Lieutenant General Stilwell and Major General Claire Lee Chennault as to who should receive what limited supplies trickled in over the Hump, it remained nothing short of an engineering miracle that the Burma Road was completed at all. What drove the men assigned to build the Burma Road was, as Prime Minister Churchill later wrote, the American "can do spirit," which accomplished the impossible insofar as the construction of the Burma-Ledo Road was concerned.[75] Despite the heroic efforts of the ATC to feed the tiger by air over the Himalayas, "the turning point in the critical transportation situation was the opening of the Stilwell Road (the combined Ledo and Burma Roads) in January 1945, when Chinese forces from India and China routed the last Japanese block of the road to China."[76] After the removal of the Japanese threat from northern Burma (and indeed all of Burma by June 1945), "additional support, including the sorely needed vehicles, flowed by road," into China

A U.S. Army Combat Engineer stands proudly next to a road sign showing the distances to various locations after the completion of the Ledo Road in January 1945 (Alexander McVean Collection).

by way of Kunming to Chinese and American forces throughout China.[77] Yet, it must be always kept in mind that "transportation was the most pressing logistics problem in the CBI [theater]." In a large sense, these problems could not have been resolved had it not been for the "extensive engineer projects for roads, rail improvements, pipelines, and airfields." Also, without the skillful use of native labor and resources, the Burma and Ledo Roads could never have been built to the scale that they, in fact, were by Army engineers. In a large sense, the Burma and Ledo Roads were not just a testament to General Stilwell's insistence that they be built, but more so to the men who labored day and night, in enemy-held territory, the oppressive heat, the monsoons, and in the dismal, fetid swamps. Without their Herculean efforts, the Burma and Ledo Roads would never have been completed either on time or, possibly, at all.

At War's End: August 1945–February 1946

Even with the completion of the Burma-Ledo Road, work did not, however, cease on the road as the engineers constantly repaired and upgraded monsoon-damaged portions of this mammoth engineering project or, as in the case of Captain King, shifted work back to India, where "additional troops and equipment arrived at Calcutta to insure" that communications between India and Burma remained intact.[78] Arriving in theater with the 1875th Combat Aviation Regiment in February 1943, King remained with that outfit until re-assigned at war's end in August 1945 to become its S-3 Operations Officer. The lieutenant remained in this position only a couple of months when the Army re-assigned him first to the 45th General Service where he served as its supply officer and later with the 76th Ordnance Base Depot, Panitola, India, near Ledo. After serving in India and later China, Captain King left for home in February 1946, where he was separated from active service with an honorable discharge. He later earned a master's degree in chemical engineering and practice and had a successful 37-year career with the Gulf Oil Corporation. He now lives in Pittsburgh, Pennsylvania, with Carolyn, his wife, whom he married in 1948. Captain King, who was immensely proud of his service in China-Burma-India during the war, later authored a book that detailed the part he and his outfit, the 1875th Aviation Engineer Regiment, played in the building of the Ledo-Burma Roads.

Corporal Alexander McVean likewise remained in China until the war's end when the Army rotated him home to his native Philadelphia, Pennsylvania. Prior to his departure from China, McVean and his comrades had heard the news of the two atomic bombs being dropped on Hiroshima and Nagasaki. While McVean voiced some regret that the atomic bomb had been dropped on civilians, he nevertheless agreed that it was the correct thing to do insofar as its use on two military targets—Hiroshima and Nagasaki. Like all veterans who fought the Japanese, the dropping of the two atomic bombs meant that they would survive World War II. Indeed, the Army corporal added that the dropping of the two bombs was, the right thing to do. He based this opinion on his experiences in Burma where he and his comrades experienced first hand the Japanese soldier's determination to fight on and if necessary die. McVean specifically said, "The Japanese would never have surrendered ... and, in fact, they would have fought to the death." McVean dismissed the critics who in later years regretted the dropping of the two bombs and was, emphatic in his assertion that "it was the Japanese who started this slaughter at Pearl Harbor in Hawaii ... with the sneak attack."[79] As for his service in China-Burma-India during the war, Corporal McVean was very praiseworthy of Lieutenant General Joseph W. Stilwell, whom the corporal fondly called "the GI's general.... He ate with us, he slept with us ... he was right there with us ... he was my idea of a general." On a lighter note, McVean noted with some satisfaction that the men in CBI were not totally forgotten by the American public. Indeed, the Army corporal recalled that while in Burma, Bob Hope and actress Ann Sheridan appeared at a USO show in the middle of the Burmese jungle as they worked on the Ledo Road. He jokingly stated that after Miss Sheridan left, the American troops, many of whom had not seen an American woman for some time, "got a hold of the toilet seat she sat on and placed it on a board with the sign, "Miss Sheridan sat here!"[80] After having accumulated the necessary 85 points for shipment back home, Corporal McVean left China in October 1945 and returned home to Philadelphia, where he later married, raised a family, and worked as an electrician. Up to his death in June 2000, McVean remained keenly aware that he participated in one of the most monumental engineering feats of the 20th century — the building of the Ledo and Burma Roads, and its contribution to the defeat of Imperial Japan in CBI.

In what was certainly an anti-climactic coda to the building of the Burma Road, Generalissimo Chiang Kai-shek, in honor of the man who had so fervently insisted on the construction of both the Ledo and Burma Roads, renamed the highway the Stilwell Road. Given the bitter animosity that existed between Chiang and his former chief of staff, this came as quite a surprise to many, including Stilwell himself, who remarked upon hearing the news of the renaming of the road in his honor, "I wonder who put him [Chiang] up to that?"[81]

Chapter 6

"A Chemical Company to the Front": Technical Sergeant Kenneth R. Quigley, 1943–1945

The war in China-Burma-India was a conflict fought over vast distances. From the distant supply depots to isolated jungle airstrips, it was a war fought by soldiers representing the different branches of the U.S. Army. These branches included the combat arms (infantry and artillery), combat support (intelligence, military police, engineers, and chemical), and combat service support (medical, veterinary, quartermaster, maintenance, motor transportation, ordnance, and chemical). Unlike the Pacific Area of Operations or the European (ETO) or Mediterranean (MTO) theaters of operations where the combat arms branches played a more dominant battlefield role, both combat support and combat service units were destined to play the dominant role in maintaining the ability of our Chinese and British allies to remain in the fight. In fact, one can say that at least in CBI, technical troops played the dominant role as they vastly out-numbered those in the combat arms. Such was the case of Technical Sergeant Kenneth R. Quigley, a member of the U.S. Army's 187th Composite Chemical Company, who operated a 4.2 Stokes Mortar and eventually found himself the only member of a chemical unit sent to CBI via North Africa during World War II. From his vantage point as a member of this composite unit in India, Sergeant Quigley pointed out that the China-Burma-India theater placed an even greater demand on the technical expertise of the U.S. Army than that of the ETO. Indeed, as the war progressed in CBI it became a theater of operations dominated by combat engineers and quartermasters as opposed to infantrymen or tankers.

With experience in both the chemical and ordnance corps, two branches of the Army's technical services that saw extensive service in CBI, Technical Sergeant[1] Quigley soon found himself, prior to the execution of Operation Shingle, the invasion of Anzio, Italy (January 1944), transferred to the CBI theater of operations and assigned to the 187th Composite Chemical Company in charge of the maintenance and distribution of chemical and other munitions to U.S. combat engineers building the Burma-Ledo Road, and to the soldiers assigned to the 5307th Composite Unit, known collectively as Merrill's Marauders. The Marauders, led by their legendary commander, Brigadier General Frank D. Merrill, were the U.S. Army's first long-range penetration group, modeled on Brigadier Orde Wingate's famed Chindits, who harassed the Japanese Army's rear areas prior to the Allied counter-offensives in Burma in early 1944. As a result of his assignment to northern Burma, T/Sgt. Quigley served alongside the Marauders during their fight for the vital airfield at Myitkyina in August 1944. As Quigley stated, the Marauders' use of the powerful 4.2" Stokes mortars and other types of munitions (to include chemical rounds) required "a good amount of ordnance" during the fight for Myitkyina. Thus, by his "incidental" assignment to CBI, Sgt. Quigley witnessed one of the most important campaigns launched against the Japanese in CBI during World War II.[2]

From Pensacola to India: 1943-1944

Kenneth R. Quigley was born in 1915 and grew up in Pensacola, Florida. Quigley, much older than most recruits, enlisted in the Army on 22 October 1943 and underwent basic combat training at Camp Claiborne, near Slidell, Louisiana. Assigned to the Chemical Corps, Quigley and his fellow soldiers learned how to operate a variety of weapons including flamethrowers, bazookas, and machine guns, the various types of chemical rounds, and the employment of the powerful 4.2" Stokes mortar while at Camp Claiborne and en route to their first landings in North Africa.[3] In fact, as their training progressed, Quigley and the other men in his company trained more and more alongside infantrymen. Indeed, as early as mid–1942, Army Ground Forces (AGF) officials believed that "concentrated" training "at the very earliest opportunity," was necessary to provide them with the fundamentals of infantry combat skills. In March 1942, in fact, the AGF ordered that "ordnance companies should begin to service weapons of infantry and artillery units near them; quartermaster companies should likewise begin to perform subsistence and sanitary functions for combat troops; chemical units should provide smoke screens for them; and medical organizations should have infantry soldiers on whom to practice first aid and evacuation." In short, as the G-1, Army Ground Forces, emphasized, because concentrated training had been approved for antiaircraft, armored, and tank destroyers elements, "it is certainly sound for nondivisional [service] units." Indeed, Lieutenant General Lesley J. McNair, commanding general, AGF, took the position that "large-scale concentration could be justified only in instances where training was so highly specialized that technical considerations outweighed the value of normal association."[4] Lieutenant General McNair, as were other senior Army officials, in fact, of the opinion that given the complexities and fluidity of the battlefield, modern combat demanded that ordnance, tankers, and chemical troops be trained as infantrymen.[5]

Training with the Chemical Corps: 1943-1944

T/Sgt. Quigley noted that training in the Chemical Corps was, indeed, concentrated. In fact, the Army sergeant recalled that the training he and his comrades went through involved a great deal of infantry-related field training such as marksmanship, small unit tactics, and the firing of weapons such as .30 and .50-caliber machine guns. Quigley noted that when "we weren't in the field, we were in the classrooms" learning about the different types of chemical munitions and chemical-related equipment.[6]

Because the chemical and ordnance troops worked near the front lines, the training outlined by the AGF was little different than that received by infantrymen in basic and advanced combat training. Organizationally, chemical training companies were organized around the platoon and company with the normal compliment for a training company being 213 soldiers though "it was frequently necessary to assign as many as 300 trainees to one company. In such cases training suffered." In addition to the training companies each Chemical Warfare Service Replacement Training Center, including Camp Claiborne, had two regiments of three battalions each, and could train a maximum of 5,112 trainees.[7] Due to the need for manpower from the various theaters, however, there existed a lack of trained cadre to properly conduct training in all branches. In fact, with a limited number of chemical companies in existence by 1943, the Army began to fill cadre positions with replacement trainees that were only slightly more knowledgeable than the trainees themselves in that they had already attended an advanced school in their various branches.

As for the length of basic combat training, it varied from post to post. By mid–1943, however, the training cycle stabilized at either thirteen weeks or, by late 1943 and early 1944, seventeen weeks.[8] With the emphasis on uniformity in the training base the Army Ground Forces mandated after 8 August 1943 that all replacement training centers were to pay particular attention to small unit training up to and including "company, battery, and troop, including at least two weeks of continuous field exercises."[9] Indeed, soldiers such as T/Sgt. Quigley experienced field-like conditions as much as possible before they transferred overseas during their advanced individual training. In fact, prior to the order from the AGF that extended basic combat training to seventeen weeks the G-1 added a special a battle course to all replacement training center training (e.g., basic combat training). The battle course consisted of an infiltration course, close combat and village fighting courses. Indeed,

> the infiltration course, the close combat course, and village fight course were introduced to prepare the trainee psychologically for experience with live ammunition and to accustom him to use his weapon under conditions more realistic than those of the range. These battle courses became one of the most characteristic features of replacement centers, the training aids par excellence of these establishments. Battle courses were conducted in carefully prepared and highly organized training areas, each designed to introduce the trainees to some phases

of the sound and fury of actual battle. For this reason they were often referred to as "battle inoculation" courses. Although used by tactical units in their basic training, the courses developed at the replacement training centers were ordinarily far better constructed and organized, and more stress was placed on their proper use.[10]

In fact, T/Sgt. Quigley recalled that one of the more demanding courses he and his comrades experienced while in basic combat training at Camp Claiborne was the infiltration course. The purpose of the infiltration course was to "accustom men to overhead fire and to the noise and effect of near-by explosions."[11] Training instructors, in fact, emphasized to Quigley and the other trainees the proper technique of moving forward under fire from machine guns and negotiating barbed wire entanglements. Indeed, as a result of the lessons learned from the Mediterranean and Pacific theaters of operation, the AGF ordered that trainees run the infiltration course at night as well as during daylight hours.[12] Soldiers, many of whom were either excited or scared often left their weapons behind as they hastily slid under the barbed wire, not daring to raise their heads or return for their weapons.

Soldiers also underwent the "close combat course" or the "blitz" course, as it was known, whereby they ran a gauntlet of pop-up targets designed to teach them how to fire small arms with speed and accuracy at surprise targets while negotiating a broken terrain. Unlike the infiltration course, there were no explosions or small arms fire overhead. Later on this changed, however, as the AGF sought to add more realism to training. T/Sgt. Quigley likewise recalled that there was a great deal of emphasis on assaulting an enemy "village." In an effort to promote teamwork and small unit tactics in what today is called military operations in built up areas, soldiers fired at fleeting targets amid the noise and confusion of battle; learned street fighting; entered and cleared houses; jumped from roof to roof and scaled walls. The culmination of this phase of training was a tactical problem that called upon the use of mutual support, cover, and movement. In order to add realism to the assault, live ammunition as well as flanking and overhead fire were employed in the taking of the village or town, while tank support appeared in the final stages of the battle. So as not to take away from the realism of the assault, the training cadre controlled only the tactical situation while the safety controls were only those inherent in normal tactical exercises. In a departure from today's semi-controlled training environment, there was more free play on each exercise. Quigley also noted that all soldiers received four hours of training in chemical warfare. Here, Quigley and other Chemical Corps troops practiced their skills by setting off chemical rounds (tear gas, smoke or other incendiaries) in the village or built-up town, and decontamination procedures.[13] By late 1944, the battle course likewise employed live artillery fire in order to expose all soldiers to the sounds of overhead artillery fire. Finally, all of the replacement training centers conducted exercises that utilized all arms in squad, platoon, and company situations that employed all infantry weapons and included overhead and flanking artillery and mortar fire. The emphasis on weapons familiarization, camouflage, cover and concealment at the replacement training centers was part of Lieutenant General Lesley J. McNair's belief that all soldiers had to possess the fundamentals of infantry combat to survive in battle. Indeed, the commanding officers of the 2nd, 3rd, and 83rd battalions believed this type of training was critical in the preparation of a soldier for the rigors of combat:

> Experience has shown that the soldier well grounded in the fundamentals of scouting and patrolling, use of camouflage, cover and concealment, and taught to move fast, will individually live to fight many battles. Next to that comes team work, an item particularly important to our mortars.... Failure in missions will be the result of poor team work. Failures in battle are inexcusable when such failures are a result of poor training.[14]

Initially, Quigley learned how to use flamethrowers, mix the napalm for the flame weapons, and became familiar with the various types of chemical weapons. He also learned the use of the 4.2" mortar and the different chemical and non-chemical rounds. While at Camp Claiborne, the native Floridian likewise learned the employment of smoke and use of smoke-generating equipment such as the portable M1 mechanical smoke generators obtained by the Chemical Corps in late 1944.

It is important to note that all of the infantry training Quigley and the other trainees received was for a purpose, due primarily to the fact that chemical troops, most notably smoke generating units, served directly with the ground forces on the front lines. Hence, chemical troops, like infantrymen, had to know how to fight and survive on the battlefield. Despite the fact that the Army, from an operational standpoint at least, designated the smoke-generator companies somewhere between combat and service units many of them came directly under the command of infantry battalions and regiments. The confusion surrounding the question to whom did the smoke generator companies belong was noted by Quigley, who recalled that as his smoke generator units prepared for the landing at Anzio in January 1944, they conducted a number of exercises using smoke-generating equipment with the infantry and took orders from an infantry officer. Quigley added that "we seemed to be trained more as infantrymen than smoke generator troops."[15]

Overseas to Oran and Italy, January–March 1944

After completion of his training at Camp Claiborne, T/Sgt. Quigley reported to the Transient Depot located in Greenville, Pennsylvania, where he and his company left for service overseas. Assigned to the 110th Ship Convoy, Quigley's unit set sail in the early winter of 1944 from Hampton, Virginia. After a 21-day voyage, the 110th Ship Convoy pulled into port at Casablanca, North

Africa.[16] In preparation for what later became the landings at Anzio midway through the Italian campaign in January 1944, T/Sgt. Quigley and his unit continued to train in laying smoke screens. Nevertheless, Quigley noted that much of the training he and his fellow soldiers received was more of an infantry nature, designed for infantry-like combat operations. Despite having been assigned to a smoke generating unit in an infantry regiment, Quigley and the other soldiers assigned to his unit remained part of the Chemical Warfare Service due in large part to the fact that the War Department considered the "operation of smoke generators somewhat technical."[17]

Army Chemical Ground Service Units Are Formed: March 1942–December 1943

While certain front-line units of the Chemical Warfare Service (CWS) remained administratively part of the Army Ground Forces other units, such as the 187th Composite Chemical Company (Quigley's unit in India) and other CWS units, were classified by the War Department as part of the Army Service Forces. In fact, "when they [i.e., the service troops] were utilized in the static defense of fixed installations they generally came under communication zone control," though administratively classified as service troops under the Chemical Warfare Service.[18] Organized in mid–1943, many of the chemical ground service units, like T/Sgt. Quigley's 187th Composite Chemical Company, were "intended to perform technical or service functions of a noncombatant nature with the field forces, under either theater, army, or communications zone control." These units included laboratory, maintenance, depot, decontamination, processing, and composite companies. In fact, many of the soldiers assigned to these support units were African Americans.[19]

Since these Chemical Ground Service units remained administratively under the Chemical Warfare Service they were trained, starting in March 1942, by experienced chemical warfare officers and noncommissioned officers in whole units or in blocks. By the end of 1943, there were eighty-nine Chemical Ground Service units organized by the War Department. Interestingly, the reason given for the activation of so many composite chemical service units was that Army officials feared that either the Germans or the Japanese might employ chemical weapons as a last resort as their situations became even more desperate on the battlefield. Indeed, Army officials maintained almost to the end of the war that once the Axis powers were placed on the defensive they (i.e., Germany or Japan) might employ gas or other chemical agents (such as sarin, a nerve agent) as a last desperate act of defiance. As events demonstrated, neither one of the Axis powers employed chemical weapons though both major adversaries had them in their arsenals when the war ended. In fact, both Japanese and German troops were trained extensively in the use of chemical weapons or poison gas. The Japanese, in fact, attached chemical warfare troops to their stronger divisions that laid smoke screens and employed tear gas in China. For their part, the Germans likewise had dedicated units and equipment for the employment of chemical gases.[20] Given this fact, one could say with some degree of accuracy that during World War II the Army took the threat of chemical and biological weapons seriously enough to prepare its soldiers to fight on a contaminated battlefield. This is illustrated in the degree of interest in the Army Service Forces' (ASF) organization of both chemical units and chemical ground service units. With this in mind the ASF in time delegated the responsibility for the command of such units to the various service and field commands, which in Quigley's case meant being placed under the overall command of Lieutenant General Joseph W. "Vinegar Joe" Stilwell, who was deputy commanding general, Allied Ground Forces, and under the over all command of Admiral Lord Louis Mountbatten's Southeast Asia Command (SEAC) which had theater responsibility for CBI.

While Quigley trained in the operation of smoke screen units and 4.2" mortars in North Africa, Army officials discovered that T/Sgt. Quigley had been a foreman in a warehouse before the war.[21] Apparently in need of trained warehousemen, the Army assigned T/Sgt. Quigley to CBI, confident that he could manage an ordnance supply warehouse that contained and distributed chemical munitions (such as smoke grenades and 4.2" mortar rounds) with little trouble.[22]

Chemical Ground Service Troops to the Front: Assam, India: Spring 1944

Indeed, while training in Oran, North Africa, Quigley recalled being called into his first sergeant's office one day and told that he was being re-assigned. Curious as to where he was going, Quigley asked his first sergeant where he was going. In turn, the first sergeant pointedly told him, "You'll find out!" Placed on a British ship heading for Karachi, India, the ship carrying Quigley made its way through the Suez Canal on its way to Karachi. After his arrival in this crowded Indian city Quigley proceeded on to Bombay where he was assigned to the 187th Composite Chemical Company. After a brief stay in Bombay, Quigley boarded a train and made his way for Camp Aanchabara, a British base, outside the city of Calcutta in the northern part of the Naga Hills in Assam Valley at the base of the Himalayan Mountains.[23] Here, his commanding officer gave Quigley the task of managing a warehouse filled with 4.2" mortar shells, chemical rounds, napalm, smoke pots (for smokescreens), dynamite, and empty shells (for chemical warheads to be inserted).

Technical Sergeant Quigley pointed out that the 187th Chemical Composite Company was co-located with British troops who, the Army sergeant recalled, "fed us and housed us in their barracks and let us drink their beer!"[24]

T/Sgt Kenneth Quigley (second from left) and comrades pose for a photograph outside their quarters somewhere in India in late 1944 (Kenneth R. Quigley Collection).

Quigley, in fact, remembered that it was some time before the American troops saw or tasted an American beer such as Blatz. Indeed, it wasn't until some U.S. Army combat engineers working on the Ledo Road provided Quigley and his comrades with a few cases of Blatz (as well as Camel and Lucky Strike cigarettes) that they were able to enjoy "a cold American one," the sergeant mused. Overall, T/Sgt. Quigley recalled that relations with the British were "very good ... as we were all there together doing the same job."

As for relations with the Indians, Quigley recalled that they were very helpful and would "help us in any way." Like all American units in CBI, the men of the 187th adopted bashaboys, or native Indian lads, who swept their quarters, did chores and other odd jobs for a few rupees every month. Quigley added that the American GIs were fascinated with the sights they saw while in India, such as elephants and other beasts of burden used by the natives (and Allied troops) to do everything, including use as a mode of conveyance. When not on duty, Quigley and his squad rode the elephants, played baseball and took in the local sights. As for the elephants, Quigley and his comrades remained amazed at the friendliness that these large animals displayed toward them. Quigley noted that he and his men were under strict orders, however, not to eat the local foods or drink the water unless it had been first purified or prop-

T/Sgt Kenneth Quigley (3rd soldier — left to right) poses with other members of the 187th Composite Chemical Company in front of some elephants and their drivers (Kenneth R. Quigley Collection).

erly prepared. Quigley proudly said that unlike many of his friends, he "never once came down with malaria or dysentery" while at Camp Aanchabara. As for relations with the Chinese, Quigley noted that his company came across very few Chinese soldiers as they were "with [Brigadier General Frank D.] Merrill in Burma."[25]

In Support of Merrill's Marauders: Assam to Myitkyina, January–August 1944

In January 1944, Lieutenant General Stilwell began his long-awaited Hukawng Valley offensive designed to re-take Northern Burma (see Map #10). Spearheading the drive were the Chinese 22nd and 38th Divisions as well as the first American combat troops, the 5307th Composite unit commanded by Colonel (later Brigadier General) Frank D. Merrill. Made up of veteran U.S.

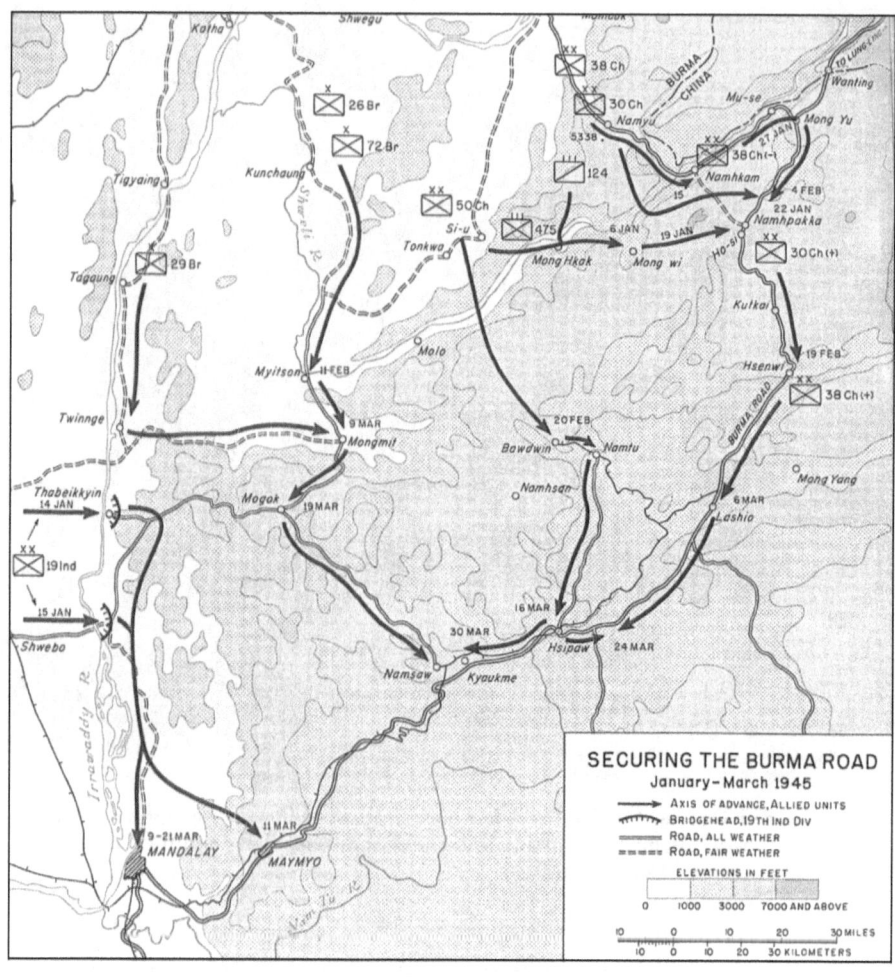

Map 10. The Hukawng Valley Campaign, January–February 1945

Army soldiers, many of whom had served in New Guinea and on Guadalcanal, the 5307th Composite Unit had been modeled after the British long-range penetration group known as Chindits.[26] Formed into a composite unit, the Marauders initiated their campaign in January 1944 in order to harass the Japanese 18th Division. T/Sgt. Quigley's 187th Chemical Composite Company played a vital role in Merrill's campaign as it was their mission was to supply Merrill's force with 4.2" mortar shells and other types of ordnance. This included smoke grenades and explosives-filled munitions. In fact, as Merrill's Marauders drove further and deeper into Burma, T/Sgt. Quigley was given the task of setting up a mortar dump 60 miles from the Burma-India border where the Marauders frequently sent re-supply teams in aircraft to pick up ordnance, flame-thrower liquids (i.e., napalm), ammunition, and rations as they advanced along the Hukawng Valley. Quigley recalled that as the spring went into the summer months of June, July and August, the fighting became more intense as Merrill's force drove toward the vital airfield of Myitkyina (see Map #11). Quigley complimented the many pilots and crews of the C-46s and C-47s that flew constant re-supply sorties to Merrill's Marauders and Chinese forces. Quigley said that to him and his comrades on the ground the pilots who flew these dangerous missions, oftentimes in the face of Japanese fighter activity, were among the greatest men they had ever known.[27]

As for the 187th's daily routine, Quigley noted that it was his job to "constantly monitor the ordnance in my warehouse, as it could ignite or go off if left on the shelf too long." Armed with his experience as a warehouse foreman, T/Sgt. Quigley said, "I was responsible for a lot of ordnance and that this was vital in keeping Merrill re-supplied and fighting." The Army sergeant praised General Merrill whom he said "was the greatest general I had ever known or heard of." Quigley recalled that after Merrill's troops took Myitkyina in August 1944 and had handed it over to the Chinese forces that accompanied Merrill's Marauders during the campaign, these same Chinese troops lost it to a powerful Japanese counterattack. Quigley noted that shortly thereafter Merrill's force had to re-take the airfield in a bitterly-fought battle that left the battlefield littered with dead Japanese, American, and Chinese troops.[28]

On the Ledo Road

Quigley made special mention of the fact that while in Assam during Merrill's campaign to re-take Myitkyina, he came across the U.S. Army combat engineers then building the Ledo Road. Among these combat engineers were many quartermaster and other logistical units supporting the building of this vital road network into China. Quigley noted that the majority of these units were comprised African American soldiers. Indeed, over 60 percent of the troops sent to the China-Burma-India theater were African Americans, many of whom formed the bulk of the quartermaster and support units building the Ledo-Burma Road into China.[29] Despite the racial attitudes of the time, T/Sgt Quigley noted that there were few incidents between the white and black soldiers, "as we were all in the same boat together." The Army sergeant was, in fact, full of praise for the African American soldiers, whom he called "some of the hardest workers and finest men I have ever known."[30]

From Myitkyina to the End of the War: 1944-1945

T/Sgt. Quigley remained in Assam and at Camp Aanchabara and managed the 187th Chemical Composite Company's warehouse until the end of the

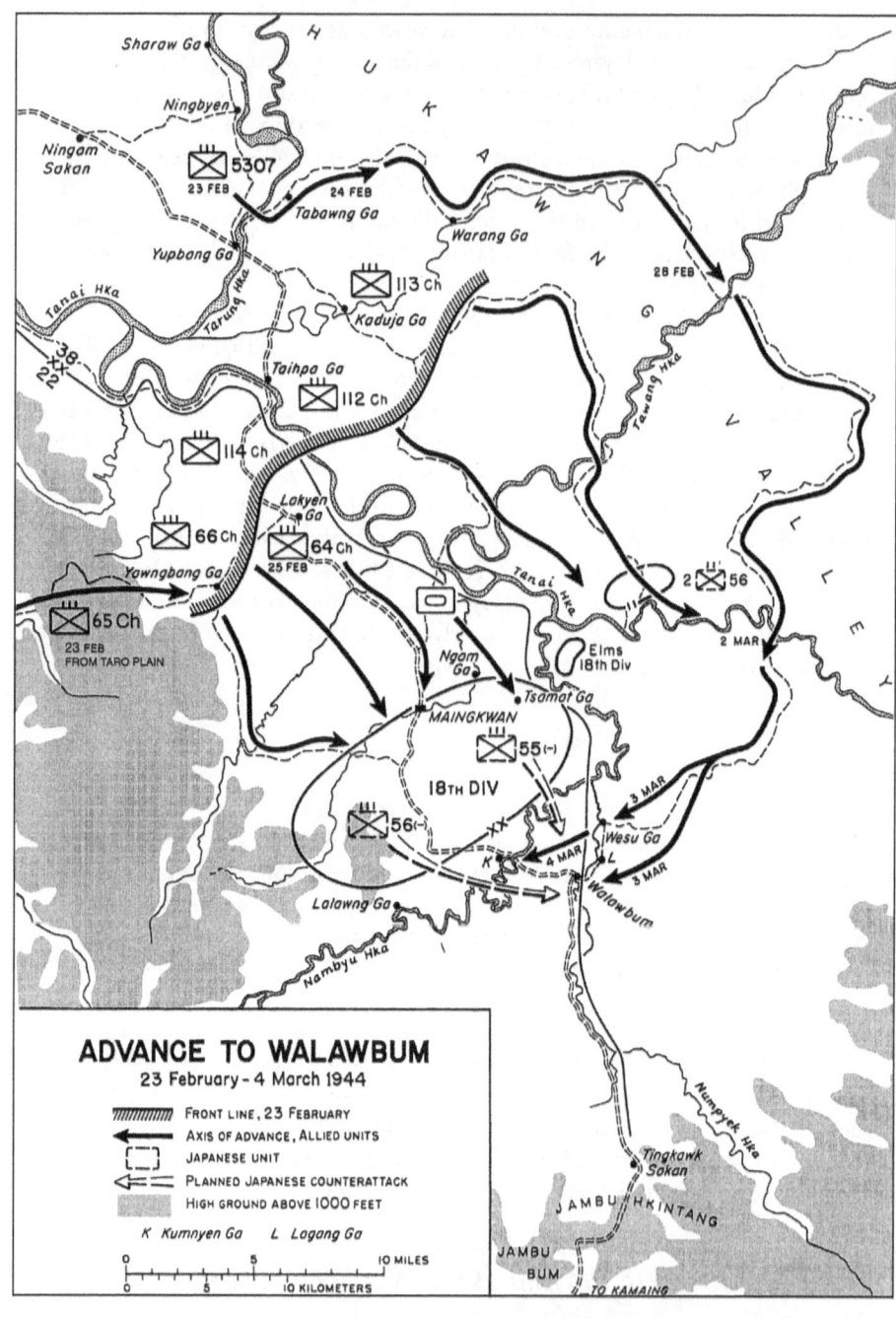

Map 11. Merrill's Marauders drive on Myitkyina, January–August 1944 (Romanus and Sunderland, *Stilwell's Command Problems*, p. 144).

war in September 1945. After the Japanese surrender on 1 September 1945, Quigley and his comrades received word that they would be going home ... or so they thought. After packing the warehouse up the 187th proceeded across India back to Karachi where they awaited demobilization and transportation home. Either due to red tape or the Army's slowness in processing the men for discharge, T/Sgt. Quigley and his men instead stood guard duty and took in the sights of postwar Karachi. After discovering that Quigley's unit had yet to be demobilized, Army officials assigned them to kitchen police duty or to military police units. Quigley, however, due to his rank, was lucky, as he was assigned to a noncommissioned officers club as a daytime manager. Still in Karachi by November 1945, the club manager treated Quigley to a traditional Thanksgiving dinner with turkey and all the trimmings. Unfortunately, no word had been received as to when he and the rest of the unit would be going home. Quigley and the other members of the 187th Composite Chemical Company, in fact, spent the remainder of 1945 in Karachi awaiting word of their demobilization. Finally, in mid–January 1946, Quigley's paperwork arrived and the Army sent the 187th Chemical Composite Company to Fort Lewis, Washington, where the unit was finally deactivated and the soldiers mustered out of federal service. Proud of his service during the war though glad to be going home, T/Sgt. Quigley boarded a train and returned home to Pensacola, Florida, in February 1946 after being gone for nearly two and one-half years. Re-united with his wife, Minnie, and daughter Patricia, who was only four months old when he left Florida for the Army and was now nearly three, Quigley quickly adjusted to civilian life and resumed his life with his job as a traveling salesman and his family.

Proud to Have Served in a Not-so Forgotten Theater

T/Sgt. Quigley, who is now 91, today lives in Pensacola, Florida, where he still works three days a week as a retail clerk and plays 18 holes of golf when not working. Upon reflection of his service during the war Quigley remains proud of his service in China-Burma-India. Unlike many veterans of the CBI theater, Quigley frankly admitted that he never thought of having served in a "forgotten theater."[31] Instead, the Army veteran was the first to admit that the theater and actions that took place there "were vital to the defeat of the Japanese," and that the service by the 187th Chemical Composite Company as well as the Hump pilots, engineers, and quartermaster troops should not be forgotten as they all served for one purpose — the defeat of Imperial Japan and the liberation of China.

Chapter 7

"Keep 'em Flying": Corporal Anthony R. Silva, U.S. Army Air Forces, In-Flight & Ground Maintenance Support in China-Burma-India, 1944–1945

The mission to support both Chiang Kai-shek's Nationalist Forces as well as Major General Claire Lee Chennault's 14th Air Force was both complex and at times difficult for both the pilots who flew the missions and the men who serviced the airplanes. As the pilots and crews of the Assam-Burma Ferry Command, and later the Air Transport Command, flew countless sorties over the Hump, air maintenance and ground support personnel performed equally demanding missions in keeping the aircraft and men flying. One of the thousands of mechanics who worked in appalling conditions that included ankle deep mud, tropical humidity, rain, mosquitoes, and monsoons was Corporal Anthony Silva, Jr. Corporal Silva served as a flight engineer and as an aircraft mechanic servicing C-109s and later in the war C-54 aircraft in India. Like many young men who were sent to CBI, Corporal Silva and his comrades endured long hours on the flight line and in the air to keep 'em flying.

Basic Training to China-Burma-India: 1943-44

Corporal Silva entered the Army in 1943 and went through basic training in Atlantic City, New Jersey. After basic training, the Army assigned Silva to the U.S. Army Air Forces' Mechanics School located in Gulfport, Mississippi. After successful completion of the course of instruction in Gulfport, Silva reported for further training to the Curtiss C-46 factory plant located just outside of Buffalo, New York. Here, Corporal Silva learned to service the C-46 Commando transport. After completion of the Curtiss school, Silva and many of his comrades were transferred to Rosecrans Field, St. Joseph, Missouri, where they served as flight engineers and mechanics on the C-46s flown by pilots and crewmen assigned to fly the sturdy transport aircraft.[1]

After a brief tour of duty in St. Joseph and later Nashville, Tennessee, Silva received orders for the China-Burma-India theater. Shortly thereafter Silva and his fellow flight engineers and mechanics embarked for India via the traditional route starting in Nashville, and from there to West Palm Beach, Florida, then directly across the Atlantic to the Azores and then on to Africa. Once in Africa, Silva and his fellow ground crewmen flew onto Karachi, where they boarded a train across India to Dacca which was, according to Silva, "not too far from our final destination at Tezgaon." Silva added that this was a "long, drawn out trip."[2]

Assigned to the 1345th Army Air Forces Base Unit, Squadron C, Silva recounted that upon their arrival at Tezgaon on 16 September 1944, the GIs were surprised to find no aircraft there. The corporal attributed this to the fact that the base was an older base abandoned by the British and converted for use by the U.S. Army Air Forces. "Tezgaon," Silva added, "had, in fact, been a British base before the Americans took it over," and was in a deplorable state of disrepair. Nevertheless, what surprised Silva and his comrades the most was the absence of any aircraft. Silva said that "we were shocked" at this fact because, "here we were, in the middle of a war without any airplanes. Our flight engineers had no aircraft. They finally arrived. We went from literally no airplanes to about 192 airplanes and, as time went on, more and more airplanes arrived. Pilots, in fact, radioed to the engineer below, 'Hey, aren't you guys going to build us some hangars?'"[3]

As for the planes, they did not arrive for a couple of weeks. Once the planes arrived, the base once again hummed with activity as C-109s landed and took off carrying their precious cargo of aviation gasoline across the Hump over to various points in China. Silva stated that one day his line chief came over to his basha and said, "Corporal Silva ... come with me ... you are going to 'fly the Hump." After driving to a revetment, Silva looked over and saw a huge airplane parked inside. The corporal stated that the plane, a C-109 (a converted B-24), was one which he had never seen before. The line chief told Silva and the other airmen that this was "one large gas tank" that we are going to "fly over to China." Silva said that our function aboard the plane was to act as a flight engineer during flight which included in-flight maintenance. "The maintenance crew for each aircraft consisted of 5 men, three were flight engineers and the other two strictly ground mechanics. While all five were aircraft mechanics three of us were [specifically] flight engineers. The reason for five crewmen was so that one was ready to depart on the next flight, one was asleep from the last flight, and the third flight engineer joined the other two. Ground mechanics worked on the plane between flights. Once the plane took off for the return trip, the one who slept during the last flight going across the Hump acted as the flight engineer and insured that the flight was prepared for the next flight without any trouble." Indeed, Silva's pilots and crew were lucky, as the days of a solitary crew performing major maintenance operations on one airplane was quickly becoming a thing of the past as base commanders became hard-pressed by an operations tempo that called for round-the-clock flight operations. Silva added that "non-maintenance operations that could not be readily adapted to production-line maintenance, or PLM as this system was referred to, were still performed by the five-man in-flight maintenance crew in order that ground maintenance crews worked on all not just their assigned solitary aircraft."[4]

As for flight operations themselves, Silva stated that the planes were routinely overloaded and, in fact, exceeded what the pilots considered a safe load. Despite this fact, however, the planes managed somehow to take off. Silva stated that because the C-54 could carry more weight, it "had relatively few problems in getting airborne even if it were overloaded."[5] In fact, considering the missions that the planes received, "the planes held up very well," Silva added, "as they were rugged and very reliable."

Aviation Maintenance in China-Burma-India, 1944-45

While the both the tonnage and air transport command increased in size and scope so too did the struggle to maintain the vast fleet of transport aircraft that operated on a twenty-four hour, seven-days-a-week schedule. Indeed, as the emphasis shifted to the utilization of all aircraft (both fighters and transports) in the re-supply efforts in China and Burma, a natural by-product of this effort naturally fell to aircraft maintenance, "long a sore spot in India-China operations."[6] In fact, Major General William H. Tunner "insisted upon increased efficiency and upon a fuller exploitation of the existing facilities" in order that the airlift might achieve its maximum potential. As a part of this, Tunner set out to streamline maintenance. In July 1944, a technical inspector from the Army Air Forces proposed the introduction of the system already in use at stateside Training Command bases which was the establishment of production line maintenance at the Assam stations. This procedure called for the "towing of aircraft through a succession of stations, at each of which was a fresh group of maintenance men," who performed specific maintenance operations "at which they were presumably skilled." General Tunner, in fact, not only adopted this idea but also began a massive construction program that witnessed an increase in hangar and apron construction necessary to accommodate any production line maintenance program.[7] While there remained much skepticism on the part of base commanders and engineering officers to go over to such a streamlined system of aircraft maintenance, Lieutenant Colonel Robert B. White, the division aircraft maintenance officer, himself a strong advocate of PLM, attempted to "combat their skepticism by stressing the efficiency of the new system."⁸ Corporal Silva emphasized, however, PLM was not designed to replace the five-man maintenance crews assigned to each flight. In fact:

> the main point was that P.L.M. did not abolish assigned maintenance crews. P.L.M. was used to perform *all major inspections, engine replacements, etc.* Those types of maintenance activities that were readily integrated into station-to-station movement through a hangar, where each station was manned and equipped for specific functions [Silva's emphasis].
>
> The five-man maintenance crew was still assigned to a specific aircraft where they performed all other maintenance activities, such as unscheduled failures that could not be brought into the middle of scheduled PLM activities.⁹

Once fully implemented, there was some residual resistance to PLM as some base commanders either ignored the order or delayed its implementation. In an effort to get PLM off the ground, division headquarters in Assam "exerted on the bases a degree of pressure," which in and of itself was self-defeating as some PLMs were hastily organized and thereby negated their effectiveness. The division maintenance officer nevertheless officially inaugurated the concept of production line maintenance on 16 February 1945. As Silva noted upon his arrival at Tezgaon, the airfield contained few revetments or hangars, and had very few hangar and parking facilities.¹⁰ These and the lack of other buildings made an already bad situation worse as pilots and base commanders hastily built temporary structures to protect the aircraft from the elements. In fact, "some base commanders and maintenance officers ... many of whom were already reluctant to change over to a system they felt would result in a temporary loss of efficiency," simply refused the order or, as was often the case, implemented the system slowly.

Not only were base commanders reluctant to introduce PLM on their respective bases but pilots were likewise distrustful of the quality of PLM. Many pilots, in fact, "preferred the old way of doing things, in which each airplane was the direct responsibility of a given crew." While General Tunner acknowledged that some commanders had refused to implement PLM, he nevertheless reported to the War Department that "PLM ... [was] ... an overwhelming success," and had resulted in a rise in the number of aircraft available for flight operations on a monthly basis. In fact, if we are to believe reports from the Air Transport Command's maintenance personnel, the average percentage of available aircraft rose from "78 percent in January to 85 percent in July." In recognition of the supposed success of PLM Tunner likewise reported that "there was a 25 percent reduction in the time required for 100-hour inspections, while the quality of those inspections had improved." As for individual aircraft, Tunner reported that the introduction of PLM was the reason for the "steady increase in daily utilization of C-54 aircraft at Kurmitola [Silva's newly-assigned base that was only a few miles from Tezgaon] from an average of 7.51 hours in April to 11.65 hours in July."¹¹

In order to ease the logistical burden as well as increase the number of aircraft available to fly over the Hump the Air Maintenance Division came up with the solution of "assigning one type of aircraft to any given base." By March 1945 this streamlined system of aircraft maintenance by aircraft type greatly assisted in the increased amount of tonnage being carried over the Himalayas into China from bases in Assam and Bengal. In fact, "use of the Assam [and Bengal] bases and of the high Hump routes had been at best a desperate matter of expedience, dictated by the presence of the Japanese forces in Burma."[12] By March 1945, with the eviction of the Japanese from northern Burma "it was most natural to fly increasing amounts of cargo directly from Bengal to China." With bases poised closer to the India-Burma border, and emergency airfields now located at Myitkyina and Yunnanyi, "planes based in Assam could fly farther south and at lower altitudes than in previous years." This lower altitude likewise meant that greater use of the C-54 could take place. This in turn meant that more cargo could be funneled into China. In fact, the Douglas C-54 Skymaster, arguably one of the best and perhaps most flexible transports used by the United States Army Air Forces during World War II, due in large part to the four very reliable engines, could fly from bases near Calcutta (Barrackpore) and in eastern Bengal, and from there directly onto Kunming (see Chart #1).

Even before the introduction of PLM, however, the numbers of serviceable aircraft available to the Air Transport Command increased substantially. Indeed,

> the total number of aircraft available for Hump operation increased substantially at the beginning of 1945, but thereafter it remained practically constant. The average number in commission for the Hump service in December 1944 was 249.6; in January 1945, 287.4; in February, 336.8; in April, 325.9; in July, 332.[13]

As has been noted, the primary responsibility of Silva and the other ground crew members was to keep 'em flying. The introduction of PLM, in fact, contributed greatly to a more efficient use of the limited assets available in the CBI theater. Indeed, like the pilots who flew the planes, the crews worked just as hard if not more so in maintaining an air fleet that by 1945 was both bruised and battered by the enemy and nature. When not involved in air resupply operations crews spent long hours on the ground, fixing, sweating, and oftentimes swearing as the mechanics fought an enemy more elusive than the Japanese to keep the supplies flowing to the Chinese, British, and American forces fighting the Japanese. Likewise, India, where many of the American air bases flying the Hump were located, like many parts of southwestern China, "was not a perfect base.... The climate and sanitary conditions were especially bad in those portions of India nearest to China, where the major part of the U.S. effort would necessarily be exerted. More than one hundred inches of rain a year fell in many places in Assam, one spot receiving more than 1,000 inches. Intestinal disease, malaria, plague, and smallpox were endemic. Also, the difficulty of obtaining good fresh food in Assam made it worth while to fly perishables from

China to India occasionally on returning transport aircraft. Soldiers (and airmen) grew tired and listless because of vitamin deficiency."[15]

Chart #1
The Transition to PLM and Aircraft Availability
March 1945

Assam Bases	Aircraft Type	Total # of Planes
Chabua	C-46	48
Sookerating	C-46	48
Mohanbari	C-46	48
Misamari	C-46	48
Tezpur	C-87/C-109	30
Jorhat	C-87/C-109	30
Shamshernager	C-87/C-109	
Tezgaon	C-54	39.314
Kurmitola		

The factors that hampered air operations likewise affected ground support operations. It is a fact that the same meteorological and climatic conditions that affected flight operations placed an even greater strain on an already tenuous maintenance capability that by 1945 supported 'round-the-clock air operations. Despite the opposition to PLM, the air maintenance system put into place on 1 May 1942 by Brigadier General Elmer E. Adler blossomed into one of the most efficient commands assigned to both the Tenth Air Force and later the Air Transport Command. Colonel Robert C. Oliver, who replaced Brigadier General Adler on 14 August 1942, "continued to build upon the organization that he had inherited" from his predecessor who had activated the Tenth Air Service Command in early May 1942 in New Delhi.[16] Eventually, the command's personnel came from Headquarters and Headquarters Squadron, the 51st Base Group's 54th Air Base Squadron, both based in Karachi, and the 59th Material Squadron, which Colonel Oliver divided into detachments and spread across airfields in India and China. Reinforced from the 3rd Air Depot Group, which arrived in Karachi on 16 May 1942, the command found itself based at Agra. By the time Colonel Oliver assumed command of the Air Service Command it had units based at Agra, Allahabad, Chakulia, Bangalore, Dinjan, and Chabua in India, and Kunming in China.[17] The primary mission of the Air Service Command was to repair, overhaul, salvage and, in conjunction with the Hindustan Aircraft Corporation located at Bangalore, manufacture a limited number of aircraft.

Overall, the introduction of production line maintenance or PLM by Brigadier General William Tunner was a major factor for the eventual success of the airlift to China and British forces in the field. The introduction of PLM

> took an aircraft through maintenance stations, with experts performing the technical chores in a standardized manner. It replaced a complete mishmash of maintenance organizations and practices. Until its institution, no two bases

were alike. Some used a few specialized crews to perform engine changes and periodic inspections, while others relied on the crew chief system to perform almost every maintenance task associated with a given airplane. General Tunner directed PLM whenever and wherever practical and separated maintenance from operations. The wing trained and assigned maintenance specialists; crew chiefs remained, but no longer would these mechanics attempt all the maintenance tasks of a specified aircraft. Each base commander had to appoint a director of aircraft maintenance directly responsible to the base commander.... After some experimenting and growing pains, the system worked superbly. Operational-ready rates climbed to 85 percent and inspection downtime dropped 25 percent.[18]

By the end of the war in August 1945 the Air Transport Command to which Silva and his crew were assigned numbered some 21,000 men and consisted of 367 airlift airplanes of all types (C-46s, C-47s, C-54s B-24s, C-87s, and C-109s).

In order to get an idea of the conditions faced by American ground crews servicing the growing armada of transport and fighter aircraft in the China-Burma-India theater, one only has to look at the ground operations that existed in China as mechanics and ground crewmen struggled to keep the transports and fighters airborne. Major General Claire Lee Chennault wrote that the repair effort was a battle in and of itself. Indeed, the conditions which the ground crews of the American Volunteer Group (AVG) faced in China prior to the entrance of the United States in the war after December 1941 typified the conditions Silva and the other ground crews later faced throughout CBI from 1942 until the end of the war:

> Working conditions on the fields were incredibly bad. Pilots and mechanics sweltered in the sticky, oppressive heat of the East China summer and shivered in the cold rains that broke heat waves. There were no hangars or shelters for planes. Few mechanics had coveralls. To save their only change of clothes, they worked in shorts and shoes, burned by the sun, soaked by rain. To keep our battered and worn planes flying, they worked from before sunrise to long after dark with only the light or a smoky kerosene lamp on hand flashlight to guide them.[19]

Chennault likewise noted the lack of spare parts and other essential services deemed necessary to maintain air operations during the early days of the air war in China prior to the United States entering the war:

> There were no spare parts and few tools. Even such simple tools as wrenches and pliers were at a premium. The 75th Squadron at Hengyang had only two sets of hand tools belonging to former A.V.G. mechanics to service the entire squadron. Administrative facilities were even more scanty. At Hengyang, the 75th set up shop with one Chinese pencil, a sheaf of rice paper, and an ancient portable typewriter borrowed once a week from a Presbyterian missionary. Its administrative staff consisted of a first sergeant and a mechanic who could also type. At Kweilin the 76th functioned for more than a year with only one ground officer, Captain Byron Smith, who served as adjutant, executive officer, personnel officer, supply officer and mess officer.[20]

Chennault's comments applied not only to the situation found in the CBI theater but, in fact, throughout the Southwest and South Pacific areas, two theaters ostensibly well-supplied as they constituted major theaters of operations. Army Master Sergeant Robert Foye (who was later commissioned and reached the rank of major) recounted similar conditions faced by the ground crewmen of the 67th Fighter Squadron based at Tontouta, on Noumea in the Southwest Pacific:

> Mechanics had only the simple 1st Echelon maintenance tools and only about 10 kits of these for the entire squadron. No special tools of any kind. Even the truck tools were at a premium.... No replacement parts.... Rain, mud, mosquitos [sic]. Mechanics worked sopping wet. Pvt Jones worked on the tail assembly sitting in six inches of water, so wet from the rain he never knew the difference. Rain poured down their faces and necks— still they worked on, passing the scanty wrenches from one to another. Not a growl from any man.... Work day from five A.M. until dark. Cold (sometimes hot) chow at noon, and back to work right away. No transportation during the first five days and the men had to walk two miles to work and home again through the mud.... Every man to his job, and never a growl except when one section chief would hold up another: "Come on! This is War— keep'em rolling!"[21]

Master Sergeant Foye wrote that in order to make up for the shortages in tools and other equipment necessary to service the airplanes, his mechanics oftentimes improvised or fashioned tools from spare parts or made their own wrenches:

> Once mechanic (Hartfield) improvised tools by cutting wrenches and welding on extensions. Servicing funnels made from gallon cans with makeshift spouts soldered to the corners. (Incidentally, 67th should have patent on the gas drum washing rack—one drum split in half and resting on a V-shaped cut in the other. Door cut in bottom half for the fire. Result: A practical G.I. messkit wash stand.)[22]

Foye added that with spare parts in such short supply, crews re-used old parts. As was often the case, the high-voltage spark plugs found on the Allison engines of the P-400 or P-39 Aircobras were oftentimes patched up with ordinary friction tape or, in the case of ignition harnesses, stripped from wrecked airplanes. Chennault wrote that the Allison engines found on the P-40E Warhawks often went 300 hours over their scheduled overhauls before servicing. Likewise, the 4-ply tires that arrived in theater from India oftentimes tore apart upon the first landings on the rocky and rugged Chinese runways. Engine oil was filtered and re-used and, there was always a shortage of tail-wheel tires. Sometimes, Chennault added, "Maintenance problems were too great even for the ingenuity and energy of the ... ground crews."[23] Nevertheless, the crews, working nonstop from dawn to dusk and sometimes beyond, labored on. Flight officer Tom Barnard, who flew as a part of the Army Air Force's Project 7-A, recalled that the American Airlines maintenance crews were very innovative in dealing with the chronic shortages of parts, tools, and suitable buildings and equipment to service the transport aircraft. Barnard said, "Workstands were constructed out of bamboo but the fragile bamboo stands swayed perilously in the wind, so empty oil drums were put into use, welded together and footholds cut in the sides so the mechanic could climb up to reach the engines. Even the motor hood of ground vehicles served as engine stands."[24]

Despite the trickle of supplies into CBI after 1943, problems of maintenance persisted, some man-made and others caused by nature. In CBI, the extreme heat, humidity and dust compounded the lack of spare parts or equipment. In order to avoid daytime maintenance operations most "maintenance work was normally carried out at night because, as one ATC officer reported, 'Maintenance work cannot be accomplished because shade temperatures from 100 degrees Fahrenheit render all metal exposed to the sun so hot that it cannot be touched by the human hand without causing second degree burns.'"[25] The heat and especially the humidity likewise produced a great deal of rot and rust while the thick dust fouled engines and other parts on the airplanes. This in turn increased the wear on them and forced an already overworked maintenance force to overhaul them more frequently.[26]

Corporal Anthony Silva takes a break on one of the landing gear wheels of a B-29 at an air base in India (Anthony R. Silva, Jr., Collection).

Undoubtedly, however, the most serious problem faced by maintenance personnel in CBI was "the chronic lack of spare parts and engines." In fact, in 1942, the reason for the airlift's failure to keep abreast with the demands of Chennault's Fourteenth Air Force was in large part the number of planes grounded by a lack of spare parts. Indeed, for 1942, "only nine of the thirty-four transports assigned to the Hump run were actually flyable, the rest grounded for want of spare parts." By the end of 1943, the situation still remained critical with over 100 transports of the ATC grounded due to a lack of spare parts. The ATC's maintenance command, in fact, figured that at any given time, 4 percent of the fleet would be grounded due to a lack of spare parts. When that figure had been surpassed, "a condition of critical scarcity was considered to exist."²⁷ This problem persisted well into 1944 and was corrected only in January 1945. Up to that time, however, the monthly average of planes out of commission for 1944 was normally 5.3 percent of aircraft (see Chart #2).

In order to increase the availability of aircraft to the Hump airlift General Harold George, the ATC's commanding officer, instituted a shuttle to increase the flow of spare parts to the CBI theater known as the Fireball Express. General George recognized

> the fact that nothing was more vital to the expansion of the lift than an adequate flow of parts and engines. Operating under ATC contract, Pan Am crews made a weekly flight to carry the parts in most demand direct from the Air Service Command Depot at Fairfield, Ohio to the Tenth Air Service Command Depot at Agra. Flying C-87s stripped of camouflage paint to give them an extra 5 mph airspeed, the express crews used the Florida-Brazil-West Africa-Sudan route to India, making the round trip in seven days.²⁸

In the end, "the increased flow of parts added greatly to the number of aircraft in service on the hump run." Because of the lack of parts, in both the Southwest Pacific and China-Burma-India theaters, "the crew chiefs violated every imaginable rule in the book just to keep the airplanes flyable." In fact, in both these theaters of war, "Every airplane in commission soon became an example of the ground crew's ingenuity and resourcefulness." Foye perhaps summed it up best when he wrote, "It would have given the experts at Chanute Field the Holy Horrors," to know that even the basic rules of servicing an airplane were violated repeatedly by air crews struggling to keep them in the air.²⁹

As Mel Christler wrote, this ingenuity and resourcefulness had its more memorable moments. Pilots had a code that they relayed to their respective bases that indicated the flight status of their plane for the next day's operations. When a pilot signaled, "Positive," it meant that the plane would be able to turn around for the next day without any major repairs. If he signaled "Negative," Christler wrote that it was a no go and that the plane required servicing.³⁰ Despite these and other maintenance problems, Christler wrote that during his tour of duty in CBI, "the maintenance was good and most of the bugs were out of the

Corporal Anthony R. Silva, Jr., USAAF, poses in his Class "A" uniform (Anthony R. Silva, Jr., Collection).

AIRCRAFT IN INDIA — CHINA DIVISION
DAILY AVERAGE — SEPTEMBER 1944

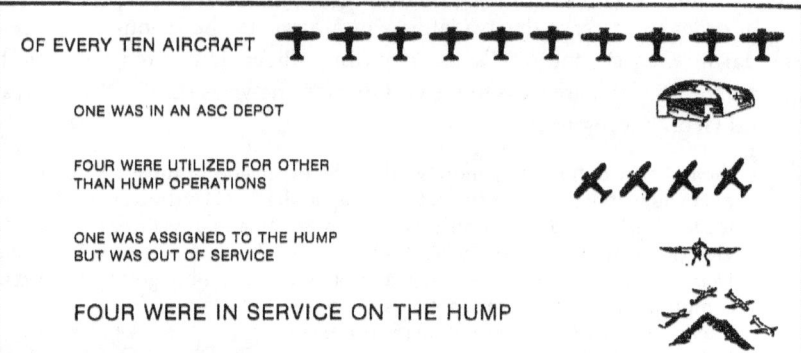

OF EVERY TEN AIRCRAFT

ONE WAS IN AN ASC DEPOT

FOUR WERE UTILIZED FOR OTHER THAN HUMP OPERATIONS

ONE WAS ASSIGNED TO THE HUMP BUT WAS OUT OF SERVICE

FOUR WERE IN SERVICE ON THE HUMP

TOTAL PLANES ASSIGNED TO ICHD (Daily Average)	372
Less: Planes in Hands of ASC Depots	34
Planes Assigned to Other than Hump Operations	151*
Total Planes Not Available for Hump Assignment	185
Planes Assigned to Hump Operations	187
Less: Planes Out of Service	42
PLANES IN SERVICE ON HUMP	145

*Total of 151 planes consisted of 9 C-87s, 13 C-46s, 108 DC-3s, and 21 miscellaneous.

Chart 2. Daily Availability of Aircraft — China Division, September 1944 (Miller, *Airlift Doctrine*, p. 56).

operation." This in turn meant that more gasoline and supplies would reach General Chennault's 14th Air Force as well as Chiang Kai-shek's forces.

Perhaps the most appreciative of the efforts of the mechanics and ground crewmen were the pilots who were attached to the various air forces serving throughout CBI. One of these pilots, First Lieutenant Donald S. Lopez, who flew P-40Es in China during the war wrote in his postwar memoirs that the ground crews

> deserve a tremendous share of the credit for the fine performance of our squadron. They got up before dawn every day to ready the airplanes for the morning missions. They performed their arduous tasks late into the night in all kinds of weather to keep their charges in top shape. They refueled the fighters from 55-gallon drums with hand pumps and strained the fuel through chamois to filter out the water, rust, and other sediment, and they did it in the broiling sun in the short periods between missions. At the same time, the armorers clambered on and under the hot wings, manhandling the heavy bombs and ammunition belts and changing gun barrels when necessary. Every night the guns were care-

fully cleaned and lubricated, and the airplanes were inspected for damage, while plugs (twenty-four per engine) were changed if necessary, new magnetos were installed, and carburetors were adjusted. This monotonous work was done day in and day out without the relief of days off, which the pilots got regularly; and without the exhilaration of flying exceedingly unmonotonous missions.[31]

Lieutenant Lopez added:

The ground crews, especially the crew chiefs, fought the enemy vicariously through their pilots. They thrilled with every victory and successful mission, suffered when the airplane was damaged or the pilot was wounded, were devastated when their pilot was lost and overjoyed when he turned up safe. They received few promotions and fewer medals, but their dedication was unequaled.[32]

The official history of the Fourteenth Air Force best summed it up: "Mechanics worked all night in the steamy heat to repair damage from missions, replace worn parts, and have a full complement of planes ready for a dawn takeoff. As fast as planes returned from combat, armorers hung new loads of demolition and frag bombs under the wings and reloaded the guns ... as pilots dashed to the alert shack in order to report a just-completed mission, and be briefed on the next target before they were back in the cockpits on a new mission."[33]

Lieutenant Lopez credits the efficiency of this system to the excellent noncommissioned officers that comprised the ranks of the crew chiefs on the flight line. Indeed, without these experienced soldiers, the China airlift operation would've floundered as C-46s, C-47s, C-54s and the rest would have remained idle or abandoned on the many airfields in India, China, and later Burma. They, and the rest of the ground crews were the unsung heroes of not only the CBI theater but also of the entire Allied war effort during World War II.

In addition to the lack of proper tools, spare parts, and overworked crews, the living and working conditions throughout CBI and the Southwest Pacific were for the most part, very spartan and in many cases deplorable. Both the pilots and crews, eaten alive by malaria-carrying mosquitoes as they worked on the flight line or slept in their tents, tormented by hordes of rats and poisonous snakes at night (especially the krait), as well as being subjected to poor food, lack of proper washing facilities and mail, substandard sleeping accommodations or a general lack of suitable barracks topped off by being at the end of an already precarious supply line, there is little wonder that morale was often as low as it was among the ground crewmen who served in CBI during the war. General Chennault wrote:

Living conditions were bad. Food was good by Chinese standards, but Americans found it hard to stomach a steady diet of fat, greasy pork, sweet potatoes, bean sprouts, and rice. One Chinese cook at Lingling fried his fish in tung oil and made the entire base sick. Dysentery, yellow jaundice, and malaria were prevalent. Once the entire 11th Bomb Squadron was forced to suspend operations for a week because most of its flight personnel had dysentery. There were no flight surgeons for the squadrons. Colonel Thomas Gentry, A.V.G., chief flight surgeon, who joined the Army, was assigned to a non-combat outfit in Kunming. Wounded and sick were cared for by medical missionaries who happened to be in the area. All during American air operations in China we found missionaries of all creeds and nationalities to be a never failing source of help whenever we needed it.[34]

Chennault added:

> Smoky kerosene lamps in hostels were too dim for reading or writing. Even beds were soggy in the steaming heat. Green mold appeared overnight on shoes and equipment. There were movies but no sound equipment. The men were so starved for entertainment they watched the silent talk lines and tried to read the actor's lips. Some bases were without soap, razor blades, and cigarettes for months at a time. The C.A.T.F.[35] worked and fought under conditions far worse than those of the A.V.G. without the spur of higher salaries and combat bonuses.[36]

In conditions that resembled those found in CBI, Master Sergeant Foye said, "Men literally dropped on their knees with cramps at the rig before they would ask for relief [from the flight line because of dysentery]."[37] By late 1943 into early 1944, this situation was gradually corrected, though it might be added that throughout the war both CBI and the Southwest Pacific Theaters remained at the end of a very precarious supply line that didn't improve until the end of the war in Europe in May 1945.

Other problems that hampered the proper servicing of the aircraft were the lack of suitable all-weather airdromes and the slow progress of airfield construction. In CBI, in fact, the only all-weather airfield in existence was owned by the Royal Air Force and shared by the CATF and Tenth Air Force. Eventually, with the arrival of more combat engineer units from the United States, thirty-four airfields were soon under construction at Jorhat, Mohanbari, Sookerating, Chabua, and Tezgaon.[38] Outside of the fact that Sir Archibald Wavell, the governor-general and viceroy of India, remained less than enthusiastic about a plan to facilitate China's ability to participate in the war effort, the native laborers, many of whom were women, refused to work in the rain or during religious holidays or, as occurred in mid–1942, when Japanese forces threatened to invade Assam — the most exposed part of India nearest to Burma. As news of the Japanese advance spread among the native labor force, many of them simply "melted away at an alarming rate." Added to the refusal of Indian women to work was Mahatma Gandhi's anti–British activities that translated eventually into anti–American sentiment that caused him to lead many strikes among the native dockworkers. This in turn led to many delays in getting the much-needed supplies over to Chiang's Nationalist forces and Chennault's Fourteenth Air Force. Despite repeated assurances from American military and diplomatic officials that American involvement in India was merely to defeat the Japanese and assist Chiang, Gandhi feared that "the Americans were there simply to assist British rule."[39] Another problem with the local natives was

India's caste system. For Americans, the unfortunate aspects of their own segregated society paled in comparison to India's complex socio-economic scale. Yet for Hump pilots like Merlin C. Newell or flight engineers like Tony Silva, India (or Pakistan) was a strange, exotic land, and the men had little or no knowledge about the local way of life and "less about their government."[40] Newell wrote, however

> We were acquainted with some things, however, because we saw them. We knew something of their labor system and a little about their caste system. We were not there very long before we knew that one Indian would not do another's work. It was supposedly their theory that to do another's work was to throw him out of a job. The coolie would not shine shoes, the *Basha* [personal servant] would not sweep, the sweeper would not carry your baggage. The windows in our bash were dirty. The *Basha* would not wash them, because he shined shoes and made beds. The sweeper would not wash them, because it was his job to sweep. The coolie would not and neither would the water carrier, because it was their job to carry water. We would not, because we were pilots, and the windows stayed dirty.
>
> The so-called professions and skilled jobs were reserved for the male population. He was the laundryman, the tailor, the baker, and the barber. The lower classed women were used for simpler things like hauling rocks and plowing. The Dhabi did our laundry. His skill usually ran out before our clothes reached us again. He could remember how many shirts, socks, and trousers we sent, but he couldn't remember the size or color. Thus, we had a common laundry pool. If we got our own clothes back, it was the exception. If we got something back we could wear, we wore it; and if we didn't, we turned it back and hoped for a better selection next time.
>
> It soon became evident we couldn't tip these boys. Every tip they got they regarded as a raise in salary. Before long, some camp had an over-abundance of labor. The British came hunting their "wogs" or "Worthy Oriental Gentleman" and cussing the damned Americans for raising the wages again.[41]

Both Newell and Silva added that while on leave they saw the utter filth the average Indian native lived in. Newell added, "We've seen the hovels they live in, smelled their filthy quarters.... We've seen them lie dead and naked in the streets, and we've seen the despicable holes the untouchables live in. If this, then, makes one an authority on India — we are authorities to a man."[42]

In addition to the Indian labor problems was the failure of the American combat engineers to arrive in theater during 1942 and 1943. Due, in part, to the reams of red tape and the demands of the other theaters, primarily in the North Africa and later Italian theaters of operation, many combat engineer units either failed to materialize or were diverted at the last moment. Not until both President Franklin D. Roosevelt and Prime Minister Churchill "put their authority directly behind the program" could a major effort be put forward to build the necessary bases and thereby increase the tonnage going over the Hump.

The exception to the shortage of suitable airfields and airdromes occurred in China, where Generalissimo Chiang Kai-shek was able to mobilize the hundreds of thousands of coolies into a potent labor force to build the necessary facilities. Technical Sergeant Robert Boehm recalled that one of his most lasting memories of China during the war was the sight in one village of a large number of coolies dragging huge stone roller over gravel and rocks in order to flatten them into a hardened surface.[43] Indeed, the lack of suitable airdromes and airfields was never a problem in China as occurred in neighboring India.

One situation that improved nearly right away was the personnel shortage. Besides the streamlined maintenance system, PLM, the increased availability of aircraft to the supply effort can be directly linked to the increased number of American maintenance and other support-type personnel assigned to Hump bases, a number which grew moderately in 1945. Indeed, from a December 1944 total of 17,032 personnel (the month Silva arrived at Tezgaon), the numbers grew slightly to 19,025 in January 1945 and reached their peak in April of that same year to 22,359. With the commencement of demobilization in the summer of 1945, the numbers began to decrease slightly. In addition to the 22,000 American personnel assigned to bases throughout India, there were 2,530 Army Air Force maintenance personnel (December 1944) assigned to bases in Southwestern China. By the war's end in August 1945 this figure rose to 5,959 American service personnel assigned to the ATC, Major General Claire Lee Chennault's Fourteenth Air Force and the Twentieth Air Force. In addition to the military personnel assigned to the China-Burma-India theater, there were 47,009 civilians, mostly involved in loading and unloading transports working for the Army Air Forces.[44]

Daily Flight Operations Over the Hump

The increased number of airplanes and men in turn translated to more tonnage reaching both the British XIV Army in its campaign to drive the Japanese out of Burma, in assisting in the re-supply efforts of Chiang Kai-shek's beleaguered Nationalist forces, as well as both the Fourteenth and Twentieth Air Forces in their air campaign against the Japanese in China, Formosa, and the Japanese home islands. Corporal Silva recalled one instance, in April 1945, when there was a "maximum effort" to get as much gasoline across the Hump into China as possible. The Army corporal, whose plane flew three separate sorties that same day in flights that normally took six hours into Kunming recounted that as soon as the planes landed ground crews that had been waiting on the runway or its edges appeared and began to unload the 55-gallon aviation fuel drums and the other supplies carried by the planes.[45] Silva also recalled that there was some Japanese air activity still menacing the Hump flights. As for the presence of Japanese fighters over the Hump, Silva stated that the American transports such as the C-109 that he and his fellow crewmen had transitioned to were fortunate in that they rarely encountered enemy planes due to the heights (28,000 feet) at which they traveled. Also, late in the war (1944-45), newer models of the C-87 came armed with a single .50-caliber tail gun and an electrically-operated upper turret with twin .50-calibers and with two .50 caliber machine-guns mounted in the nose of the airplane. The nose guns could, in fact, be fired by pulling the "D" handles located on either side of the throttle quadrant and fired by a thumb button on the pilot's control wheel. Despite this, however, flying still remained a hazardous job as planes still crashed into the side of the rugged Himalayas or ran into enemy fire either from the air or on the ground up until the summer of 1945.[46]

Silva commented that air operations continued round the clock. In particular, Silva remembered that for his squadron, flights into China started as early as 7:30 A.M. or could occur as late as 11:00 A.M. The C-109 crewman emphasized, however, that flights could take place "at any time ... though most operations occurred in daylight hours." Corporal Silva said that "there was no rule that you took off at a certain time during the day. If you were going to take off in the morning, you normally did it in late morning as there would always be fog and you couldn't see the end of the runway."[47] Silva added that since most planes were loaded by crews who worked throughout the night, taking off could occur at any time in the morning. When asked if the flights had already been scheduled or if a set pattern of flight operations had been set for certain areas, Silva emphasized that there was no set schedule or pattern to the flights, as air operations occurred all the time and went just about everywhere where they were needed the most. Silva recalled that one particular morning, about 6, the flight officer came over to their tent and said, "Wake up men, we're flying today.... Get outta bed and get over to the plane!" Silva said, "We never asked where we were going or how long we would be gone," as flights occurred non-stop daily. Silva added that they rarely if ever remained overnight at any particular base. The average daily utilization rate of each aircraft flying the Hump was 8.8 hours though this number oftentimes changed depending upon the mission or operation.[48]

As for maintenance, Silva said, "Occasionally we had to change an engine ... and when we did have to change engines we stayed on the job until it was done. I remember one case there we were on the job 35–40 hours continuously. You know, to change a couple of engines to get the plane back in the air." Silva stated that while the repairs were going on, "there was nobody there looking over our shoulders saying you should be pushing that or this. You got your assignment and went out and you did it. That was pretty much your job."

As for weather, Silva recalled that air operations were only rarely affected by the weather. The only time operations were suspended was during the monsoon. In fact, after Lord Louis Mountbatten assumed command of Southeast Asia Command (SEAC), flight operations were to take place non-stop and were carried on in sunshine and rain, through the summer heat and by 1944 through the dreaded monsoon season. Silva remembered that during his time in CBI, "there was no period of diminished operations. The weather didn't make any difference. Whenever the airplane was loaded and if the weather permitted, you took off." As for accidents, Silva stated that these occurred quite frequently as "we were definitely in violent weather, oftentimes in wind that gusted to 150 mph ... a lot of rough weather. Icing normally built up on the wings. We flew in upthrusts that tossed us around like ping pong balls." Silva added, however, that "you didn't really think much about it then as most of us were 18 to 20 years old."

As for the weather and its corrosive effects upon the C-109s and other aircraft at Tezgaon and Kumitola, Silva stated that the aircraft he flew experienced very little if any of these problems. Contrary to popular opinion that heat and humidity retarded engine performance and promoted aircraft wear and tear, Silva stated that if anything "the heat and humidity might have, in fact, helped the aircraft as the engines developed more power and ran smoother with high humidity."

Unlike Hall's or Goodman's command, however, Silva's squadron had been assigned to fly supplies to the XX Air Force. It might be noted that the XX Air Force (until its deactivation in the spring of 1945) competed with Chennault's Fourteenth Air Force for the meager supplies trickling over the Hump into China. In fact, by the time the XX Air Force had ceased air operations and the air war over the Pacific had shifted from Chinese bases to those located on Saipan, Iwo Jima, and later Okinawa, the command had accounted for nearly 12 percent of all supplies coming in over the Hump. As for supplies coming in over the Himalayas, "Gasoline and oil accounted in 1945 for nearly 60 percent of all net tonnage carried eastbound over the Hump. Ordnance supplies (including motor vehicles, dismantled for the Hump crossing, and appropriate spare parts, as well as bombs and ammunition) amounted to approximately 15 percent of the total lift. The balance, roughly a fourth of the total, included passengers, a relatively small quantity of Air Corps technical supplies, PX supplies, and a larger proportion of Quartermaster supplies."[49] In addition to the supplies were the thousands of passengers, primarily "thousands of Chinese troops ... transported from China to India" and back again for "training and combat." Planes carried other valuable war-essential commodities including "silk, tungsten, tin, mercury, and even green tea." Silva stated, however, that the bulk of the cargo his plane transported into China consisted of fuel and ordnance and later on, Chinese troops.

As the tempo of allied ground operations intensified in CBI after April 1945, Silva's plane as well as those in his command began transporting Chinese troops from India or Burma into China, to bases in or near Shanghai. In fact, this mission began to surpass the transporting of supplies insofar as the airlift was concerned. Silva recalled that after take off his plane would normally land at bases midway, empty about half of their fuel and then pick up a contingent of Chinese soldiers whom they then transported either into China near bases in Shanghai or elsewhere. After dropping the Chinese troops off, the American crews returned to the midpoint or to the other bases where they had deposited the spare fuel drums, filled their tanks and flew home.

Chart #3
The Types of Aircraft Used as Transports in China-Burma-India During World War II, 1941–45[50]

	C-46	B-24J	B-25 J	C-47	C-87	C-109*
Wingspan	108'1"	110'0"	67'7"	95'0"	110'0"	110'0"
Length	76'4"	67'2"	52'11"	64'6"	67'2"	67'2"
Height	21'.9"	18'0"	16'4"		18'0"	18'0"
Wt. Loaded (lbs)	50,000**	65,000	35,000	30,000	65,000	65,000
Range (mi)	1,200	2,100	1,350	2,125	2,100	2,100
Ceiling (ft)	27,600	28,000	24, 200	23,200	28,000	28,000
Max speed (mph)	269	300	272	230	300	300
Bomb/Cargo (lbs)	12,000	8,800	3,000	7,500	8,800	8,800

*The C-109 was the tanker model of the C-87 and was used extensively over the Hump after 1943 by the USAAF.
**Normally, the gross weight of the C-46 was 48,000 lbs with the capability to carry an extra 2,000 lbs for a total of 50,000 lbs.

Facilitating the airlift of troops (and supplies) into China were the newer, more powerful aircraft converted into transports by the ATC. Serving alongside the venerable C-46s, C-47s, and C-109s was the Douglas DC-4 or (military C-54) or Skymaster. The C-54 Skymaster was both a transport and cargo carrier that came equipped with four Pratt & Whitney R-2000 radial engines that produced a speed of 265 miles per hour. The C-54 could climb to 26,600 feet and had a maximum range of 3,800 miles. With a length of 93 feet 11 inches and a wingspan of 117 feet 6 inches the C-54 carried a maximum load of 73,000 lbs. In fact, the Skymaster in time became the airplane of choice when long range and a heavy payload were required. Unfortunately, however, "the C-54 ... could not be used on the northern Hump route and did not see service in the airlift" until the recapture of Myitkyina in August 1944. Nonetheless, the C-54 could carry 70 percent more payload than the C-46. With this in mind and an eye aimed on increased tonnage over the Hump into China, Headquarters ATC had hoped to build a fleet of some 272 C-54s.[51] The plan ultimately fell short of its objective during the first few months of 1944 January–April, "because the ATC could not send enough C-54s to CBI ... to carry the required volume." By the war's end, on 1 September 1945, the Army Air Forces had over 1,000 C-54s in operation throughout the CBI theater.[52]

As for how the pilots and crews felt about the various transports used by the ATC, Silva stated that "the C-109 was ... [a] ... bare-bones ... low comfort ... (aircraft).... The Flight Engineer didn't have a seat or anything and sat on the chute on the floor. You may not stand up until the plane reached cruising altitude. Then life is pretty much easier until the plane is ready to come in for a landing. You set up the various controls, then the descent, monitor the fuels, and do whatever has to be done during the flight or after the landing."[53] As for mechanical liability of the planes and parts Corporal Silva stated that "there were some things that were very reliable. Well, some electronic parts, for instance the governors had these little resistors that would burn out. The little things that would require some type of activity that would keep them going." Silva recounted that during one flight, they were already about an hour and a half out from base, at mid-point, when two engines failed on their C-109.[54] Fortunately, Silva added, "we were at the highest peak of the Hump on this route, so we continued to our destination as our altitude remained the same as the terrain altitude decreased."[55]

Overall, however, of the types of transports used, the C-47 was judged to have been the best overall transport utilized by the ATC in the CBI theater. In fact:

> the C-47 had qualities of stability that resulted in it being assigned almost all air-dropping missions. It was easy to load and balance the C-47 so long as the cargo was tied down as far forward as possible. When the aircraft was in flight, cargo could be dragged to the door and kicked out without upsetting the transport's balance. In the case of the C-46, cargo had to be arranged in the fuselage literally with slide rule precision lest the craft's flying qualities be adversely affected. Nor could the cargo be shifted readily when the aircraft was in flight for the same reason. Therefore, the C-46 and the four-engined C-54 were most useful on the Hump, while the stable, sturdy, and dependable C-47 was excellently adapted to dropping supplies from low altitudes.[56]

The reasons for the increases in Hump tonnage from 1943 to 1945 point toward better and more aircraft, a much-improved system of maintenance (PLM), and an increase in personnel due, in large part, to the prioritization by both President Roosevelt and Prime Minister Churchill of China as a major theater of operations against the Japanese on the Asian mainland. Indeed, after the Trident conference of 12–25 May 1943, held in Washington, D.C., both leaders agreed that while major ground operations in Burma were to remain limited in nature, priority would be given to an increase in supplies going to Chiang Kai-shek's Nationalist forces. This in turn meant that emphasis was given to the diversion of more airpower in the form of transports to the ATC. Part of this increase in aircraft allotment was the arrival of the B-24, the C-54, and C-109 in India to the ATC's growing fleet of C-46s and venerable C-47s. As Silva noted, by the time he arrived at his second base of Kumitola near Tezgaon, there were some "192 four-engine airplanes" at these two bases.[57] Silva recalled that when he arrived in the theater, the effort seemed to go to support Chennault and that the routes flown were normally east and north instead of south and east. Despite this increase in the numbers and types of transports as well as the direction of the re-supply effort, the only major obstacles that remained were the tenuous, oftentimes acrimonious relations with the natives of China and India (see Chart #3).

Relations with the Natives in China and India

Silva recalled that the American air crews had little if any direct contact with the Chinese or Indians. In fact, the only sustained contact with the former was when the planes landed and the Chinese crews unloaded the fuel or cargo carried by the transports. Corporal Silva stated that he and his crew did not have "a great deal of contact with them [i.e., the Chinese]." Silva added that "the only real contact that I would have had with them was when the airplane landed and the crew left the aircraft and crew chief remained and he worked with the Chinese and unloaded the airplane. You know you cannot say that there was any kind of social activity between us because 99 percent of them didn't speak a single word of English." As for Silva's impressions of China, the corporal bluntly stated that it was "very, very backward. I would imagine that most of the areas we went into other than Shanghai or Kunming they probably hadn't changed for thousands of years. Very, very primitive."[58]

Despite the primitive conditions American soldiers encountered in China, they nonetheless marveled at the "industrious" nature of the average Chinese peasant working at the various U.S. bases. Sergeant H. C. Sterling, who served as a radio operator in CBI, recalled that there was a "resourcefulness" among the Chinese coolies assigned to build the many airfields used by the ATC and other Allied pilots and crews. Sergeant Sterling recalled that at one base:

> There were 15,000 coolies working on the Luliang Army Air Base while building and maintaining the several 12,000 foot runways. They all worked in family groups, each group leaving a small pile of rocks on the corners of a day's work. They would beat aimlessly on the rocks all day long, with chips flying into their eyes until many were rendered totally blind, but this did not seem to worry them nor did any other minor injury, such as losing a leg. Several times the U.S. Army engineers made the mistake of appointing Chinese foremen to supervise this aimless horde, which was a great error, since these workers look upon a foreman as a spy and feel that they are not to be trusted to do their work alone. The Chinese are very strict about this code, and would die rather than take orders from anyone. He must do things his own way or not at all. He can best be shown a hundred times just how to accomplish a task and will do it your way that one time to please you, but will always, repeat always, smile warmly and do it his own way on the next move.... To do anything another man's way under orders makes a Chinaman lose much face and when he loses his face, his livelihood is gone too, since he never will be trusted again and must leave his local community for keeps and start life anew somewhere else.[59]

Relations with the Natives in Assam and Bengal

As in China, relations with the natives in India bordered on the curious though they were marked by the same mistrust and suspicions as they were with the Chinese. Unlike their British allies, who had controlled India since the 18th century through the Raj or local princes, American pilots and ground crewmen knew very little about the peoples or lands of the sub-continent. With air bases located in Assam and Bengal, the American airmen, enlisted crews and support personnel collectively viewed India as backward with towns that had little in the way of sanitation. Indeed, most of the towns where U.S. airmen were stationed during the war were disease-infested. As above-mentioned, Indian women, many of whom worked in the wool or small cottage industries that characterized Indian village life, worked according to their own schedules and practices. With many Indian males serving in the ranks of the British or Commonwealth armies throughout the Middle East, Italy, and in Burma, Indian women constituted a sizable portion of the labor force. On the other hand, much of the work, insofar as railway, port, airfields, and highway construction, remained in the hands of the Royal Engineers and native organizations such as the Central Public Works Department or some other civilian governmental organization. In fact, "whether civilian or military organizations controlled a particular project, the work was usually done by Indian contractors employing their own labor gangs."[60] There was a reluctance as well on the part of the British Governor-General, General Sir Archibald Wavell, to mobilize the entire Indian population. With Indian troops fighting on the different fronts the "Government of India had to realize that there was a point beyond which the patient farmer (or woman worker for that matter) could not be overworked."[61]

The influx of American and British engineers and build up of the country's infra-structure nonetheless was bound to change the average Indian who lived within proximity of an American base. Indian women and children operated laundries on American air bases and worked in the Hindustan Civil Air Plant while bashaboys or houseboys cleaned the barracks, washed clothes and did other odd jobs for the Americans for a couple of rupees. Silva stated that in his four-man tent the Americans all chipped in some fifteen rupees a month each "or something like that" for their bashaboy, a young man about fifteen years old named Sabu Chandra-di. Silva added that "this young fella used to relish in the fact that he knew more about our government than we did. He could name off everybody from the president right down the line through all of the secretaries. He was smart as a whip."[62] Other Indian work gangs worked on the docks or on the flight lines unloading and loading transports for the next day's operations. It is important to note that the war in CBI came as an economic boom for many segments of Indian society. Indeed, in a country where the annual income was approximately 60 rupees ($20 U.S.), there was concern among British officials that the influx of capital would result in inflationary tendencies in the Indian economy, and thus sought to cut back military production in favor of the production of civilian goods. Indeed, one could say with a good deal of accuracy that much of the opposition to the use of native labor in Assam or Bengal came not from local Indian leaders but from the British themselves who feared that inflation might rise in wake of the war's economic impact on a particular region or province. Nevertheless, the Indian native proved to be hardworking and very reliable as the tempo of operations increased into 1944-45.

The Endless War in China-Burma-India: 1944-1945

In addition to the increased tonnage in supplies going over the Hump, the ATC's transports began, in late 1944 into early 1945, to carry Chinese troops into both Burma and China from bases in neighboring India, where thousands of them had been in training in preparation for offensive operations against the Japanese. Starting in late March 1945, the Japanese, in one of their largest offensives of the war, launched the *Ichi Go* offensive, aimed at the bases of the Fourteenth and XX Air Forces in Chengtu, Kweilin, and Liuchow as well as others throughout East China. The overall Japanese objective was to "destroy the backbone of the Chinese Army and possibly cause the collapse of Chiang Kai-shek's government, as well as annihilate all Chinese (and Allied) resistance and thereby knock China out of the war once and for all."[63]

In order to meet this enemy offensive, and either defeat or at least slow the advance of the Japanese Army, Chiang Kai-shek ordered all Chinese forces in Burma and India airlifted into China. From 1 April to mid-May 1944, the ATC diverted a significant number of transports flying supplies over the Hump to lend assistance and ferry in Chinese troops to meet this emergency. Between 1 April and 11 May 1944, ATC pilots, in Operation Rooster, flew over 1,648 sorties in order to transport 25,136 Chinese troops, 2,178 horses, and 1,565 tons of supplies into China in order for them to blunt the Japanese offensive.[64] In fact, "Without the assistance of the ATC, the Chinese defense of east China would have collapsed far more quickly and enabled the Japanese to open the Yangtze drive before preparations for its defenses were complete."[65] Silva said, "We [his squadron] always picked up the Chinese troops in China, and flew them to where they were most needed." During Operation Grubworm in the spring of 1945, ATC pilots flew in the entire Chinese 14th and 22nd Divisions (some 25,096 troops) from bases in Burma into China to meet the renewed Japanese effort against the numerous Allied airfields. Silva stated that the vast majority of flights that he and his squadron participated in headed east or north, normally from some midpoint between Kurmitola and Shanghai, as well as many smaller bases in China. First Lieutenant Don Downie, a Hump pilot who flew out of Chabua, India, recounted that on most return trips from China, "We would draw a load of forty or more Chinese troops headed for either training in [Ramgarh] India or combat in Burma."[66]

Despite the best efforts of the pilots and crews of the ATC's India-China Division (all Air Transport Command wings were raised to division status on 1 July 1944), the Japanese Ichi Go offensive nonetheless placed a severe strain on the transport command's ability to support the Fourteenth Air Force, Chiang Kai-shek's needs, and the British and Commonwealth forces in Burma. In fact, it might be noted that at one point during the Japanese offensive, the Joint Chiefs of Staff reportedly considered ending all assistance to China due to the mismanagement of the re-supply efforts as well as the acrimonious relationship between Stilwell and Chennault that had existed since the former's arrival in theater in February 1942. In the end, however, General George C. Marshall as well as the other service chiefs "decided that such a course of action would greatly strengthen the Japanese will to fight."[67] In the end, after briefly considering making Stilwell overall theater command over Chennault, President Roosevelt finally agreed to relieve the former and instead appoint Major General Albert Wedemeyer as China theater commander in the fall of 1944.

"The Men in the Greasy Coveralls"

With the start of the Japanese Ichi Go offensive, as well as the desire to increase the bombing of Formosa and the Japanese home islands in the summer and fall of 1944, "the pressure for more lift increased as consumption of supplies in China reached a new high." To meet this increased demand and with the capture of Rangoon by Lieutenant General William J. Slim's Fourteenth Army in May 1945, General George Stratemeyer, who had been appointed theater air commander in Burma after the Trident Conference in May 1943, "assigned to the airlift the tactical units of his air force whose primary mission had been completed (keeping the British supplied)." General Stratemeyer not only reinforced the ATC with more transports but also re-assigned the 7th and 308th Bomb Groups, the 443rd Troop Carrier group, the 3rd and 4th Combat Cargo Groups, as well as the 12th Airdrome Squadron to the Hump airlift. Stratemeyer also reorganized the ground crews into more efficient teams and pushed for adoption of PLM throughout CBI. The Burma theater air commander likewise called for better air traffic control, loading, and reporting procedures in order to cut down on accidents and over-loaded planes.

The efforts by General Stratemeyer had a positive effect upon airlift operations which saw an overall increase in the amount of tonnage going over the Himalayas. In fact, from the start of the airlift in the spring of 1942 to war's end on 1 September 1945, Hump pilots had managed to lift some 650,000 tons of supplies to Chiang Kai-shek's Nationalist forces (in China and Burma). Under the leadership of Major General William Tunner, Hump pilots and crews also had facilitated Slim's advance down the Irrawaddy and aided in the re-capture of Rangoon in the spring of 1945. With the introduction of Stratemeyer's reforms and the tireless work of the thousands of pilots, crewmen, mechanics, and loaders, "the Hump reached its peak in the summer of 1945," and enabled the Allies to tie down some one million Japanese troops on the Asian mainland.[68]

Of course, the unsung heroes of this massive accomplishment in CBI were not just the pilots and crews. Included in this group were, as Corporal V. Fair, himself a mechanic on the flight line in CBI, wrote, the men in the greasy coveralls, who held in their blister-ravaged hands wrenches and looked skyward each day as the planes flew in and out with greased-stained faces and, "dreamt of no reward or gain ... didn't come here [in CBI] to make headlines ... [but only] came here to make 'em fly."[69]

The End of the War in China-Burma-India

When asked about the period right before V-J Day on 1 September 1945, Silva stated that emphasis of his squadron was to shuttle as many Chinese troops into China as was possible. In fact, Silva added that besides the airlift of Nationalist troops into China (mostly near Shanghai), other squadrons also shared this responsibility of disarming and processing the thousands of Japanese troops that now became prisoners of war on the Asian mainland. As Silva and his fellow aviators transported Chinese troops into China, the war that had been on hold since 1937 broke out again, this time between Chiang Kai-shek's Nationalist troops and the communists led by Mao Zedong. "Stuck in the middle of this fight," Silva said:

> When we were going into places, I want to say Kunming, but I'm not sure, but that they [the Nationalist troops and Communist troops] were fighting, they were shooting at each across the runway even as we flew into there. There was a civil war going on, whether it was from major factions or whether it was local warlords, I don't know, if you will, but the idea that everybody had was that Communists Chinese versus the Nationalist Chinese that were fighting each other.[70]

When asked if at any time the pilots felt themselves in danger during the war, and especially as the Chinese civil war erupted upon Japan's surrender, Silva stated, "We were always aware of it, weary of it, but we were never bothered by it. There was, in fact, a lot of strange things that happened over there."[71] One of these, Silva stated, were the thousands of Chinese pounding big rocks into little rocks and then crushing them with a huge roller to flatten and press them into the ground to make a runway.

Another sight Silva recalled was when the plane was about to land and how the Chinese, working on the airfield would "separate and as the plane passed them by, would come back together and continue working." Silva noted that occasionally, as the Chinese resumed work on the runway, one of them would run across the path of the plane in order to "chase spirits or dragons away" that haunted them with the belief that the plane's propellers would "chase these demons away. Tragically," Silva said, "many Chinese, most of them women, would be killed by the spinning propeller."

What China lacked in technology she made up her vast pool of manpower. This could be seen on a day-to-day basis, whether flying over the construction of the Burma-Ledo Road or in the construction of the numerous airfields throughout China as vast gangs of Chinese peasants pulled huge stone rollers over a sea of gravel created by this seemingly unlimited pool of manpower. Corporal Silva stated that these rollers were normally 20 feet in diameter, "huge things" pulled by hundreds of Chinese with ropes. Silva added that there would be women as well as men among the people pulling these rollers.

Silva stated that one of the severest problems encountered in China was pilferage. The corporal said that one of most enduring memories of China was the poverty that he and his fellow Americans saw on a day-to-day basis. Indeed, this poverty in turn encouraged pilferage. In fact, Silva stated that many of the brass fuel fittings of his aircraft were often taken by the Indians or Chinese who in turn made things out of them in order to sell and make a little money to feed their families. Silva emphasized that one of the most memorable aspects of his service in both China and India was the extreme poverty and density of the population, much of it crowded into the major cities of Karachi, Dakka, and Shanghai. Corporal Silva added that he could not believe the mass of humanity that could live in such a congested area and under such unsanitary conditions.

The Chinese Soldier

As for the Chinese soldiers that Silva and his fellow crew members came across, the Massachusetts native noted that "that they were poorly armed and clothed, in uniforms that looked as though they were quilted and baggy." Silva added that all of the Chinese soldiers either wore a steel British-style helmet or a baseball cap with a very narrow bill adorned with a Nationalist symbol superimposed in the center of the cap. As for their gear, they normally wore all of their equipment or carried it with them. Silva noted that one of the squads of Chinese soldiers he saw "carried more gear than they should have been carrying or had." Silva added that "this in turn caused the airplane to be at times overloaded as we packed them into the plane like sardines. Once aboard, they would sit on the floor and they would occupy almost every square inch of the floor of the airplane." Silva added that the Chinese soldiers "were usually very dirty, and the smell was overpowering!" Silva stated that the American crews would take "'bug bombs' with their caps off and throw them in the back of the plane in order to kill the lice, etc., in order to diminish the smell in the air." Silva reiterated the fact that many Chinese soldiers never made it into China for upon landing in Shanghai, the manifest would occasionally be short one or two Chinese soldiers who had been thrown or shoved out of the airplane during the flight. "Furthermore," Silva stated, "we never went back into the cabin when the plane took off." Silva said that as a precautionary measure in case, for instance, the Chinese became mutinous, the crew and pilots wore their .45 caliber pistols in the plane and, in fact, everywhere they went. Silva added that "you wore that .45 constantly, day and night. It was never further than an arms-reach away."

The End of the War: September–December 1945

For Silva and his crew, it seemed as if the war would drag on into 1946 as flight operations continued across China. As experienced by U.S. Marines, soldiers, sailors, and airmen throughout the major Pacific theaters, Silva stated that the Japanese in Burma were no different, and were, in fact, more determined than ever to fight to the end in China. He said that the Japanese, despite the fact that defeat was now on their doorsteps, "refused even to consider surrender" in China. When asked if he ever noticed that the hard fighting was in fact, coming to an end, Silva said, "If anything, as the months progressed, the activity [in CBI] kept increasing. Only after V-J Day, in September or October 1945, did things seem like they were slowing down." After thirteen months of continuous operations in CBI, and after having accumulated sufficient points in theater to go home, Corporal Anthony Silva received orders on 15 December 1945 to begin the long journey home. After flying into West Palm Beach to turn his airplane over to inspectors, he and his crew enjoyed a lavish meal that Silva said was excellent. After enjoying his meal and short stay in Florida, he and his crew boarded a flight home bound for Westover Air Force Base in Massachusetts on 19 December 1945, and as he noted, "we were ready to go home."

China-Burma-India: The Forgotten Theater

When asked, "Why has the war in China-Burma-India been forgotten by historians?" Silva bluntly stated that "CBI was, in fact, forgotten even during World War II. I think that this was the main reason. You know, there was little if any publicity given the war in CBI, as most of the publicity here in the United States, as I understand it, was given to the European theater of operations ... and a bit to [Field Marshal Erwin] Rommel in North Africa and that sort of thing, but relatively little on activities in India or China." Silva added that for himself and his fellow soldiers who served in CBI the real question was, "'What was going on over there [i.e., in Europe]?' There was very little publicity of what went on in CBI."

Silva attested the reason for this general lack of knowledge of the events in CBI was the fact that at times it seemed like it was "Confusion-Beyond-Imagination," as there "was so much going on in CBI, I am sure there must have been some coordination though at times it didn't seem like anyone had control of anything." Silva illustrated this fact with the comment that at Tezgaon or Kunming, "there would be planes flying in from a mission and planes taking off, fuel tankers landing ... a tremendous amount of activity, and it didn't seem organized!" Silva stated that when he returned home most people didn't seem to care about China-Burma-India or the fact that he had served there as the war was now over. This lack of knowledge of the fighting in CBI affected Silva as well before he entered service in 1943. Indeed, it was only when Silva and his unit were flying over Africa did it dawn on him that there was, indeed, fighting going on halfway around the world in China.

After the war, with his service as an crewman aboard a C-109 well behind him, Anthony Silva went to work as a superintendent for an aircraft maintenance and training facility prior to re-entering government service as a member of the Federal Aviation Administration (FAA) as an aviation safety inspector. After retirement from the FAA, Silva remained active with that agency, working part-time as a designated air worthiness representative. He and his wife, Marie, currently live in Spring Hill, Florida, and to this day he remains very proud of having served in the China-Burma-India theater during World War II. Near his home in nearby Weekewachee, Florida, Silva and other former CBI veterans meet regularly to reminisce over their experiences in America's "forgotten front," and specifically remember the sacrifices they and their comrades made while "feeding the tiger."

Chapter 8

"Road Builders and Jungle Warriors": African American Soldiers and the War in China-Burma-India & the Southwest Pacific Area of Operations, 1941–1945

Though trained as infantrymen during the interwar period (1919–41), African Americans served primarily as heavy laborers and in quartermaster units during World War II under enlisted and junior officers who were predominantly black and senior officers who were predominantly white. This in turn led to the creation of segregated units, a trend that carried on into the post–World War II Army. This condition also served as the antecedent for today's problem in minority advancement in the U.S. Army.[1] In fact, the problems associated with African Americans in the combat arms began as a result of the Army's policies during World War I, when over 380,000 African American soldiers served in France, 42,000 of them in combat units.[2] Unfortunately, due to the decisions on the part of both General John J. Pershing, commanding general of the American Expeditionary Forces (AEF), and the Army High Command, the two African American combat divisions (92nd and 93rd) saw combat duty while attached to the French Army and not with the AEF.

While historians remain divided over the combat performance of both the 92nd and 93rd divisions, it is very clear that the majority of white company and field grade officers during World War I, many of whom became "the Army's senior commanders of World War II," shaped their opinions, which was by and large negative, of the performance of black soldiers from their contacts with all-black units while in France.[3] These and other opinions on the performance on African American soldiers heavily influenced Army planners during the interwar era and carried well into the fourth year of the U.S.'s involvement in the Second World War as the United States engaged in a multi-front war in the Pacific, European, and Mediterranean theaters of operations.

It is a fact that African American troops eventually saw front-line service as infantrymen during the last months of the war in Northwestern Europe (December 1944 through 7 May 1945), and in the Italian theater of operations during the same period. These two theaters were not, however, the first real test of combat for African American soldiers. The black combat experience began in both the Southwest Pacific Area (SWPA), and in the jungles of Burma (1942–1945). Here, black troops participated in major and minor combat operations against the Japanese Army as well as laborers building the Ledo-Burma Road. The fact remains that due to the concentration of large Japanese forces and too few Allied troops blacks inevitably saw greater frequencies of combat in these two Pacific theaters than did their contemporaries in the Mediterranean (MTO) or European theaters of operation (ETO) during World War II.

The critical role played by African American troops, as both infantrymen and road builders in the SWPA and CBI theaters during World War II, is important given the influence that the war had on post–World War II trends in the 1950s and 1960s.[4] As occurred toward the end of World War I, Army leaders during the same period in World War II (1944–1945) used the performance of African Americans in that conflict as a gauge to best measure the utilization of blacks in integrated combat units. Even more important, however, is the impact World War II had on the decision to utilize blacks in combat support (CS) and combat service support units (CSS) in the postwar era, and how these decisions affected the current demographics of the U.S. Army insofar as the number of blacks in the combat arms. In short, one can conclude that World War II had, in effect, a direct impact on the decision by many black soldiers to select both combat support and combat service support units as their units of choice to serve in. One can say with a fair degree of accuracy that the black historical experience in the nation's wars during the 20th Century has been the predeterminant factor on why black males to this day select combat support and combat service support units instead of combat arms. Indeed, it is important to note the link SWPA and CBI had in the legacy of the service performed by African Americans during World War II. For it was in both theaters that African Americans played an important if not crucial role in both combat and combat service support as they participated in the refinement of aerial re-supply and jungle warfare.

African Americans and the War Department, 1919–1941

Before any discussion can take place concerning the role played by African Americans in the Pacific theater of operations and more specifically the China-

Burma-India theater during World War II it is necessary to understand the War Department's policies concerning the use of Negro troops in combat as abovementioned. The War Department's policies of using African American troops in a combat service support role had its inception in the post–World War I debate over the role of Negro soldiers in the Army, and more specifically in a combat role. It could be said with some truth that the interwar policies (and debate) over the value of African American soldiers left its mark on the Army for the next thirty years as the senior leadership debated the lessons of the World War and the value of the Negro soldier in combat.[5]

This debate was briefly resolved with the issuance of Plan 1922 which in part stated, "Military realities and not 'social, ethnological and psychological' theories must be the deciding factors in determining the use of Negro manpower." Army planners conceded that although Negros were citizens, entitled to all the rights of citizenship, and were an "appreciable part of our military manhood," the realities of the time were such that the arguments of lower aptitudes and intelligence, as well as inherent prejudices of the time, assured that when war came, African Americans would be excluded from combat units for all the same reasons (or excuses) used during World War I. Furthermore, as the Army (and during World War II the Marine Corps) assigned increasing numbers of African Americans to a combat service support role, it became increasingly clear that the Army's manpower policies were based more on past, erroneous perceptions rather than battlefield realities.[6]

As for the use of Negro soldiers in service units, the 1922 plan called for the exclusion of African American troops from general service units based on their educational background and lack of technical skills. As early as 1921, in fact, the chief of engineers voiced strong opposition to the allocation of Negroes to general service units. In commenting on the Negro's lack of technical skills, the Army's chief engineer pointed out that these units "required officers and men with considerable technical skill and that their duties 'compel these troops to be exposed to the same conditions of fire and all the severe circumstances of front line fighting ... without the opportunity to relieve the nerve strain by returning the fire of the enemy.'"[7] He went on to recommend that all engineer units, except auxiliary (separate) battalions, be white or, "if troops of other colors, that the personnel be specially selected." In response to the chief of engineers' memorandum on the use of Negroes in combat engineer units the War Department replied that it had no plans to "restrict the use of Negroes to any particular types of organization in any branch of the service" insofar as corps area assignment to the Organized Reserves was concerned. The War Department did not, however, discard the Chief of Engineers' suggestions and, instead, filed them for further consideration in the event of large scale mobilization.

By 1928, plans formulated by the War Department called for the assignment of Negroes in the Regular Army to inactive Regular Army ammunition trains, engineer auxiliary battalions, and quartermaster units. For a decade, the decisions concerning Negro troops and their mobilization during a national emergency virtually disappeared until 1938. Indeed, by the eve of World War II, the Army had "no comprehensive plan for the employment of Negro troops in time of war in existence."[8]

This exclusionary policy remained in effect until 1937, when the War Department examined its wartime mobilization and manpower plans. A new plan, later adopted in 1937 and labeled the 1937 Plan, called for Negro manpower to be maintained at a ratio approximately in proportion to the total manpower available, that is, from 9 to 10 percent, with the ratio of combat troops to service troops to be the same as that of white troops.[9] Thus, of the 5.81 percent of African Americans in the Army's Protective Mobilization Plan (PMP), the largest numbers were assigned to the Infantry, Engineers, and Quartermaster Corps.

As a result of the War Department's 1937 and subsequent 1940 plans, the chiefs of the arms and branches who opposed the assignment of African Americans to their respective branches were able to effectively block both the integration of combat units and the assignment of all–Negro units to the combat arms. By December 1941, armed with the stereotypes and myths that blacks were "docile, tractable, and good natured," the War Department had effectively if not purposely created a system whereby blacks were assigned more often to combat support and combat service support units.[10]

In fact, in the months before the war began, War Department officials concluded that Negroes would fill segregated units. Furthermore, the Army Plan of 1940 stated that all–Negro units "did not need to be employed separately." The authors of this plan believed that Negro units should be kept small and used in attachments or assignments to larger white units. A less widely held view was that these same Negro units could be used as part of white divisions only if they were to operate successfully on the battlefield.

In any event, when war came on 7 December 1941, the War Department set about to convert many existing African American combat units from combat arms (infantry, armor, and artillery) to combat support and combat service support units as part of a larger manpower policy. Despite the intense political pressure and lobbying efforts by leading Negro and white politicians (including the first lady — Mrs. Eleanor Roosevelt), as well as black civic groups such as the NAACP, the War Department proceeded to convert many former all-black infantry and artillery units into combat service support troops (quartermaster, transportation, engineers, etc.).

Road Builders and Jungle Warriors: The Building of the Burma–Ledo Road, 1942–1945

With the decision to build a road capable of linking up with the old Burma Road having been made by the Combined Chiefs of Staff in the summer of

1942, the United States Army began shipping vast quantities of equipment to India in order to prepare for the arrival of the first American engineer units that would execute the construction of the Burma Road. Among the first two units to be engaged in construction of this vital road were the 45th Engineers General Service Regiment (Combat) and the 823rd Engineer Aviation Battalion, both of which were Negro units that had already been in Assam building airfields as well as working on other projects. Both the 45th Engineers and 823rd Aviation Engineers could justifiably boast that they were the first American engineer units in the China-Burma India theater of operations. These two American engineer units shortly thereafter joined a bridging and several pioneer units of the British Army working on the road. In addition to the British pioneer troops and American engineers were some 8,000 local laborers.[11] Actual construction of the Ledo Road officially began on 15 December 1942.

The first section of the road to be built ran approximately 103 miles from Ledo through the Patkai Mountains to Shingbwiyang. The road was to be built through territory that had yet to be surveyed though it had been used by refugees fleeing into India during the retreat from Burma. Among the obstacles faced by the engineers were the five mountain ranges of the Patkais, steep gorges, hairpin curves, swollen streams, and landslides that oftentimes sent tons of rocks, dirt, and mud onto the freshly bulldozed roads. Finally, the dense jungle that surrounded the engineers on both sides of the road blanketed the entire area. This dense jungle canopy likewise provided an excellent cover for the Japanese troops who waited in ambush for the approaching American columns. The engineers had to stop work and virtually hack a path with machetes out of the jungle in order to expand and widen the road and certain points. To their credit, the soldiers of the 45th and 823rd Engineers made steady progress as they hauled some 100,000 cubic feet of earth away, clearing a path for the graders, rollers, and rock crushers to lay the road bed. The engineers, using equipment that had previously been sent to India via Lend-Lease, and within three months of having taken over construction of the road from the British, made considerable progress. Indeed, by 1 January 1943, the road had progressed five miles. Toward the end of February, the engineers had made their way to the Mile 43.3 marker.[12] Unfortunately, this was where the work came to an abrupt halt as they came to the India-Burmese border. One of the main reasons for this sudden halt in construction was that the engineers had outrun their supply lines. More importantly as they reached the border with Burma the engineers came ever closer to the front lines. This in turn contributed to the numerous enemy sightings that forced the engineers to take both defensive and sometimes offensive measures that included active patrolling in order to prevent a Japanese surprise attack from annihilating the undefended engineers working on the Ledo Road. Despite the ever-present threat from the jungle-wise Japanese troops, the engineers labored day after day, through the monsoon and the oppressive heat and humidity, driving bulldozers and graders, felling trees, building numerous pontoon bridges, and blasting away huge boulders. In the meantime, other African American units arrived in theater to assist in the work of the 45th and 823rd Engineers. By the late fall 1942, soldiers belonging to the 60th Ordnance Company, a unit composed of black enlisted personnel and white officers organized in Burma, began to rush ammunition to the forward troops (both American and Chinese), while members of several laundry and salvage units repaired disabled or broken machinery.

First Combat Operations in Burma: 1 April 1943

Even as the engineers of the 45th Regiment labored on the first sections of the Burma Road, they likewise engaged in some of the first major combat actions with the Japanese by an American ground unit. Armed with reports of enemy activity near their lines, the soldiers attached to the 45th Combat Engineers fanned out along the road in search of the enemy troops that had been reported in their sector. While the engineers played cat and mouse with several elusive enemy snipers, there was no large body of Japanese troops to be found. As a precautionary measure, however, Colonel John Arrowsmith, the commanding officer of the 45th Regiment, ordered patrols at all times to be carried out in order to forestall any enemy attack. These patrols, however, met no resistance. When the sightings of enemy troops diminished, the regiment's intelligence officers assumed that the Japanese had been dissuaded from attacking such a large formation and had melted back into the Burmese jungle.

"Kickers and Packers": Aerial Re-Supply in SWPA and CBI, 1943–1945

As portions of the Ledo-Burma Road began to connect with each other, African American quartermaster and transportation companies convoyed supplies forward as the construction workers labored on. Meanwhile, members of the all-black 518th Quartermaster Battalion arrived in theater at Dinjan and Sookerating. The battalion, split into two locations, performed valuable service in preparing the supplies air-dropped to locations throughout Burma and taken into China by the famed Hump pilots of the Assam-Burma-China Ferry Command or the soon-to-be renamed Air Transport Command (July 1942) (see Map #12). Indeed, members of the two detachments that belonged to the 518th Quartermaster Battalion rode the C-47s and C-46s and pushed or, more correctly, kicked the supplies out of the cargo doors to the troops below.

As both the SWPA and CBI operated under almost identical conditions, a brief comparison of the two theaters is worthwhile to illustrate their common features. These features included troops fighting over terrain that ranged from rugged mountains and mountain trails to the dense, disease-infested, fetid jungles to swampy morasses. Oftentimes, and at the end of precarious sup-

Map 12. Aerial Re-supply in Burma: The Aerial Sector, 1943–1945 (detail from map in Miller, *Airlift Doctrine*, p. 140).

ply lines, the soldiers in both SWPA and CBI came to depend on aerial re-supply in order to maintain the momentum of attack or, in the case of the engineers in India and Burma, to speed the construction of the Ledo Road into Burma. With the loss of Burma to the Japanese in May of 1942 and the subsequent sev-

An African American soldier sits atop and guides an elephant pressed into service by the combat engineers to haul heavy logs and beams into place on the Ledo Road. Elephants proved extremely useful in the dense Burmese jungle (Alexander McVean Collection).

ering of the supply lifeline into China via the old Burma Road, Allied leaders decided, prior to the commitment to the aerial resupply of China via the Hump, that the main priority would be the construction of a road (i.e., the Ledo Road), leading into China after northern Burma had been recaptured from the Japanese. In fact, until the recapture of Myitkyina in August 1944, "Allied strategy became one of opening a new land route from India to China across northern Burma in addition to defeating the Japanese in Burma."[13] Experiments in aerial resupply in SWPA were later refined in CBI and played an important part in the Allied victory there.

Necessity was the mother of invention in both SWPA and CBI. After the expulsion of British, Indian, and Chinese forces from Burma, and with it the severing of the Burma Road, the Allied leaders in CBI embarked upon a strategy to re-supply their over-extended forces both from the air and over land via a road cut out of the jungle. With the failure of the first Allied offensive to retake the port of Akyab in December 1942, due in large part to the Allies' inability to supply its spearhead, Allied commanders sought a solution that would take into consideration the lack of suitable airfields and Burma's hostile terrain.

Indeed, in CBI as in many of General Douglas MacArthur's operations in SWPA, "air supply was the 'chief and often only means of supplying Allied ground forces in action against the enemy.'"[14] As a result of the reorganization of the theater that broke CBI into British and American spheres of responsibility and the creation of the Southeast Asia Command under Admiral Lord Louis Mountbatten, the U.S. Tenth Air Force assumed administrative command of the 443rd Troop Carrier Command's (TCC) four squadrons until May

1944, when the TCC came under the command of the commanding general, Third Tactical Air Force. Under both re-organizations, the TCC "became the air transport force for the Combat Cargo Task Force that flew in support of the U.S. combat engineers working on the Ledo Road and Merrill's Marauders, as well as Lieutenant General William Slim's Fourteenth Army." The TCC likewise flew missions in support of Brigadier Orde Wingate's Long Range Penetration Group or Chindits. In their effort to find a solution to the vexing problem of supplying Allied forces in the field Allied planners looked to the solution used by General MacArthur's forces in SWPA. This was later acknowledged in the official history of aerial re-supply during the Burma campaign:

> Information concerning the use of transport aircraft for supply of American and Australian troops in Papua filtered into Allied headquarters in Southeast Asia, however, and when combined with the earlier experience in Burma, this information did make an impression. As a result there was a growing desire to see what could be accomplished in Burma by using air transport to supply ground troops operating against the enemy in the jungle.[15]

Indeed, it is a fact that aerial re-supply operations based on the experiences on New Guinea were replicated in CBI. In a postwar history of the Services of Supply in CBI this latter fact was confirmed:

> Based on information received from other theaters, principally the Southwest Pacific where troops under conditions comparable to those in the Ledo area had been successfully supplied by air dropping, it was authoritatively decided to adopt the aerial re-supply method. On 4 March 1943 arrangements commenced for experimental dropping of food and supplies to troops in the forward area.[16]

The first units assigned to kicking duty were the 60th Laundry Company and the 3477th Ordnance Company, "who both packed and kicked out the baskets and parachute bundles." Both consisted entirely of African American soldiers. The first mission on which the 60th Laundry and 3477th Ordnance companies employed air dropping occurred on 6 March 1943 using C-47 Dakotas of the Air Transport Command flying out of Chabua. So successful was the mission that Allied leaders decided to create a permanent dropping unit. With personnel from the 3841st Quartermaster Truck Regiment as the packers and kickers and the 3304th Quartermaster Truck Company as the receiving unit, the ATC was able to divert "four aircraft per day from the 'Hump' route until June 1943 when the 2d Troop Carrier Squadron of the Tenth Air Force picked up the mission, increasing available aircraft from 4 to 10."[17]

The kickers and packers of the 518th Quartermaster Battalion (Mobile) rapidly became legendary in their ability to sustain forces in isolated areas of Burma during Slim's offensive. An example of the efficacy of aerial re-supply came during Brigadier Charles Orde Wingate's first Chindit mission when aircraft from the Royal Air Force dropped some 303 tons of food and supplies to the British and Gurkha forces on the ground.[18] When Chinese troops launched their long-awaited offensive in the Hukawng Valley in November 1943, the kickers and packers of the ATC supplied nineteen Chinese and two Indian divisions as well as several American units by air.

Until its de-activation in December 1944, the officers and men of the 518th Quartermaster Battalion, all of whom had less than ten days of instruction on how to pack, load, and kick supplies, rolled up an impressive record. Indeed, the 518th even experimented with various loads such as delivering the first 75-mm pack howitzer air-dropped into Burma. Other items air dropped included: (1) oil and gasoline stored in 55-gallon drums; (2) delicate medical supplies including generators and bulky operating tables; (3) blood plasma; (4) and foodstuffs including ducks and fresh eggs.[19] All personnel were trained in all phases of air dropping so that if a person or skill were to be lost, it could be quickly duplicated on the spot. The 518th trained members of other organizations including members of the Royal Air Force's 177 Wing, 194 Squadron. Members of the 518th were "proud that it used only its own personnel, other than local labor, for less technical work, and that it never allowed the planes of the air cargo squadron to remain idle while waiting for packaged supplies."[20]

As the official history from the Royal Air Force's 177 Wing recounted, the success of Lieutenant General Slim's forces during the Arakan campaign was due to the combined air and ground operations that repulsed a major Japanese thrust aimed at the Eastern border of India. In a subsequent operation, C-47s and C-46s belonging to the Royal Air Force maintained a 'round-the-clock aerial re-supply effort that supplied three British divisions (5, 7, and 26), preventing them from being cut off. It was truly a "combined operation":

> The requirements of an Army in action, and their packing for air-supply, were the responsibility of the R.A.F., though volunteer Kickers out of the Army were welcomed, and did a fine job. The Dakota's maximum useful load was 7500 lbs (3¾ short tons), adjustable in relation to the fuel required for the flight. Loads with parachutes were ideally dropped from 600'–700'. Sometimes the nature of the terrain prevented aircraft going so low. "Free" dropping—of items which were not unduly affected by impact—was usually from about 100'. Quite frequently parachutes failed to open. When this happened and the load was ammunition, the result could seem quite unfriendly.[21]

The intensity of the fighting can be seen in the fact that the transports of the 177 Wing, 194 Squadron were forced to fly 2 sorties per plane in a period of less than twenty-four hours. In fact, in sorties that took nearly 4½ to 5 hours to complete, pilots of the 177 Wing managed to drop in one period in February 1944 some 3,995 tons of supplies in flight operations that occurred mostly at night in order to avoid Japanese fighters and anti-aircraft guns. Indeed, the intensity of the battle and the subsequent aerial resupply effort can be seen in the fact that starting on 10 February at 3:45 P.M., and in operations that lasted until 8:45 the next morning, on 11 February 1945, aircraft from the wing flew 36 sorties.[22] It could be said that the techniques and procedures perfected by the 518th Quartermaster Battalion (Mobile) changed the course of the war in Burma in favor of the Allies.

During General Stilwell's offensive to re-take northern Burma and especially the strategic airfield at Myitkyina, the kickers of the 518th and other units were able to drop a total of some 7,309 tons of supplies to the attacking ground forces. In fact, the efficiency of the airlift can be seen in the fact that Brigadier General Frank Merrill's long-range penetration force, known as Merrill's Marauders, received 15 tons per day that was mostly air-dropped at pre-arranged locations. In fact, according to Ray Lewallen, who served as a flight engineer with the 3rd Combat Cargo Squadron, 1st Group, and who spent the majority of his time as kick master stationed at Myitkyina, most of the freight air-dropped to Merrill's Marauders, and the Chinese and British armies, took place at about 500 feet and in all kinds of weather including the monsoon.[23]

By the time Merrill's Marauders had taken Myitkyina, some 20 percent of the tonnage going to his and Stilwell's Chinese forces had been airlifted to designated airfields or drop zones while a further 42 percent were dropped or kicked, and 38 percent parachuted into Allied lines.[24] The tempo and dangers of the airlift can be seen in the fact over 100 transports crashed or were reported as missing due to enemy fighter activities, crashes, and other mishaps.[25] A postwar synopsis of air supply operations over Burma likewise recorded that over 50 percent of the kickers and personnel involved in aerial resupply were African American soldiers. This was an impressive record, given the racial segregation policies that hampered the full integration of black troops in the U.S. Armed Forces.[26]

Members of the 518th meanwhile likewise served as forward aerial liaison troops in order to assist members of the 3304th Truck Company in receiving its supplies via aerial re-supply. In one of the major Chinese offensives of the war in CBI, members of the 3304th trucked supplies into the Hukawng Valley until it too was relieved by other units when the ATC shifted the re-supply effort to air delivery via C-46s. Meanwhile, the 518th continued to perform its vital forward-area spotting duties admirably and in time became known as one of the premier air-dropping units in the CBI theater. As above-mentioned, the 518th also served as a training outfit for other air cargo units, teaching its members how to pack, load, and kick supplies from a moving aircraft.[27]

After the monsoon season of 1944 (May–October), construction on the Ledo portion of the Burma Road continued. With the addition of other all-Negro units, including the 1327th Engineer General Service Regiment and 352nd Engineer Regiment, both of which had been assigned to U.S. forces in Persia (Iran) building airfields and roads for the supply routes heading north toward the Soviet Union, the main emphasis for all U.S. engineer units after 1944 in CBI was the completion of the Burma Road.

With the completion of the Burma Road in February 1945 linking Ledo, Assam, with Kunming, China, and other major supply routes running through northern Burma, the task now became one of convoys and convoy security. For this task, the Army assigned 58 truck companies under three groups and eleven battalions to the Motor Transport Service. Of these, 52 of them were manned entirely by African American soldiers. The three group and nine battalion headquarters were also composed of Negroes. In short, African American soldiers comprised a large percentage of the engineer general service, maintenance, dump truck, pontoon, engineer aviation,[28] and combat engineers maintaining the Stilwell Road.[29]

Discipline and Morale Among the African American Soldiers in CBI

The army that the African American soldiers entered was, unfortunately, a segregated one. Therefore, it was inevitable that the discriminatory practices faced by Negroes in the United States soon found their way to all of the major wartime theaters where African Americans served, including CBI. Unlike the other theaters where morale among the African American troops was quite low, the isolation of the CBI theater and the lack of amenities for both black and white soldiers kept racial incidents to a minimum. In fact, the relationship between black and white soldiers in CBI remained amicable. Corporal Alexander McVean, a combat engineer who served in CBI and helped in building the Ledo and Burma Roads stated that there was very little trouble between the white and black soldiers. If anything, in fact, white troops were for the most part praiseworthy of the abilities of and service performed by African American troops in CBI. Technical Sergeant Kenneth Quigley, who served in an ordnance company in Burma, stated that the African American troops he came across were "outstanding fellas ... who did a fantastic job in carving out those mountains and widening those narrow curves."[30]

Both Quigley and McVean stated that the black troops they observed while in India and later in Burma came into their areas right after they arrived themselves. Corporal McVean added that he and his fellow soldiers had the responsibility to clear the area of any Japanese before the African American units arrived. McVean recalled that he and his fellow combat engineers would oftentimes remain in an area if resistance was heavy and protect the flanks of the rear echelon units in order that they could carry out their mission.[31] While there were some problems between white and black soldiers, the majority of the problems experienced by African American troops were the same ones experienced by white troops: service in a faraway and oftentimes isolated post with little or few amenities. Despite these and other problems, the relationship between white and black soldiers remained amicable. In fact, "morale among the Negro units on the road was judged to be higher than that of whites." It is also a fact that unlike the majority of American troops, black soldiers who served in CBI saw the completion of the Stilwell Road as a major accomplishment. The 858th Engineer Aviation Battalion, for instance, discovered that most of "its troops were proud of the fact that of all the Engineer Battalions in the IBT [India-Burma Theater], the 858th Engineer Aviation Battalion had been given the honor of going to China."[32] It might be added that it was not lost among the men of the 858th that they had broken new ground, insofar as its acceptance as a major American unit.

The only problems that occurred regarding the presence of so many African American soldiers were in India and China, where the native Indians (and Chinese) were exposed to American racial policies that had reminded them of their own caste system. The second problem occurred in China where Generalissimo Chiang Kai-shek voiced strong objections to the presence of Negro troops in China. The Nationalist Chinese leader went so far as to ask General Stilwell that "Negro units not be used east of Kunming ... unless the tactical situation demanded it." While both Stilwell and his successor, General Albert Wedemeyer, at first adhered to the generalissimo's request, both men later ignored the order due to the shortage of drivers and pressing needs of the Fourteenth and Twentieth Air Forces.[33]

The outstanding performance of the 858th typified the majority of African American units throughout CBI and the other Pacific theaters. In fact, throughout CBI and elsewhere in the Pacific, African American combat support and combat service support units demonstrated remarkable efficiency when trained and led properly. One could, in fact, say that "their work in the difficult projects assigned to them in India and Burma, when all of their problems of training and background are considered, was a tribute to the ... adaptability and speed with which officers and men could learn both manual and leadership skills, when need was greater than original skill or outlook."[34]

Jungle Fighters: A Reassessment

The proud record of achievement of the 858th Engineer Aviation Battalion and other combat service support units demonstrated that if trained and led properly, African American troops could and would fight. Unfortunately, the mixed performance of the 93rd Division (African American) on Bougainville in combat against the Japanese led, after the war, to one of the most bitter postwar historical debates on the abilities of the African American soldier in combat. One might add that this was a debate that was not resolved until the Vietnam War cast aside any doubts as to the abilities of the black soldier in combat.

Among the first African American units to see major combat in World War II was the 24th Infantry Regiment, which saw action on the island of Efate, New Hebrides, as part of Task Force 9156 (4 May to October 1942), as a mobile striking force until re-assigned as service troops. While individual battalions of the 24th Infantry conducted patrols on Guadalcanal and later on the Green Islands, north of Bougainville, and engaged small enemy formations in what were little more than skirmishes, the effectiveness of black troops in combat remained a topic of concern at General Douglas MacArthur's headquarters in the Southwest Pacific Area (SWPA), and in Washington, D.C. In fact, the War Department had already made preparations to send the 93rd Division, composed entirely of African Americans, to MacArthur's theater. In an "Eyes Only" message to Lieutenant General Millard P. Harmon, Army chief of staff General George C. Marshall advised him that only when the 93rd was deemed fully prepared for combat would it be sent to the Pacific theater of operations and more importantly, to General MacArthur's command in SWPA.

Even as the 93rd Division crossed the Pacific Ocean, it became the subject of an intense debate as to its future performance in combat. In fact, even before elements of the 93rd Division first saw combat during the Bougainville campaign, in the Northern Solomons, the 1st Battalion, 24th Infantry and the 25th Regimental Combat Team experienced its first major combat on the island. From all accounts, Major General Oscar Griswold, the commanding officer of the XIX Corps, into whose sector these untried combat units were given their baptism of fire, appeared quite pleased with the initial performance of the African American troops. In fact, in commenting on the combat performance of the 1st Battalion, 24th Infantry and 25th Regimental Combat Team, General Griswold informed General Harmon that from all accounts, both units were "as good as any division that had not seen action."[35]

In subsequent actions, units and soldiers from the 1st Battalion, 24th Infantry and 2nd Battalion, 25th Infantry performed very well under fire. Indeed, Private Wade Fogg of Company F, 2nd Battalion, 25th Infantry won the regiment's first Bronze Star when he silenced three Japanese pillboxes and killed 20 enemy troops.[36] Unlike in World War I, when commanders fed black units into combat without first properly training them or commanders who led African American units or had them assigned to their command in the Pacific, both Major General Griswold and Brigadier General Robert Beightler, the commanding officer of the 37th Infantry Division, had not made the mistake of throwing untried combat troops into the most dangerous areas of the front. Both officers instead eased these African American soldiers into combat by sending them into action with more experienced units. On Bougainville, in fact, General Griswold insisted on sending each battalion of the 25th Infantry attached to individual infantry regiments of the American Division into action. Thus, the latter events involving Company K of the 3rd Battalion, 25th Infantry, long held as an indictment of the poor performance of African American soldiers under fire, appear to be more of an aberration than a definitive accounting of the abilities of the Negro soldier under fire.

Company K and a Breakdown of Discipline: April 1944

In order to prevent an enemy counterattack, Company K, led by Captain James Curran, a white company commander, was given the order to establish a blocking position. Along with its four black platoon leaders, Company K set out from its base in the pre-dawn hours of 6 April 1944 to a point located near an abandoned Japanese hospital. When the 1st and 3rd platoons came under fire, the men responded by the book and reportedly killed two Japanese soldiers. It was then, however, that the tactical situation broke down as a panic set in and the men began to fire their weapons into the dense jungle and at each other. In short, fire discipline and junior leadership broke down even as Captain Curran and his non-commissioned officers attempted to restore fire discipline and order. Informed of the situation, battalion headquarters ordered Company K to fall back and re-organize.[37]

A subsequent battalion investigation concluded that the men of Company K panicked, due in large part, it was later reported, to their poor leadership and lack of jungle training. As the investigation further illustrated, many of the problems encountered by Company K pointed to the Army's pre-war decisions on manning, officering and training Negro troops. General Griswold's investigation of Company K's performance specifically concluded:

1. The unit had had little jungle training; consequently, as individuals or as a unit, they were not prepared to handle adequately problems encountered in jungle operations. Most individuals showed willingness to learn from white troops, however, their ability to learn and to retain what has been taught is generally inferior to that of white troops.
2. In general, morale of all soldiers was high. However, units as a whole seemed to be unduly affected by reports and difficulties encountered by other elements of the command. Morale of the officers, especially white, seems rather low. Much of this attitude can be traced to the lack of responsibility demonstrated by their junior colored officers and non-commissioned officers.
3. In general, discipline seems satisfactory, however, there is a tendency on the part of junior colored officers to make the minimum effort to carry out instructions. This tendency exists among the enlisted men when they receive instructions from these junior officers. As a rule colored officers do not have control of the enlisted men, On the other hand, those units having a large proportion of white officers appear to be better controlled, trained, and disciplined.
4. Initiative is generally lacking especially among platoon commanders and lower grades.
5. Field sanitation is generally inadequate.
6. To date, the 25th Infantry, though supposedly better trained than the 1st Bn., 24th Infantry has not progressively improved to the extent of the latter unit.[38]

In short, the performance of both the 1st Battalion, 24th Infantry and 25th Infantry convinced many in Washington, D.C., most notably Secretary of War Henry L. Stimson, that only with white officers could black soldiers be used effectively in combat, and even this without further training. Undersecretary of War John J. McCloy, however, differed with the opinion of Secretary Stimson by adding that the experiences of Company K were an "exception" and should not be used to judge all black combat soldiers.[39]

It must be added that the experiences of the 93rd Cavalry Reconnaissance

Troop, which remained on Bougainville, was much different than that of the 93rd Division, as that unit performed excellent yeoman service throughout the remainder of 1944 until it too was relieved and sent elsewhere in February 1945. Perhaps the best defense of Company K's actions on Bougainville came from its regimental commander, who later wrote that "had this organization been given prior instruction and been accompanied by an experienced platoon of the 164th Infantry in its initial action, the results would have been far different."[40] Many of the problems of indiscipline and poor fire discipline encountered by African American as well as white units in general, in fact, stemmed from the lack of proper training. Indeed, the poor black performance can be tied directly to an indifferent War Department that negated the experience of African American combat troops during World War I. The results of this policy or lack thereof led to the type of disasters encountered by units such as Company K in SWPA, CBI, and elsewhere during World War II. One last problem that led to Company K's poor battlefield performance was the Army's ill-conceived pre-war policies of placing poorly trained white (and in a few cases black) officers, many of whom did not want to be there in the first place, with inexperienced or poorly-trained troops. Inevitably, this policy likewise contributed to the types of fiascoes encountered by Company K and other units on Bougainville and elsewhere.

"The First In, the Last Out": A Summary

One must be careful to cite the War Department's failure to adequately prepare black soldiers for combat once war began. Indeed, much of the blame for Company K's failures can be directly traced to the policies adopted during the interwar era, when conscious decisions were made concerning the manning, training, and leading of these all-black units. For it was during the interwar era that the War Department established its guidelines in the use of African Americans in combat. While African Americans received high praise for their work in combat service support units, particularly in the CBI and European theater of operations, they have been unfairly judged on their overall performance in combat. As the records illustrated, African Americans who served in units such as the 1/24th Infantry Battalion and 25th Infantry Regimental Combat Team performed admirably when led and trained properly.

During World War II, blacks eagerly sought to prove that they were willing to stand beside their white countrymen and fight as combat soldiers. As events unfolded, however, the Army's leadership denied African American soldiers this opportunity. Instead, they were placed in segregated combat service support units. Unlike the situation that occurred during the Vietnam War thirty-three years later, "where a disproportionate number of Black soldiers served in infantry units, and suffered a higher percentage of casualties than their white counterparts," African American soldiers during World War II were denied the right to fight, and instead used as heavy labor or stevedore troops.[41]

It was not until the Vietnam War (1965–1973) that black soldiers proved beyond a doubt that they were just as efficient in combat as they were in combat service support units. When properly trained and led by competent officers, blacks as well as whites performed well in combat. As the experiences of Company K suggested, if a unit is not well trained or led, order and fire discipline can rapidly break down as they did on Bougainville in April 1945.

As for the service of black troops in CBI, it was to their credit that their performance was well appreciated. The hard work and dedication of the African American soldiers who worked on the Ledo and Burma Roads, as well as the members of the various ordnance, maintenance, supply, and support companies who accompanied the combat troops in Burma and into China at war's end, demonstrated that blacks were very capable in carrying out the tasks assigned to them throughout the course of the war in CBI. This was well demonstrated by members of the 518th Aviation Battalion who pioneered the use of kickers and packers while serving in CBI. Used extensively by both the Americans and British in CBI and elsewhere, the 518th Aviation Battalion's work contributed largely to the victory in CBI in September 1945, as well as to the method of aerial resupply used in Burma during World War II as well as the Korean War (1950–53), and later in Vietnam (1965–1973).

It was no small tribute that the first Army engineer unit sent to China to work on the Stilwell Road was the 858th Engineer Battalion, "which moved in May 1945 to maintain the road from the Salween River to Kunming. This unit, the only Negro Battalion sent to China, remained there until V-J as one of two battalions then working on the China end of the road. In units, with the white 71st Light Pontoon Company attached for maintenance between the Salween and the China border, they eventually worked nearly five hundred miles east of Kunming."[42] In a large sense, African Americans were the first ones in, and the last ones out to serve in the CBI theater during the entire war. Their impressive record of service was matched only by their skill in how they operated the machinery that built the Burma Road, and the fortitude they displayed in the face of a segregated Army in the field.

Chapter 9

"The Forgotten Theater of World War II": Reflections of Service in China-Burma-India, 1941–1945

Undoubtedly, the China-Burma-India Theater was one of the greatest logistical efforts ever undertaken by the U.S. Army. Besides the primary mission of supplying Chiang Kai-shek's beleaguered Nationalist forces, the men (and women) who served in CBI during World War II maintained a supply line that began in the United States and ended in Kunming, China, a distance of some 16,000 miles. With bases in India, Burma, and China, the U.S. Army and U.S. Army Air Forces likewise maintained a logistical and maintenance infrastructure that would not be duplicated until the commencement of the U.S. efforts during the Vietnam War in 1965.

Responsible for maintaining this tenuous supply line were the men of the Air Transport Command, Quartermaster Corps, Ordnance Corps, Chemical Warfare Services, and the combat engineers who built the Ledo-Burma Road. For the Americans who served in CBI, the war became one of long distances over hostile terrain, among peoples of different races and cultures, and one fought over terrain that was as forbidding as was the climate that it was fought in. Yet they endured for nearly three years with little rest, few amenities, and with little if any acknowledgment from the American people back home. They were, in fact, the forgotten soldiers and airmen of a theater by-passed and oftentimes brushed aside as irrelevant and unimportant in the overall grand strategy of the war effort against Japan. What follows are the war experiences of these intrepid warriors in the forgotten theater of World War II in their own words as they fought and flew, built and cursed in a savage land inhabited by a determined adversary.

"Flying the Hump": The Air Effort in China-Burma-India, 1941–1945

Colonel C. V. Glines, U.S. Air Force, recalled that "flying the Hump" from bases in India to Kunming, China, was a dangerous affair. Indeed, as Colonel Glines noted, the air routes used by American pilots were "considered ... [to be] ... the most dangerous ever assigned to air transport." Colonel Glines' account provides an excellent synopsis of why and how the Army Air Forces set out not only to re-supply Major General Claire Chennault's Flying Tigers but also to maintain a steady, uninterrupted flow of supplies to Chiang Kai-shek's Nationalist Forces from early spring 1942 to October 1945:

"Flying the Hump"

In mid–December 1941, in the wake of Japan's massive land, sea and air offensive in the Far East and its attack on Pearl Harbor, the Allies had no doubts about the need to support China fully to keep it in the war. China's forces would tie down Japan on the mainland. In any event, General Claire Chennault's China Air Task Force, the "Flying Tigers," had to be supplied.

Suddenly, in March 1942, supplying China became immeasurably harder. Japanese forces cut the Burma Road — the only overland path to China — and all land supply ceased. The Allies came back with a response unprecedented in scope and magnitude: They began to muster planes and pilots to fly over the world's highest mountain range. The route over the Himalayas from India to Yunnanyi, Kunming, and other locations in China was immediately dubbed the "Hump" by those who flew it.

Though relatively short, the route is considered the most dangerous ever assigned to air transport. The reason is apparent from this description contained in the official Air Force History. "The distance from Dinjan to Kunming is some 500 miles. The Brahmaputra Valley floor lies ninety feet above sea level at Chabua, a spot near Dinjan where the principal American valley base was constructed. From this level, the mountain wall surrounding the valley rises quickly to 10,000 feet and higher.

[The Air Force History continues ...] "Flying eastward out of the valley, a pilot first topped Patkai Range, then passed over the upper Chindwin River Valley, bounded on the east by a 14,000' ridge, the Kunmon Mountains. He then crossed a series of 14,000–16,000 foot ridges separated by the valleys of the West Irrawaddy, East Irrawaddy, Salween, and Mekong Rivers. The main "Hump" which gave its name to the whole awesome mountainous mass and to the air route which crossed it, was the Santsung Range, often 15,000 feet high, between the Salween and Mekong Rivers."

Pilots had to struggle to get their heavily laden planes to safe altitudes, there was always extreme turbulence, thunderstorms, and icing. On the ground, there was the heat and humidity and a monsoon season, that, during a six-month period, poured 200 inches of rain on the bases in India and Burma.

If the U.S. was to conquer such obstacles, it would have to build an organization to ensure the smooth flow of planes, people, and supplies. The seeds of such an organization already existed. On May 29, 1941 ... the U.S. Army had created the Air Corps Ferrying Command. Out of this small organization grew the

U.S. Army Air Transport Command, under the command of Major General Harold L. George.

"It seems almost incredible," General William H. Tunner remarked in his memoirs, "that up until three o'clock in the afternoon of May 29, 1941, there was no organization of any kind in American military aviation to provide for either delivery of planes or air transport of material."

When the Japanese closed the Burma Road, the U.S. devised an initial plan that called for sending 5,000 tons of supplies each month over the Hump into China as soon as possible. American C-47s delivered the first, small load of supplies in July 1942. It was a meager beginning. If the resupply effort was to be greatly expanded, airfields would have to be built, pilots would have to be trained, and transports would have to be manufactured and ferried to the China-Burma-India (CBI) theater.

The air transport task in the CBI fell first to Major General Lewis H. Brereton, commander of the Tenth Air Force. The Ferrying Command was to deliver seventy-five C-47s to the CBI, but some were diverted to support British forces in North Africa. Of the 62 that finally reached the theater, about 15 were destroyed or lost, and many of the rest were out of service for long periods due to a shortage of parts and engines.

It was obvious that the theater air commander should not be responsible for a supply route reaching from factories in the U.S. to destinations in China. On October 21, 1942, Air Transport Command (ATC) officially took over the task.

Operations under ATC began in India on December 1 [1942]. The original small air transport unit was established as ATC's India-China Wing. As air transport activity increased, it became the India-China Division, comprising several wings. "Every drop of fuel, every weapon, and every round of ammunition, and 100 percent of such diverse supplies as carbon paper and C rations, every such item used by American forces in China was flown in by airlift," General Tunner said later.

Tonnage flown across the Hump increased slowly. Thirteen bases were established in India and six in China. Curtiss C-46s gradually replaced the Douglas C-47s and C-53s. Consolidated C-87s, the cargo version of the B-24, and some war-weary B-24s were added. In December 1942, 800 net tons were delivered to China. In July 1943, 3,000 tons were delivered. The target was 5,000 tons per month., but General Chiang Kai-shek, the Chinese [Nationalist] leader, wanted more.

"Safer to Bomb Germany"— Increases in tonnage came at a great cost. In the last six months of 1943, there were 155 accidents and 168 fatalities. General Tunner commented in his memoirs, perhaps somewhat facetiously, "It was safer to take a bomber deep into Germany than to fly a transport plane over the Rockpile [i.e., the Himalayas] from one friendly nation to another."

Aircrews were in short supply. Those on hand were flying more than 100 hours per month. Pilots, most of whom had never before flown a twin-engine aircraft, were quickly recruited from among basic flying training school instructors in the Air Training Command. They were sent to bases at Assam, Karachi, and later Gaya, India, for checkout in the C-46. Accidents mounted. Spare parts soon were in short supply. Maintenance personnel were inexperienced and worked under severe handicaps. Colonel Edward H. Alexander, commander of the India-China Wing, reported, "Except on rainy days, maintenance work cannot be accomplished because shade temperatures of from 100 to 130 degrees Fahrenheit render all metal exposed to the sun so hot that it cannot be touched by the human hand without causing second-degree burns."

In November 1943, the ATC Ferrying Division opened the "Fireball" run from Florida to India. C-87s and, later, C-54s were put to work flying high priority parts from the Air Service Command depot at Patterson Field, Ohio, to India. The aircraft were based at Miami, and crews were stationed at key points along the routes to Brazil, Central Africa, and India.

Emergency shipments from the States could arrive in CBI in as little as 4½ days after order placement. In the organization of the complex Hump operation, a key player was Brigadier General Cyrus R. Smith, president of American Airlines, who served as crew chief to General George. General Smith acted as a troubleshooter. In the fall of 1943, after the operation suffered many accidents, he visited the theater to report on conditions.

"We are paying for it in men and airplanes," General Smith reported. "The kids here are flying over their head — at night and in daytime — and they bust [the aircraft] up for reasons that sometimes seem silly. They are not silly, however, for we are asking boys to do what would be most difficult for men to accomplish; with the experience level here, we are not going to pay dearly for the tonnage moved across the Hump ... With the men available, there is nothing else to do."

One of the unforeseen requirements was for the establishment of a search-and-rescue organization. Many crews, forced to bail out or crash-land, struggled for weeks, despite injuries, burns and disease, to find safety. Terrain was so rugged that survivors would spend an entire day traveling one or two miles.

In the beginning weeks, when a plane was down, the first available transport crew went in the first available aircraft to conduct the search. This quickly proved unsatisfactory At Chabua, Captain John L. "Blackie" Porter, a former stunt pilot, started "Blackie's Gang," with two C-47s. His gang carried Bren .30 caliber machine guns. The co-pilot carried one on his lap, while the other was kept in the cargo area. They sometimes carried Thompson machine guns and hand grenades. In 1943, virtually every rescue of crew members was due primarily to the efforts of "Blackie's Gang."

"The Search for Eric Sevareid" — One of the first of Blackie's rescue missions was a search for the twenty members and passengers, including CBS correspondent Eric Sevareid, who had bailed out of a C-46 in the Naga hill country of northern Burma. The area was populated not only by Japanese, but also by headhunters. The men were found, and supplies were dropped. Lt. Col. Don Flickinger, the wing flight surgeon, and two medics parachuted to assist the survivors. A ground party walked in and took them to safety.... After many such successes, the US created a special search-and-rescue organization with Captain Porter as its commander. He was lost in action in December 1943 while on a search mission.

Soon, however, more was requested, and more was delivered. Brigadier General Earl S. Hoag, in charge of the India-China Wing at the beginning of the year, predicted that his men would deliver 77,000 tons during the last six months of 1944. His estimate was too conservative; more than twice that much was delivered. The rapid rise stemmed from a sharp increase in the number of aircraft and men, assigned to back up decisions made by President Roosevelt, British Prime Minister Winston Churchill, and the Combined UK–US) Chiefs of Staff at a June 1944 strategy meeting.

General Tunner took command of ICD-ATC in August 1944. A 1928 West Point graduate and strict disciplinarian, he made many changes in the interest of efficiency. One significant innovation was the introduction of production line maintenance function, the brainchild of Lt. Col. Bruce White, a former executive with Standard Oil of New Jersey in China. Planes brought in for maintenance would pass thru 3–10 stations as if on a factory production line. At each station, a plane would go through different maintenance functions. A rigorous inspection completed the procedure. If approved, each aircraft would be test-flown before being sent back to the line. The concept became standard practice throughout the Army Air Forces on bases with large numbers of a single type aircraft.

When General Tunner arrived, pilots rotated out after 650 hours of flying time. Many pilots were flying as much as 165 hours a month in order to pile up the time and go home quickly. General Tunner's flight surgeon reported that fully half of the men were suffering from operational fatigue. Several accidents stemmed directly from such fatigue. General Tunner immediately increased the number of flying hours to 750. "It didn't make the pilots happy," the General wrote later, "but it kept quite a few of them alive."

"The Accident Rate Declines"— He appointed Robert D. "Red" Forman as chief pilot, and, as training improved, the accident rate began to decline. When General Tunner took over the India-China Division, 4-engine C-54s were being introduced. They could carry three times the load of the C-47s and would eventually replace them and the C-46s. As the Air Force history states, the operations [in CBI] brought airlift into "the age of big business."

General Tunner felt his hard-nosed management approach would result in improved efficiency and performance. "I had been sent to this command to direct American soldiers, and while I was their commander, by God, they were going to live like Americans and be proud they were Americans." General Tunner inaugurated malaria-prevention spraying operations, using stripped-down B-25 "Skeeter Beeters." According to Tunner, this, combined with the use of repellents and mosquito nets, drove down the incidence of disease.

In 1944, General Tunner changed the route of the C-54 flights, creating a more direct flight to China. This placed the transports over 150 miles of Japanese-held territory and within range of Japanese fighters. To defend his aircraft, he requested and received fighter protection. "Enemy action was of little consequence" afterward, he reported.

"Search and Rescue"— Another area that needed improvement, as far as General Tunner was concerned, was the search-and-rescue capability, which he called "a cowboy operation." He appointed Major Donald C. Pricer, a Hump pilot, as commander of the unit and assigned to the job four B-25s, a C-47, and an L-5, all painted yellow. One of the first tasks was to pinpoint all known aircraft wrecks in the theater, the better to eliminate "duplication of work, for, after all, aluminum was scattered the length and breadth of the route." It was during this period, moreover, that the helicopter was introduced into the theater and began to prove its potential as a rescue vehicle.

"Jungle Survival School"— General Tunner ordered each base to establish a jungle indoctrination camp, with mandatory attendance for all new arrivals in the theater. Newcomers had to spend time in the jungle under supervision of trained guides. The general encouraged introduction of competition into the operation and challenged each unit to beat its own records and those of other units. He authorized the publication of a newspaper, with prominent display given to tonnages carried over the Hump by individual units. He also encouraged the creation of press releases. One told of training elephants to load drums of gasoline quickly aboard aircraft. The photo that accompanied this story reached hundreds of newspapers.

The success of the Hump operation under the ATC became apparent from statistics released on August 1, 1945. On that day, the command had flown 1,118 round trips, with a payload of 5,327 tons. A plane crossed the Hump every minute and twelve seconds; a ton of material was landed in China four times every minute. All of this was accomplished without a single accident. When the war was over, Air Force historians added up the figures. The peak month was July 1945, when 71,000 tons of cargo were carried. Some 650,000 tons of gasoline, munitions, other material, and men had been flown over the Hump during the airlift, more than half of the tonnage delivered in the first nine months of 1945.

Besides helping to defeat Japan, the Hump operation was the proving ground for mass strategic airlift. The official Air Force history comments: "Here, the AAF demonstrated conclusively that a vast quantity of cargo could be delivered by air, even under the most unfavorable circumstances, if only the men who controlled the aircraft, the terminals, and the needed material were willing to pay the price in money and men."[1]

Not all flights were accident-free. John F. Jones, who flew the Hump air route during World War II, recalled the procedure if, in fact, the crew had to bail out of the aircraft in one of the many transports used by the U.S. Army Air Forces in China-Burma-India.

"SOP for Bailing Out or Crash Landing — Before or At Landing"

1. Ascertain position of the aircraft to facilitate speedy orientation with the ground.
2. Check for Escape Packets, pistol belts, etc.
3. In the event of a bailout, transfer all items of food and equipment to pockets.
4. For crash landing, transfer items of food and equipment to pockets, taking in addition whatever food is available from aircraft, plus Tommy gun, helmet, etc., that can be conveniently carried.
5. Finally, destroy all secret equipment, documents and the aircraft. ABOVE ALL, KEEP YOUR HEAD — demoralization has killed more crews than has the emergency itself.

"Walkout Procedure"

1. As quickly as possible, head for the hills, dense jungle or elephant grass. In enemy territory, do not waste time looking for other crew members — in all probability you will meet them in the normal course of events.
2. Avoid rain trails, railways, road clearings, creek beds, villages and natives other than Kachins.
3. If you have crash landed, by all means travel together for mutual protection and assistance. The first few hours are the most critical, so move quickly.
4. Bivouac — Make camp in dense jungle or elephant grass, away from trails, streams or villages. Build a low shelter, and remain in hiding for 24–36 hours, depending on time of landing. Build no fires, make no unnecessary noise, and do not move about unnecessarily. During daylight hours, orient yourself on your map and plan your route of evasion consistent with terrain, district, and previous instruction. If enemy searching parties pass nearby,

freeze — it is only remotely possible that they will see you. Avoid panic, and remain in hiding. However, if you are actually discovered, take off, but fast — do not attempt to shoot it out, as repercussions may be in order if you are captured.

5. EXTRA HINTS — In traveling, avoid leaving a trail. Make no unnecessary noise. By all means, follow a regular schedule of hiking, and resting (50 minutes and 10 minutes in rolling country, 20 minutes and 10 minutes in mountainous country). Travel should cease not later than 1700 hours and building of shelters accomplished in remaining daylight.

"Clothing and Equipment"

1. Cap — In bailing out, a peaked flying cap should be tucked into a pocket or inside coveralls to insure its possession on the ground. If you crash land, take your helmet, it will be invaluable to you in protecting you against the sun, head injuries in dense jungle, also in cooking, washing, collecting rainwater, and as a fairly comfortable pillow.
2. Sox — Wool sox should be worn, and two extra pairs carried in a pocket. Sox should be washed and changed daily. Proper care of feet is imperative.
3. Shoes — G.I. shoes are a must. The high topped combat boots are better still, if available, as they permit the tucking in of trousers to keep out leeches, ticks, gravel, etc. Two extra pairs of shoes laces should be carried in a pocket. They will be invaluable in building shelters, tying equipment to pistol belt; also, lacking leggings, or high-topped boots, trousers may be tucked inside sox secured by shoe laces, to keep out leeches, ticks, gravel, etc.
4. Weapon — .45 automatic in a holster and ammunition clips should be worn at all times in aircraft to insure their possession on the ground. If you crash land take tommy gun with ammunition for self-defense and killing game.
5. Pistol Belt — Necessary for carrying other vital equipment.
6. Canteen — On pistol belt, including canteen cup which you will need for cooking.
7. Compass.
8. Pocket knife in pocket, preferably the G.I. or Boy Scout type.
9. Lighter — In pocket, the larger the better, will supply fire for 2 to 3 weeks.
10. Money-belt or escape pouch should be carried at all times while in aircraft to insure its possession on ground. Intelligence Officer has briefed you on its contents and how to use them.
11. Dog-Tags and AGO Cards — to identify you as a soldier or officer of the U.S. Army in the event of capture.
12. Jungle pack — On parachute; Pack contains:
    - Ground to Air Code
    - Survival Book
    - 6 Chocolate Bars
    - Red Flare
    - 20 Rounds .45 ammunition
    - 1 pair leather gloves
    - First Aid kit — Type B-4 (Frying pan insert)
    - Matches — Water Proof bottle
    - Oil Stone
    - Fish hooks and line
    - Compass
    - Jungle Knife
    - Head net (mosquito)

The only purpose for your taking your weapon and ammunition, pistol belt and canteen, compass and jungle survival kit, and money belt on a flight is to save your life on the ground. Otherwise, in the confusion of leaving the aircraft in a forced landing, you will most likely leave this vital equipment behind. Carelessness will mean disaster for you on the ground.² [Appendix 1]

During the Second World War, the Army Air Forces called upon the nation's growing airline industry to supply it with experienced pilots and aircraft to transport troops and material over vast distances. Among the airlines that responded to the call for aviators and aircraft was American Airlines. In 1991, the United States Air Force, the successor to the Army Air Forces (USAAF), recognized the massive contribution made by American Airlines and the pilots who braved the weather, terrain, and enemy fighters to assist in the resupply of China. For the surviving pilots and the relatives of those now deceased, the Air Force awarded to the pilots and crews of Project 7-A, who flew the C-87 transports. Flight Officer Tom Barnard, an employee of American Airlines who flew C-87s out of Tezpur during the war, along with Captain Bill James, accepted the medals for the pilots and crews who could neither be there or were deceased. The experience these pilots and crewmen brought with them to CBI cannot be underestimated as the addition of the American Airline crews greatly "accelerated operations over the India-China route," and made possible "the doubling [of the] ... number of transports in service in the India-China division, by greater efficiency in maintenance and repair, loading and unloading of cargo to reduce the length of time planes spent on the ground and by an increase in the number of airfields in the area. The accrued benefits of pilot-training programs also were noticeable."³ A trained communicator, Tom Barnard brought his skills to CBI and assisted in the extension of the communications and weather detecting systems in a theater that had virtually neither until the massive commitment of pilots, crews, airplanes, and support personnel in mid-1943. Within a year, C-46s, flown by Army Air Force personnel, many of them trained pilots and crews, averaged two round trips per day into Burma and China.⁴ Below is Flight Officer Barnard's account of a special unit, Project 7-A, put together by the U.S. Army Air Forces to fly supplies to Chiang Kai-shek's Nationalist Forces, Major General Claire Lee Chennault's Fourteenth Air Force, and the combat engineers building the Ledo-Burma Road. Mobilized in July of 1942, the pilots and crewmen of the airline industry contributed greatly to the victory over Japan in CBI through the thorough application of their skills as pilots, radiomen, and mechanics.

"AMERICAN AIRLINES, THE 'HUMP' AND PROJECT 7-A"

On a sweltering Sunday afternoon last July, when everyone in the company felt he had had about all the excitement he could bear for one season, a telephone call came through from the ATC⁵ in Washington which touched off what will probably go down in American Airlines history as our greatest war assignment. We were asked to establish a base in India to fly supplies into China over the

Burma Road of the Air, those 28,000' high Himalayas termed the "Hump" is an excess of under-statement by those who have flown it.

Within 24 hours Project 7-A was under way. Plans had been formulated for moving planes, men, and equipment to India, and Ted Lewis started south with a bale of secret instructions from all departments. At 4 A.M., on the 6th day after the phone call, Ted was in Natal. By noon he and Walt Hughen had opened their secret orders, held a meeting of all station personnel and decided who should go on and who should stay. By night the first plane was en route to India with Walt Hughen in charge.

Tired, rain-soaked and half sick, the first crews arrived at the India base early in August, ten days after the first call was received. The monsoon season was at its height. The heat was intolerable. The camp was a mudhole, and the airport was little better. Goats and Brahman cows were still in possession of the barracks. In spite of all this, our first plane went over the "Hump" the following day with a load of ammunition for beleaguered China. It took a couple of weeks before the full complement of C-87s assigned to the project had arrived, but it took just one day for every plane to get into action once it was there, thanks to the heroic work of the maintenance men under Vic d'Ailoia. On the first two Hump trips an Army co-pilot accompanied our crew for the purpose of checking the territory. After the third trip, our complete 5-man crews manned the planes, and within a few weeks' time we were returning the compliment by teaching newly-arrived Army flight crews and ground crews how to manage the C-87s and keep them flying.

Those were trying days. Even after the boys got the cows and goats driven out of the barracks, they swear they never knew when they might wake up to find one staring them in the face. Runways were flooded, and lighted at first only by gasoline flares. Later, when the rains stopped, the animals chose the runways as their favorite grazing grounds, and often a jeep went clattering down to clear them out of the way before a plane could take off. Flight crews had to learn to fly the Hump on instruments with no navigational facilities available. The weather made it impossible for them even to see the terrain below them; and maintenance men had to keep the planes on schedule with no spare parts other than those which our planes had taken over, no shelter from the rains, no lighting facilities for night work, and no workstands. But American Airlines men do not lack ingenuity. Workstands were constructed out of bamboo but the fragile bamboo stands swayed periously in the wind, so empty oil drums were put into use, welded together and footholds cut into the sides so the mechanics could climb up to reach the engines. Even the motor hood of the ground vehicles served as engine stands.

Camp quickly organized into a working unit with Joe Whitford as station manager and Joe Barry as chief dispatcher. Departments organized — mess, quarters, supplies, laundry and recreation — one man made responsible for each.... All the boys on this India project returned with a very realistic approach to the Indian problems. In their own barracks, there were 8 castes of several different religions, and it took more than a dozen natives just to serve breakfast, for some could handle one kind of food — cleaning, serving the food and washing the dishes. Wives please note! And took their turn at flying the Hump.

Walt Hughen returned to this country [i.e., the United States] in September (1943), and Chuck O'Connor succeeded him in command. Ted Lewis went over with two replacement planes in September and stayed until the project was taken over by the Army the first of December (1943)....

With the passing of the rainy season, operations were put on a 24-hour basis, and it seemed as though some of the boys never did get any time to sleep, for our planes were taking off before dawn and returning by moonlight. At the height of our operations, we were averaging almost six round trips per day. During the entire time, we made 1,075 crossings of the Burma Road of the Air and carried almost 5,000,000 pounds of cargo, mostly bombs and gasoline into China. Regardless of the weather, the planes went through. On exactly one day throughout our entire operations in India were all planes grounded because of the weather, though often it was necessary to land at some base in China other than the designated one. Many of the crews never saw the jagged peaks beneath them for a month after they had made their first flight. When the weather improved, enemy air alerts brought new problems, but the boys took those in stride too and flew over the higher mountains on a round-about course which put them out of the reach of the single-motored Zeros. Thanks to our pilots' consummate skill in flying, we lost no planes through enemy action.

On every man's lips when he returned was the story of [Captain] Toby Hunt, beloved captain who went down with his ship after his crew had jumped to safety. Unable to make a landing at all in China because of the weather, Captain Hunt was returning to base to refuel when engine trouble developed over the mountains. They found his body by the wreckage of his plane only 20 miles from base. Had he tried to make those last few miles and save his plane instead of jumping to safety himself? No one will ever know, but we salute a gallant gentleman and a great flier.

This was not Captain Hunt's first rendezvous with death. But they missed by a hair's breadth the first time. Flying on instruments 20,000' over the Hump a few weeks earlier, Captain Hunt found he could not hold altitude because of ice. The load had to be lightened. Back to the cabin went the crew, without oxygen, to release the cargo door. Even after the safety catches had been pulled, the door still jammed. Then big Wes White, navigator, picked up Flight Engineer Taggart, held him chest high so that he could use both legs as battering rams. The door gave way. Still without oxygen, the men wrestled 14 full drums of fuel to the open door and sent them hurtling into the mists below. Both crew and plane were saved. Toby's day had not yet come.

Towards the end of the summer (1943) better weather, better food — brought in from China — better health, a lighted runway with approach lights, a 24-hour standby on radio facilities, installation of radio ranges and an improved flow of spare parts, for which "Monk" Bolling and Jim Lecompte must take a bow, improved operating conditions considerably, but it was never a cinch, as any Burma Roadster will tell you. A "Burma Roadster," by the way, is anyone who has flown the Hump and added a Burma Roadster bill to his short-snorters.

The Army took over operations December 1 (1944), and the last ship we had been operating left India that day for New York. Project 7-A had ended, and the men who carried it out had already been assigned to other jobs. Joe Whitford in his last report to Ted Lewis, written the day it was over, summed up the feeling of the men when he said, "We shall probably forget the records we put on the books and the hours flown and the tonnage moved, but we shall never forget or regret the fact that we stuck it out when the going got really tough. Only those who slopped through the mud and rain of the monsoon, or felt common sorrow in the loss of a fellow worker, or ate corn-willy and hot dogs, or jumped in the outdoor shower, or chased goats and cows out of the compound will understand the common feeling binding all on this project."

This is the story of American Airline's part in the operation in India. It is but a small part of the work which has been going on out there, ever since April

1942. We are proud that we were asked to do it and we think we did a good job. But there isn't a man who doesn't admit that it would have been impossible without the friendly cooperation of the Army, who helped us from the moment we landed, tired and rain soaked last August until our last ship took off in December.[6]

Born in State Center, Iowa, in 1919, Major Glen Norell, USAF (Ret.), enlisted in the Army Air Corps in 1940, and graduated with the rank of staff sergeant pilot in April 1942. Promoted first to flight officer and then to second lieutenant, Lieutenant Norell received orders overseas to China-Burma-India in June of 1943. Assigned to fly C-46s over the Hump for his base in Chabua, India, to Kunming, China, Norell, who retired a major, flew 63 missions. Discharged in 1946, the Air Force later recalled him to active duty during the Korean War, where he served two tours in England prior to his final discharge in 1953. Major Norell provided an interesting account of the time he was forced to bail out of his aircraft over Burma due to mechanical problems.

"Bail-Out Over Burma"

I arrived in the CBI theater of war in June 1943, and was assigned to an ATC base at Chabua, India, to fly C-46s (Commando) over the "Hump." The Hump was the Assam-China air route established after the Burma Road was closed from India to China, over the high Himalaya Mountains of Northern Burma. Aircraft flying this route carried war materials and personnel into China from 1942 through 1945.

My 42nd mission over the Hump was a night flight from Chabua, India, to Kunming, China. Before gaining cruising altitude and the 1st ridge, a mountain range on the western side of Burma, we experienced severe carburetor ice. The flight was in May 1944, during the monsoon, or rainy season, when the inherent weakness of the C-46, carburetor ice, was most prominent. Full carburetor heat and maximum carburetor de-icing fluid injection would not keep the engines running. We had lost one engine and the other one was surging. We were losing altitude and down to 14,000 feet. As Aircraft Commander, I radioed the "MAYDAY" call and gave the command to jump.

I landed in some trees that stopped me about 4 feet from the ground. It was dark, it was raining and it was a bit discouraging, but when it became light I got going down the river to the southeast, which could take you into Japanese territory. I couldn't see chopping my way up the hill, through the jungles. There were several waterfalls, where the vegetation on the sides was rotten and it was treacherous climbing down. You knew if you fell and broke a leg, you would never get out. I drank water from the springs just as it came out of the ground, and did not get anemic dysentery as my co-pilot did. I had adequate rations in my parachute back pack to eat for the short period I was in the jungle, but you were advised to watch the monkeys and eat what they ate, if you had no rations. I did not see many animals in the jungle, and the only problem was the leeches. They would get on your body and you never knew it. They would swell from about ⅛" to ½" in diameter after sucking your blood. I saved my parachute, rip cord and pilot chute, and wrapped myself in the parachute at night to keep away from the leeches.

After about 2 days moving down the river I came to a trail. I went up the trail 100 yards and found a lean-to. It finally quit raining, I had taken all my clothes off to dry them, when two oriental soldiers walked around the corner. They were closer to my .45 pistol than I was, not knowing of they were Japanese or Chinese, I gave them the old "Ding Hao." They turned out to be Chinese, they gave me a "Ding Hao" back and were going to walk right on by me. I got them stopped and tried to get them to go to NW, but they would not, so I followed them SE and that afternoon, we walked into Shingbwiyang, Burma.

I got a hop back to Chabua in a troop carrier C-47. It is a standard policy that if you are involved in an aircraft accident or incident you get right back into the aircraft and fly. Therefore, I was on another Hump flight the next day and again we momentarily lost both engines over Chabua on our return flight. The remainder of my 63 combat missions were accomplished without a major event. I was thankful to return to the States in November 1944 and to see my wife, Mildred, and our son Stanley, who was then 10 months old and I had never seen.[7]

"Flying with the 4th Combat Cargo Group"

Frank Garcia, a radio operator assigned to the 14th Combat Cargo Squadron, 4th Combat Cargo Group recalled his services in China-Burma-India as being one of the most interesting periods of his life:

> Drafted into the Army Air Corps on 13 March 1943, and had basic training in Monterey, CA. Was shipped from basic training to Radio Operator & Mechanic School in Sioux Falls, SD. After graduating was assigned to P-47 Fighters, in Wilmington, NC & [from there] to Pocatello, ID. My main duties with fighters was converting the radio equipment to British V.H.F. sets for shipping and fighter units to England. Was transferred in June '44 to 4th Combat Cargo Group, which was being activated at Syracuse AAB in New York. We trained in C-47s. From there we moved to Bowman Field at Louisville, KY and converted over to Curtiss C-46s. In November of '44 group was deployed to the CBI via South America, Africa, and on to Karachi, India, and our final destination, Sylhet, in Assam Province of India. My group, the 4th Combat Cargo, was involved in the Northern and Southern Burma Campaigns and flying the Hump to Kunming, Nanning, Kweilin and other fields in China. Also ferrying units of the Chinese Army. After the "Big Bang" in Japan, I rotated back to the United States and discharged October '45.... While in the service I was awarded the Air Medal with Oak Leaf Cluster, and the Distinguished Flying Cross with Oak Leaf Cluster, plus the other campaign medals that went with the Theater of Operations.[8]

"The Lifeline of the Hump Air Routes"

Frank R. Vierling was chief of the maintenance section for the 130th AACS, 4th Wing, U.S. Army Signal Corps, and stationed in Kunming, China. Originally slated to become a flight engineer on a B-29, Vierling remained in Kunming as head of the transmitter maintenance group located there. He recalled that the unpredictable, oftentimes violent weather and local conditions played havoc with the vital transmitting equipment used by Hump pilots to hone in

210   CHAPTER 9

ROUTE FOX INSTRUMENT DEPARTURE PROCEDURE

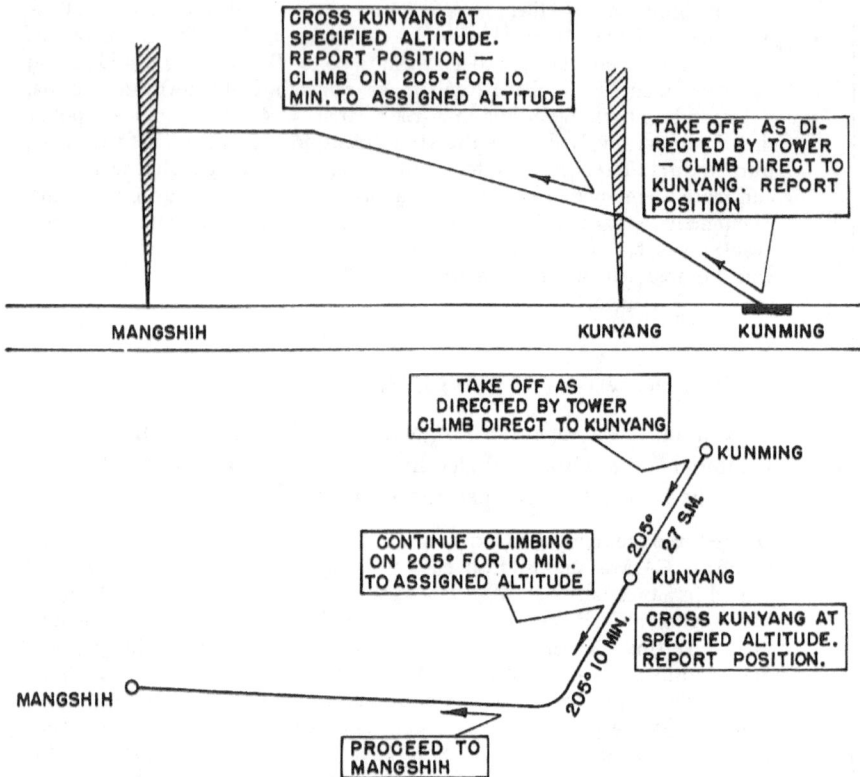

TAKE OFF AND LEAVE TRAFFIC PATTERN AS DIRECTED BY TOWER.
AFTER LEAVING TOWER FREQUENCY, NOTIFY KUNMING CONTROL THAT FLIGHT
IS IN PROGRESS GIVING TIME OFF.
PROCEED CLIMBING DIRECT TO KUNYANG — CROSS KUNYANG MARKER AT ALTITUDE
AS DIRECTED BY A.T.C.
CONTACT KUNMING CONTROL GIVING POSITION REPORT OVER KUNYANG MARKER
PROCEED CLIMBING ON 205° FOR 10 MINUTES TO ASSIGNED ALTITUDE.
PROCEED AT ASSIGNED ALTITUDE TO MANGSHIH.

Diagram 1. Instrument Flying into Kunming, China (Hump Pilots Association).

on the beacons placed near Kunming and other airfields and transmitted signals used to guide pilots in flying into China via instruments [see Diagram #1]:

> I was slated to be part of the B-29 operation, but was held at Kunming and never left. I believe our AACS radio station there was one of the largest, if not the largest, radio station overseas.
> We had a great crew dedicated to keeping the planes in the air. In my time there, we only had one major outage. A C-6 didn't make it over the village at

the end of the runway and crashed. The village was razed and the people given new sites (no one checked with us) directly over our underground cables. These were the lifelines between our remote locations (receivers, tower, etc.) and their associated transmitters. In making mud bricks, the Chinese workers cut into our two 104 wire cables. Lines their hoes didn't cut were soon shorted out by water. We had "key down" on all transmitters! We quickly established tower service and a few other vital links with a couple of abandoned field wires strung in the trees. These were from the original installation and had been abandoned for years. Operators were moved to the transmitter building to send their messages "in the blind."

Rain, (as you know, there was lots of it) always plagued us with partial outages, but we could work around a few shorts, total outages proved how vital this need was. One of the first messages received reported that poles were being cut into the mountain and cables were being flown in from the United States. In short, the order the Signal Corps had new overhead lines in and our underground cables were repaired for spares.[9]

Lieutenant Dennis G. Chandler, a bombardier with the 12th Bomb Group, 434th Bomb Squadron and stationed at Fenny, India, attended the University of California at Berkeley until called to active duty in February 1943. First assigned to Navigation School at Monroe, Louisiana, he was given further schooling at the B-29 Bombardiering School at Roswell, New Mexico, prior to his assignment to Victorville Air Force Base where he remained for three months as an instructor prior to volunteering to fly in B-25 medium bombers. After he trained with other B-25 crews in Columbia, South Carolina, the Army assigned Chandler to the 12th Bomber Group, 43rd Squadron in February 1945. He arrived in Fenny, India, just as Lieutenant General William Slim's Irrawaddy Offensive began (January 1945). Flying in support of the advancing British troops, Chandler and the rest of the 434th participated in the recapture of Mandalay and Rangoon from the Japanese. His squadron provided vital close in air support to the British and other Commonwealth troops (Indian and Gurkhas) in the Burma theater. He remained with the 434th until he volunteered to fly transports for the ATC based out of Kunming as a navigator to India and to towns located in China's interior (Chi Chiang, Liuchow, and Nanning). Lieutenant Chandler remained in the Army Air Forces until his discharge in February 1946. After his discharge from the service, Lieutenant Chandler completed his degree in engineering and worked as a materials testing engineer until he retired in 1986.[10]

Hump pilot Don Yarger, who flew with the 12th Combat Cargo Squadron, the 3rd Group, 333rd & 332nd Troop Carrier Squadron, 513th Group, out of Myitkyina, Shanghai, and Kiangwan provided a brief account of his career in China-Burma-India:

> My career in the CBI did not last near as long as most but it did have some disheartening phases. The first event was on the way to that theater via the southern route — South America, Ascension Island, Africa, Egypt, Iran and India. Between Natal, Brazil and Ascension our aircraft sprung leaks in both oil screen

gaskets due to faulty lock nuts having been installed at Natal. After a very eventful crossing with the skill of the pilots and the radio man helping the rescue craft (B-17) locate us, we did land safely at the Ascensions. Myself (Flight Engineer) and the Navigator had been very busy advising the pilots, taking location readings and hand pumping oil from the reserve cabin tank out to the engines. When we landed at the Ascensions we had 5, 6 and 7 gallons of oil left in the two nacelle tanks and the reserve cabin tank.

My crew that I trained with and went to the China-Burma-India and Myitkyina, Burma with consisted of Lawrence A. Wilkerson, Pilot; Ralph M. Raymer, co-pilot; Charles M. Shull, Radio Operator; and myself the Flight Engineer. Shull and I had graduated in the same High School Class of 1943. We met at Bergstrom Field and were able to be assigned to the same crew, Chuck and our pilot were both killed the night of August 4-5, 1945 near Mangshi, China. They hit a mountain during a heavy storm. They still being checked out by instructors who were also killed and were probably due to go home soon.

Incidentally, the plane that we flew into CBI, was left at Agra, India, with 100 hours on it. After the war ended and we flew all of the aircraft into Shanghai to turn over to the Chinese. I found that aircraft on Kingwan Airfield, had 180 hours on it and our aircraft we were using had many, many more hours than this.[11]

Lieutenant Colonel Dempsey W. Welch, U.S. Air Force (Ret.), maintained a detailed diary of his services in China-Burma-India. Beginning in 1944 when he embarked for India via Hampton Roads, Virginia on 29 August 1944 and arrived in Bombay, India, on 7 October after a six week journey, Lieutenant Colonel Welch provides an excellent glimpse of wartime Bombay and later being attacked by Japanese fighters at Myitkyina, Burma, after Merrill's Marauders and Nationalist Chinese forces captured that vital airfield in August 1944:

Lieutenant Colonel Welch's Wartime CBI Diary

29 August '44 ... left Camp Patrick Henry for Hampton Roads, VA, boarded ship at 2300 hrs 30 Aug '44 en route to India.

3 Sep '44 ... arrived Cristobal, Panama Canal Zone, remained overnight on ship. (Sure would have loved to have gotten off ship and visited the first Army unit I belonged to) Co I 14th Infantry, Fort Davis Canal Zone, was stationed there from Dec 1927 to Sept 1930.

4 Sep '44 ... started through the Panama Canal arrived on the Pacific side Panama City, Panama 1900 hours. Entered the Pacific Ocean 6 Sept '44. Crossed the Equator at the Galapagos Islands. Our transport was the General A. E. Anderson (a Navy Transport). The Navy Sailors gave us a Royal Initiation to Davy Jones Locker for our first crossing of the Equator.

17 Sep '44 ... Crossed the International Date Line, that is where I lost one day of my life, never gained it back until my return to "Uncle Sugar Able" in Sept 1945.

20 Sep '44 ... Arrived in New Zealand, 23 Sept arrived in Melbourne, Australia. Ship docked in the harbor but we could not get off the ship. Received a royal welcome from the Aussies. We could buy souvenirs from them by lowering a piece of string from the ship. We would swap cigarettes for beer, magazines and etc.

24 Sep '44 ... Departed Melbourne for Bombay, India. We stayed on the ship until the 9th October. We were loaded on a troop train and went to Asval, India arriving at Camp Beal (a British camp) Staging Area.

11 Oct '44 ... departed Camp Beal for Calcutta, India by train. Life was miserable on the train. It was hot, about 110 degrees and the mosquitoes were as large as hummingbirds. We had K-rations for the entire trip of 4 days. The Engineer and Fireman on the engine would stop about 5 times per day and would get out the cab for tea. They would draw hot water from the engine's boiler and make their tea. This would give us a chance to get off the train and take exercises to loosen up our stiff bodies. We were greeted by beggars and children at every stop with their arms out-stretched saying, "Baksheesh Sahib." Which we gave them cigarettes, K-rations, and candy bars. We were about 25 miles out of Calcutta when the train stopped for the engineer and fireman's usual cup of tea. They wandered off to a little village across the track, and we had a couple of Black boys (from Alabama) who had worked on the railroad, so they climbed up into the cab of the engine, blew the whistle, opened the throttle, and were in Calcutta in about 30 minutes.

15 Oct '44 Arrived in Calcutta, debarked from the train and while walking in front of the depot we had to be careful where we stepped as the natives were lying all over the sidewalks. Some were sleeping but most were dead — died from starvation. (It is the custom in India that if someone dies on the streets, they cannot be moved until a relative or person of the same Cult can identify them. Otherwise they will lay there until the Vultures and Jackals can devour them. When they are identified they are carried to the Burning Ghatt on the banks of the River where they are stacked on cords of wood, then burned).

... Left Calcutta, India for Kanchapara, India. We were billeted in an English (It was an English Tea Plantation). Two officers were assigned to a Basha. We had a house boy assigned to us who took care of our beds and laundering. We had a large Basha which was the kitchen and dining room — we went first class as the dining room was air conditioned — ha ha! The air conditioner consisted of a large sheet of matting about 3' wide and 12' long which was suspended from the ceiling. There were two ropes tied to the bottom of the mat at the center and one rope ran outside at the end of the basha and the other rope ran outside at the opposite end of the Basha where two native women sat on their haunches and pulled the ropes back and forth, thus moving the mat which in turn moved the air, which made the Basha somewhat cooler. The grounds were immaculate — the grass (similar to our Augustine) was mowed daily, (not lawn or power mowers), but older India women would get down on their knees (5 or 6) in a line and would snip the grass short with their fingers.

18 Oct '44 Well our short vacation was over. We were loaded onto 2½ ton trucks and headed for Bangapore, an ATC base. At 0800 hours we boarded ATC C-46s en route to Myitkyina, Burma, arriving 6 hours later at 1400 hours. Japs were dug in at the end of the strip, C-46 planes were burning after being strafed by Jap Zeroes. Dead Japs were lying all over the strip, Merrill's Marauders were driving the few Japs that were left off the air strip. They finally succeeded in driving the Japs, 20 miles from Myitkyina.

19 Oct '44 Drew supplies for making camp. Camp area was an old battlefield full of booby traps, fox holes, and dead Japs that the vultures and jackals were making a meal of.

20 Oct '44 Put up Army G1 pyramidal tents. Two officers to a tent. Eight GIs to a tent. After putting up tents we immediately dug a large hole beside the tent and covered with logs and sand bags—from 2 to 6 persons per hole in case of bombing by the Japs.

21 Oct '44 Went downtown in Myitkyina. Town was complete destroyed. Found a water well that was full of Jap rifles and Samurai swords. I retrieved a rifle and sword for souvenirs.

21–26 Oct '44 Nothing unusual. Pretty quiet at night & usual camp duties during the day.

27 Oct '44 1845 hours one Jap fighter (Zero) and one Bomber (we called the bombers "Maytag Washing Machines") surprised us. I was in my tent writing my wife a letter. The ground shook like an earthquake — bombs exploding and machine guns strafing the C-46s that were on a landing strip. They destroyed 6 planes.

28 Oct '44 Received 5 letters from my wife — the first since leaving the States on 30 Aug '44.

29 Oct '44 1830 hrs Japs back again, but our Ack-Ack drove them away — no damage.

30 Oct '44 Found a Jap skull — large hole thru it just above where ears were. Gave it good cleansing in hot soapy water and gave it to my tentmate, the squadron dentist.

1–3 Nov '44 0450 hours 5 Jap Zeroes came over, circled, over camp (evidently trying to locate our gasoline storage tanks. We had two very large tanks; the engineers had them covered with camouflaged netting which made them almost impossible to see from the air. Was in my bunker in nothing flat. The area was sprayed with tracer ammo and our Ack-Ack downed one of the Zeroes. Later on, I retrieved some pieces of the aluminum and windshield and made watch bands out of them.

6 Nov '44 Got one letter from my wife. This day was our 14th wedding anniversary and here I am 20,000 miles from Home.

7–20 Nov '44 Nothing unusual. 21st to 24th moved into a new camp area.

25 Nov '44 1900 hrs, we had taken the fuselage of an old C-46 and moved it off the edge of the landing strip and set up a movie projector in the nose of the plane. About 1900 hrs one evening we were all out there sitting on the ground and watching a movie when two Jap Zeroes came in low. (We did not get an alert.) They were strafing the area where we were as the light from the projector could be seen from the air. We were lucky as they over-shot us on the ground, but they destroyed several of our planes that were parked on the apron (set them all afire). They made only one pass, but they sure did some damage.

26 Nov '44 Two Jap bombers came over (1830 hrs). Just had time to get into my bunker. They came in low, right over the air strip, and started dropping their bombs about 200 yards from my tent. A third one came over (after the first ones dropped flares) and he found our gas tank storage area. We hit one of the tanks and we had one helluva explosion and fire. Thought it would never burn out. We were pretty worried for if they had had any more fighters to follow thru, they sure could have wiped us out with all the light that was coming from the gas tank fires.

26 Nov '44 Nothing much happened. (*sic*)

27 Nov '44 We received word that the Merrill's Marauders and the Mars Task Force had just captured the Jap Air Strip in Bhamo, and that was the last Jap fighting in Burma.[12]

The Backbone of the Air Transport Service— The Venerable Douglas DC-3

Mr. Donald W. Douglas, founder of the Douglas Aircraft Corporation that built one of the most successful designs for transport aircraft — the sturdy DC-3 — was, in fact, one of the main architects of victory in China-Burma-India during World War II. In a speech given in 1955 to the Necomen Society, in San Francisco, California, Douglas "told all about the Douglas aircraft" and how they won World War II.

> If you traveled by air during World War II, in any theater, it is probable you traveled in an airplane built by Douglas, because the Douglas DC-3, and later DC-4, were the backbone of our military air transportation program. I remember at one time seeing so many Douglas planes on the line in India, bound for the Hump and China, that I thought I was on the flight line at the Santa Monica plant. And, if you have traveled by air since the War, it is probable that you travel with Douglas, because the Douglas-built transports have been the most popular in the world; they are as well known abroad as in our own Country.
> Then came the now famous DC-3. This is an ideal time and most certainly the right place publicly to acknowledge our debt of gratitude to my good friend C. R. Smith for his part in the development of the DC-3. His tremendous faith in us and in the future of air travel, his boundless energy and clear vision and his uncanny knack of making and inspiring the right decision at the right time, were the catalytic agents that greatly influenced us in taking the steps to build that famous and historic airplane. The first DC-3 flew in Dec. 1935. It had a gross weight of 24,000 pounds and carried 21 passengers. A few airplanes were designed as sleepers. Before production ceased on this model and its variations, 803 had been built as commercial airplanes and 10,113[13] as military versions. In addition to the 1,541 in airline operation, it is estimated that approximately 3,000 are still flying and that additional hundreds are in private service by corporations and individuals. And these figures, also are conservative.
> Over the years people have told us that without question the DC-3 is the best known and most beloved airplane ever built in aviation history. Its exploits in WWII are endless and legendary. Affectionately known in the military services as the "Goony Bird," it was equally at the time useful from the Burma Road to Alaska, from New Guinea to Panama, and from the Yalu River to Tasmania. In many lands and in many languages, it became a household word. The British called it the "Dakota" and before the war, in Baghdad, street urchins used to point to the sky when KLM's airliners lumbered by and say, "there goes a Dooglas Douglas." Major Mahmoud Al Hindi told me in 1940 that the word "Douglas" was uniformly applied to all airplanes in Arabia shortly after KLM's DC-2 flew over the country for the first time on its way to Melbourne in the London-to-Australia race.
> It would take days to recount the exploits of the DC-3 (C-47) in the last war. This branch of the "DC" family was praised and honored everywhere. In award-

ing Douglas the Exceptional Service award, the Air Force said the airplane ranks as "the best single airplane ever built." With Montgomery at El Alamein, with Eisenhower in Normandy and in the Battle of the Bulge, and with MacArthur and Kenney in the Pacific, it was unequaled and indispensable. If I seem to linger a bit too long in telling the story of this aging member of the family, it is because, like millions everywhere, I love the "Old Faithful." It will always remain close to my heart.[14]

Hump pilot Eugene D. "Gene" Adams of Marietta, Georgia, flew C-46s with the 16th Combat Cargo Squadron, 4th Group at Sylhet, Argatala, Myitkyina and Chittagong from November 1944 to July 1945:

> I had been flying as a 1st Lieutenant glider tow pilot at Camp Mackall, NC from 21 August 1943 to 9 July 1944 when I was ordered to Syracuse AFB, NY, 16th Combat Cargo Squadron, 4th Group as a first pilot. Captain Leslie W. Bray was the C.O., and 1st Lieutenant Wilfred R. Pieper was Ops Officer. I trained pilots in C-47s at Syracuse and Bowman Field, Louisville, KY, until August 19 when our Group Executive Officer, Major Walter F. Wilbur, 2nd Lieutenant John A. Stallings, and I went to Reno, NV, per General [Henry] "Hap" Arnold's plan to arrange for C-46s and instructor pilots to come to Bowman to convert our Group to C-46s. We were then sent to Baer Field, Fort Wayne, Indiana, getting ready for overseas assignment and picking up new C-46 aircraft to take overseas. We practiced 1000' short field landings (empty) at Standiford next to Bowman, but did not know yet that they were to give us the skills to get into and out of dirt strips not too much longer than that in Burma.
>
> We staged out of Morrison Field, West Palm Beach, FL, and I believe the Group had 100 C-46s (25 each for 13th, 14th, 15th, and 16th Squadrons). We left Morrison 19 November 1944. Colonel Wilbur chose to fly in my C-46, #4477310. I felt honored. I seem to remember that he had several thousand hours as an airline pilot and held an engineering degree from MIT. We also had 1st Lieutenant Sydney Halem as our Navigator. We swapped pilot and co-pilot time for each hop from Morrison to Borinquen at Puerto Rico to Atkinson (British Guiana?) to Belem to Natal. Then across the Atlantic to Ascension Island (volcanic island in the middle of the Atlantic) to the coast of Africa, landing at Accra. Then NE to Kano (Nigeria) to El Fasher to Khartoum to (Aden) Masira Island to Karachi to Sylhet in Assam Valley. We were glad to get to Sylhet because it was our destination. Half way around the world. My notes show trips to Barrackpore; Dec 12 Load 5980 pounds to Tulihal; Dec 13 to Imphal to Yazagyo to return the same day with 9162 pounds; On Dec 14 it was Tulihal before returning to Sylhet[15] ... but it is evident that I was hauling about 2750 gallons of fuel a day from supply point Imphal to Yazagyo. Nobody today would think of putting 55 gallon drums lined up on each side of the open floor, secured only with small ropes to keep them from sliding. Imagine 25 steel drums at 384 lbs each, loosely held from upward movement, falling over and rolling around should we encounter much turbulence. It would have been a disaster. I tried to check the "tie-downs" but we always were uneasy. Fortunately, we did have fairly smooth air for flying these loads. Also, we had no alternative but to fly the loads that the British[16] put in the aircraft. But, we must remember that we were just youngsters. And that is why the oldsters sent us there. "The difficult we did immediately. The impossible took a little longer. Tra-La-La! We lived in fame or went down in flames and nothing could stop the Army Air Corps."
>
> My notes show that I continued hauling 17 loads of 10,000+ each from 17 to

31 Dec with Dec 20, 25, and 27 as only days off. (Literally, "*My Little Assam Dragon*.") All loads were now food instead of gas but Dec 31 was 2 loads totaling 19,994 lbs of ammo. These note end Jan 29, 1945 showing 31 loads averaging over 10,000 lbs each for Jan. For security reasons I coded some of them G, A., GF, FR, GR, R, G, and two W's, but don't remember what the codes meant.

I quit logging loads, dates and places in my notes. We never saw any tonnages reported for our Combat Cargo Sqdrns. We were never mentioned in any papers. In fact, we rarely got a newspaper or had time to read it anyway. When we did see a news item we saw where ATC "The non-combatant" Air Force exhibited their tonnage in a Service newspaper. I suspect that all our loads hauled were reported as ATC tonnages anyway.

We moved to Agratala for awhile and then to more permanent base at Chittagong which served as our base of operations until the Southern Burma Campaign ended in May or June 1945. While at Chittagong we flew usually three loads a day into Central Burma to as many 39 "named" landing areas. One day in late afternoon I talked the crew into taking a 4th round trip "to help the war effort." It meant getting back late and still getting up at 0400 hours the next day, but they volunteered to come with me.

We flew in fuel and empty drums back; bombs or ammo in and empty cases back. A C-46 with its floor covered with bombs doesn't look like 10,000 lbs. It isn't — it is 12,000 lbs. The take-off runway at Chittagong ended where the Boy of Bengal begins. The wall between the runway and the water was only a few feet high as I remember, but we did have to be airborne before we got there or we would hit it with the landing gear. We just did make it off over the short wall with the 12,000 lb load. With no other obstructions we used the bay to our advantage to gain as much altitude possible before heading east across the mountains toward Burma.

We flew personnel from combat zone to combat zone; wounded British and Indian soldiers out of many areas; and blood in special containers from one place to another. We liked to haul canned peaches or canned boned chicken from Australia, because if a box got broken we were allowed to open a leaking or damaged can and eat delicacies that were lacking in our K-Rations or the chow line at our base in Chittagong.

We hated to haul "G-Oil" (coconut oil for Indian soldiers who could not eat animal fat) because it leaked into the aluminum airplane and could not be washed out. I heard of one airplane ruined from hauling dry cement that got into the fuselage structure and couldn't be removed. And, another time that some unlucky pilot got a load of live cattle. The lightest load we ever had, filling all cabin spaces, was hundreds of wicker baskets of chicken feathers for stuffing mattresses and pillows in some hospital. If that load ever got loose at altitudes the natives in remote Burmese villages that never had seen our airplanes on land would swear that the "Big Bird" had lost all his feathers.

From our base at the harbor of Chittagong we flew loads across the mountains to northern Burma, south to Central Burma, specifically from North of Mandalay, south on both sides of the Irrawaddy River and the "bombed out" central highway and railway going to Rangoon. I got a little rest from flying while 310 was getting both engines changed. I was sent to serve as airstrip commander at Indiangali and at Lewe. We heard over a field radio that Germany had surrendered. My base was at Chittagong until Rangoon was evacuated by the Japanese. We then went to Myitkyina to help the ATC fly loads into China. I flew one flight into Kunming, remained overnight, and returned to Myitkyina the next day.

I had 87 points and was able to be one of the first to go home on "Green Project" (as passenger) by Air along the same route except that we made the flight from Dakar to Natal and on to our flight destination: Miami, FL. I had flown 352 Combat Cargo Missions (flights) and logged 532.40 pilot hours in the CBI. I was awarded the DFC w/1 Clusters, the Air Medal w/2 Clusters, and most of the campaign medals and clusters of the rest: Central Burma and India-Burma, Asiatic-Pacific Theater, etc. but thankfully, no Purple Heart. Someone on the troop train from Miami to Camp Chaffee, AR stole my short-snorter (roll of friends' signatures on bills of all countries), Chanel No. 5 perfume, and silk hose gifts I got in Cairo. But, I got home with a Jap rifle and radio. All I have left is a Ghurka Knife and the headphones of the radio. I do have copies of orders and my Form 5, and could furnish the Army with copies of some of our records that were said to have been destroyed in a warehouse fire.[17]

"Detached Service with the Service of Supply"

Major Samuel A. 'Sam' Curcio made three flights over the Hump as a priorities and traffic officer–ferrying division-route supervisor from February 1943 to May 1945 based at Jorhat, Kunming, and ATC Headquarters located in Calcutta. Major Curcio wrote that

> although I did serve in the CBI from 2/1/43 to about 5/15/45, I was neither a pilot or a "bona fide crew member." When I arrived in the CBI on or about 2/1/43 (Chabua), I was assigned to Mohanbari as an Assistant Priorities and Traffic officer. My job was to unload the freight cars loaded with 7.92 rifle ammunition, guns of all kinds, and the drums of gasoline. These had come on the flat boats up the Bramaputra River to the rail head — then transferred on the freight cars on the small tea gauge railways which ran along the runway. We stored the ammunition in big bamboo warehouses along the railroad siding. The bombs went to a secluded guarded bomb dump, and the gasoline to a similar dump which was hidden away in the jungle near the field.
>
> After a month or so I was placed on detached service with the S.O.S. (Service of Supply) and sent to Jorhat — a field under construction about 90 miles South of Mohanbari and Chabua. My job was to coordinate the shipments of material coming into the new field and keep Headquarters advised of the progress of the construction. For awhile I was the only American on the base, although the British were actually in charge of construction. There were several thousand Indian Coolies breaking up large rocks into small rocks. (All those small rocks made an excellent base for a good landing surface, especially when the rains came on down). I recall that both General Stilwell and General Chennault were most anxious to have the base completed and in operation P.D.Q.[18] Building the runway was slow so we had one heck of a time putting them together with the aid of some former auto mechanics. The Indian workers didn't take too kindly with having the rock crushers put them out of work, so to calm them down we only used one for awhile. Until the runway was completed the planes landed on the grass strip along the runway.
>
> We shipped bombs, gasoline, ammunition to the fledgling 14th Air Force in the spring of 1943, many of the pilots of which had been members of the original Flying Tigers. The Japanese would send their photo planes to take pictures, particularly when, in the latter part of 1943, the runway was extended (to accommodate the B-29s which began flying in to refuel on their way to bomb

Manchuria). Once in awhile we would have a "red alert" but the P-40s and then later the P-47s and P-51s would get up and chase away the Jap bombers which weren't shot down. I remember meeting my old college friend, Harry Staulcup (a fighter pilot-P-47s), at Jorhat.

I remember so clearly that in early January 1944, a C-87 carrying bombs and gasoline exploding on take off (almost 300 yards from the end of the runway) and our new commanding officer was killed when he went to see if he could help at the crash site. Bombs were exploding in the fire which consumed the aircraft. A friend, Captain Robert Jordan of Dallas, Tx, was severely injured and sent back to the States to recuperate from those injuries. We never heard from him after that. Finally, Jorhat was completed and went into 24 hour operation with C-47s, C-46s, C-87s and C-109s. Our plane went to Kunming, Chengkung, and Chengtu. Some of the C-47s went into Yunnanyi.

In early 1944 I was transferred to Kunming and put in charge of the Priorities and traffic office there to help speed up the loading and unloading of the transports. Everybody was obsessed with "turn-around-time." After spending about a year in China, I was promoted to Major and sent to Calcutta. I was designated Division Route Supervisor and traveled all over India, China, and Burma, making inspections and then preparing reports for the Commanding Officer of the CBI. With that title, I got the red carpet treatment everywhere I went in the theater. I had no other bosses except the Commanding General. In May 1945, I had had enough and was rotated back to the U.S.A.

Our flying units sustained substantial losses in men, planes, and material. Many of our unarmed and unescorted transports took off and were never heard from again. Air Medals and DFCs were awarded for missions flown over the Hump. I'm sure others have questioned as I often have, if our efforts did shorten the war. On the other side of the coin, we did keep China in the war and did earn a Presidential Unit Citation. We did haul pipe used in building an oil pipeline into Burma and helped reopen the Burma Road. All of this did keep many Japanese soldiers in China and may have contributed to an earlier end of the war.[19]

Clarence Linebach on Flying the Hump

Clarence "Linn" Linebach, who served as director of operations of the 1330th Army Air Forces Burma, in Jorhat and Barrackpore recalled that

the weather at times was so bad that for the first two months I flew the Hump, I didn't see the mountains. I remember the ice from the props hitting the fuselage with such force it sounded like men with hammers beating on it. I remember in the Assam Valley during the rainy season, there was water everywhere and the natives were camped on any little high spot they could find. I remember how inefficient our C-87s and C-109s were, sometimes using as much gas for the trip as we off-loaded in Chengtu down to Kunming, 50 to a load in a C-87. You can imagine what a mess 50 airsick Chinese could make, so our crew chiefs removed cargo doors from C-87s, thinking they surely wouldn't let the soldiers fly in a plane without doors. It didn't make any difference, they were loaded in anyway but then we had the problem of leaving Chengtu with 50 troops and arriving at Kunming with 48 or 49.

One of our crewmen on one trip saw a Chinese soldier push another out the door in flight to the great enjoyment of the others. Anyway, it wasn't too long

"Allies of a Kind." An American combat engineer poses with his Chinese counterpart. Chinese troops provided flank security and cleared the jungles of the Japanese as the American engineers labored to build the Ledo Road after January 1945 (Alexander McVean Collection).

after that I received a wire from Hastings Mill saying, "Please replace the doors on your C-87s, we are losing our Allies en route."[20]

Air Transport Command pilot Alfred "Al" Lang, who flew from bases in Tezgaon, Kurmitola, and Dacca from January to November 1945, recalled his days flying the Hump into China:

> Took off from Tezgaon with load of gasoline barrels. Arrived 5 hours later over Kunming (200' in fog). Held at least 3 hours over Kunming on instruments, holding on non-directional beams. Kunming finally went "0 visibility" and the tower said, "Everybody take off for Luliang." Everybody did, Luliang was stacked every 500' to 20,000'. Held another 3 hours at Luliang and finally got on ground, pulled on to taxi strip and watched next plane coming in. On final approach, he never pulled out, flew it straight into the ground with a load of mortar shells on board. When the plane hit, it immediately was a ball of flames. Rest of the planes had to land the remainder of the night down wind right into the exploding shells. The story is— 2 hours later the whole crew walked into operations; only 1 crew member had a cut on his forehead. But no one knew how they had gotten out.
>
> Flying C-109s from Kurmitola to Chengtu, we all left gas at Chengtu except enough to get us back to Myitkyina. After leaving Myitkyina, we ran into head winds and arrived at Kurmitola in a monsoon thunderstorm. No problem except C-109s had no windshield wipers. We could see the field with no problem on down wind, and base leg, but turning on final approach vision was blocked out. I made six passes at the field with no luck. The engineer said, "Lt. ... you better get her on the ground, the gas is gone clean out of sight in the gas sight gauges." The next time around I dropped landing gear and flaps, and came in very low. I saw the runway lights pass beneath my left wing and I said, "cut the power," and the co-pilot did. I kicked the left rudder, then the right rudder, and we were scooting down the wet runway. We finally got stopped and pulled into the revetment. I told the engineer to stick the gas tanks. He came back and said, "Lt., there was hardly enough to wet the bottom of the stick."
>
> In Dacca, there was a little Anglo-Indian orphanage. They didn't have very much, but were thankful for what they got since they were outcasts from both the Indian community and the English. A group of guys from both Tezgaon and Kurmitola thought we might do something for them. We scrounged the bases' scrap yards and came up with enough junk to build the kids a playground, sliding boards, sand boxes, etc. Sometimes later the bases were breaking up and we managed to scrounge up about 25 porcelain sinks that were being scrapped because the porcelain was "chipped." The kids only had little basins to wash in, but they did have a roof tank. We built in the sinks with scrap lumber and piped them in with scrap plumbing. So finally the kids had a place to wash with stateside sinks. The men were both officers and enlisted men, working together for the kids.[21]

A B-29 Bombing Mission over Yawata, Japan

One of the main objectives of Major General Claire Lee Chennault in the China-Burma-India theater during World War II was to launch a massive bombing campaign against mainland Japan from airfields based in China. B-29 pilot Herman K. Sigrist, who trained on B-29s at Salina, Kansas, recalled his experiences in CBI and specifically on one particular bombing mission over Yawata, Japan, a major steel producing city fueling the Japanese war machine.

> Took my training on B-29s at Salina, KS. We flew our plane over with stops at Dayton, Ohio, Presque Island, Maine, Gandu Lake, Newfoundland, Africa, Egypt, and finally Kharagpur, India, which was to be our home base. We flew gasoline over the Hump between missions and put in storage so that we could fly missions out of China. Crossed the Hump about 15 times, flew several straight missions. Flew one interesting mission after the Naval Battle of the island of Formosa. We got to fly in and photograph all the damage. What a sight that was.
>
> We flew a mission over Yawata, Japan, took some flak in the nose wheel well and ran out of fuel. Could not make radio contact for straight in landing, so all of us in the back bailed out. The nose gear would not come down, so they crash landed close to the runway. I am enclosing the story of this mission. I can't remember the date of our crash but I think it was Oct 1944 [see Appendix #2].
>
> After returning to India we were given a new pilot and a brand new plane that had just been received. So we had to remove all the armor plating and take the cannon out of the tail turret to save weight so we could put in extra bombs. On 20 November 44 we flew back over the Hump to our base in China. On 21 November 1944 we took off on a mission over Amuri, Japan. Got a flak burst in #3 engine over target — propeller would not feather; knew we could not make it all the way back. No one wanted to bail out again, so we headed for Vladivostok, Russia. Landed there and were interned. They sent us about half way across their country to a place called Tashkent. There we met up with about 119 other Americans. Some were Navy and the rest Air Force.
>
> In late January '45 we were put on a train for a day and on trucks and taken there to Tehran, Iran. There we were met by our own people (G2 Washington, DC). From there we were taken to a tent city outside Cairo, Egypt, and given good food and plenty of beer and some money to gamble. We stayed there for about a week and then flew us to Naples, Italy, and put up on a Liberty Ship and were sent to the States — New York. From there we got to come home for 30 days and were restricted to the Continental limits of the U.S., and could not tell anyone where we had been. All the AF had to report to Miami Beach, FL, after leave to a Major Hiett for further orders. Stayed in Florida about 2 months and was given the choice of any place in the U.S. we wanted to be stationed. I took Lackbourne, in Columbus, Ohio, 55 miles from home. Stayed there until after VJ day when I received a telegram from Major Hiett telling me to go to the intelligence officer on base and tell him everything. I then had enough points to receive my discharge.[22]

Lieutenant Ruth Firsching Heckinger, an Army nurse who served in the China-Burma-India theater during the last months of World War II in Asia, maintained a detailed diary of her experiences while in China. This service included duty as a nurse aboard a C-47 ferrying patients from Kunming to hospitals in India. Flying to India across the traditional way from Homestead Flying Field, Florida, to North Africa and then on to Calcutta in a C-54, Lieutenant Heckinger's journey included a chance meeting with a famous Flying Tiger pilot, Colonel Robert Lee Scott, who was aboard the same plane en route to India.

An Army Nurse's Diary

April 1945: Me! 21 years old and in North Africa—Casablanca, yet! Enroute to the land of Mystery and Romance—India!! Flew over from Miami alone—that is, not a part of a group like all others because I injured my back on the diving boards at the Floridian Hotel and a conscientious medic insist that I stay for diathermy treatments; so all my buddies left without me and when I was finally cleared for take-off, I was the only girl aboard but in good company: a general, a famous colonel (Bob Scott), the Homestead base commander and two dozen cute pilots who razzed me unmercifully for hanging out with the brass—well, I couldn't help it if they were clustered around me "protectively" ... the general, two colonels and I were invited into the cockpit of what they told me was a "deluxe" C-54 (no bucket seats). My first time in an airplane and I'm sitting behind the wheel (pardon me, stick).

May 1945: Finally got to Calcutta after a week of incredible adventures. There's nothing like traveling on your own surrounded by a couple of armies bent on protecting the little kid. The fact that I was a lieutenant and a nurse meant nothing to these guys; I was just a little girl from home that needed watching over. Once a pilot put earphones on me and told me what to say: "Benghazi Tower, this is the Green Hornet coming in on a downwind leg. Over." There was complete silence from the tower, then came landing instructions, then, "If that pilot is Bergen, I can't wait to see McCarthy," and there were six men with binoculars watching us come in. I ate in the EM's Mess that night. Left Karachi in a B-24 and when we stopped at Agra, they had me waving to the tower from the hatch. When we took off again, the pilot decided to give me a novel view of the Taj Mahal and buzzed it! I had no idea what a feat that was until I saw him wipe the sweat off his brow.

July 1945: Night duty is two straight weeks of twelve hour tours and if there's an extra job like accompanying a convoy, it's 16–18 hours before we get off. Well, we get two days off before going back on days. Last week I did a favor for a pilot friend; he was assigned to bring back a load of ambulatory patients from Kunming and told me how nervous he was doing this without medical personnel aboard, so I said, what the hell, I've got two days off, I come mit. He was delighted and I got the rare chance to fly the "Hump." Wow! What a sight! Stark, jagged, bony, gargantuan molded lumps of Earth thrown at the sky and showing a snarling countenance to those presumptuous enough to dare cross over black rover!! A hostile personality, as much of an enemy as the Japanese. So the trip was a little scary, but mostly awesome and I'll do it again if they ask me. So life is an incredible adventure. A lament in one ear, perhaps, but always a song in the other.[23]

Major General Perry M. Hoisington, USAF (Ret.) and Colonel Raymond K. Childress, USAF (Ret.) were both members of the 462nd Bombardier Group, 58th Bombardier Wing of the 20th Air Force, known affectionately as the Hellbird Group. They flew bombing missions in B-29s, known as "flying coffins" due to the many hazards presented in flying this rather large airplane over mainland Japan. They recalled the splendid support offered by the C-46 pilots of the ATC in ferrying precious gasoline and ordnance into bases into Kunming and Chengtu. In a postwar letter to a group of former Hump pilots General Hoisington and Colonel Childress remembered the many perils associated with flying the Hump during the war and thanked them for their great contribution to what they termed a "great flying accomplishment."

"Pure Gallantry in Action"

> Our appreciation is intended for you all for the Herculean job you did in support of the air effort launched from China; in particular, the B-29 long-range missions against targets in Mongolia and Japan. I visited and flew the "Hump" with you in your C-46s to express the appreciation of the 58th Bomb Wing and the 20th Air Force for the great effort you contributed to the war against Japan. But this could in no way represent fully the admiration all us B-29ers had for your great flying accomplishment. Having made the trip across the Himalayas a number of times in all kinds of weather we are well aware of the hazardous aspects of flights over this poorly mapped area while flying B-29s. We can only imagine them being at least in the "flying coffins."
>
> Once, upon arriving over China, it can vividly be recalled the entire western part was covered with a low layer of clouds and a number of you were circling above the clouds with no place to land as all fields were "socked in." That was certainly one peril you all had to face that we didn't as we normally had enough gas on board when flying the Hump to go back to our point of departure. Early on you were facing the threat of being attacked by Japanese fighter planes whereas we would have loved it if they had tried us on for size.
>
> Without question the war time "Hump" operation will stand out as one of the greatest feats of flying in aviation history. There were never enough medals to pin on the chests of those of you who made these flights. It was pure gallantry in action. It will never be forgotten![24]

One of the more interesting accounts of flying the Hump is from Liu Fang, widow of China-born Hump pilot Wu Zidan, who described her late husband's activities and the importance of the China airlift by the ATC pilots and crews to aid China in its war against Japan. Written as a memorial to her late husband, Mrs. Fang's account highlighted the little known contributions made by Chinese pilots who, like their American colleagues, braved the tortuous route of the Himalayas in order to supply their countrymen with aviation gasoline, ordnance, and other vital logistical support during World War II.

Flight Over the Hump

> What does the word "Hump" here mean? Never heard it before. Indeed, most young people today have very little knowledge or ... (are) ... totally ignorant of that by-gone period in which the Chinese and American people, in order to defeat the Japanese aggressors, pioneered an aerial transportation line across the CBI border. As the widow of a Chinese Humpster and witness to that period of history, I feel obliged to write down what I know about it so that people may have a correct understanding of that historical episode and the difficulty in bringing about our happy life today.
>
> In March 1942, the occupation of Rangoon and other major cities in Burma by the Japanese troops deprived China of all the international outlets, both on land and by sea. At this critical juncture, requested by the Chinese government,

the U.S. government, out of the over-all consideration of the anti-fascist war as a whole, decided to blaze a new trail to China no matter what difficulties had to be surmounted.

As the result of the active and meticulous joint planning by China and the U.S., an air corridor from India to China was opened. Between May 1942 & VJ Day in August 1945, defying the most fickle climate, the Chinese and American crews operated more than 1,000 transports flying over the western ranges of the Himalayas along the CBI border on a more than 1,200 kilometer long air line, succeeding in transporting over 7,000 tons of materials, both military and civilian. Directly and indirectly there were over 100,000 people involved in the above operations, which contributed in a great measure to the defeat of the Japanese aggressors. For the above great achievement was, of course, paid a great price — a loss of over 500 airplanes and 1,500 people.

However, on the scene of that fierce warfare, people often only see the heroic fight with the enemy on the front stage to the neglect of outstanding contributions made by unknown heroes on the back stage. For instance, known far and wide in China are the meritorious deeds of the "Flying Tigers," formally known as the American Volunteer Group (AVG) and later changed to the 14th AF — headed by General Claire Chennault in fighting the intruding Japanese occupation forces in North China and Japanese Islands carried out by B-29 heavy bombers launched from airfields in Chengdu, Hazhong and other places, and the military victories scored by the Chinese expedition armies in the battlefields of India and Burma.

But relatively much less known is the fact that the guns, ammunition, napalm, and various other types of supplies the armies and air forces were equipped with were flown over the Hump. A slogan, popular then in war-time rear China reads: "A drop of gas is a drop of blood." It reminded people of the priceless worth of every single item flown in by air.[25]

Robert A. "Stumpy" Stumpf, who served as a radio operator aboard a Douglas C-54 transport recalled that missions over the Hump, dependent primarily upon good flying weather, could occur at any time, in bad weather or good, and during the day or at night. Oftentimes, these missions could be extremely long and hazardous. As Robert Stumpf recalled, flying over Burma often resulted in flying practically on "gas fumes" as conditions necessitated extra flying hours and maneuvers to avoid crashes or becoming lost. He specifically recalled one such mission when the gas gauges on his C-54 read "empty!"

Lost: Courtesy of the Hump

I had just returned to my tent after seeing the evening movie when the runner came to inform me that I was alerted for another flight. After being up all day I felt more like hitting the sack than hauling a load of gas to China, but because I was in the army, I had to do the latter. The crew, including me, griped while riding down to Operations in a bouncy GI truck. Operations was the Office where we got our orders and weather information before taking off. I remember distinctly one of my friends, "Berky," who worked in operations, telling my pilot and me that he didn't blame us for not wanting to fly at 11 o'clock at night.

Finally, after Wezzie, our pilot, had signed all the clearance forms and red tape papers, we got out to the plane.

It was our best type of transport, a 4-engine Douglas C-54 loaded with maybe 35 55-gallon drums of 100-octane gasoline. I left my parachute near the rear door and climbed over the barrels to the crew compartment. There I checked the radio equipment while the pilot, with the help of the co-pilot and flight engineer, taxied to the runway and checked the 5800 horses in the engines. The control tower cleared us and, streaking between the straight rows of runway lights, we lifted slowly into the moonless night.

In the darkness the monotonous throb of the engines sounded reassuring. Very few lights seen on the flooded plains of India at night but later we would see the fires of the Burmese hill people who evidently have more wood to spare. The needle of the radio compass still pointed back to our home base. When Wezzie tunes in the station which is one hour ahead of us, we will be able to follow this compass arrow in the right direction. That station will be our first check point. When we fly over it, I will send our position, altitude and other data to home base.

Meanwhile I listened for weather reports over the radio, hunt for ever-fading American music on the dial or just think of home. Soon Wezzie called me and said he could not get our checkpoint on the compass. I tried my trained ear but not a sound could be heard. When by dead reckoning we judged that we were over the station, the compass still had not verified our figuring. Not knowing your exact position is serious business over the Hump.

We were in Burma so I called Myitkyina and asked for a bearing. They said we were 10 miles south of them and to fly north. Wezzie refused to do this because we were only 14,000' up and there might have been mountains to the north if the bearing was incorrect. I asked Myitkyina to show us a light. They complied but we could not spot their beam through the cloud blanket. Still uncertain of our location, Wezzie did a 180 degree (turned around) and headed back home. Since we had traveled east for an hour, it was logical that by flying west for about an hour, allowing for wind, we would be home. Mother Nature was snickering quietly to herself. When 2 hours had elapsed and we had not found home, we knew we were lost. Being "somewhere" almost 3 miles high over the Hump at two in the black morning with a limited supply of gasoline is a good definition of the word "lost."

For the next 2 hours I talked with a station in upper Assam obtaining northward bearings which my pilot would not fly for safety reasons. About 4 o'clock my voice gave out so I switched to using Morse code. Still all the stations would give me were bearing heading north while Wezzie continued shuttling in various other directions. A poll taken among our crew members assured everyone that we were definitely in the CBI Theater of Operations, but all 3 countries got votes.

About daybreak 3 distant ground radio operators gave me a "fix" which was supposed to pinpoint our exact location. Alas, the "fix" as plotted on the map did not match the locale or direction of the river we were flying over — proof positive that it was defective. A little after sunrise, at about 6:30, we spotted a small landing strip in the jungle below but could not tell whether it was Jap or Allied controlled. We decided to risk a landing since our gas gauge was flirting with the word "empty." As we circled lower I made out 2 or 3 American transports and a flock of British Spitfire and Hurricane fighters. On our final approach we got a green light from the tower and made our landing. An American lieutenant came up to the cockpit and Wezzie asked him a simple question —"Where are we?" We had arrived at a British fighter strip 20 minutes north of the Jap lines. Wezzie said to me, "STUMPY, we've been flying north for over an hour and if my arithmetic is correct we have just come from a hundred miles behind Jap lines." So we went off and got some breakfast.

My frustration as a flight radio operator was complete when immediately after landing, I called our home field and received their reply as clear as a bell. I was calling from what we learned was a place called Kan, Burma, and named "Fox Dog" in code. After a very sparse breakfast shared with us by the few GIs there, the problem of little or no gas in our wing tank was attacked. We still had almost 2000 gallons of high-octane fuel as cargo but the logistics of getting it into the wing tank could prove hazardous. Our pilot dickered a trade with the English — gallon for gallon. and so as American drums of gasoline were being unloaded from our cargo section, a gasoline truck pumped petrol into our wing tanks — gallon for gallon. Since a British imperial gallon was 20% larger than a U.S. gallon, we took great pride in beating the Redcoats as our Revolutionary forefathers had done many years before.[26]

Hump pilot Ed Crumpacker recalled his experiences while on a re-supply mission to China and the difficulties experienced in unloading the high octane fuel carried in 55-gallon drums ferried by the majority of pilots in China-Burma-India.

A Hair Raising Experience

One of the methods for rapid unloading of cargo was devised by myself and my crew to handle fifty-five gallon drums of gasoline which weighed over 350 pounds. A load of that nature was the most dreaded for several reasons and particularly the fire hazard aloft. Our planes came equipped not only with vehicle loading ramps but other load handling equipment, including a wider ramp which hinged at the cargo door sill. We found we could prop the end of that ramp up to a 45-degree angle with a drum standing on end on the ground. Then we would put a large truck tire carcass adjacent to the bottom of the barrel. When we would "free" roll the loaded drums out the cargo door and down that ramp, the tire would absorb the impact and the energy would be transferred laterally so the drum would roll a substantial distance across the ground. Thus we could unload 28 55-gallon drums of gasoline in a neat row in that fashion. But first we had to get one drum out on which to set the lower end of the ramp. We had already discovered that a full drum could be unloaded onto soft soil by dropping it at an angle from the cargo door. The only damage resulting was a slight flattening of the drum on one side. Thus our system was complete. The only difficult job was rolling the drums down the inclined floor of the cargo compartment to the cargo door without their getting away from us.

One of my most hair raising experiences occurred while hauling one of those full loads of 28 55-gallon drums of gasoline. In spite of fighter cover, many felt safer flying "on the deck," as close to ground as possible, taking advantage of our camouflage paint to protect us from above, and being close enough to ground to make too fast a moving target for ground fire. This was considered dangerous up to 4,000' in altitude. Terrain inside Burma was flat so this could be accomplished safely by remaining at a relatively fixed height just above the ground. But we were faced with a problem of exposure descending from altitude after we crossed Chin Hills at about 9,000'. They ran in a N-S direction and consisted of a series of ridges gradually increasing in height going from India into Burma. I had discovered that the ravine between the last two ridges drained to the south and entered the plan not too far south of our normal course. Thus I devised a method of descending between those ridges so that by the time I arrived at the end of the ravine I would be at the level of the Burma plain, and thus well hidden all the way. However, I did not consider it safe to use that same route on the way back since we would be climbing in the ravine, and if we lost an engine there might not be enough room to turn around.

On a mission loaded with gasoline drums one bright and sunny morning, after we had reached altitude we became a bit too complacent for the second time as we were cruising over the mountains. As is common in such cases of inattention we thought we had arrived over the last ravine before we actually had. I signaled to him that I was going to start the let down and he nodded his approval. I then throttled back and commenced the descent. In the course of things we seemed to be approaching the bottom of the ravine sooner than we normally would. Before I realized what we had done, we rounded a slight curve between the walls of the two ridges and suddenly came upon a box canyon with nowhere to go except back the way we had come. I immediately put maximum continuous power on the engines and hugged the right side of the canyon as I began as slow a climbing turn to the left as possible. We barely cleared the tops of the trees surrounding the small village located there and commenced our climb back out. I did not level off until we were well above the highest which seemed a minimal risk at this point. What had happened was that we had gone down into the ravine second from the end, which drained to the north rather than the south. I have often thought what an enormous ball of fire we would have made with all that gasoline aboard if we had not cleared those tree tops.[27]

Mr. Tommy C. C. Tengg, a fore-chief engineer from Xian, China, who served aboard a C-47 with the Chinese Army Air Corps (CAAC), provided an interesting insight into the operations of the Chinese National Aircraft Corporation (CNAC) from the Chinese viewpoint. While there are language difficulties (as well as political overtones), which at times make Tengg's account difficult to comprehend, his story nonetheless illustrates the difficulties Hump pilots faced in CBI during World War II.

Remember the "Over Hump" Flight

I was born in 1919 at the middle of the Yangtze River and graduated from the Aeronautical Engineering Department of Southwest Associated University (the Tsinghua, Peking and Nan-Kai 3 universities united 1938–46 to establish continuity of their education responsibilities, Kunming, China).... As soon as I passed 4th year exam, CNAC Chief Pilot Mr. McDonnell came to Kunming Airport from Calcutta in summer 1944 to superintend in receiving co-pilot entrance exam and test to satisfy CNAC urgent demand for the lack of flight crews. Fortunately, I was accepted by Mr. McDonnell, (a fat fellow) and joined CNAC to go to Calcutta for 2-month Link Simulator Training. At first trip flight, Captain Robertson, and Co-pilot F. C. Lee flight crew, I joined them as a training co-pilot about 10 trips. Lee recommended to Robertson for my successful short run maneuverable flying rapid progress, so Robertson reported to Mr. Robertson for my successful short-run maneuverable flying rapid progress, so Robertson reported to Mr. Phillips (tall man always with sunglasses whole daytime), Operation Manager to let me put formally on schedule as co-pilot to fly between India and China.

When I began to fly in the airline courses, such as Kunming-Dinjan-Suifoo (Sichuan Province), etc., I flew with many Americans and only a few American-Chinese pilots. For example, A. Hing, B. Fong, B. Huong, Golden Pan, Antoson, Moonai, Sydney (tall fellow, later DC-4 pilot), Winner; but most of them such as Blackmore, Bohr, Barl, Caltlen, K. L. Ma (crashed at neighborhood of Dragon Gate of West Mountain, Kunming, after takeoff and climbing period), Koolson, Harmer, Scholff, Smith and Son Wallson were died in the aircraft crashes.

I could remember the Capt Robertson, Blackmore, Snydy, Smith and Winner were my good flight crew partners. They taught me a lot of flying technical maneuverabilities and experiences with kind, frank, and very good friendly helps, but without any selfish conservation, only because we united together to fight against Fascist for a same target toward the cooperated success for the victory of the Allies and the world people during World War II. We fought shoulder-to-shoulder closed to our arms proceeded owing to the isolation of war-occupied area by Japanese troops' aggression to cut off the land transportations with Allies and China so that Sino-American flight crew members cooperated closely together to build an "Air Transportation Bridge" between India and China, actually between all the allied people and supporting main force of whole Chinese people.

One thing should be remained in heartsore and heartsick for the memory of the death of my two college schoolmates H.W. Chu and T. J. Sheng. On 8-31-44 No. 97 C-47 was missed during the "Over Hump" flight course. Capt. Koolson jumped from his cabin with parachute, only one of crew survived and others (R/O Y. W. Fie) two were killed. Chu is also my schoolmate in Senior High. He studied Foreign Language in our university, a very wise, healthy and handsome young fellow. Sheng studied Electrical Engineering in our university, is a little short than me, quiet, and studied very hard. On 1-6-45 No. 7 CNAC C-47 was also missed over Hump Flight region due to strong gusts to move the a/c off course due north. All of flight crews (Capt Wallen, R/O Y.S. Liu) were killed.

Japanese enemy attacked Pearl Harbor—U.S., Great Britain and China declared war openly to world people at same time against Fascist Japan, so the international situations were to be changed on a sudden. As soon as a wide territories of Burma and eastern part of India were rapidly occupied by Japanese troops, more than all, Rangoon (Mar 7), Myitkyina (May 8), and Lashio (May 24), all possible air passage way could be adopted by Allies that is the NE Indian RR terminal station Sardiya where a Dinjan Airport is located at the north as an airway starting point to Kunming and Nibin (Suifoo Sichuan Province). The straight air distance from Dinjan to Kunming is about 900km (to Nibin 1,100km), but along Burma-China boundary Korrigoon Mtns. Situated north-southward in middle of the airway almost just resist a large area of this air route and the height reaches around 3,000–5,000m, continuously laid up from Tibet thru Yunnan Province to Burma as an obstacle to seen any lightning coming from ground during night flights. The thunderstorm and storm-bound surge will occur from May to October every year. Sometimes sudden blast of gusted wind blew very hard or puff of wind blew in fitful gust, so the turbulent air waves produced strong and variable bad weather which could make your a/c suddenly move up and down, pitch, roll and yaw, the strong turbulence will shoot airplane rapid drop down almost several thousands feets, maybe crashed on a hillside of the mountains if your ship control manually.

There were no reliable and accurate aerial maps and charts for actual ground positioning flight to make the ship flying on course. There were also no modern equipped communication and navigation equipments on C-47 or DC-3 (early operated with old type DC-2). There was even no one weather station between the Sardiya and Dalee (western city in Yunnan Province) to provide weather forecast about "Over Hump" flight region information and the weather facilities. Many and many great mountain ranges and the bleakish valleys covered with wide forest-sea that no people could live in this area unless the animals. There will be no cookery foods for eat and pure water for drink in high altitude forest-sea if crash happened and the flight crew fortunately survived on the ground unless the only way hungry and thirst make you waiting for to the death.

The twin-piston-engine C-47 or DC-3 has max service ceiling about 7,000m, but average cruising altitude "Over Hump" flight around 5,000m. When we crossed over all mountain ranges and valleys seemed to be endless, hence we often change course or heading and flying altitude. When climbing or descending just like going along hump-back. In passing thru the valley level flight you look at left and right mountains or hill just like crossing between two humpbacks. When forward mountain is facing to you as an obstacle in the flying just like sitting on the fore-hum-back of camel. Therefore, we called as the "Over Hump" Flight, that's the most dangerous, difficult and glorious historical flight during World War II period, I think.

May 1942 to September 1945 total actual operation period has 3 years plus 4 months, completed transportation mission approximately 33,500 passengers and 55,000 tons of cargo and post. Aircraft in operation began from 10 (July 1942) to 45 (Sept. 1945), including C-53, C-47, DC-3, and C-46 (C-46 joined CNAC fleet on June 1945). The aircraft utilization of "Over Hump" flight is very higher than any other airline at that time. For example, average flying hour of one aircraft reached 8 hours 56 minutes per day in 1944, each flight crew member over 100 flying hours per month (as for me 120 hours per month, max 160 hours). It is the highest record in historical Chinese Civil Aviation (See Chinese Modern Civil Aviation History).

During period of "Over Hump" Flight total flight accident have 48 a/c including 26 crashes, a/c damages 22, and flight crew members 75 sacrificed for sake of following reasons: (1) terrible bad weather; (2) very dangerous high altitude mountain ranges area; (3) urgent transportation missions and plans; (4) flight crew from co-pilot promoted to pilot too fast. For example, the new coming pilot should have at least half year "Over Hump" Course Flight practice and then to be checked out to captain. Co-pilot should have at least over 5,000 flying hour experience then to be promoted to pilot. (5) Aircraft over loading (C-47 total takeoff weight is 24,000 lbs, but usually adopted 27,000 lbs—over-load, 3,000 lbs); (6) Course too long for C-47, there is no reserve airport for emergency landing; (7) crew member flew too much, for lack of rest, physical exercise and tour; (8) poor ground facilities, such as communication and navigation, weather, air traffic control, aircraft maintenance and repair ground equipments, etc.

Over Hump flight operation is a kind of heroic anti–Fascist action. It is one of cooperation of American and Chinese flight and ground personnels to support the world people fighting together arm-to-arm & shoulder-to-shoulder against Fascist aggression, especially to Japanese enemy in the Asia battlefield. This successful and noble task has been accelerated rapidly the World War II to be pre-ended and got the final glorious people's victory. There seems to have a

One of the best airplanes of World War II — the Douglas C-47, affectionately called the "Gooney Bird" by the Americans or "Dakotas" by the British, flies over the jungle canopy somewhere over New Guinea during World War II (Leo J. Daugherty Collection).

high desirable requirement to erect a charming monument both in the U.S. and China as a memorial to the dead fighting fellows to fulfill our expectations.

American Over Hump Association had been established several years ago in U.S. Many members, families and familiar friends visited to China several times and Xi'an. Wish you have a happy traveling tour and wish all of you good health and wise.[28]

Humpster Alex Kaplan recounted his experiences flying the Hump and over the infamous Bermuda Triangle in December 1945. He provided an interesting sidelight on the controversy of the missing Navy squadron that disappeared over the Bermuda Triangle on 5 December 1945.

The Hump and the Bermuda Triangle

I made 100 trips and everyone was an adventure. I left Myitkyina in August 1945 after the bombs were dropped. I made a few trips to Karachi ferrying troops to India's east coast for their boat trip home. In the latter part of September 1945,

> I went on temporary duty in Bangkok, Thailand. We flew between Saigon and Rangoon so that we would always have an aircraft in Saigon to evacuate the OSS,[29] if necessary. By December 1945, I was on my way home on a C-54 out of Dum-Dum (Operation "Pipeline"). An interesting event occurred out of Santa Maria in the Azores. We were headed for Bermuda that night and I was operating the radio. I could pick up New York stations and I was in constant contact with LaGuardia airways, but could not talk with Bermuda. LaGuardia relayed all weather info and reported clear weather and good communications. I could not contact Bermuda with our "75 watt liaison" transmitter until we were a few minutes away. After landing in Bermuda, and having breakfast, we headed for West Palm Beach, FL. Bermuda operations asked us to listen and look for some downed Navy flyers. That was the morning of December 6, 1945. I didn't realize till many years later that Dec. 5, in the afternoon, the famous Navy squadron and rescue planes were lost in the "Bermuda Triangle." I definitely encountered electromagnetic interference even though the weather was clear and communications to LaGuardia were fine.[30]

Humpster Sherman Legas recalled an evening spent on guard duty in the pouring rain when he confronted someone he thought was an intruder to his assigned post at Sookerating in March 1944:

A Near Miss on Guard Duty

> It happened at Sookerating in March 1944 at the time the Japanese were making their big push up the Imphal-Kohima Road. They were supposedly within 30 miles of Sookerating and it was anticipated that they would have spies and infiltration well in advance of the main force. Thus, at Sook[erating] and the other Assam bases, a high state of alert existed.
> Everyone, officers included, were required to pull guard duty. I lived in the officers tent area and when my turn at guard duty came I was assigned a beat along the edge of the area. One end of the beat terminated at the near end of a basha. The next sentry's beat terminated at the other end of the same basha. We were told to signal "okay" to each other at the end of each beat from our positions on opposite ends of the basha porch.
> The night was miserable, raining and most of our beats were slippery mud at the end of the basha where my post or beat terminated. I was armed with an M-1 Carbine loaded with 16 rounds, 15 in the magazine and one in the barrel and the weapon "on safe." My weapon was semi-automatic, but in practice I had fired the whole clip in about 3 seconds on a number of occasions. (I had the duty as the squadron armaments officer and had access to all the ammo I wanted).
> After a number of wet, miserable, mud slogging beats at the ends of which my buddy sentry, "Fatty," and I exchanged proper signals from opposite ends of the basha porch, I again approached the signaling point. I was slithering along the end of the basha approaching the corner of the porch and at that moment saw a man hiding in what appeared an ambush for me at that corner. It was too late for me to stop so I threw myself forward about 8' and landed on my knees and butt in a deep squat facing the person. My carbine butt was in the middle of my belly and I was pointing it at him up and down with frantic jerking on the trigger. *My Weapon did not fire,* — the safety was still "ON." Then I heard Fatty's familiar, soft voice say, "Hey, what are you doing?" My blood turned to

ice water and when I was able to speak again in a few moments I said, "Fatty, you damn fool, I was trying to kill you! What are you doing hiding on my post?" "Well, geez, I was just going to give you a little scare!"

I've thanked God many times that I was prevented from ending this practical joke in a tragedy.[31]

Lieutenant Royce A. King recounted his experiences in liberating a former Japanese prisoner of war camp in late August 1945. As Humpster Ray Lewallen, Royce's flight engineer, wrote, "It was a very sad situation because of the living conditions." Lewallen added that the liberation of this POW camp was also dangerous "because the Japanese in the area did not know that the war was over."

MISSION TO A PRISON CAMP

Late in August 1945, my squadron, the 3rd Combat Cargo Squadron, 1st Group moved from Myitkyina, Burma, to Luliang, China, near Kunming. Luliang and Kunming bases were very familiar to us as we used them for refueling stops the past months transporting the Chinese 50th Division, and gas over the Hump from Burma to Nanning, China. The Chinese had been in combat during the retaking of Burma.

I was bunked with my friend, Hank Ketchum, again, as we were in India, Burma and before as cadets in Advanced Twin Engine School. We were crewed together as replacement pilots in C-47s since March. Luliang left a lot to be desired for comfortable accommodations we expected, having been in tents in India and Burma. We were in a barracks type structure with crumbling walls and ceiling. Steel cots, held together by ropes and we lay on paper thin mattress. An added feature were the rats that came and went from holes in the walls, even in the daytime. Fortunately, the squadron was moved to Kunming a couple of weeks later where we were four to a room and fewer rats.

Our trips out of Kunming were east, moving troops to Luichow, or bringing back U.S. personnel that were in east China and were now starting home. August 28th, my flight was to assign two C-47s for a mission to a prison camp at Weihsien in north China. I drew one of the assignments.

We were to take in relief supplies, radios and several Chinese officers to act as interpreters as it was still garrisoned by the Japanese. My plane was #907, one I had flown before with its crew chief, T/Sgt Ray Lewallen. My diary doesn't state who the other crew members were, as we switched co-pilots within the flight. The other pilot could have been Lt. Simmons, only wished I'd recorded all the names daily.

Weihsien is only 1200 miles NE of Kunming on a peninsula out in the Yellow Sea across from Korea. So soon after the Japanese surrender, refueling bases were few in northern China, so we were required to load barrels of gas with the other cargo before leaving Kunming. Also had nine Army and Navy people as passengers to drop off at Hsian en route. Loads like this, cargo passengers and barrels of gas, I was glad to be up front as pilot and not back in the cargo section.

Mid-morning Aug 29th we were loaded and waiting our turn to takeoff. The other C-47 from our squadron, loaded as we were, was crewed by Lts. Knaack and Bostwick. While we sat we witnessed one of our C-47s crash while attempting to take off on a much shorter strip. Kunming is at 6000' and when loaded we needed as much runway as you could get. We later learned that the radio man was killed but pilots Lts. Wilenberg and Jury, plus the crew chiefs were suffering from burns. Our turn came and we were airborne later than I'd liked, as a few hours later we ran into weather that forced us to RON at Liangshan. The base was near enough to the city and several of us rode in by rickshaws. The city had a wall around it, and I was impressed by the big, ornate gate that we rode thru in the city. Following some signs I was directed to an art show in a small school building. I bought two watercolors by Prof. Cho York to take home for Christmas gifts. At least then I thought I'd be home by Christmas, but it was not to be.

We were up at 0530 on the 30th. Some of the gas from our barrels was used to top off our tanks. It was a slow process as Chinese soldiers used a hand pump to get into our wings. It was a little disturbing to find out that one barrel we carried was filled with oil instead. It was lucky we were up early as we had a tire blow out before takeoff. Many strips in China were crushed rock, some fist size, and hell on tires of loaded planes. Some planes carried spare tail wheels all mounted in the event that some base couldn't service the problem. Our blow out was a main wheel anyway, but a ground crew had us going in an hour. Flew on about 500 miles to Hsian and discharged our passengers. I think they were glad to get off after all our problems. We took on more cargo and two barrels of gas. We were fully loaded now and learned that we would be the first ground contact to those interned at Weihsien by either American or Chinese.

From Hsian to Weihsien is about 600 miles. We arrived about 1800. My diary says, "after getting lost a bit." The field itself was well camouflaged with the hangar looking like small rolling hills from the air. Knaack's plane arrived soon after with a load much like ours. I kidded them that they would not have found the field at all had I not been on the ground for them to see. We parked about 30 yards apart on the deserted airfield and waited. It was decided to stay aboard the plane and see about transport in the morning. It was getting dark and had no hint as to where the Japanese were. It was totally dark when we heard a truck engine some way off. The truck lights would be on, then off, as it approached across the field. With its lights off, the Japanese truck pulled alongside our plane and stopped. After some conversation among the Chinese soldiers, several approached the truck and I followed along.

I had a large flashlight and lucky me, pointed it at the cab. There sat a neatly uniformed Japanese officer staring back. He was holding a ceremonial sword on his lap and as he stepped down, I noticed the pistol on his hip. Knaack and I moved to the rear of the truck and pointed our flashlights up to the rack. There we saw 5 soldiers with rifles pointed down at our group. We promptly switched our lights off! The conversation between Chinese to Japanese, and then to the American officer who came with the other plane, indicated that the Japanese officer was inviting us to come with him. It was explained that we were to stay with the aircraft and have him return with transport in the morning.[32]

Guards were posted and K-stations were passed around. My canteen of water tasted real good to us up front. A C-47 cockpit is a cold and cramped place to try to sleep with only my A-2 jacket for warmth. Sometime later we heard some gun fire away off and in the morning learned that some Chinese soldiers had later came to the other plane to explain that there had been some "bandits" in the area, and they had driven them off. Dawn was welcome as we were all chilly and hungry and wondering what would come next. Some trucks came across the field and later and backed up to our cargo doors. We all helped load out the crates and boxes, then climbed atop the load to ride to the camp some three miles away.

I noticed as we approached the camp it appeared to be a mission or school. It was surrounded with a wall, and guard towers. The whole area about the size of three football fields. Soldiers opened a large wire gate and we passed into the camp compound where there were some brick buildings, other wooden structures and a few trees. The Japanese soldiers bowed to us to us as we passed by. I wasn't prepared for what happened next. A throng of people appeared and were shouting and clapping and surrounded the trucks. Later learned that 1500 civilians, American, British and French were held here, some as long as the war. Missionaries, oil company employees with families, and some laborers who had been caught by advancing Japanese armies during the earlier years of the war.

The officers and enlisted men we had brought in took charge of the cargo from the trucks. I wandered around answering questions from the people and listened to their stories. The children, most of whom had been born here, asked questions about our uniforms and wings. We all ended up giving away our insignia from our sun tans, the little Army Air Corps prop and wing, my silver bar and even some .45 bullets. They told how a week earlier a bomber had dropped clothing and supplies to them. That accounted for the weird assortment of G.I. clothing many wore, knit stocking caps and some too large pants and shirts. Although thin, most looked healthy that I saw. A Frenchman followed along with me, explaining his time there. His English mixed with French, made it a little difficult. I did learn that village Chinese would come to the fence with milk, eggs, and other food that went mostly to the children, so some bartering was done. He explained to me that food was not the best for the adults.

A Catholic nun was in a group that questioned me, and upon learning that I was from Iowa, asked if I knew where Cedar Rapids was. My wife was working for a dentist there while I was overseas. The sister had a brother-in-law in Cedar Rapids who hadn't heard from her for years and asked if I wouldn't contact him. I readily agreed to and wrote my wife about it upon my return to Kunming. This alone made the trip a happy one for me. I also promised the kids I would buzz the compound later that afternoon when we left for Hsian. We swooped low over the camp and made a wide sweeping turn for another pass. We watched the people looking up and waiving . I was glad to have had this mission for sure.

Later we learned that two other C-47s were dispatched to Mukdon, Manchuria and brought out Gen. Jonathan Wainwright[33] from a prisoner of war camp there. He was the last Commander of American forces in the Philippines, a prisoner since the fall of Corregidor, May 16, 1942. It would have been real a pleasure to have met the hero of Bataan.[34]

Despite its reliability as a transport aircraft, C-47s experienced mechanical failures. Jack D. Goodrich, who served as a Hump pilot with Squadron B, 1348th Army Air Force, Burma, based out of Myitkyina, recalled one such episode he and his crew experienced while flying over to Burma in Asmara, Ethiopia.

Breakdown Over Asmara, Ethiopia

Our group, destined to be Squadron B at the 1348th AAFBU in Myitkyina, Burma, left Nashville, TN; hedgehopped across the traditional African route;

and assembled in Calcutta in late January 1945. En route we had some interesting experiences. As we crossed Africa, we heard of a base referred to as the "Garden Spot of Africa." It was on ahead of us at a place called Asmara. Supposedly, it was a prime rest area for Italian military personnel during their war with Ethiopia. At each stop across the way, the stories became grander and more vivid. The only hitch was that Americans were only to use the base as a navigational aid to check before turning toward Aden. The base was manned by British military who, in our biased opinion, didn't want their Shangri-La inundated with a bunch of Yanks. How to enjoy the forbidden occupied more and more of our thoughts and conversations as we headed East. When we left Khartoum on our last leg we made up our minds on a sure fire plan. About twenty-minutes out from Khartoum and heading for Asmara we called back and said that we were having trouble with one of our engines (there was nothing wrong with either of them). Our base suggested that we return, but we said that we would carry on and keep them informed. When we felt that we were too far away to return, we called again to say that the problem was increasing. After several minutes, the Khartoum tower informed us of the Asmara airfield and said that it might be necessary to land there. If high fives were known at that time, the four of us, pilot, co-pilot, navigator and radio operator, would have been slamming hands in the aisles.

There was only one problem to make the incident realistic. We should come in on one engine. Since the pilot had been an instructor in C-47s before requesting overseas duty, a single engine landing in a brand new aircraft was a snap. We contacted Asmara, received landing instructions, dropped flaps as requested, feathered the left engine and started a straight approach. Still a long way from the field the pilot said, "O.K., drop the gear." I dropped the lever, glanced at the window, saw the gear begin to start down and then became fascinated and a bit embarrassed at the fire trucks and ambulances lined up near the runway. Everything was going according to plan until the tower operator said with a very British accent and reserve, "Ho Yank, we see you are having a bit of trouble with your engine, but do you really want to land with your wheels up?" We were only a few hundred feet off the runway and coming down fast when we both realized what had happened, yelled, "Selector Valve!" and switched the selector from the feathered left engine hydraulic pump to the right engine. The pilot did a fine job holding the plane off the runway until the pressure built up and the gear lowered. It seemed as though the gear locked in place and the wheels hit the runway within the same second.[35] We could well imagine what would have happened if we had wrecked a perfectly good aircraft for a lark. We would probably be getting out of Leavenworth just about now. However, nothing happened, and our youthful buoyancy bounced back in time to continue our "plan."

A lot of people arrived at the ramp to see if we were all right, but the one we quickly singled out was the crew chief responsible for repairing the engine. We had wrapped a carton of Camels and stuffed some cash in a bag, and while presenting this to him, intimated that we would like to stay in Asmara for a day or so to see the sights. He laughed as he slipped the Camels under his arm, and even suggested a couple of pubs that we might enjoy. We thought it was unfair that three of us should be able to go off together and leave our radio operator in a strange environment, so we stripped our insignia (we didn't think the Brits would recognize or even care about a bare uniform) and planned to meet our radio operator where the lorries left the base for the town. He spoke Italian with a heavy Brooklyn accent, but we were sure he was an accomplished linguist. We were no sooner seated in the first "night club" than we had four smiling girls of the house join us. Their English was only one step above, "Hey JOE, What do you know," but they knew how to signal the bartender and order more champagne for the table. Most of our conversation consisted of a few words, partially understood and much arm waving. It was amazing how fast a couple of bottles could disappear, but at the local low price, it seemed OK. Soon the bartender would signal us and with a big smile use a circular motion with his finger asking if we wanted another round for our table — we thought. We didn't become suspicious until everyone else in the place was smiling at us and bottles of champagne were everywhere. We conferred, using Pig Latin, that we had used as children and concluded that we were being taken for a roll. When we asked for the check and saw 43 bottles of wine, we had all our fears confirmed and the exits seemed to be a long way from us. Again, using our secret language, we wadded as much money as we had, threw it on the table, said, "Keep the change," and walked toward the door smiling and waving all the way. We almost made it. We were only a few steps from the door when the girls had unfolded and counted the money, and decided there was a bit of a shortage. There were only four American uniforms in town and five seconds later they were running down the middle of the street toward the return lorry. We took to the street because there were fewer cars and bicycles than there were people on the sidewalks, and we needed space between us and sounds of the shouting behind us.

Fortunately a lorry was ready to leave for the base; we jumped aboard as the driver closed the door, mumbled something about "Damn Yanks" and pulled out into traffic leaving a long line of shouting people falling farther and farther behind. Early the next morning we found the British crew chief, convinced him that one night in Shangri-La was enough and took off for Aden. I have often wondered what the British base commander thought when confronted by a group of irate townspeople describing four men in non-descript uniforms who drank their wine and paid only partially. They wouldn't have gone into detail as to how such a large quantity was sold, and the British C.O. probably vowed to impound the next yank plane and crew until he could safely dispose of them.[36]

Besides Hump pilots, flight crews, and ground maintenance personnel, combat engineers, infantrymen, quartermasters and what today would be labeled combat support and combat service support personnel also served in China-Burma-India. Among this latter category was Stephen Kalista, a member of the 1111th Signal Company, 44th Air Service Group, who had been assigned to Dinjan, India. Prior to his death in 1995, Kalista gave us a look at the role played by signalmen in the war in CBI and their vital contribution to the Allied victory in August 1945.

A Signalman at War

I enlisted in the U.S. Army Signal Corps, was inducted 8 September 1942. Basic training at Sea Girt, New Jersey. Went to Fort Monmouth for Radio Repair Training. After completion of 3 courses in 10 months, I went to Jefferson Barracks, MO, an Air Corps pool. Spent days getting additional training in the use of guns, lots of physical exercises, Saturday parades, etc. Transferred to New Orleans Air Base. After several transfers went to the newly-organized 1111th Signal Co. We later transferred by 6x6 trucks to Barksdale Field, LA.

Later the 1111th Signal Co. went by troop train to Lakeland, FL. While there, the company did various things like play "capture the flag." Packed up our test equipment, etc., for overseas deployment. Our VHF radio team went to Orlando AF for a refresher course on VHF radio equipment. Members were: Kalista, Clark, McDonnel, Carter? We had one lesson on how to swim at the Lakeland Community Pool. I still could not swim! We transferred to Camp Patrick Henry, Va., for shipment overseas. Italian POWs did KP duty at this base and were always smiling. I was able to get a pass—visited my brother, Joe, and his wife at Fort Myers, VA. He was an M.P. stationed at Fort Myers, VA ... [and] ... guarded Tomb of Unknown Soldier, etc. Because of a heavy snowfall, I missed the bus and was almost AWOL.

The 1111th Signal Company and about 4,000 plus G.I.s boarded the USS *General Butner*, a troop ship at Newport News, VA, and left on 23 April 1944. The Red Cross girls gave us sewing kits, books, no kisses. Our ship went unescorted to Capetown, South Africa. We were given a 12-hour pass—visited Capetown, bought food, etc. We only had two meals on the boat—breakfast and supper—Starvation! Our troop ship continued to Durban, South Africa—went into harbor—we picked up British Corvettes and a troop ship. Because of the rough weather around Africa, the ship stayed close to shore—it still tilted—garbage cans flew all over the place. By the way, we slept on hammocks stacked 4 high; washed our clothes and took showers in salt water with regular soap—had diarrhea.

Our next stop was Mombassa Harbor, Kenya Colony (the land of Mau-Maus). Remember them—cut off British soldiers heads. On to Bombay, India, arrived 25 May 1944. Bombay was bombed out. An ammunition ship exploded in the harbor about a month before we arrived. The Bombay fire dept. was destroyed—half the city was destroyed by fires, etc. We loaded cattle cars (Indian troop train) and headed for Calcutta area. The cars had park benches—two stacks—we used these as beds. During our journey we were not allowed to drink Indian water or purchase any food or vegetables or fruit except bananas—no showers?—one day we ran out of drinking water. The Indian railway used ... different gauge railroads. We arrived at air base (Sylhet and Asansol) near Calcutta. Don't remember much of our stay there. Several of us went TDY (temporary duty) on a C-47 plane (Gooney Bird) to Dinjan Airfield (home of Combat Cargo C-47 & C-46 outfits). Slept in two-man pup tents. During heavy monsoon season several inches of water were in the tent. Had to dig a ditch around the tent. One day while digging the ditch, lightning struck nearby. I ran into the tent. I was using a shovel with *steel*!

We laid telephone lines. Did not have transportation—put an iron bar through cable reel—two men held the bar and we walked along and laid the telephone line while walking long distance. The telephone line was placed along the end of the airplane runway—line was broken several times when planes came in too soon on runway. In one case someone built a paper fire on top of the line. Our transportation improved—we borrowed a Jeep. At Fort Monmouth we learned to place telephone lines in trees by using a long rod while riding in back of 6x6. These lines were connected to U.S. Army EE-5 telephone—those with a hand-operated ringer. The British used D.C. power in India. We installed a H.C. generator at a tea plantation house—must have been for a Colonel. A Red Cross woman was installing curtains in the house. Our two-man pup tents did not have a light bulb.

Later when the 1111th Signal Co., 44th Air Service Group joined us, we lived in 4-man British white tents. One light bulb per tent, dirt floor and net to keep out malaria mosquitoes. At the beginning, no showers available. Got water from a local pump and used metal helmet to wash face and shave. When we had heavy rains, I would strip down and shower outside tent. We would walk to water pump, strip down (skinny dip?) and body wash ourselves using water from helmets. The Indians were very modest. I guessed they were shocked to see a group of naked GIs wash themselves. The poor people of Calcutta would open a water hydrant in Calcutta and lift up their clothing, throw water under their private parts. Some bathed in the Hoogley River where bones of cremated bodies were thrown in the water.

Our tent was never guarded. I do not recall any thefts of tents by the local Indian population. Our first toilet was a "slit" trench complete with a shovel and a roll of toilet paper on a tree limb. At night we used flashlights. Conditions improved somewhat when they installed showers and an outhouse. This took me back to my childhood days in Pennsylvania [Coaldale, PA.] where we, too, had an outhouse.

Well getting back to the 1111th Signal Co., 44th Air Service Group, stationed at Dinjan Airfield, we had airborne radar repairmen (3rd Echelon repair), teletype repairman, etc. All airborne radio used in C-47s, C-46s, etc. plus marker beacon sets, radio compass, etc. Our six man group (MOS 951) only repaired the command set SCR-522 (VHF Radio). When there was a need to align radio sets without outside interference, a screen room was constructed inside the basha repair shop

The 1111th Signal Company had 100 enlisted men. Capt Molkenthen was our Commanding Officer, Lt Schoenig, our Signal Officer, Lts Cole and H. Opencensky. Our 1st Sgt was Sgt. Lilly. He later developed an illness and was sent back to the States. My team leader went back to the States to go to O.C.S. We had a mobile unit which in some cases went to the runways for radio repair work.

The 44th Air Service Group consisted of the following units: 1) Headquarters & Headquarters Squadron; 2) 497th Air Service Squadron; 3) 498th Air Service Squadron; 4) 1080th Quartermaster Co.; 5) 1111th Signal Co.; 6) 1573rd Ordnance Supply & Maintenance Co.; 7) 1574th Ordnance Supply & Maintenance Co.; 8) 2116th Quartermaster Co.; 9) 2117th Quartermaster Co. It is to be noted that Marvin Sledge, our last C.O., of the 44th Air Svc Gp. was also formerly C.O. of the 52nd Air Svc Gp in Burma. I was a member of both units.

After the war with Japan ended in Aug 1945, I and the V.H.F. repairman started to smash the SC 522 radios with sledge hammers! The 1111th Signal Company was alerted to ship back to the U.S.A.! Couple days later I was in Myitkyina, Burma for 4 months. Good planning by Army. I never forgave for this move. I would like to quote from a letter which I sent to my parents on 18 Sept 1945. As you read it you will see what the Army did to me.

"We arrived in Burma in September 1945. The 1009th Signal Co. did not exist as a unit. About 20 members (low points) left Myitkyina in Oct 1945. Others left for USA. Except for turning boxes inside out, playing M.P looking for stolen trucks, operating switchboard, doing art work and developing and printing film negatives, I sat around doing nothing until December 1945. Left for Camp Kanchapara near Calcutta. Left Calcutta on Jan 27 on *S.S. Marine Panther*, Arrived 25 Feb 1946. Because of illness on boat, did not get discharged until 11 August 1946."[37]

Jim Beamon, a base operations officer with the 20th U.S. Army Air Forces, stationed at a base located in the central part of India, provided a rare view as to the operations of a forward air base in India during a Japanese air raid. As Beamon wrote, "The base was a combat type cargo operation, located adjacent to the Headquarters of the 20th Air Force, which was a B-29 bomber operation."

Christmas 50 Years Ago

Both these operations [i.e., bomber and cargo] required flying from rear bases in India to forward bases in North China. Flight time involved was 18–20 hours round trip, many times as much as 30 hours without sleep, also flying over the very treacherous Himalayan mountains called the "Hump," under the most severe weather conditions in the world, many hours over enemy territory where aerial attacks were frequent.

In order to supply the medical needs of these two large operations, a General Hospital was established on our base. It was staffed with the highest level of personnel and equipment to take care of all types of casualties. To break the long hours of duty and the adverse living conditions, a small Xmas Eve party was organized by the staff to celebrate the glorious holiday of Xmas. A small service band from base personnel was acquired for entertainment and the 20 some nurses on the base supplied the partnership for dancing. The evening started off in a fashion conducive to a typical holiday celebration. Sometimes earlier I had made the acquaintance of a Major who, at the time, was head of the Dental Department of Pennsylvania Medical School. He invited me to be his guest at this party, which I readily accepted. He was not only interesting, but a joy to talk to.

While enjoying some of the festivities of the evening the party was abruptly interrupted by an announcement from the Officer-of-the-Day, who happened to be one of the nurses, that the base was under a One-Ball alert,[38] which meant that the enemy aircraft was headed in our direction, about 20 miles out, and that we were to evacuate the club building, dousing all lights and the personnel return to their barracks area, which generally was the safest area in case of an aerial attack.

Japanese air bases were such a long distance from our base a raid was not impossible, but improbable and was not supposed to happen. The participants of the party made no effort to accept this order from the Officer-of-the-Day as for real, and continued with the activities. In a very short time the OD appeared again and with much more forceful language that we were now under a Two-Ball alert, which meant that an enemy air raid was imminent and headed in our direction. A raid to most now became a possibility and the OD's orders were beginning to be taken seriously. In a few minutes a Three-Ball alert was announced, which meant the enemy was about 5 minutes out and our bases were their target.

As Operations Officer, I was charged with all activities on the flight line and the airstrip. This included security of the area and safety of the personnel. Upon receiving the last alert I went outside to discover the entire area was under a complete "black-out" including our air base which was about 2 miles distance. I then began to realize my responsibility to the flight line and the personnel that worked there. Slowly I felt my way to the flight line in my jeep in a very "pitch-dark" evening. This 2 mile drive back to the base not only seemed the longest I had ever driven but the loneliest. One had the feeling that the world had deserted you.

Arriving at the base and knowing no security measures had been taken, I ordered all personnel to return to their respective barracks area. I asked the tower operator to remain because he would be my only line of communications with H.Q. Many of the personnel, realizing that two of us were staying, wanted to remain. Being charged with their safety, more forceful orders were issued.

In a very short time aircraft were overhead and then things began to happen. Explosions began to be heard, the sky became a glowing red. I then realized our B-29 base was the target and not us, and hoped our base would not be their secondary target. In a short time the area took on an air of quietness, ending what we hoped was the completion of an unusual event. A preliminary assessment of casualties and damage to aircraft and building revealed it was minimal. No doubt they had to sacrifice bomb load to cover the long distance. But had it not been for the small number of aircraft involved, the damage and the casualties would have been much greater.

I had been in an aerial raid in North Africa and many in North China, but none seemed to have the lasting and telling effect as this Christmas Eve raid in India. Rarely, in 50 years, does a Christmas Eve pass without some inner feeling reminding me of this sad event."[39]

Flying could be and was a dangerous undertaking even without the presence of enemy fighters. The B-24s, C-47s, C-46s, and C-87 that traversed the Hump were, in fact, "flying bombs." In addition to the hydraulic and fuel lines powering the aircraft and the landing gear, they carried aviation fuel in 55-gallon drums lashed together by ropes that sometimes broke loose and rolled about the cargo area causing leaks, spills and toxic gases. A spark, either on impact from landing, from an unconnected wire, or a leak from a hydraulic system onto a hot exhaust tube could and did turn a Dakota or Commando into a funeral pyre that brought instantaneous death to the pilot, co-pilot, crew members, and personnel on the ground. Bob Friedman, a pilot in a C-46 recalled one such incident over Chengkung, China:

On Fire at Chengkung

After almost 50 years, I wish could contact the crew (co-pilot, flight engineer and radio operator) who were with me when the left wing of our C-46 nearly burnt off during a night takeoff from Chengkung. It happened October 14-15, 1944, but the story began about a year before at C-46 School at Reno. Did you ever notice the short stub of tubing protruding from the left nacelle about a foot behind the engine exhaust stack, directly in the exhaust stream? I wondered what it was for and why it was located where it was. The Curtiss tech. rep. explained: "it was vent the hydraulic fluid from the 'up' side of the landing gear actuator cylinder. If it was ever necessary to crank the gear down manually, you pulled the handle, the fluid vented out making it possible to crank down the gear." I thought that seemed an unlikely place to dump hydraulic fluid — into the hot exhaust. NOT TO WORRY said he, "think about it, if you are cranking down the gear, you wouldn't be at full throttle and the exhaust wouldn't be streaming that far back." Sounded reasonable — but remember, the hydraulic system of the C-46 was a plumber's nightmare. It leaked and didn't always work as designed.

The flight to Chengkung was my 60th round trip, 600 hours on the Hump. This should have been my last trip. It almost was! On our return flight from

Chengkung to Misamari, early that Sunday morning, we took off to the south. It was still darkly. As the gear came up, the left side of the aircraft let up. Something had gone wrong with the plumbing and the hydraulic fluid was dumping into the exhaust stream. It was like a blow torch. Of course, we didn't know that then. All we could see was a wing on fire! Instinctively I pulled the extinguisher, throttled back and turned to the right, toward the lake and, with about 500' terrain clearance, nursed the plane around to an approach. The fire was still burning but not as brightly. Coming over the end of the runway, I called for gear down, not realizing that all of the fluid had pumped overboard. I was going to get it on the ground, gear or not, but the crew chief had anticipated the problem. He was standing by with one of the extra cans of fluid we carried. When I called for the gear. I shut down both engines and as we rolled to a stop on the runway we were already exiting via the rear steps. Fire trucks extinguished what fires still burned. Then we got to look at the damage. The underside of the left wing was burned away. You could see the sparks. The airplane was a total loss. Why it didn't blow up or come apart in the air I will never know. We were lucky.

We deadheaded back to Misarami on the next plane. I checked into Base Ops. They had us listed as crashed and written us off as dead. When I got to my basha, my basha mates (Pipkin & Hancock) had also heard that I was dead. They were sorting out my stuff. Several pilots who had been in the air around Kunming that night told me they had seen the fire light up the night sky. No one from operations, maintenance or supply asked me to account for the burned airplane.

The following day I made my 61st and the 62nd round trip two days later. After one more Hump flight, my 63rd, I rotated home in November.[40]

Appendix 1

Table of Organization of the 516th Quartermaster Truck Regiment, Tehran, Iran, 1942–1944

```
        ┌─────────────────────────┐
        │  516th Quartermaster    │
        │     Truck Regiment      │
        └─────────────────────────┘
```

1st Battalion	2nd Battalion	3rd Battalion

This chart illustrates the organization of a standard Quartermaster Truck Regiment. Each Battalion had sixty 5-ton or 2½-ton GMC Trucks.

Appendix 2

Observations of Ground Search Party Investigating Wrecks of C-47s #812 and #767

Headquarters — Air Jungle Rescue Unit
Tingkawk Sakan, Burma — 4 December 1944[1]

Subject: Observations of Ground Search Party Investigating wrecks of C-47s #812 and #767

To: Commanding General, Tenth AF, Hq., APO 218

04 November 44 — We left Kawata Bum at 0900 hrs. All walking was uphill and required trail cutting now. At 1030 hrs we bumped into a huge black bear. It is hard to say who was the more surprised, the bear or us. I believe that Sin Wanaw was under the influence of opium and Saki, because his gun went off before we could fire a shot; hence, the bear got away. Sin was heartbroken. We arrived at the next ridge at 1200 hrs and pitched camp.

05 November 44 — We departed at 0810 hrs and crossed the mountain. The going was extremely tough. We had to cut the entire route thru bamboo and Jagger palms. We headed south down ridge we supposed C-47 #767 to be on, and we pitched camp where we found water. The L-5 came over and dropped streamer message saying we were ½ mile due east of #812. The nights have become unbearably cold. A blanket and our clothes are not sufficient for sleeping. The food drop was lost over the ridge.

06 November 44 — Since we were on the same ridge as was #767, we decided to search for this plane. We had no luck. The underbrush and the vine bamboo was so thick that we wondered if we would ever be able to find it. The liaison plane came over at 1400 hrs and dropped us water, rice. Natives are all out of opium, and have fever and headache. I dosed them with aspirin and finally when they threatened to return to their villages, I gave them three toulas I had in my jungle kit. Of my party of 18 men, 16 are chronic opium smokers. From 0700 hrs. to 0800 hrs it is impossible to move them, as this is "their" hour, and they are in a semi stupor.

07 November 44 — The L-5 dropped us exact course to #812 and so we moved to the adjoining ridge. John Tongwa found #812 at 1400 hrs. The L-5 came over and dropped food. Hasty inspection of #812 shows, pilot, co-pilot and engineer burned to the point of near cremation.

08 November 44 — There is nothing we can do until L-5 drops shovel. We went to plane, laid bones of three men out and searched. I found part of a money belt, a ring on

the finger of Edward L. Winston, and burned diary. Found GI dog tags on Hiram T. Hovick. Spent rest of day felling over 300 trees for food drop clearing. Plane came over and circled #812, but heavy overcast prevented them from coming near us. The natives are out of opium and rice. There are very grumbly, we are also running short of food. Regardless of the natives' decision, we are determined to stick out the search. I sent most of the natives with the 3 enlisted men to search for #767. Ukya Nu and I with several coolies further enlarged clearing and put up very large signals stating we had found #812, also asked for food. We only have 2 flares left. Surely hope weather lifts, I don't approve of fasting. Plane dropped 2 signals and rations at 1330 hrs. Message gave results of election returns.

10 November 44 — L-5 came over, but weather prevented contact. Nights are freezing, and prevents sleeping.

11 November 44 — Natives are extremely restless and grumbly. Want more rice, vegetables and opium. I had a very stormy argument with leaders. They threatened to leave, but I managed to quell open distrest [sic] temporarily. Drop down ridge — still have to search for #767. Oh unhappiness! Suffering Saints! It's me birthday. Doc and the boys of the 90th have sent me a quart of Schenleys, 100 proof, 27 bottles of beer, 4 cartons of cigarettes, a box of cigars, and a wealth of candy, crackers and gum. We are happy with the world and a little tipsy. We got the two head guides and the interpreter that way too. They are in a little better humor now. We killed a couple of large baboons for the natives. At least I'll be warm tonight. I have a parachute to wrap in.

12 November 44 — The entire camp is out in search of #767. The booty for discovery is Rs/40. L-5 dropped rice, food, and a shovel. We dug graves and fixed aluminum head stones for them. Killed several more baboons for the natives.

13 November 44 — Held burial service at 0900 hrs for Hiram T. Hovick and two officers, names unknown. L-5 came over and dropped a message. Glory be! I'm a first Looey [i.e., First Lieutenant]. It literally came from the sky. They dropped a streamer over #767, but we did not get note in time to observe. L-5 came over again at 1400 hrs and dropped compass and distance to #767. Will move to that ridge tomorrow.

15 November 44 — I stayed in camp today and worked on a new clearing. The others went out searching. A C-47 saw my signals to the L-5 and thought I was in distress. They circled for a full hour. This is no isolated occurrence, for I've experienced this five times already since this search began. Although I was not in distress, their alertness will some day save lives for they dropped me a note and spent much of the time getting a fix on me. L-5 dropped food, cream, potatoes, sugar and salt. Men returned tired, disorganized and luckless. Head man from Maitung sent two new men and present of 8 eggs.

16 November 44 — Searched all day for #767. No luck. Returned to camp exhausted. No one could possibly imagine the roughness of such country without being down trying to cut his way through it.

17 November 44 — John Tongwa, and Sin Wanaw went out to hunt for the plane. Myers and I in desperation took a coolie and decided to cut a direct compass course to #767 despite terrible terrain and thickness of underbrush. By accident we blundered on wreckage of #767 at 1345 hrs. We had stopped to eat lunch only 25 ft from it. I had decided to climb a tree located just on the other side of the wall on bamboo. Myers having decided to climb the tree next to it got up and cut through the 4 ft wall of vine bamboo. He shouted, "I've found it!" The plane was a mass of torn metal. After a hasty examination we left. The L-5 circled while we were there.

18 November 44 — We left for #767 at 710 hrs. Woodham and I lost patience with the guide and blazed our own way. We beat the main party to the wreck. The tail of the ship was about 25 yds away from the fuselage. Upon close examination, we feel certain that one man left the wreck alive. Another and perhaps two, lived after the crash for awhile.

They had endured agony, no doubt. A cot had been set up outside the plane and a parachute tied over it as a shelter. All jungle kits had been opened and bare necessities taken out. A trail had been cut about 3 months previous to our coming upon it. About ¼ mile from wreckage a lean-to had been built. I am of the opinion that a white man built it, as it was not made of bamboo but trees. Furthermore, the trees were hacked by an inexperienced cutter. It was impossible to follow the trail due to the poor cutting and the rapidity of the growth of the vine. bamboo. We believe that one man was alive for some time, because he was lying on his back at the back of the plane. He had a trench coat under him, a musette bag under his head and a parachute over him. He was Cpt. Morris Berger, only partial decomposition had set in. Lt. John R. Morris was found in his radio compartment. Lts. Mall and DeLoach had been killed instantly. Lt. Turbeville had evidently attempted to bail out. His chute was open and the harness straps broken loose. He was about ten feet from the wreck, on his back. A piece of step ladder had broken his neck. Personal possessions were found on all. Dog tags were found on all but Cpt. Berger. The engine and nose of the plane were buried in the mountains, and covered up with vine bamboo. An elephant just charged up to camp. We scared him away by firing in the air. We finished the graves today.

19 November 44 — We went down to #767 at 0800 hrs and arranged bodies, and spent several hours on the graves. L-5 failed to show up. The natives had no rice, and refuse to leave tomorrow. I gave them our rations, and they have promised to leave.

20 November 44 — We left #767 at 0720 hrs and traveled over 8 miles by 1115 hrs. We are camping tonight at Kawata Bum. L-5 came over at 1145 hrs and circled #767. I climbed tall tree and signaled him from that distance by mirror flashes. This is the first time hrs. weather has permitted communication by this method. We plan to reach Maitaung by 1300 hrs. Tomorrow the head man has invited us to a "blowout" there.

21 November 44 — We reached Maitaung before 1200 hrs. Before we had reached the village proper, we had stepped in for Saki, in several homes. All night the villagers (Kachins) brought presents of fish, chicken, rice, beans, etc., our interpreter has never showed up and we have sent search parties to comb the hills for him.

22 November 44 — We have combed the hills but there is no sign of him. More search parties are out. Today, all of us are rather ill. The villagers have brought us over 44 quarts of Saki and many other presents this morning. I have doctored all the villagers. Babies and adults are covered with what appears to be syphilitic sores. I used weak (diluted) iodine on the babies, and Sulfanilamide on the oldsters. We took group pictures of ourselves with the men and women. John Tongwa and Sin Wanaw left for home. It was like saying good-bye to old friends. Rumor has it that our lost interpreter is on the road to Banti. We shall leave for there in the morning. If we stayed any longer, our two elephants could not carry our bags.

23 November 44 — We had intended to leave at 0600 hrs but after shaking hands and saying good-bye to the head man, our coolies and the villagers, receiving fine gifts, we left at 0800 hrs. At old Maitung I got rides for Myers, Hoffman and Woodham, in a jeep. I walked elephants to Namti, 10 miles away. I stopped at Naylung Dean at 1300 hrs. Had food and said good-bye to head man. Arrived at Namti at 1530 hrs. exhausted and sick. Drank coffee at SOS and slept at bizarre.

24 November 44 — We got up at 0500 hrs packed and ready to leave for Mogaung after settling with Mr. Jones, British Civil Affairs Officer, and the lost interpreter. The latter had found his way to Namti after being in the jungle without food for 2 days. He had taken trail to Nawlu and followed a stream to the Myitkyina-Mogaung Road. Avn. Engineers had taken him to Namti Junction after finding him. Arrived at Mogaung at 0930 hrs. Proceeded to Pahok and arrived there at 1030 hrs. The L-5 from Air Jungle Rescue that had kept contact with us in the jungle, took me home to Tingkawk Bakan. Did I say home? It feels like it now!

Chapter Notes

Preface
1. Winston S. Churchill, *The Second World War: Closing the Ring* (Boston: Houghton Mifflin Company, 1951), pp. 560–1.
2. Ibid., p. 561.

Chapter 1
1. The best accounts on this phase of the war in China-Burma-India include Wesley Frank Craven and James Lea Cate's *The Army Air Forces in World War II: Volume 1: Plans and Early Operations January 1939 to August 1942* (Washington, DC: Office of Air Force History, Government Printing Office, 1983), hereafter cited as Craven and Cates, *AAF in World War II: Vol. I*; S. Woodburn Kirby, et al., *The War Against Japan: Volume II: India's Most Dangerous Hour* (London: HMSO, 1958), pp. 1–77, hereafter cited as Kirby, *War Against Japan*, Vol. 2; Charles R. Romanus and Riley Sunderland, *United States Army in World War II: The China-Burma-India Theater: Stilwell's Mission to China* (Washington, DC: U.S. Army Center of Military History, Government Printing Office, 1987), pp. 1–143, hereafter cited as Romanus and Sunderland, *Stilwell's Mission to China*.
2. See Robert Lee Scott, *Flying Tiger: Chennault of China* (New York: Berkeley Medallion Books, 1959), hereafter cited as Scott, *Chennault of China*; Russell Whelan, *The Flying Tigers: The Story of the American Volunteer Group* (New York: Viking Press, 1943), hereafter cited as Whelan, *The Flying Tigers*.
3. Romanus and Sunderland, *Stilwell's Mission to China*, p. 143; Kirby, *War Against Japan*, Vol. 2. pp. 50–99.
4. Roy S. Cline, *United States Army in World War II: The War Department: Washington Command Post: The Operations Division* (Washington, DC: Center of Military History, 1990), p. 221, hereafter cited as Cline, *Washington Command Post*.

5. For the bitter debate over the two competing strategies to defeat and drive out the Japanese forces in CBI see Major General Claire Lee Chennault, *Way of a Fighter: The Memoirs of Claire Lee Chennault* (New York: Putnam, 1949), pp. 309–23, hereafter cited as Chennault, *Way of a Fighter*; Romanus and Sunderland, *Stilwell's Mission to China*, pp. 313–89.
6. See Winston S. Churchill, *The Second World War: Closing the Ring* (Boston: Houghton Mifflin, 1951), pp. 560–1, hereafter cited as Churchill, *Closing the Ring*.
7. Ibid., p. 561.
8. Field Marshal Lord Alan Brooke, *War Diaries, 1939–1945* (Berkeley: University of California Press, 2001), hereafter cited as Brooke, *War Diaries*.
9. Ibid. See Field Marshal Alan Brooke's entries for 14 May 1942, pp. 403, 20 May 1942, p. 407, and his extremely critical comments on Chiang Kai-shek and his wife, Mei-ling Soon (Madame Chiang), dated 23 November 1943 pp. 477–81.
10. See Churchill to Major General Sir Hastings Ismay, 7 January 1942, in Warren F. Kimball, *Churchill and Roosevelt, The Complete Correspondence: I. Alliance Emerging* (Princeton, NJ: Princeton University Press, 1984), p. 321, hereafter cited as Kimball, *Churchill and Roosevelt: 1. Alliance Emerging*.
11. Winston Churchill, *The Second World War: The Grand Alliance* (Boston: Houghton Mifflin, 1950), p. 686.
12. Romanus and Sunderland, *Stilwell's Mission to China*, p. 11.
13. Prior to the U.S. involvement in World War II, planners in both the Navy and War Departments formulated five war plans dubbed "Rainbow." These included Rainbow 1 which called for a hemispheric defense of North America to prevent a violation of the Monroe Doctrine; Rainbow 2 which called for a hemispheric defense as outlined in Rainbow 1 and protection and defense of U.S. interests in the Pacific; Rainbow 3 again called for a hemi-

spheric defense though it outlined that U.S. interests in the Western Pacific be defended; Rainbow 4 was a reiteration of Rainbow 1 though it called for the use of combat troops in the southern part of the South American continent or to the eastern Atlantic; Rainbow 5 called for the defense of the hemisphere though it called for the dispatching of U.S. combat forces to either Africa or Europe "as rapidly as possible ... in order to effect the decisive defeat of Germany or Italy, or both." After the Japanese attack on Pearl Harbor, Rainbow 5, or Plan D, which called for a "Germany First" strategy, was used. See Cline, *Washington Command Post*, pp. 55–8.

14. Barbara Tuchman, *Stilwell and the American Experience in China, 1911–45* (New York: Macmillan, 1970), p. 234.

15. Chennault, *Way of a Fighter*, p. 234; Romanus and Sunderland, *Stilwell's Mission to China*, pp. 92–3; and Lieutenant General Lewis H. Brereton, USA, *The Brereton Diaries, The War in the Air in the Pacific, Middle East, and Europe, 3 October 1941–8 May 1945* (New York: Morrow, 1946), pp. 111–3.

16. Chennault, *Way of a Fighter*, p. 234.

17. Lieutenant Colonel Charles E. Miller, USAF, *Airlift Doctrine* (Montgomery, AL: Air University Press, Maxwell Air Force Base, March 1988), p. 50, hereafter cited as Miller, *Airlift Doctrine*; Romanus and Sunderland, *Stilwell's Mission to China*, pp. 202–4.

18. The Air Service Command was first established on 1 May 1942 under the command of Brigadier General Elmer E. Adler and was based at New Delhi, India. Oliver assumed command on 1 August 1942. Romanus and Sunderland, *Stilwell's Mission to China*, p. 200.

19. Ibid.

20. Tuchman, *Stilwell and the American Experience in China*, p. 234; Captain Edward Goodman, USAAF, interview with the author, 30 June 1994. Notes in possession of the author, hereafter cited as Goodman interview.

21. William H. Tunner, *Over the Hump* (Washington, DC: Office of Air Force History, 1985), p. 75.

22. Goodman interview.

23. Ibid.

24. Interview with Captain David C. Hall, USAAF, by the author, Madison Township, Ohio, 15 July 1994, in possession of the author, Part 1, Side A, hereafter cited as Hall interview.

25. William J. Slim, *Defeat into Victory*. 3rd ed. (London: Macmillan, 1988), p. 242.

26. Ulysses Lee, *United States Army in World War II: The Employment of Negro Troops* (Washington, DC: Center for Military History, 1994) pp. 616–17, hereafter cited as Lee, *Employment of Negro Troops*.

27. Romanus and Sunderland, *Stilwell's Mission to China*, p. 269; Michael Schaller, *The U.S. Crusade in China: 1936–1945* (New York: Columbia University Press, 1979), p. 120.

28. Chennault, *Way of a Fighter*, pp. 250–88; See "Air Power Rather than Army Reform" in Romanus and Sunderland, *Stilwell's Mission to China*, pp. 315–54.

29. Ibid.

30. Alan Brooke, *War Diaries*, pp. 490–2 and 503; Romanus and Sunderland, *Stilwell's Mission to China*, pp. 179, 182, 226, 271; Louis Allen, *Burma: The Longest War, 1941–1945* (London: Phoenix Press, 1984), pp. 472–80.

31. Romanus and Sunderland, *Stilwell's Mission to China*, pp. 320–27.

32. See Reginald Cleveland, *Air Transport at War* (New York: Harper & Brothers, 1946), pp. 149–234.

33. Charles R. Romanus and Riley Sunderland, *United States Army in World War II: The China-Burma-India Theater: Stilwell's Command Problems* (Washington, DC: Center of Military History, 1987), p. 11.

34. Ibid., p. 212.

35. Ibid., p. 213.

Chapter 2

1. Interview of Technical Sergeant (T/Sgt.) Robert Boehm, U.S. Army, by Leo J. Daugherty, 7 July 1994, Parma, Ohio, hereafter cited as Boehm interview, Pt. 1, Side 1. In possession of author.

2. See Chapters 17 and 18, "Hitler's Grand Design" and "Operation Edelweiss," in Earle F. Ziemke and Magna E. Bauer, *Moscow to Stalingrad: Decision in the East* (Washington, DC: Center for Military History, 1987), pp. 349–81; and Earl F. Ziemke, *Stalingrad to Berlin: The German Defeat in the East* (Washington, DC: Center of Military History, 1987), pp. 18–22.

3. For the single best account of the massive effort to supply the Russians see T. H. Vail Motter, *United States Army in World War II: The Middle East Theater: The Persian Corridor and Aid to Russia* (Washington, DC: Office of the Chief of Military History, HQ Department of the Army, 1952), hereafter cited as Motter, *The Persian Corridor*.

4. Benjamin King, Richard C. Biggs, and Eric R. Criner, *Spearhead of Logistics: A History of the United States Army Transportation Corps* (Newport News, VA: U.S. Army Transportation Center, 1994), p. 167, hereafter cited as King, et al., *Spearhead of Logistics*.

5. Ibid., p. 168.

6. Ibid.

7. Boehm interview, Pt. 1, Side 1.

8. King, et al., *Spearhead of Logistics*, p. 167.
9. Ibid., p. 168.
10. Motter, *The Persian Corridor*, pp. 326-7.
11. Boehm interview, Part 1, Side 1.
12. Ibid.
13. Ibid.
14. General Joseph W. Stilwell, *The Stilwell Papers*, edited and arranged by Theodore H. White (New York: Sloane, 1948), pp. 107-19, hereafter cited as Stilwell and White, *Stilwell Papers*; Field Marshal Lord Alan Brooke, *War Diaries, 1939-1945* (Berkeley: University of California Press, 2001), pp. 215-26, hereafter cited as Lord Alan Brooke, *Diaries*.
15. Lord Alan Brooke, *Diaries*, p. 215.
16. Romanus and Sunderland, *Stilwell's Mission to China*, pp. 313-5; King, et al., *Spearhead of Logistics*, pp. 169-172.
17. Charles F. Romanus and Riley Sunderland, *United States Army in World War II: China-Burma-India, Time Runs Out in CBI* (Washington, DC: Center of Military History, 1999), pp. 313-4, hereafter cited as Romanus and Sunderland, *Time Runs Out in CBI*.
18. Boehm interview, Pt. 1, Side 1.
19. King, et al., *Spearhead of Logistics*, p. 171.
20. Charles F. Romanus and Riley Sunderland, *United States Army in World War II: China-Burma-India Theater: Stilwell's Mission to China* (Washington, DC: Center of Military History, United States Army, 1987), p. 221, hereafter cited as Romanus and Sunderland, *Stilwell's Mission to China*.
21. See Mary H. Williams, *The United States Army in World War II: Chronology 1941-1945* (Washington, DC: United States Army, Center for Military History, 1994), pp. 382-3, hereafter cited as Williams, *Chronology*.
22. Formerly the Burma-Ledo Road renamed in honor of Lieutenant General Joseph W. Stilwell who had been replaced by Lieutenant General Albert Wedemeyer as the commanding general of all U.S. forces in CBI.
23. King, et al., *Spearhead of Logistics*, pp. 174-5; Alvin P. Stauffer, *United States Army in World War II: The Technical Services: The Quartermaster Corps: Operations in the War Against Japan* (Washington, DC: Office of the Chief of Military History, Department of the Army, 1956), pp. 55-97; Robert W. Coakley and Richard M. Leighton, *United States Army in World War II: The War Department: Global Logistics and Strategy, 1943-1945* (Washington, DC: Center of Military History, United States Army, 1986), pp. 500-29, and 725-36 respectively.
24. A "Tommy Gun" was the .45-caliber Thompson sub-machinegun carried by U.S. soldiers and Marines during World War II.

25. Boehm interview, Pt. 1, Side 1.
26. "Flyboys" was the term American soldiers gave to the pilots and air crews that flew over the Himalayas or "Hump" as it was referred to. Boehm interview, Pt. 1, Side 1.
27. Ibid.
28. Boehm interview, Pt. 1, Side 2.
29. Ibid.
30. Romanus and Sunderland, *Time Runs Out in CBI*, p. 318.
31. Motter, *The Persian Corridor*, p. 327.
32. Romanus and Sunderland, *Time Run Outs in CBI*, p. 318.
33. Sergeant Boehm is referring here to his wife, Mrs. Grace Boehm, whom he had married prior to leaving for the Army in 1942.
34. Boehm interview, Pt. 1, Side 2.
35. Ibid.
36. For an excellent history of Merrill's Marauders see Charlton Ogburn, Jr., *The Marauders* (New York: Harper & Brothers, 1959) and; James E. T. Hopkins, and John M. Jones, *Spearhead: A Complete History of Merrill's Marauder Rangers* (Baltimore: Galahad Press, 1999).
37. Boehm interview, Pt. 1, Side 2.
38. Ibid.
39. Ibid.
40. Ibid.
41. Ibid.

Chapter 3

1. See Leo J. Daugherty III, "Supplying War: Inter-service and Inter-Allied Cooperation in China-Burma-India," *Joint Forces Quarterly*, Summer 1996, no. 12:102, hereafter cited as Daugherty, "Supplying War"; and Colonel Marshall comments in "Hauling Gas from India to China in a B-24," in John G. Martin and Janet M. Thies, et al., *China Airlift: The Hump*, Vol. 3 (Paducah, KY: Turner, 1992), p. 141, hereafter cited as Martin and Thies, et al., *The Hump*, Vol. 3.
2. See Captain Edward M. Goodman Biographic sketch in Martin and Thies, *The Hump*, Vol. 3, p. 236.
3. Janet Beighle French, "'Flying Over the Hump': Daredevil on Mission to Save China," *Cleveland Plain Dealer*, June 28, 1992, p. 4-G, hereafter cited as French, "Flying Over the Hump."
4. Ibid.
5. Ibid.
6. See Hall Comments on Martin B-26s in Captain David C. Hall interview, Part 1, Side 1, loc. cit.; also, "Bomber Falls Near M'Cool; 2 Pilots Live," *The Tribune* (Gary, IN), August 7, 1942.
7. French, "Flying Over the Hump," p. 4-G.

8. A. B. Feuer, *General Chennault's Secret Weapon: The B-24 in China* (Westport, CT: Praeger, 1992), p. xxii, hereafter cited as Feuer, *The B-24 in China*.
9. Ibid.
10. Interview with Captain Edward M. Goodman, September 30, 1994, Berea, Ohio, p. 1, hereafter cited as Goodman interview notes, p. 1.
11. Jeff Ethell and Don Downie, *Flying the Hump in Original World War II Color* (St. Paul, Minnesota: Motor Books International, 2004), p. 96, hereafter cited as Ethell & Downie, *Flying the Hump*.
12. Feuer, *The B-24 in China*, pp. xxii–xxiii.
13. Ibid., p. 2.
14. Ethell & Downie, *Flying the Hump*, p. 96.
15. Wesley Frank Craven and James Lea Cate, *The Army Air Forces in World War II: Volume Six: Men and Planes* (Chicago: University of Chicago Press, 1958), p. 28, hereafter cited as Craven and Cate, *Men and Planes*.
16. Ibid.
17. Goodman interview notes, p. 1.
18. Martin and Thies, *The Hump*, Vol. 3, p. 140.
19. Ibid., p. 141.
20. French, "Flying Over the Hump," p. 4-G.
21. Martin and Thies, *The Hump*, Vol. 3, p. 140.
22. Captain Edward Goodman, USAAF, interview with the author, September 30, 1994, Berea, Ohio, hereafter cited as Goodman interview. French, "Flying Over the Hump," p. 4-G.
23. Feuer, *The B-24 in China*, p. 13.
24. Martin and Thies, *The Hump*, Vol. 3, p. 140.
25. Feuer, *The B-24 in China*, p. 13.
26. Martin and Thies, *The Hump*, Vol. 3, p. 141; French, "Flying the Hump," p. 4-G; Feuer, *The B-24 in China*, p. 13.
27. See Frank Roth, et al., request by Robert Underbrink, "Request for Copy of the Aluminum Trail," in the *China-Burma-India Hump Pilots Association Newsletter*, Winter 1994/1995, p. 20.
28. Feuer, *The B-24 in China*, p. 55.
29. Martin and Thies, *The Hump*, Vol. 3, p. 142.
30. "'ETA' or Estimated Time of Arrival."
31. "'ADF' or Automatic Direction Finder."
32. Martin and Thies, *The Hump*, Vol. 3, p. 144.
33. Feuer, *The B-24 in China*, p. 54.
34. Ibid.
35. Martin and Thies, *The Hump*, Vol. 3, p. 143.
36. French, "Flying Over the Hump," p. 4-G.
37. Martin and Thies, *The Hump*, Vol. 3, pp. 143–4.
38. Feuer, *The B-24 in China*, p. 13.
39. Ibid., pp. 13–4.
40. Martin and Thies, *The Hump*, Vol. 3, p. 144.
41. Feuer, *The B-24 in China*, p. 56.
42. Goodman interview.
43. French, "Flying the Hump," p. 4-G.
44. See Chennault's comments in Feuer, *The B-24 in China*, p. 163.

Chapter 4

1. The Flying Tigers adopted this name from the "Tiger Shark" artwork found on the noses of their P-40 Warhawks. Robert Lee Scott, Jr., *Flying Tiger: Chennault of China* (New York: Berkeley, 1959); Charles R. Bond, Jr., and Terry H. Anderson. *A Flying Tiger's Diary* (College Station, TX: Texas A&M University Press, 1993).
2. See Chapter 14, "Commitments to China," in Wesley Frank Craven and James Lea Cate, *The Army Air Forces in World War II: Volume I: Plans and Early Operations. January 1939 to August 1942* (Washington, DC: Office of Air Force History, 1983), pp. 484–513, hereafter cited as Craven and Cates, *I: Plans and Early Operations*; John G. Martin, *It Began at Imphal: The Combat Cargo Story* (Manhattan, KS: Sunflower University Press, 1988), p. 1, hereafter cited as Martin, *It Began at Imphal*.
3. The Tenth U.S. Army Air Force was activated at Patterson Field, Dayton, Ohio, on 12 February 1942.
4. Charles F. Romanus and Riley Sunderland, *United States Army in World War II: China-Burma-India-Theater: Stilwell's Mission to China* (Washington, DC: Center of Military Army, 1987), p. 79, hereafter cited as Romanus and Sunderland, *Stilwell's Mission to China*.
5. Ibid., p. 163.
6. Craven and Cate, *Vol. 1: Plans and Early Operations*, pp. 501–2.
7. General Joseph W. Stilwell, *The Stilwell Papers*, arranged and edited by Theodore H. White (New York: Sloane, 1948), p. 38, hereafter cited as Stilwell and White, *Stilwell Papers*.
8. Captain Goodman was commissioned a second lieutenant in the U.S. Army Air Corps and after flight training, ferried B-25s and B-26s to North Africa prior to his assignment to the Assam-Burma-China Ferry Command in the spring of 1943. He was stationed with the 97th Transport Squadron, 28th Group, Station 5, flying C-87s and B-24s based out of Tezpur in Assam. While assigned to the Assam-Burma-China Ferry Command, Captain Goodman flew over 700 hours and 82 round trips over the

Hump. Captain Edward M. Goodman, interview with the author, April 14, 1994, hereafter cited as Goodman interview; Also see John G. Martin, and Janet M. Thies, *China Airlift: The Hump*, Vol. 3 (Paducah, KY: Turner, 1992), p. 236, hereafter cited as Martin and Thies, *China Airlift*, Vol. 3.

9. Ibid., p. 61.
10. Ibid.
11. Ibid.
12. Ibid., p. 62.
13. Hugh G. Earnhart, director, Oral History Program, Oral Interview Transcript with Captain David C. Hall, USAAF, October 12, 1994, Department of History, Youngstown State University, Youngstown, Ohio, p. 1. The interview is on repository at the Maag Library, Youngstown State, hereafter cited as Earnhart, Hall Oral History Transcript.
14. Ibid., p. 2.
15. Ibid., pp. 2-3.
16. Ibid., p. 3.
17. Captain David C. Hall, USAAF, interview with the author, Madison, Ohio, July 15, 1994, in possession of the author. Part 1, Side A, hereafter cited as Captain David C. Hall Interview, Pt. 1, Side A.
18. Ibid. The Fourth Cargo Command Group consisted of the 13th, 14th, 15th, and 16th Squadrons. Hall was in the 14th Squadron.
19. Ibid. Hall said the C-47 had a Wright 1350 horsepower engine while the C-46 had a Pratt-Whitney R2000 horsepower engine and possessed 50 percent more combat cargo carrying capacity than the former. Captain David C. Hall Interview, Pt. Side A.
20. Ibid.
21. Ibid.
22. Hall Oral History Transcript, p. 4.
23. Winston S. Churchill, *The Second World War: Closing the Ring* (Boston: Houghton Mifflin, 1951), p. 560, hereafter cited as Churchill, *Closing the Ring*; Ray S. Cline, *United States Army in World War II: The War Department: Washington Command Post: The Operations Division* (Washington, DC: Center for Military History, 1990), pp. 213-221, hereafter cited as Cline, *Washington Command Post*.
24. Benjamin King, Richard C. Biggs, and Eric R. Criner, et al., *Spearhead of Logistics: A History of the United States Army Transportation Corps* (Fort Eustis, VA: United States Army Transportation Command, 1994), p. 174, hereafter cited as King, et al., *Spearhead of Logistics*.
25. For the best description of the controversies surrounding the China-Burma-India Theater, see Chapter 8 in Charles F. Romanus and Riley Sunderland, *United States Army in World War II: China-Burma-India Theater:*

Stilwell's Mission to China (Washington, DC: Center of Military History, 1987), pp. 262-310, hereafter cited as Romanus and Sunderland, *Stilwell's Mission to China*.
26. Ibid., p. 251.
27. Stilwell and White, *Stilwell Papers*, p. 183.
28. Romanus and Sunderland, *Stilwell's Mission to China*, p. 253.
29. Ibid., pp. 252-3; Major General Claire Lee Chennault, *Way of a Fighter: The Memoirs of Claire Lee Chennault*, edited by Robert Hotz (New York: Putnam, 1949), pp. 220-27, hereafter cited as Chennault, *Way of a Fighter*.
30. Romanus and Sunderland, *Stilwell's Mission to China*, p. 255.
31. Ibid., pp. 322-3.
32. Ibid., p. 325.
33. Stilwell and White, *Stilwell Papers*, p. 143.
34. For an excellent look at the strategic situation in CBI during 1943-1944 see Chapter XII in Cline, *Washington Command Post*, pp. 213-33, and; John Ehrman, *Grand Strategy: Volume V: August 1943-September 1944* (London: HMSO, 1956), pp. 123-33, hereafter cited as Ehrman, *Grand Strategy: V*.
35. Cline, *Washington Command Post*, p. 221.
36. Ibid., pp. 221-9.
37. Ehrman, *Grand Strategy: V*, p. 132.
38. Ibid., p. 153; For an excellent account of the war in Burma and of the Allied effort to recapture Burma, see Louis Allen, *Burma: The Longest War, 1941-1945* (London: Phoenix Press, 1984), pp. 150-420, hereafter cited as Allen, *Burma: The Longest War*.
39. Ehrman, *Grand Strategy, V*, p. 148.
40. Ibid., p. 149.
41. President Franklin D. Roosevelt, "Personal and Secret. From the President to the Former Naval Person [Prime Minister Winston Churchill]," dated 24 February 1944 in Warren F. Kimball, et al., *Churchill and Roosevelt: The Complete Correspondence: II: Alliance Forged, November 1942-February 1944* (Princeton, NJ: Princeton University Press, 1984), pp. 755-6, hereafter cited as Kimball, et al., *Churchill and Roosevelt*.
42. Ibid., p. 756.
43. Churchill, *Closing the Ring*, pp. 560-1.
44. See diary entry dated 25-26 May 1942 in Lieutenant General Lewis H. Brereton, USAAF, *The Brereton Diaries, 3 October 1941-8 May 1945* (New York: Morrow, 1946), p. 126, hereafter cited as *Brereton Diaries*.
45. Chittagong, in fact, was where the U.S. Army's Air Transport Command (ATC) stationed Captain Hall's 14th Squadron. See Hall Oral History Transcript, p. 4.

46. Churchill, *Closing the Ring*, p. 564.
47. Ibid., pp. 565–7.
48. Ibid., p. 567; Allen, *Burma: The Longest War*, pp. 173–230;
49. King, et al., *Spearhead of Logistics*, p. 174.
50. Captain David C. Hall Interview, Pt 1, Side A.
51. Anthony March, "Fourth 'Com-Car' Supplies British," *Phoenix* 2, (June 16, 1945), no. 4: 3–5. Published by the 4th Combat Cargo Group.
52. Ibid., p. 5.
53. Ibid., p. 3.
54. Ibid.
55. Captain David C. Hall Interview, 9 September 1995, Madison Township, Ohio, Pt. 1, Side 1, hereafter cited as Hall Interview II.
56. Hall Oral History Transcript, pp. 4–5.
57. Merrill's Marauders were members of the 5307th Composite Unit (Provisional) modeled after Orde Wingate's long-range penetration force known as the Chindits. They were led by Brigadier General Frank D. Merrill, a member of Lieutenant General Stilwell's staff. See Charlton Ogburn, Jr.'s, *The Marauders* (New York: Harper & Brothers, 1959); U.S. War Department, *Merrill's Marauders* (Washington, DC: Center for Military History, 1945, reprinted 1990); James E. T. Hopkins, *Spearhead: A Complete History of Merrill's Marauder Rangers* (Baltimore: Galahad Press, 1999).
58. Hall Oral History Transcript, p. 6.
59. Ibid., p. 7.
60. Captain David C. Hall Interview, Pt. 1, Side A.
61. Martin, *It Began at Imphal*, p. 44.
62. Ibid.
63. Ibid., pp. 44–5.
64. The Marauders that Captain Hall flew into Burma were combat engineers who adopted the title from the famous long-range penetration force that had already seized Myitkyina in August 1944. Corporal Alexander McVean, who served in this group said that the engineers "took this title after their arrival in Burma to began building the connection to the old Burma Road." Corporal Alexander McVean, U.S. Army, interview with the author, Philadelphia, Pennsylvania, April 8, 1995.
65. Hall Oral History Transcript, p. 8.
66. *Brereton Diaries*, 26 May 1942, p. 126.
67. Field Marshal Sir William J. Slim, *Defeat into Victory* (New York: Collection Reprints, 1961 and 1988), p. 309, hereafter cited as Slim, *Defeat into Victory*.
68. Ibid., p. 336.
69. Martin, *It Began at Imphal*, p. 45.
70. Goodman Interview.
71. Hall Oral History Transcript, p. 9.
72. Ibid; see Wesley F. Craven and James Lea Cate, *The Army Air Forces in World War II. Vol.6: Men and Planes* (Chicago: University of Chicago Press, 1958), pp. 1–45, hereafter cited as Craven and Cates, *Men and Planes*.
73. Captain David C. Hall Interview, Side 1, Pt.1.
74. Hall Oral History Transcript, p. 12.
75. Captain David C. Hall Interview II Side 1.
76. See General George C. Marshall letter to Winston S. Churchill: Memorandum for Field Marshal Wilson, 3 April 1945 in Larry I. Bland and Sharon Ritenour Stevens, et al., *The Papers of George Catlett Marshall, Volume 5: The Finest Soldier": January 1, 1945–January 7, 1947* (Baltimore: Johns Hopkins University Press, 2003), pp. 113–4.
77. Hall Oral History Transcript, p. 9.
78. Captain David C. Hall Interview II Side 1.
79. Captain David C. Hall Interview, Side 1, Pt.1.
80. Captain David C. Hall Interview II, Side 2.
81. Ibid.
82. Hall Oral History Transcript, p. 13.
83. Ibid., p. 14.
84. Ibid.
85. Captain David C. Hall Interview, Pt. 1, Side 2.
86. Hall Oral History Transcript, pp. 11–12.
87. Captain David C. Hall Interview II, Side 1.
88. Hall Oral History Transcript, p. 14.
89. See Brigadier General Smith's comments in Craven and Cate, *Men and Planes*, p.132.
90. Goodman interview.
91. Craven and Cate, *Men and Planes*, p. 123.
92. Ibid., p. 138.
93. Ibid.
94. Ibid., p. 139.
95. General Joseph W. Stilwell was replaced by Lieutenant General Albert C. Wedemeyer on 31 October 1944 after Generalissimo Chiang Kai-shek requested that the former be removed from the CBI theater due to his disagreements with the Chinese leader's policies and his clashes with British officials. See Barbara W. Tuchman, *Stilwell and the American Experience in China, 1911–1945* (New York: Macmillan, 1971), pp. 460–509.
96. Ibid., p. 254.
97. Wesley F. Craven and James L. Cate, *The Army Air Forces in World War II: Volume V: The Pacific: Matterhorn to Nagasaki, June 1944 to August 1945* (Chicago: University of Chicago Press, 1953), p. 220, hereafter cited as Craven and Cate, *Matterhorn to Nagasaki*.

98. Martin, *It Began at Imphal*, p. 49.
99. Craven and Cate, *Matterhorn to Nagasaki*, p. 255.
100. Martin and Thies, *China Airlift*, Vol. 3, p. 153.
101. Ibid., pp. 153–4.
102. King, et al., *Spearhead of Logistics*, p. 174.
103. Captain David C. Hall Interview II, Side 1.
104. Hall indicated that Colonel Baird had already gone home and was flying for the airlines, and thus he did not know his successor. Ibid., *Sides I and 2*.
105. Hall Oral History Transcript, p. 17–18.
106. Ibid., p. 18.
107. Ibid.
108. Ibid., p. 19.
109. Slim, *Defeat into Victory*, p. 454.
110. Winston S. Churchill, *The Second World War: Closing the Ring* (New York: Houghton Mifflin, 1951), p. 561.

Chapter 5

1. Karl C. Dod, *United States Army in World War II: The Technical Services: The Corps of Engineers: The War Against Japan* (Washington, DC: Office of the Chief of Military History, 1966), p. 387, hereafter cited as Dod, *The Corps of Engineers: The War Against Japan*.
2. Ibid.
3. Ibid., pp. 387–9.
4. Ibid., p. 386, and; Cline, *Washington Command Post*, p. 226.
5. Alan Brooke, *War Diaries*, 17 January 1945, p. 646.
6. Interview with Corporal Alexander McVean, U.S. Army by Leo J. Daugherty III, Philadelphia, PA., April 8, 1995. Part 1, Side A, hereafter cited as McVean interview, Part 1, Side A. For training, see Robert R. Palmer, Bell I. Wiley, and William R. Keast, *United States Army in World War II: The Army Ground Forces: The Procurement and Training of Ground Combat Troops* (Washington, DC: Center of Military History, 1991), pp. 460, 542–551, hereafter cited as Palmer, et al., *Procurement and Training of Ground Combat Troops*.
7. Palmer, et al., *Procurement and Training of Ground Combat Troops*.
8. McVean interview, Part 1, Side A.
9. Ibid.
10. Ibid.
11. Ibid.
12. The Japanese referred to these women as "comfort girls." They were essentially forced into prostitution to provide sexual entertainment for the troops. See Louis Allen, *Burma: The Longest War: 1941–45* (London: Phoenix Press, 1984), pp. 590–99.
13. Ibid.; also see Dod, *The Corps of Engineers: The War Against Japan*, pp. 443–475.
14. William C. King, *Building for Victory: World War II in China, Burma, and India and the 1875th Engineer Aviation Battalion* (Lanham, MD: Taylor, 2004), p. 65, hereafter cited as King, *Building for Victory*.
15. Ibid.
16. See Charles F. Romanus and Riley Sunderland, *United States Army in World War II: China-Burma-India Theater: Stilwell's Command Problems* (Washington, DC: Center of Military History, 1987), p. 274, hereafter cited as Romanus and Sunderland, *Stilwell's Command Problems*.
17. Field Marshal Lord Alan Brooke, *War Diaries, 1939–1945* (Berkeley: University of California Press, 2001), pp. 210–11, 215, and 235 respectively; Winston S. Churchill, *The Second World War: Closing the Ring* (Boston: Houghton Mifflin, 1951, pp. 559–61, hereafter cited as Churchill, *Closing the Ring*.
18. Churchill, *Closing the Ring*, pp. 559–60.
19. Ibid., p. 561.
20. King, *Building for Victory*, p. 99.
21. Ibid.
22. Dod, *The Corps of Engineers: The War Against Japan*, p. 432; James W. Dunn's, "The Ledo Road," in Barry W. Fowle, et al., *Builders and Fighters: U.S. Army Engineers in World War II* (Fort Belvoir, VA: Office of History, United States Army Corps of Engineers, 1992), pp. 327–46.
23. Ibid.
24. Ibid., p. 432.
25. Ibid., p. 433.
26. Ibid.
27. Ibid., pp. 433–4.
28. King, *Building for Victory*, pp. 99–100.
29. Dod, *The Corps of Engineers: The War Against Japan*, p. 434.
30. Ibid., pp. 434–5.
31. Ibid., p. 435.
32. Hsu Long-hsuen and Chang Ming-Kai, *History of the Sino-Japanese War (1937–1945)*, translated by Wen Ha-hsiung. Second ed. (Taipei, Taiwan: Chung Wu, 1972), pp. 398–9, hereafter cited as Hsu and Chang, *Sino-Japanese War (1937–1945)*.
33. Ibid., p. 399.
34. General Joseph W. Stilwell, *The Stilwell Papers*, edited and arranged by Theodore H. White (New York: Sloane, 1948), p. 277, hereafter cited as Stilwell, *Stilwell Papers*.
35. Roosevelt refers to Lord Admiral Louis Mountbatten, the newly appointed commander-in-chief, Southeast Asia Command (SEAC), at the Quadrant Conference. See Roosevelt to

Churchill, 29 January 1944, (R-454), in Warren F. Kimball, et al., *Churchill and Roosevelt: The Complete Correspondence: II: Alliance Forged* (Princeton, NJ: Princeton University Press, 1984), p. 690.

36. Ibid., Roosevelt to Churchill, 18 February 1944, (R-471), *loc. cit.*, p. 732.

37. Dod, *The Corps of Engineers: The War Against Japan*, p. 442.

38. King, *Building for Victory*, p. 111.

39. Dod, *The Corps of Engineers: The War Against Japan*, p. 443.

40. McVean interview, Part 1, Side A.

41. King, *Building for Victory*, p. 122.

42. McVean interview, Part 1, Side A.

43. Reginald M. Cleveland, *Air Transport At War* (New York: Harper & Brothers, 1946), p. 213.

44. Dod, *The Corps of Engineers: The War Against Japan*, p. 443.

45. Ibid.

46. Ibid.

47. Ibid., p. 444; Hsu and Chang, *Sino-Japanese War, 1937–1945*, pp. 399–400; For an excellent account of Merrill's Marauders see Charlton Ogburn, Jr., *The Marauders* (New York: Harper and Brothers, 1959); and James E. T. Hopkins, *Spearhead: A Complete History of Merrill's Marauder Rangers* (Baltimore: Galahad Press, 1999); Gary J. Bjorge, *Merrill's Marauders: Combined Operations in Northern Burma in 1944* (Fort Leavenworth, KS: Combat Studies Institute, U.S. Army Command and General Staff College, 2003).

48. Ulysses Lee, *United States Army in World War II: The Employment of Negro Troops* (Washington, DC: Center for Military History, 1994), p. 610, hereafter cited as Lee, *Employment of Negro Troops*.

49. Ibid., p. 611.

50. Ibid., pp. 15–50.

51. Ibid., pp. 618–9.

52. King, *Building for Victory*, p. 111.

53. Ibid.

54. Lee, *Employment of Negro Troops*, p. 612.

55. Ibid., pp. 615–18.

56. Dod, *The Corps of Engineers: The War Against Japan*, p. 463.

57. McVean interview, Part 1, Side B.

58. King, *Building for Victory*, p. 122.

59. Ibid., p. 125.

60. Ibid., p. 134.

61. Ibid., pp. 138–9.

62. Lee, *Employment of Negro Troops*, p. 615.

63. Ibid.

64. Ibid.

65. See Churchill, *Closing the Ring*, pp. 360–1, 375; Alan Brooke, *War Diaries*, p. 646.

66. Donovan Webster, *The Burma Road* (New York: Perennial, 2004), p. 317, hereafter cited as Webster, *The Burma Road*.

67. King, *Building for Victory*, pp. 134–7; Dod, *The Corps of Engineers: The War Against Japan*, pp. 474–5.

68. Dod, *The Corps of Engineers: The War Against Japan*, p. 473.

69. General George C. Marshall to Lieutenant General Daniel I. Sultan, January 25, 1945, in Larry I. Bland and Sharon Ritenour Stevens, editors, *The Papers of George Catlett Marshall: Volume 5: 'The Finest Soldier': January 1, 1945–January 7, 1947* (Baltimore: Johns Hopkins University Press, 2003), pp. 40–1.

70. McVean interview, Part 1, Side B.

71. Dod, *The Corps of Engineers: The War Against Japan*, pp. 474–5.

72. General George C. Marshall to General Thomas T. Handy, 27 September 1945, in Bland and Stevens, *The Papers of George Catlett Marshall: Volume 5: 'The Finest Soldier,' January 1, 1945–January 7, 1947*, pp. 316–6.

73. Ibid., p. 316.

74. King, *Building for Victory*, p. 170.

75. Churchill, *Closing the Ring*, pp. 560–1.

76. Benjamin King, Richard C. Biggs, and Eric C. Criner, *Spearhead of Logistics: A History of the United States Army Transportation Corps* (Fort Eustis, VA: U.S. Army Transportation Center, 1994), p. 175.

77. Ibid.

78. Dod, *The Corps of Engineers: The War Against Japan*, p. 475.

79. McVean Interview, Part 2, Side A.

80. Ibid.

81. Webster, *The Burma Road*, p. 328.

Chapter 6

1. Hereafter abbreviated as T/Sgt.

2. Technical Sergeant Kenneth R. Quigley, U.S. Army, telephone conversation with the author, August 23, 2005, subject, "Service in India and Burma in WWII." Notes in possession of the author, hereafter cited as Quigley phone conversation.

3. Ibid.

4. Robert Palmer, Bell I. Wiley, and William R. Keast, *United States Army in World War II: The Army Ground Forces: The Procurement and Training of Ground Combat Troops* (Washington, DC: Center of Military History, 1991), p. 528, hereafter cited as Palmer, et al., *Training of Ground Combat Troops*.

5. Ibid., pp. 385–423.

6. Quigley phone conversation.

7. Leo P. Brophy and George J. Fisher, *United States Army in World War II: The Tech-*

nical Services: The Chemical Warfare Service: Organizing for War (Washington, DC: Center of Military History, 1989), p. 279, hereafter cited as Brophy and Fisher, *Chemical Warfare Service: Organizing for War.*

8. Ibid; Robert R. Palmer, Bell I. Wiley, and William R. Keast, *United States Army in World War II: The Army Ground Forces: The Procurement and Training of Ground Combat Troops* (Washington, DC: Center for Military History, 1991), p. 380–408, hereafter cited as Palmer, et al., *Procurement and Training of Combat Troops.*

9. Palmer, *Procurement and Training of Combat Troops*, pp. 384–5.

10. Ibid., p. 387.

11. Ibid.

12. Ibid.

13. Quigley phone conversation.

14. Brophy and Fisher, *The Chemical Warfare Service: Organizing for Combat*, p. 306.

15. Quigley phone conversation.

16. Ibid; T/Sgt Kenneth R. Quigley, "Comments," written responses to a questionnaire from author, dated November 7, 2005. Questionnaire in possession of author, hereafter cited as Quigley, 'Comments.'

17. Quigley phone conversation; Brophy and Fisher, *The Chemical Warfare Service: Organizing for War*, p. 307.

18. Ibid.

19. Brophy and Fisher, *The Chemical Warfare Service: Organizing for War*, pp. 308–9.

20. See Leo J. Daugherty III, *Fighting Techniques of a Japanese Infantryman, 1941–1945: Training, Techniques and Weapons* (St. Paul, MN; Motorbooks, 2002), pp. 31 and 49; also, U.S. War Department, *Handbook on German Military Forces*, Introduction by Stephen E. Ambrose (Baton Rouge: Louisiana State University Press, 1990), pp. 155, 322–23, and 518–37.

21. See both Quigley phone conversation and "Comments." Quigley asserted as much since as he had related that he had placed this information on his induction papers when asked about his civilian employment.

22. Ibid., "Comments," p. 1.

23. Quigley phone conversation.

24. Ibid.

25. Ibid; Quigley "Comments."

26. Literature on the 5307th Composite Unit or "Merrill's Marauders" as they became known, is both abundant and excellent. Included in this group are the official histories: Hsu-Long-Hsuen and Chang Ming-Kai, *History of the Sino-Japanese War (1937–1945)*, translated by Wen Ha-hsiung (Taipei, Taiwan: Chung Wu, 1972), pp. 398–429; Charles F. Romanus and Riley Sunderland's *United States Army in World War II: Stilwell's Command Problems* (Washington, DC: Center of Military History, 1985), and; Charles F. Romanus and Riley Sunderland's *United States Army in World War II: Time Runs Out in CBI* (Washington, DC: Center of Military History, 1958); Major General Sir Woodburn Kirby, *The War Against Japan: Volume III: The Decisive Battles*, (London: HMSO, 1961); perhaps the best narrative of Merrill's Marauders was written by a former Marauder, Charles Ogburn, *The Marauders* (New York: Harper & Brothers, 1959); Gary J. Bjorge's excellent monograph, *Merrill's Marauders: Combined Operations in Northern Burma in 1944* (Fort Leavenworth, KS: Combat Studies Institute, 1996); Alan Baker's *Merrill's Marauders* (London: Ballantine,1972); Michael Calvert's *Chindits: Long-Range Penetration* (London: Ballantine, 1973); D. D. Rooney's, *Stilwell* (London: Ballantine, 1971); The most detailed histories of the Marauders is Shelford Bidwell's, *The Chindit War: Stilwell, Wingate and the Campaign in Burma: 1944* (New York: Macmillan, 1979); the most recent and most detailed history of the Marauders is James E. T. Hopkins and John M. Jones' *Spearhead: A Complete History of Merrill's Marauder Rangers* (Baltimore: Galahad Press, 1999) and Mir Bahmanyar's, *Shadow Warriors: A History of the U.S. Army Rangers* (London: Osprey, 2005).

27. Quigley phone conversation.

28. Ibid.

29. Ulysses Lee, *United States Army in World War II: The Employment of Negro Troops* (Washington, DC: Center for Military History, 1994), pp. 610–18.

30. Quigley phone conversation; Quigley, "Comments."

31. Ibid.

Chapter 7

1. Corporal Anthony R. Silva, U.S. Army Air Forces, interview with the author, Spring Hill, Florida, February 28, 1998. Tape in possession of author. Part 1, Side A, hereafter cited as Silva Interview, Pt. 1, Side A.

2. Ibid.

3. Ibid.

4. Comments by Anthony Silva, Jr., to Leo J. Daugherty III, 15 September 2006, re: Manuscript. "Comments" are in possession of author. Hereafter referred to as Silva, "Comments."

5. Silva Interview, Pt. 2, Side A.

6. Wesley Frank Craven and James Lea Cate, *The Army Air Forces in World War II: Volume Six, Men and Planes* (Chicago: University

of Chicago Press, 1958), p. 140, hereafter cited as Craven and Cate, *Men and Planes*.
7. Ibid.
8. Ibid.
9. Silva, "Comments."
10. Ibid; Silva Interview, Pt. 1, Side A.
11. Craven and Cate, *Men and Planes*, p. 141.
12. Ibid., p. 141.
13. Ibid.
14. Ibid.
15. Charles F. Romanus and Riley Sunderland, *United States Army in World War II: China-Burma-India Theater: Stilwell's Mission to China* (Washington, DC: Center for Military History, 1987), pp. 202–3, hereafter cited as Romanus and Sunderland, *Stilwell's Mission*.
16. In fact, 1 May 1942 to be precise.
17. Romanus and Sunderland, *Stilwell's Mission to China*, p. 200.
18. Lieutenant Colonel Charles E. Miller, USAF, *Airlift Doctrine* (Montgomery, AL: Maxwell Air Force Base, Air University Press, 1988), p. 55, hereafter cited as Miller, *Airlift Doctrine*.
19. Major General Claire Lee Chennault, *Way of a Fighter: The Memoirs of Claire Lee Chennault*, edited by Robert Hotz (New York: Putnam, 1949), p. 186, hereafter cited as Chennault, *Way of a Fighter*.
20. Ibid.
21. Martin Caidin, *The Ragged, Rugged Warriors* (New York: Dutton, 1966), p. 315, hereafter cited as Caidin, *Ragged, Rugged Warriors*.
22. Ibid.
23. Chennault, *The Way of a Fighter*, p. 191.
24. Project 7-A was the assignment of a select group of American Airlines pilots, crew, and stewardesses (who served as nurses) to the China-Burma India by the U.S. Army Air Forces. See Flight Officer Tom Barnard's, "American Airline ATC Personnel Received Official Credit for World War II Service: 'Burma Roadster,'" *China-Burma-India Hump Pilots Association Newsletter*, Autumn 1991, pp. 21–3.
25. William J. Koenig, *Over the Hump: Airlift to China* (London: Ballantine Books, 1972), p. 62, hereafter cited as Koenig, *Over the Hump*.
26. Ibid., p. 62.
27. Ibid., p. 63.
28. Ibid.
29. Caidin, *Ragged, Rugged Warriors*, p. 316.
30. Jeff Ethell and Don Downie, *Flying the Hump: In Original World War II Color* (St. Paul, MN: Motorbooks, 2004), p. 98, hereafter cited as Ethell and Downie, *Flying the Hump*.
31. Donald S. Lopez, *Into the Teeth of the Tiger* (Washington, DC: Smithsonian Institution Press, 1997), pp. 170–71, hereafter cited as Lopez, *Teeth of the Tiger*.
32. Ibid., p. 171.
33. Ibid.
34. Chennault, *Way of a Fighter*, pp. 186–7.
35. Chinese Air Task Force.
36. Chennault, *Way of a Fighter*, p. 187.
37. Caidin, *Ragged, Rugged Warriors*, p. 316.
38. Koeing, *Over the Hump*, pp. 63–4.
39. Romanus and Sunderland, *Stilwell's Mission to China*, p. 202.
40. See Merlin C. Newell, "The Yank in India," *China-Burma-India Hump Pilots Association Newsletter*, Autumn 1991, pp. 23–5.
41. Ibid., p. 24.
42. Ibid., p. 25.
43. Koenig, *Over the Hump*, p. 64, and; Technical Sergeant (T/Sgt) Robert Boehm, U.S. Arm, interview with the author, Parma, Ohio. Pt. 1, Side 1. Interview in possession of author.
44. Craven and Cate, *Men and Planes*, p. 141.
45. Silva Interview, Pt 1, Side A.
46. Ethell and Downie, *Flying the Hump*, p. 103.
47. Silva Interview, Pt. 1, Side A.
48. Miller, *Airlift Doctrine*, pp. 55–6.
49. Craven and Cate, *Men and Planes*, p. 146.
50. Ethell and Downie, *Flying the Hump*, p. 86; Koenig, *Over the Hump*, p. 62.
51. Koenig, *Over the Hump*, p. 146.
52. Ibid., p. 56.
53. Silva Interview, Pt. 1, Side A.
54. Ibid.
55. Silva, "Comments."
56. Charles F. Romanus and Riley Sunderland, *United States Army in World War II: China-Burma-India Theater: Stilwell's Command Problems* (Washington, DC: Center of Military History, 1987), pp. 99–100, hereafter cited as Romanus and Sunderland, *Stilwell's Command Problems*.
57. Silva Interview, Pt. 1, Side B.
58. Silva Interview, Pt. 1, Side A.
59. See Sergeant H. C. Sterlin, USAAF, "Mama-FooFoo," ('Starvation in Silk Pants') as reprinted in Harry G. Howton, et al., *China Airlift—The Hump* (Dallas: Taylor, 1983), p. 142.
60. Karl C. Dod, *United States Army in World War II: The Technical Services: The Corps of Engineers: The War Against Japan* (Washington, DC: Office of the Chief Military History, 1966), pp. 392–3.
61. Romanus and Sunderland, *Stilwell's Command Problems*, p. 279.
62. Silva Interview, Pt. 1, Side B.
63. Koenig, *Over the Hump*, pp. 133–4.
64. Ibid., p. 135.

65. Ibid.
66. Activated on 26 August 1942, the Ramgarh Training Center was part of Lieutenant General Joseph W. Stilwell's "Y" plan to train and equip thirty Chinese divisions. See Romanus and Sunderland, *Stilwell's Mission to China*, pp. 214–8; Ethell and Downie, *Flying the Hump*, p.37.
67. Koenig, *Flying the Hump*, p. 135.
68. Ibid., p. 150–5.
69. Corporal V. Fair, "The Man with the Wrench," *China-Burma-India Hump Pilots Association Newsletter*, Autumn 1993, p. 27.
70. Silva Interview, Pt. 1, Side B.
71. Ibid.

Chapter 8

1. This chapter originated from a paper the author delivered at a U.S. Army Center for Military History Conference held in Washington, D.C., in July 2004; See Major Ronald P. Clark, U.S. Army, "The Lack of Ethnic Diversity: Why Are There so Few Black Infantry Officers in the U.S. Army?" Master's thesis, U.S. Army Command and General Staff College, U.S. Army Command and General Staff College, Fort Leavenworth, KS, 2000, pp. 19–20, hereafter cited as Clark, "Lack of Ethnic Diversity in the Infantry."
2. Ibid., p. 19.
3. Ulysses Lee, *United States Army in World War II: Special Studies: The Employment of Negro Troops* (Washington, DC: Office of the Chief of Military History, 1966), pp. 5–6, hereafter cited as Lee, *Employment of Negro Troops*.
4. Clark, "Lack of Ethnic Diversity in the Infantry," pp. 20–22.
5. Ibid., pp.18–35.
6. It must be noted that the Marine Corps did not start recruiting African Americans into its ranks until 1942. Trained as Marines at Montford Point, N.C., African Americans nevertheless were restricted to segregated combat service support or Force Troop units and antiaircraft units. See Henry I. Shaw and Ralph W. Donnelly, *Blacks in the Marine Corps* (Washington, DC: History and Museums Division, HQMC, 1975), pp. 2–13; A more recent study on the subject is Colonel Alphonse G. Davis, USMC (Ret.), *Pride, Progress, and Prospects: The Marine Corps' Efforts to Increase the Presence of African-Americans (1970–1995)*, Washington, D.C., History and Museums Division, HQMC, 2000), pp. 1–5; also see Major Charles D. Melson, USMC (Ret.), *Condition Red: Marine Defense Battalions in World War II* (Washington, DC: History and Museums Division, HQMC, 1996).

7. Lee, *Employment of Negro Troops*, p. 35.
8. Ibid., p. 36.
9. Ibid., p. 42.
10. Ibid., pp. 43–50.
11. Ibid., pp. 610–1.
12. Ibid., p. 611.
13. Lieutenant Colonel Charles E. Miller, USAF, *Airlift Doctrine* (Montgomery, AL: Maxwell Air Force Base, Air University Press, 1988), p. 139, hereafter cited as Miller, *Airlift Doctrine*.
14. Ibid.
15. Ibid., p. 141.
16. Ibid.
17. Ibid., p. 142.
18. Ibid.
19. Lee, *Employment of Negro Troops*, p. 616.
20. Ibid.
21. See Harry C. Howton, David J. Orth, and Janet Thies, et al., *China Airlift—The Hump, Volume II* (Paducah, KY: Turner, 1983, p. 211.
22. Ibid.
23. Ray Lewallen, "Reminiscences," *China-Burma-India Hump Pilots Association Newsletter*, Summer 1994, p. 5.
24. Miller, *Airlift Doctrine*, p. 143; For an account of the total tonnage dropped to Merrill's forces see Alan Barker, *Merrill's Marauders* (New York: Ballantine Books, 1972); Gary J. Bjorge, *Merrill's Marauders: Combined Operations in Northern Burma in 1944* (Fort Leavenworth, KS: Combat Studies Institute, 2003; Charlton Ogburn, Jr., *The Marauders* (New York: Harper & Brothers, 1959); and James E. T. Hopkins, in collaboration with John M. Jones, *Spearhead: A Complete History of Merrill's Marauder Rangers* (Baltimore: Galahad Press, 1999), hereafter cited as Hopkins, et al., *Spearhead*.
25. Hopkins, et al., *Spearhead*, p. 752.
26. Charles F. Romanus and Riley Sunderland, *United States Army in World War II: The China-Burma-India-Theater: Stilwell's Command Problems* (Washington, DC: Center of Military History, 1987), p. 104.
27. Lee, *Employment of Negro Troops*, pp. 615–7.
28. Ibid., p. 617. This unit, the 858th Engineer Aviation Battalion, in fact, remained in China until V-J Day in September 1945.
29. Ibid., pp. 616–7.
30. Technical Sergeant Kenneth R. Quigley, U.S. Army, telephone conversation with the author, November 7, 2005, re: African Americans in CBI.
31. Corporal Alexander McVean, U.S. Army, interview with the author in Philadelphia, Pennsylvania, April 8, 1995.

32. Lee, *Employment of Negro Soldiers*, p. 619.
33. Ibid., p. 620.
34. Ibid.
35. See Harry A. Gailey, *Bougainville: 1943–1945. The Forgotten Campaign* (Lexington, KY; University of Kentucky Press, 1991), pp. 174–5, hereafter cited as Gailey, *Bougainville*.
36. Ibid., p. 178.
37. Ibid., p. 179; Lee, *Employment of Negro Soldiers*, pp. 506–8.
38. Lee, *Employment of Negro Soldiers*, pp. 513–4.
39. Gailey, *Bougainville*, p. 182.
40. Lee, *Employment of Negro Troops*, p. 516.
41. Clark, "Lack of Ethnic Diversity in the Infantry," p. 20.
42. Lee, *Employment of Negro Troops*, p. 617.

Chapter 9

1. Colonel C. V. Glines, USAF, (Ret.), "Flying the Hump," reprinted with permission of the *China-Burma-India Hump Pilot Association Newsletter*, Autumn 1991, pp. 25–6.
2. John F. Jones, "'SOP for Bailing Out or Crash Landing:' Before or at Landing," *China-Burma-India Hump Pilots Association Newsletter*, Autumn 1991, pp. 29–30.
3. Reginald M. Cleveland, *Air Transport at War* (New York: Harper & Brothers, 1946), pp. 212–3. Hereafter cited as Cleveland, *Air Transport At War*.
4. Ibid., p. 213.
5. ATC or Air Transport Command.
6. Flight Officer Tom Barnard, "American Airline ATC Personnel Received Official Credit for WW-II Service," reprinted with permission of the *China-Burma-India Hump Pilots Association Newsletter*, Autumn 1991, pp. 21–3.
7. Major Glen Norell, USAF (Ret.), "Bail Out Over Burma," *China-Burma-India Hump Pilots Association Newsletter*, Winter 1991, pp. 2–3.
8. Frank Garcia, "Reminiscences of CBI," *China-Burma-India Hump Pilots Association Newsletter*, Winter 1991, pp. 3–4.
9. Frank R. Vierling, "Reminiscences," *China-Burma-India Hump Pilots Association Newsletter*, Winter 1991, p. 4.
10. Lieutenant Dennis G. Chandler, "Reminiscences," *China-Burma-India Hump Pilots Association Newsletter*, Winter 1991, pp. 4–6; John G. Martin and Jan Thies, *China Airlift: The Hump*, Vol. 3 (Paducah, KY: Turner, 1992), pp. 206–7.
11. Don Yarger, "Reminiscences of CBI," *China-Burma-India Hump Pilots Association Newsletter*, Winter, 1991–1992, p. 16.
12. Lieutenant Colonel Dempsey W. Welch, USAF (Ret.), "Diary of Lieutenant Colonel Welch, USAF (Ret.), in *China-Burma-India Hump Pilots Association Newsletter*, Winter 1991–1992, pp. 18–9.
13. According to the editor of the *China-Burma-India Hump Pilots Association Newsletter*, "The page where this number appeared was 'smeared.'" See Donald W. Douglas, "Speech of Donald W. Douglas," given at the Pacific Coast Dinner, San Francisco, California, in *China-Burma-India Hump Pilots Association Newsletter*, Winter 1991–1992, p. 20.
14. Ibid.
15. Eugene Adams noted, "I am writing this on a computer August 12 as a 71 year old retired professional engineer from notes taken as a 23 year old more interested then in the romance of tigers and old India than in logistics." Eugene D. "Gene" Adams, *China-Burma-India Hump Pilots Association Newsletter*, Autumn 1992, p. 8. Hereafter cited as "Adams Reminiscences," *loc. cit.*
16. The British ground crews that loaded the aircraft at night. An oft-cited complaint of American crews was that the British consistently overloaded the C-46s and C-47s, making takeoff difficult.
17. "Adams Reminiscences," *loc. cit.*, p. 9.
18. P.D.Q or Pretty Damn Quick.
19. Major Sam Cucio, "Reminiscences," *China-Burma-India Hump Pilots Association Newsletter*, Autumn 1992, pp. 10–1.
20. Clarence "Linn" Linenbach, "Reminiscences," *China-Burma-India Hump Pilots Association Newsletter*, Autumn 1992, pp. 26–7.
21. Lieutenant Alfred Lang, "Reminiscences," *China-Burma-India Hump Pilots Association Newsletter*, Autumn 1993, pp. 26–7.
22. Herman K. Sigrist, "Reminiscences," *China-Burma-India Hump Pilots Association Newsletter*, Autumn 1993, p. 28.
23. Lieutenant Ruth Firsching Heckinger, "Army Nurse Diary," *China-Burma-India Hump Pilots Association Newsletter*, Autumn 1993, pp. 12–3.
24. Major General Perry M. Hoisington, USAF (Ret.), and Colonel Raymond K. Childress, USAF (Ret.), "Appreciation for a Tough Job Well Done," *China-Burma-India Hump Pilots Association Newsletter*, Autumn 1993, pp. 20–1.
25. Mrs. Lui Fang, "Do You Know About the Flight Over the Hump?" *China-Burma-India Hump Pilots Association Newsletter*, Winter 1993–4, pp. 27–8.
26. Robert A. "Stumpy" Stumpf, "Lost: Courtesy of the Hump," *China-Burma-India Hump Pilots Association Newsletter*, Summer 1993, pp. 8–9.

27. Ed Crumpacker, "Reminiscences," *China-Burma-India Hump Pilots Association Newsletter*, Spring 1994, pp. 18–9.

28. Tommy C. C. Tengg, "Remember the 'Over Hump' Flight," *China-Burma-India Hump Pilots Association Newsletter*, Winter 1995, pp. 13–4.

29. The OSS or Office of Strategic Services, organized during World War II, was the forerunner to the Central Intelligence Agency.

30. Alex Kaplan, "Reminiscences," *China-Burma-India Hump Pilots Association Newsletter*, Winter 1995, p. 12.

31. Sherman Legas, "Reminiscences," *China-Burma-India Hump Pilots Association Newsletter*, Winter 1995, p. 12.

32. According to Flight Engineer Ray Lewallen, "It was a very sad situation because of the living conditions. We spent the night in the aircraft because of Japanese in the area that did not know that the war was over." See Ray Lewallen, "Comments," *China-Burma-India Hump Pilots Association Newsletter*, Summer 1994, p. 5.

33. General Wainwright was held as a prisoner of war until liberation in August 1945. See General Jonathan M. Wainwright, *General Wainwright's Story*, edited by Robert Considine (Garden City, NY: Doubleday, 1946), pp. 233–74.

34. See First Lieutenant Royce A. King, USAAF, "Mission to a Prison Camp," *China-Burma-India Hump Pilots Association Newsletter*, Summer 1995, pp. 15–6.

35. Humpster Jack D. Goodrich added, "What a loud scraping sound would have been heard if that landing gear hadn't dropped down. That ole hydraulic selector level had to be on a good engine for any pressure to be applied." See Jack D. Goodrich, "Reminiscences," *China-Burma-India Hump Pilots Association Newsletter*, Autumn 1995, p. 18.

36. Ibid., pp. 17–8.

37. Stephen Kalista, "A Signalman at War," *China-Burma-India Hump Pilots Association Newsletter*, Winter 1995–1996, pp. 13–4.

38. These were the Chinese Jing Bao gongs that sentries banged as they ran balls up a flagpole to signal an impending air raid. For how the Americans and Chinese reacted to these raids, see Donald S. Lopez, *Into the Teeth of the Tiger* (Washington, DC: Smithsonian Institution, 1997), pp. 74–6.

39. Jim Beamon, "Christmas, 50 Years Ago," *China-Burma-India Hump Pilots Association Newsletter*, Spring 1995, pp. 22–3.

40. Bob Friedman, "On Fire at Chengkung," *China-Burma-India Hump Pilots Association Newsletter*, Spring 1995, pp. 23–4.

Appendix 2

1. See Mark Beech, et al., "Air Jungle Rescue Unit," *China-Burma-India Hump Pilots Association Newsletter*, Winter 1991–1992, pp. 24–|5.

Bibliography

Personal Papers

The Papers of General Joseph W. Stilwell, U.S. Army (deceased), Hoover Institution, Stanford University, California.

U.S. National Archives, College Park, Maryland

Adjutant General, World War II Operations Reports of the 475th Infantry Regiment, Record Group 94, ING 475-01-.03, INRG-475.-.03

Oral Histories

Technical Sergeant Robert M. Boehm, U.S. Army, Quartermaster Corps. Interview with the author, Parma, Ohio, July 7, 1994.
Captain Edward M. Goodman (deceased), U.S. Army Air Forces. Interview with the author, Cleveland, Ohio, September 30, 1994.
Captain David C. Hall, U.S. Army Air Forces. Interview with the author, Madison Township, Ohio, July 15, 1994.
Corporal Alexander McVean (deceased), U.S. Army, Corps of Engineers. Interview with the author, Philadelphia, Pennsylvania, April 8, 1995.
Technical Sergeant Kenneth R. Quigley, U.S. Army, Chemical Warfare Services. Telephone interview with the author, Pensacola, Florida, August 23, 2005.
Lieutenant Colonel Richard "Pop" Reynolds, USAF (ret.) (deceased), telephone interview with the author, 1995.
Corporal Anthony M. Silva, U.S. Army Air Forces. Interview with the author, Spring Hill, Florida, February 28, 1998.

Published Memoirs and Diaries

Bond, Major General Charles R., Jr., and Terry H. Anderson. *A Flying Tiger's Diary*. College Station, TX: Texas A&M Press, 1984.
Brereton, Lieutenant General Louis H. *The Brereton Diaries: The War in the Air in the Pacific, Middle East, and Europe, 3 October 1941–8 May 1945*. New York: Morrow, 1946.
Brooke, Field Marshal Lord Alan. *War Diaries, 1939–1945*. Edited by Alex Danchev and Daniel Todman. Berkeley: University of California Press, 2001.
Chennault, Major General Claire Lee. *The Way of a Fighter: The Memoirs of Claire Lee Chennault*. New York: Putnam, 1949.
Marshall, General George C. *The Papers of George Catlett Marshall*. Edited by Larry I. Bland, and Sharon Ritenour Stevens, et al. Volume 5, *The Finest Soldier*. Baltimore: Johns Hopkins University Press, 2003.

Slim, Field Marshal Sir William. *Defeat into Victory*. London: Macmillan, 1988.
Stilwell, General Joseph W. *The Stilwell Papers*. Edited by Theodore H. White. New York: Sloane, 1948.
Wainwright, General Jonathan W. *General Wainwright's Story*. Edited by Robert Considine. Garden City, NY: Doubleday, 1946.
Wedemeyer, General Albert C. *Wedemeyer Reports*. New York: Holt, 1958.

Articles

"Bomber Falls Near M'Cool: 2 Pilots Live." *The Tribune*, Gary, Indiana, August 7, 1942.
Daugherty, Leo J. III. "Supplying War — Inter-service and Inter-Allied Cooperation in China-Burma-India." *Joint Forces Quarterly*, Summer 1996, pp. 95–106.
French, Janet Beighle, "Flying Over the Hump: Daredevil on Mission to Save China." *Cleveland Plain Dealer*, June 28, 1992, p. 4-G.

Books

Allen, Louis. *Burma: The Longest War, 1941–1945*. London: Phoenix Press, 1984.
Bahmanyar, Mir. *Shadow Warriors: A History of the U.S. Army Rangers*. London: Osprey, 2005.
Baker, Allan. *Merrill's Marauders*. New York: Ballantine, 1972.
Bidwell, Shelford. *The Chindit War: Stilwell, Wingate and the Campaign in Burma: 1944*. New York: Macmillan, 1979.
Bjorge, Gary J. *Merrill's Marauders: Combined Operations in Northern Burma in 1944*. Fort Leavenworth, KS: Combat Studies Institute, U.S. Army Command and General Staff College, 2003.
Brophy, Leo P., and George J. B. Fisher. *The United States Army in World War II: The Technical Services: The Chemical Warfare Service: Organizing for War*. Washington, DC: Center of Military History, 1989.
Brophy, Leo P., Wyndham D. Myles, and Rexmond C. Cochrane. *United States Army in World War II: The Technical Services: The Chemical Warfare Service: From Laboratory to Field*. Washington, DC: Office of the Chief of Military History, Headquarters, U.S. Army, 1959.
Caidin, Martin. *The Ragged, Rugged Warriors*. New York: Dutton, 1966.
Calvert, Michael. *Chindits: Long Range Penetration*. London: Pan/Ballantine Books, 1974.
_____. *Slim*. London: Pan/Ballantine Books, 1973.
Carter, Carolle J. *Mission to Yenan: American Liaison with the Chinese Communists 1944–1947*. Lexington: University of Kentucky Press, 1997.
Churchill, Winston S., *The Second World War: The Grand Alliance*. Boston: Houghton Mifflin, 1950.
_____. *The Second World War: Closing the Ring*. Boston: Houghton Mifflin, 1950.
Clark, Ronald P., "The Lack of Diversity: Why Are There So Few Black Officers in the U.S. Army?" Master's thesis, U.S. Army War College, Fort Leavenworth, KS, 2000.
Cleveland, Reginald. *Air Transport at War*. New York: Harper & Brothers, 1946.
Cline, Ray S. *United States Army in World War II: The War Department: Washington Command Post: The Operations Division*. Washington, DC: Center of Military History, 1990.
Coakley, Robert W., and Richard M. Leighton. *United States Army in World War II: The War Department: Global Logistics and Strategy, 1943–1945*. Washington, DC: Center of Military History, 1986.
Craven, Wesley Frank, and James Lea Cate. *The Army Air Forces in World War II: Volume I: Plans and Early Operations January 1939 to August 1942*. Washington, DC: Office of Air Force History, Government Printing Office, 1983.
_____. *The Army Air Forces in World War II: Volume V: The Pacific: Matterhorn to Nagasaki, June 1944 to August 1945*. Chicago: University of Chicago Press, 1953.
_____. *The Army Air Forces in World War II: Volume 6: Men and Planes*. Chicago: University of Chicago Press, 1958.

Bibliography

Daugherty, Leo J. *Fighting Techniques of a Japanese Infantryman, 1941–1945: Training, Techniques and Weapons.* St. Paul, MN: Motorbooks, 2002.
Dod, Karl C. *United States Army in World War II: The Technical Services: The Corps of Engineers: The War Against Japan.* Washington, DC: Office of the Chief of Military History, U.S. Army, 1966.
Dunlop, Richard. *Behind Enemy Lines: With the OSS in Burma.* Chicago: Rand McNally, 1979.
Ehrman, John. *Grand Strategy: Volume V: August 1943–September 1944.* London: HMSO, 1956.
Eldridge, Fred. *Wrath in Burma: The Uncensored Story of General Stilwell and International Maneuvers in the Far East.* New York: Doubleday, 1946.
Ethell, Jeff, and Don Downie. *Flying the Hump: In Original World War II Color.* St. Paul, MN: Motorbooks, 2004.
Feuer, A. B. *General Chennault's Secret Weapon: The B-24 in China.* Westport, CT: Praeger, 1992.
Fowle, Barry W., et al. *Builders and Fighters: U.S. Army Engineers in the World War II.* Fort Belvoir, VA: Office of History, U.S. Army Corps of Engineers, 1992.
Gailey, Harry A. *Bougainville: 1943–1945: The Forgotten Campaign.* Lexington: University of Kentucky Press, 1991.
Heiferman, Ron. *Flying Tigers: Chennault in China.* New York: Ballantine Books, 1971.
Hopkins, James E. T., and John M. Jones. *Spearhead: A Complete History of Merrill's Marauders.* Baltimore: Galahad Press, 1999.
Howard, Michael. *Grand Strategy: Volume IV: August 1942–September 1943.* London: HMSO, 1972.
Howton, Harry G., et al. *China Airlift — The Hump.* Dallas: Taylor, 1983.
Hoyt, Edwin P. *Merrill's Marauders.* Los Angeles: Pinnacle Books, 1980.
Khera, P. N. *Official History of the Indian Armed Forces in the Second World War: 1939–1945: 2 Volumes: The Reconquest of Burma.* Calcutta: Combined Inter-Services Historical Section, Orient Longmans, 1959.
Kimball, Warren F. *Churchill & Roosevelt: The Complete Correspondence: Volume I: Alliance Emerging: October 1933–November 1942.* Princeton, NJ: Princeton University Press, 1984.
_____. *Churchill and Roosevelt: The Complete Correspondence: II: Alliance Forged, November 1942–February 1944.* Princeton, NJ: Princeton University Press, 1984.
King, Benjamin, Richard C. Biggs, and Eric R. Criner. *Spearhead of Logistics: A History of the United States Transportation Corps.* Newport News, VA: U.S. Army Transportation Center, 1994.
King, William C. *Building for Victory: World War II in China, Burma, and India and the 1875th Engineer Aviation Battalion.* Lanham, MD: Taylor, 2004.
Kirby, Major General S. Woodburn. *History of the Second World War. The War Against Japan, Volume I: The Loss of Singapore.* New Delhi–London: Natraj Publishers/HMSO, 1957.
_____. *History of the Second World War: Volume II: India's Most Dangerous Hour.* London: HMSO, 1958.
_____. *History of the Second World War: Volume III: The Decisive Battles.* London: HMSO, 1962.
_____. *History of the Second World War: Volume IV: The Reconquest of Burma.* London: HMSO, 1965.
_____. *History of the Second World War: Volume V: The Surrender of Japan.* London: HMSO, 1969.
Kleber, Brooks, E., and Dale Birdsell. *United States Army in World War II: The Technical Services: The Chemical Warfare Service: Chemicals in Combat.* Washington, DC: Office of the Chief of Military History, U.S. Army, 1966.
Koenig, William. *Over the Hump: Airlift to China.* London: Pan/Ballantine Books, 1972.
Lee, Ulysses. *The United States Army: The Employment of Negro Troops.* Washington, DC: Center of Military History, 1994.
Lewin, Ronald. *Slim: The Standard Bearer.* London: Leo Cooper, 1976.
Long-hsuen, Hsu, and Chang Ming-kai. *History of the Sino-Japanese War. 1937–1945.* Taipei, Taiwan: Chung Wu, 1971.

Lopez, Donald S. *Into the Teeth of the Tiger.* Washington, DC: Smithsonian Institution Press, 1997.
Martin, John G. *It Began at Imphal: The Combat Cargo Story.* Manhattan, KS: Sunflower University Press, 1988.
_____, and Janet M. Thies. *China Airlift: The Hump, Volume 3.* Paducah, KY: Turner, 1992.
Melson, Charles D. *Condition Red: Marine Defense Battalions in World War II.* Washington, DC: History and Museums Division, 1996.
Merrill's Marauders: February–May 1944. Washington, DC: Historical Division, War Department, June 1945.
Miller, Charles E. *Airlift Doctrine.* Montgomery, AL: Maxwell Air Force Base, Air University Press, March 1988.
Motter, T. H. Vail. *United States Army in World War II: The Middle East Theater: The Persian Corridor and Aid to Russia.* Washington, DC: Department of the Army, Office of the Chief of Military History, 1952.
Ogburn, Charlton, Jr. *The Marauders.* New York: Harper & Brothers, 1959.
Palmer, Robert R., Bell I. Wiley, and William R. Keast. *United States Army in World War II: The Army Ground Forces: The Procurement and Training of Ground Combat Troops.* Washington, DC: Center of Military History, 1991.
Rasor, Eugene L., *The China-Burma-India Campaign, 1931–1945: Historiography and Annotated Bibliography.* Westport, CT: Greenwood Press, 1998.
Romanus, Charles R., and Riley Sunderland. *United States Army in World War II: China-Burma-India Theater: Stilwell's Mission to China.* Washington, DC: U.S. Army Center of Military History, Government Printing Office, 1987.
_____. *United States Army in World War II: China-Burma-India Theater: Stilwell's Command Problems.* Washington, DC: U.S. Army Center of Military History, Government Printing Office, 1987.
_____. *United States Army in World War II: China-Burma-India Theater: Time Runs Out in CBI.* Washington, DC: U.S. Army Center of Military History, 1999.
Rooney, D. D. *Stilwell.* New York: Ballantine Books, 1971.
Schaller, Michael. *The U.S. Crusade in China: 1936–1945.* New York: Columbia University Press, 1979.
Scott, Robert Lee. *Flying Tiger: Chennault of China.* New York: Doubleday, 1959.
Shaw, Henry I., and Ralph W. Donnelly. *Blacks in the Marine Corps.* Washington, DC: History and Museums Division, HQMC, 1975.
Stauffer, Alvin P. *United States Army in World War II: The Technical Services: The Quartermaster Corps: Operations in the War Against Japan.* Washington, DC: Headquarters, Department of the Army, Office of the Chief of Military History, 1956.
Tuchman, Barbara. *Stilwell and the American Experience in China, 1911–1945.* New York: Macmillan, 1970.
Tunner, William H. *Over the Hump.* Washington, DC: Office of Air Force History, 1985.
Wardlow, Chester. *United States Army in World War II: The Technical Services: The Transportation Corps: Responsibilities, Organization, and Operations.* Washington, DC: Headquarters, U.S. Army, Center of Military History, 1991.
Webster, Donovan. *The Burma Road.* New York: Perennial, 2004.
Whelan, Russell. *The Flying Tigers: The Story of the American Volunteer Group.* New York: Viking Press, 1943.
Williams, Mary H. *United States Army in World War II: Chronology: 1941–1945.* Washington, DC: Center of Military History, 1994.

The China-Burma-India (CBI) Hump Pilot Association Newsletter

Adams, Eugene D. "Reminiscences." Autumn 1992, p. 8.
Barnard, Tom. "American Airline ATC Personnel Received Official Credit for WWII Service: 'Burma Roadster.'" Autumn 1991, pp. 21–3.

Bibliography

Beamon, James. "Christmas, 50 Years Ago." Spring 1995, pp. 22–3.
Chandler, Lieutenant Dennis G. "Reminiscences." Winter 1991, pp. 4–6.
Crumpacker, Ed. "Reminiscences." Spring 1994, pp. 18–9.
Cucio, Major Sam. "Reminiscences." Autumn 1991, pp. 10–1.
Douglas, Donald W. "Speech of Donald W. Douglas." Winter 1991.
Fair, V. "The Man with the Wrench." Autumn 1993, p. 27.
Fang, Mrs. Lui. "Do You Know About the Flight Over the Hump?" Winter 1993–4, pp. 27–8.
Garcia, Frank. "Reminiscences of CBI." Winter 1991, pp. 3–4.
Glines, Colonel C. V., USAF (ret.). "Flying the Hump." Autumn 1991, pp. 25–6.
Heckinger, Lieutenant Ruth Firsching. "Army Nurse Diary." Autumn 1993, pp. 12–3.
Hoisinger, Major General Perry M., USAF (ret.), and Colonel Raymond K. Childress, USAF (ret.). "Appreciation for a Tough Job Well Done." Autumn 1993, pp. 20–1.
Jones, John F. "SOP for Bailing Out or Crash Landing: Before or at Landing." Autumn 1991.
Kaplan, Alex. "Reminiscences." Winter 1995, p. 12.
King, First Lieutenant Royce A., USAAF. "Mission to a Prison Camp." Summer 1995.
Lang, Lieutenant Alfred. "Reminiscences." Autumn 1993, pp. 26–7.
Lewallen, Ray. "Reminiscences." Summer 1994, p. 5.
Legas, Sherman. "Reminiscences." Winter 1995, p. 12.
Linenbach, Clarence "Linn." "Reminiscences." Autumn 1992, pp. 26–7.
Newell, Merlin C. "The Yank in India." Autumn 1991, pp. 23–5.
Norell, Major Glen, USAF (ret). "Bail Out Over Burma." Winter 1991, pp. 2–3.
Sigrist, Herman K. "Reminiscences." Autumn 1993, p. 28.
Stumpf, Robert A. "Stumpy." "Lost: Courtesy of the Hump." Summer 1993, pp. 8–9.
Tengg, Tommy C. "Remember the 'Over the Hump' Flight." Winter 1995, pp. 13–4.
Underbrink, Richard. "Request of Copy of the 'Aluminum Trial.'" Winter 1994/1995, p. 20.
Vierling, Frank R. "Frank R. Vierling: 'Reminiscences.'" Winter 1991, p. 4.
Yarger, Don. "Reminiscences of CBI." Winter 1991, p. 16.
Welch, Lieutenant Colonel Dempsey W., USAF (ret.). "Diary of Lieutenant Colonel Welch, USAF. Ret.)." Winter 1991-1992, pp. 18–9.

Index

1st Battalion 131, 194, 195, 196
1st Combat Cargo Command Group 15, 79, 86, 88
1st Platoon 195
2nd Combat Cargo Group 15, 79
2nd Troop Carrier Squadron 189
3rd Combat Cargo Command 65, 100
3rd Combat Cargo Command Group 65, 79, 83, 176
3rd Combat Cargo Squadron (1st Group) 15, 191, 233
3rd Group 211
3rd Platoon 195
Third Tactical Air Force 189
4th Combat Cargo Command 65, 71, 79, 80, 81, 86, 92, 100, 102
4th Combat Cargo Group 15, 20, 67, 71, 79, 80, 83, 85, 89, 91, 97, 99, 102, 176, 209, 251
5th Indian Division 83
7th Bomb Group 52, 176
Tenth Air Force Headquarters 244
Tenth Air Service Command Depot 163
10th Engineers 117
Tenth U.S. Air Force 13, 52, 64, 189, 200
11th Brigade 78
12th Airdrome Squadron 176
12th Bomber Group 211
12th Combat Cargo Squadron 83, 211
13th Squadron 251
14th Air Force 12, 38, 60, 165, 168, 176, 193, 205, 218
14th Army 11, 104
14th Combat Cargo Squadron 71, 78, 209
14th Division 99
14th Squadron 67, 79, 251
15th Corps 86
15th Squadron 251
16th Combat Cargo Squadron 4th Group 216
16th Squadron 251
18th Imperial Japanese Army 110
XIX Corps 194
XX Air Force 89, 110, 133, 168, 170, 175, 193, 223, 224, 240

XX Bomber Command 98
20th U.S. Army Air Force 239
22nd Division 99
25th Infantry 195, 195
25th (Infantry) Regimental Combat Team 194, 196
26th Quartermaster Truck Regiment 29
37th Infantry Division 194
43rd Squadron 211
44th Air Service Group 237, 238, 239
45th Combat Engineers 114, 186
45th Engineer General Service Regiment (Combat) 127, 185
45th General Service 139
45th Quartermaster Regiment 128
45th Regiment 186
51st Base Group's 54th Air Base Squadron 159
52nd Air Service Group 239
58th Bomb Wing 224
59th Material Squadron 159
60th Laundry Company 189
60th Ordnance Company 186
71st Light Pontoon Company 125, 134, 197
75th Squadron 160
76th Light Pontoon Company 125
76th Ordnance Base Depot 139
77th Brigade 78
77th Light Pontoon Company 125
92nd Division 181
93rd Cavalry Reconnaissance 195
93rd Division 181, 193, 194
97th Transport Squadron, 28th Group 64
110th Ship Convoy 145
112th Regiment 118
114th Regiment 118
130th AACS 209
187th Composite Chemical Company 141, 147, 150, 153
209th Combat Engineer Battalion 118
236th Combat Engineer Battalion 134
308th Bomb Group 176
308th Squadron 59, 60
330th Combat Engineers 125

330th Engineers 117, 123
332nd Troop Carrier Squadron 211
333rd Troop Carrie Squadron 211
352nd Engineer Regiment 191
434th Bomb Squadron 211
443rd Troop Carrier Command (TCC) 188
443rd Troop Carrier Group 176
462nd Bombardier Group 223
475th Infantry Regiment 43
479th Maintenance Company 117
493rd Bomb Squadron 52
513th Group 211
516th Quartermaster Truck Regiment 243
518th Aviation Battalion 197
518th Quartermaster Battalion (Mobile) 186, 189, 190, 191
823rd Engineers 127, 185, 197
849th Aviation Battalions 117
858th Engineer Aviation Battalion 192, 193, 197
1009th Signal Company 239
1080th Quartermaster Company 239
1111th Signal Company 237, 238, 239
1327th Engineer General Service Regiment 191
1345 Army Air Forces 155
1348th AAFBU 235
1573rd Ordinance Supply and Maintenance Company 239
1574th Ordinance Supply and Maintenance Company 239
1875th Engineer Aviation Battalion 112, 114, 136, 139
1883rd Aviation Battalion 117, 125
1905th Engineer Aviation Battalion 117
2116th Quartermaster Company 239
2117th Quartermaster Company 239
3304th Truck Company 191
3477th Ordnance Company 189
3841st Quartermaster Truck Regiment 189
3949th Quartermaster Truck Company 24, 25
5307th Composite Unit 35, 127, 142, 149, 150
5332nd Brigade 35

Actual Instrument Flying (AI) 14
ADF 55
Adaman Islands 75
Adams, Eugene "Gene" D. 216
Adler, Brigadier General Elmer E. 159
Advanced Twin Engine School 233
African Americans 181, 182
Air Corps Ferrying Command 199
Air Force Entrance Examination 65
Air Force History 203
Air Force's Reconnaissance 61
Air Maintenance Division 158
Air Research and Development Command 61
Air Service Command 13, 159, 201
Air Service Command Depot 163
Air Training Command 200

Aircraft types: B-17 Flying Fortresses 49, 66; B-24 Liberator 14, 47, 49, 51, 55, 56, 57, 60, 61, 62, 64, 66, 86, 97, 155, 160, 200, 241; B-25 49, 60, 211; B-26 "Martin Marauders" 49, 66, 88; B-29 (bomber) 44, 106, 110, 112, 120, 133, 209, 221, 222, 223, 225, 240, 241; B-29 Bombardiering School 211; C-9s 66; C-17 66; C-46 14, 49, 51, 60, 67, 68, 71, 78, 81, 84, 86, 87, 97, 100, 102, 151, 154, 160, 165, 171, 186, 190, 191, 200, 201, 202, 205, 208, 217, 230, 241; C-46 Outfits 238; C-47 11, 14, 34, 49, 51, 60, 64, 67, 78, 83, 84, 86, 87, 88, 97, 100, 102, 151, 160, 165, 171, 186, 189, 190, 200, 201, 202, 209, 230, 233, 238, 241, 244, 245; C-53 230; C-54 (Skymaster) 154, 156, 157, 160, 165, 171, 202, 222, 225; C-87s 14, 47, 51, 61, 64, 160, 163, 205, 206, 219, 241; C-109 51, 154, 155, 160, 168, 169, 170, 171, 180; "Dakota" 215, 241; "Dakotas" 11, 84; DC-2 230; DC-3 12, 64, 215, 230; DC-4 171; Mitchell B-25 61; P-39 Aircobra 161; P-40 7; P-40E Warhawk 161, 164; P-47 219; P-400 Aircobra 161; Air Commando Group, 78
Akyab 188
Al Hindi, Mahmoud 215
Alexander, Colonel Edward H. 200
Allison, Chuck 54
Aluminum Trail 14, 49, 62
American Airlines 20, 161
American Airways 12
American, British, Dutch, Australian Supreme Command (ABDACOM) 13
American Expeditionary Forces (AEF) 181
American Volunteer Group (AVG) 3, 7, 63, 88, 160, 225
Anakim 85
Andaman Islands 18
Andrews Air Force Base 61
Anvil 75
Anzio, Italy 141
Arakan Campaign 190
Arcadia Conference 6, 9
Army Air Corps 65, 208, 209, 216, 235
Army Air Force Headquarters 59
Army Air Forces (USAAF) 23, 168, 205
Army Corps of Engineers Research and Development Lab 61
Army Ground Forces (AGF) 107, 108, 136, 142, 143, 144
Army Plan 184
Army Quartermaster 29
Army Service Forces (ASF) 36, 40, 147
Army's Protective Mobilization Plan (PMP) 184
Arnold, General Henry "Hap" 72, 94, 216
Arrowsmith, Brigadier General John C. 115, 127, 186
Ascension Island 216
Asmara 235

Index 269

Assam 14, 191
Assam-Burma-China Ferry Command 12, 13, 20, 49, 63, 105, 112, 186
Assam-Burma Ferry 77
Assam-Burma Ferry Command 35, 47, 49, 64, 72, 154
Assam Valley 219
Atlantic City, New Jersey 154
Auchinlek, General Sir Claude 75
Australia 46
AVG Chief Flight Surgeon Gentry 166

Baird, Lt. Colonel Stuart D. 71, 91
Baldwin, Staff Sergeant 80, 94, 104
Bangkok, Thailand 232
Barl 229
Barnard, Flight Officer Tom 205, 161
Barry, Joe 206
Bashaboy 92
Bataan 235
Battle for Burma 16
Beamon, Jim 239
Beechcraft 66
Beightler, Brigadier General Robert 194
Berger, Capt. Morris 246
Bermuda Triangle 231
Bhamo 130
Blackie's Gang 201
Blackmore 229
Boehm, Grace 46
Boehm, Robert 2, 24, 25, 26, 27, 29
Bohr 229
Bolero 16
Bolling, "Monk" 205
Bombay 213
Bonin Islands 133
Bostwick, Lt. 233
Bougainville 193, 194, 196, 197
Bowman Field 209
Brady, Brigadier General Francis M. 13
Bray, Captain Leslie W. 216
Brereton, Major General Lewis H. 63, 77, 85, 200
British Chiefs of Staff 76
British Chiefs of the Imperial General Staff 2, 5
British XVth Corps 77
British 5th Division 78
British Fourteenth Army 36, 64, 72, 80, 168
British-Gurkha 78
British 10th Army 71, 83
British 26th Division 78
Brook-Popham, Vice Marshal Sir Robert 7
Brooke, Field Marshal Lord Alan 5, 6, 9, 33, 106, 112, 133, 247, 253
Brown, Col. Rothwell H. 125
Buffalo, New York 154
Burma 112
Burma-Ledo Road 3, 4, 36, 40, 43, 72, 77, 132, 133, 139, 178

Burma Road 9, 11, 44, 73, 84, 106, 107, 114, 128, 131, 136, 137, 139, 140, 191, 192, 197, 200
Burma Roadster 207

Cairo Conference 5, 64
Calcutta 36, 45, 158, 213, 238
Caltlen 229
Camp Aanchabara 147, 149
Camp Chaffee 218
Camp Claiborne 142, 143, 144, 145
Camp Lee, Virginia 25
Camp Mackall 216
Camp Patrick Henry, Virginia 212, 238
Camp Shapiro 45
Cannon, Brigadier Gen. Robert M. 35
Carrier Groups 65
Carter 238
Casablanca 145
Casablanca Conference 16, 34, 71
CATF 166
CBI Border 225
CBI Theater of Operations 19, 20, 33, 36, 226
CCS 99, 105, 106
Central Pacific Area 18
Central Public Works Department 174
Chandler, Lt. Dennis G. 211
Chandra-di Sabu 174
Chanute Field 163
Chemical Corps 142, 143, 144, 145
Chemical Ground Service 146
Chemical Warfare Series 198
Chemical Warfare Service 146
Chemical Warfare Service Replacement Training Center 143
Chengkung 241
Chengtu 212, 219, 223
Chennault, Major General Claire Lee 3, 5, 7, 13, 17, 18, 19, 34, 35, 38, 39, 49, 59, 63, 71, 72, 73, 88, 106, 110, 112, 114, 119, 137, 160, 161, 166, 172, 176, 199, 205, 218, 221, 225, 247, 256; China Air Task Force 3, 199; Fourteenth Air Force 9, 13, 17, 35, 64, 71, 72, 106, 154, 162, 164, 166, 168, 170; secret weapon 49
Chi Chiang 16, 18, 19, 20, 39, 112, 114, 119, 113, 211
Chiang Kai-shek, Generalissimo 1, 2, 3, 4, 5, 6, 8, 11, 12, 14, 16, 17, 18, 20, 19, 34, 38, 39, 47, 64, 71, 72, 73, 76, 85, 106, 112, 114, 119, 132, 133, 135, 140, 160, 164, 166, 167, 175, 176, 177, 193, 198, 200, 205; Nationalist Army 5; Nationalist Chinese Forces 65; Nationalist Forces 9, 64, 65, 199, 106, 168, 205, 154, 172, 176
Chief of Imperial General Staff 112
Chief of Staff to the Minister of Defense 6
Childress, Colonel Raymond K. 223
Chin Hills 227

China 110, 191, 229
China-Burma-India Campaign 24
China-Burma-India (CBI) Theater 3, 8, 19, 20, 33, 51, 60, 61, 68, 104, 138, 140, 155, 163, 168, 171, 172, 180, 182, 186, 197, 198, 203, 212, 215, 221, 226
China Theater 134
Chindits 15, 35, 75, 78, 150, 189
Chindwin River 75
Chindwin River Valley 199
Chinese Army Air Corps 228
Chinese Army 66th Regiment 125
Chinese Civil Aviation 230
Chinese Civil War 16
Chinese Communist Troops 108, 123
Chinese 14th Division 175
Chinese "Humpster" 224
Chinese Minister of Foreign Affairs 134
Chinese National Aircraft Corporation (CNAC) 228
Chinese Nationalist Leader 200
Chinese 113th Regiment 127
Chinese 6th Army Headquarters 99
Chinese Soldiers 178
Chinese 38th Division 43, 118, 119, 125, 127, 149
Chinese 22nd Division 127, 149, 175
Chittagong 63, 91, 217
Christinson, Lt. General Sir Philip 77
Christler, Mel 163
Chu, H.W. 229
Chungking 7
Churchill, Winston 1, 2, 5, 6, 8, 9, 16, 17, 19, 73, 74, 76, 77, 78, 89, 104, 105, 112, 114, 119, 120, 133, 167, 172, 201, 247
Clark 238
CNAC 228, 230
Cole, Lt. 239
Combat Support (CS) 182
Combined Chiefs of Staff (CCS) 17, 19, 22, 34, 35, 64, 71, 74, 105, 112, 184
Combined Joint Chiefs of Staff 1, 16
Commando 241
Commonwealth 9
Communist 136
Company B 134
Company F, 2nd Battalion, 25th Infantry 194
Company K, 3rd Battalion, 25th Infantry 194, 195, 196, 197
"Confusion Beyond Imagination" 104, 180
Corregidor 235
Corridor Operation 29
Cortright, Staff Sergeant James H. 100
Crumpacker, Ed 227
Culverin 75
Curcio, Major Samuel "Sam" A. 218
Currie, Lauchlin 11
Curtis C-46 Factory Plant 154
Curtiss C-46 Transports 35, 65, 200

d'Ailoia, Vic 206
DeRoach, Lt. 246
Desert-Shield-Desert Storm 62
Dien Bien Phu 16
Dill, Field Marshal Sir John 13
Doolittle, Jimmy 48
Douglas, Donald W. 215
Douglas Aircraft Corporation 215
Douglas C-54 226
Douglas C-54 Transport 225
Downie, First Lieutenant Don 175
Dracula 18
Dum Dum 63, 79, 92

East Irrawaddy River 199
Eisenhower, General Dwight D. 75
Engineers Corps 184
Ethiopia 235
European Theatres of Operation (ETO) 182

Fair, Corporal V. 177
Fang, Mrs. 224
Federal Aviation Administration (FAA) 180
Ferry (Ferrying) Command 51, 200
Fireball Express 163
First Indochina War 16
Flickinger, Lt. Col. Dan 201
Flying Tigers 39, 47, 63, 88, 199, 222, 225, 250
Fog, Private Wade 194
Fong, B. 229
Forman, John D. "Red" 202
Formosa (Taiwan) 15, 17, 35, 106, 110
Fort Hertz 11
Fort Leonard Wood 107, 108
Fort Lewis 153
Fort Meyers, Virginia 238
Fort Monmouth 238
Fort Sutton, North Carolina 107
4.2 Stokes Mortar 141, 142, 145
Foye, Master Sergeant Robert 161, 166
French Indochina (Vietnam) 37
Friedman, Bob 241

Gandhi, Mahatma 166
Garcia, Frank 209
USS *General Butner* 238
USS *General Sherman* 45
Gentry, Colonel Thomas 166
George, General Harold 163, 201
Glines, Colonel C.V. 199
Golden Pan 229
Goodman, Capt. Edward 2, 14, 23, 47, 49, 61, 64, 95
Goodman, Mary 61
Goodrich, Jack D. 235
Goony Bird 215
Gray, Captain 45
Great Britain 229

Green, Lt. Col. William J. 117
Griswold, General Oscar W. 194, 195
Guadalcanal 150, 193
Gulfport, Mississippi 154
Gurkhas 78

Hainan 136
Hall, Amy 103
Hall, Capt. David C. 1, 2, 15, 23, 65, 66
Hampton Roads, Virginia 145, 212
Handy, General Thomas T. 136
Harmer 229
Harmon, Lt. General Millard P. 194
Hawaii 46
Haynes, Cap. Elmer H. 49, 52, 53, 54, 55, 56, 57, 61; B-24 53
Headquarters 159
Headquarters Squadron 159
Heckinger, Lt. Ruth Firsching 222
Hellbird Group 223
Hicks, Lt. Col. William E. 119
Himalayas 23, 208, 224, 225
Hindustan Civil Air Plant 174
Hoag, Brigadier General Earl S. 201
Hoffman 246
Hoisington, Major General Perry M. 223
Hovick, Hiram, T. 245
Hughen, Walt 206
Hukawng Valley 121, 123, 149, 189
Hump 14, 15, 17, 18, 37, 47, 51, 55, 62, 87, 158
Hump-Flying 56
Hunt, Capt. Toby 207
Huong, B. 229

Ichi Go Offensive 175, 176
Imphal-Kohima Road 232
India-China Division 202
Indian National Congress 121
Indian 17th Division 83
Infantry Corps 184
International Diesels 29
Iranian State Railroad 26
Irrawaddy Offensive 211
Irrawaddy River 38, 199, 110
Ismay, Major General Sir Hastings 6, 247
Iwo Jima 105, 133

James, Capt. Bill 205
Jap Figher 214
Japanese Air Force 72
Jap Zeroes 213, 214
Japanese High Command 4
Japanese Kwangtung Army 133
Japanese Army: 15th Army 77, 78; 18th Army 72, 77, 78; 18th Division 118
Joint Allied Military Council 4
Joint Chiefs of Staff (JCS) 16, 105
Jones, Mr. (British Civil Affairs officer) 203, 246
Jordan, Robert Captain 219

Kachins 246
Kalista, Stephen 237, 238
Kaplan, Alex 231
Karachi, India 102, 103, 147
Kentucky 67
Kenya Colony 238
Ketchum, Hank 233
Khartoum 216, 236
Kick Master 191
Kickers 189
King, Captain 136, 139
King, Admiral Ernest J. 16, 17
King, Lt. Royce A. 233
King, Lt. William C. 112, 114, 117, 121, 128, 130, 131, 132, 136; 1875 Aviation Battalion 114, 115
Knaack, Lt. 233, 234
Kohima Ridge 15
Koolson, Capt. 229
Korea 23, 62, 233
Korean War 197
Kunming 4, 14, 15, 22, 36, 37, 54, 56, 97, 133, 134, 136, 138, 168, 191, 197, 199, 210, 218, 219, 222, 223, 233
Kunmon Mountains 199
Kurmitola 157, 221

LaGuardia airways 232
Lakeland Community Pool 238
Lang, Alfred "Al" 221
Lashio 9, 229
Lashuka 125
Lecompte, Jim 207
Ledo, India 11, 40, 106, 191, 192
Ledo Road 21, 64, 106, 109, 110, 114, 115, 118, 120, 121, 127, 128, 136, 138, 139, 140, 185, 192, 197, 253
Ledo-Burma Road 132, 133, 182, 186, 198
Lee, F.C. 228
Legas, Sherman 232
Lend-Lease 3, 7, 11, 25
Lewallen, Ray, T/Sgt. 191, 233, 259
Lewis, Ted 207
"Liberator Express" 51
Lilly, Sgt. 239
Linebach, Clarence "Linn" 219
Lopez, First Lieutenant Donald S. 164
Louisville, Kentucky 20, 67, 68, 209
Luliang 233
Luliang Army Air Base 173

Ma, K.L. 229
MacArthur, General Douglas 77, 188, 189, 194; Southwest Pacific Forces 77
Mack Diesels 29, 40
Magruder, Brigadier General John 7
Mainland Japan 223
Makaw 125
Malay Peninsula 3, 4
Mall, Lt. 246

Mandalay 4, 9, 75
Marauders 252
Marine Corps (United States) 183, 257
S.S. *Marine Panther* 239
Mars Task Force 131, 215
Marshall, General George C. 4, 6, 9, 11, 16, 17, 18, 20, 71, 72, 73, 89, 133, 134, 136, 176, 194, 254
Marshall, Col. Ralph S. 47, 52, 54, 55, 56, 61
Martin B-26 Marauder 48, 50
Martin Marauders 48, 66
"Maytag Washing Machines" 214
Mayu Peninsular 75
McCloy, John J. (Undersecretary of War) 195
McDonnell, Mr. 228, 238
McIsaac, Col. Kenneth 118
McNair, Lieutenant General Lesley J. 142, 145
McVean, Alexander 2, 23
Mekong River 120, 199
Melbourne 213
Merrill, Brigadier Gen. Frank D. 43, 64, 127, 142, 149, 151, 191
Merrill's Marauders 11, 15, 35, 42, 43, 82, 84, 107, 110, 127, 129, 131, 142, 150, 151, 189, 191, 212, 214, 249, 255
Missouri Air National Guard 61
Mogaung 125
Molkenthen, Capt. 239
Mombassa Harbor 238
Mongolia 224
Moonai, Sydney 229
Morris, Lt. John R. 246
Morrison Field 216
Motor Transport Service 191; 516th Quartermaster Truck Regiment 29; 517th Quartermaster Truck Regiment 29
Mountbatten, Admiral Lord Louis 5, 16, 17, 19, 64, 72, 74, 75, 76, 79, 80, 85, 89, 134, 169, 188; Southeast Asia Command (SEAC) 147
Mullet, Col. DeWitt T. 133
Myers 246
Myitkyina 4, 9, 11, 14, 35, 54, 75, 76, 79, 88, 91, 99, 102, 106, 110, 112, 118, 120, 121, 127, 129, 130, 134, 142, 151, 171, 191, 211, 212, 213, 221, 226, 229, 233, 235, 239
Myitkyina-Mogaung Road 246
Myitkyina-South 99

NAACP 184
Naiden, Brigadier General Earl L. 12
Nationalist Chinese 7, 212, 136, 193
Nationalist Chinese Army 72
Nationalist Troops 108
Negro Soldiers 183
New Deli 14
New Guinea 150
New Zealand Forces 64
Newell, Merlin C. 167
Norell, Major Glenn 208

North Africa 142, 145, 146, 147, 179, 241
North Burma Air Task Force 100
Northern Solomons 133
Northwest Airlines 20
Northwest Europe 182

O'Connor, Chuck 206
Okinawa 46, 105, 133
Oliver, Colonel Robert C. 13, 159
Opencensky, Lt. H 239
"Operation Buccaneer" 75
"Operation Culverin" 76
"Operation Elephant" 99
"Operation Grubworm" 65, 99, 175
"Operation Gymnast" 12
"Operation Jackrabbit" 65
"Operation Matterhorn" 17, 133
"Operation Overlord" 16, 75
"Operation Pipeline" 232
"Operation Rooster" 175
"Operation Shingle" 141
"Operation Sledgehammer" 13
"Operation Tarzan" 75
"Operation Torch" 12
Oran, North Africa 147
Ordnance Corps 198
Organized Reserves 183
OSS 100, 232, 259

Palaus 133
Panama Canal 212
Pearl Harbor 4, 8, 229
Pershing, John J. 181
Persia (Iran) 40, 191
Persian Corridor 20, 24, 29
Persian Gulf 23, 29
Persians 27
Philips, Mr. 229
Pick, Brigadier Gen. 133, 134
Pick, Col. Lewis A. 115, 117, 118, 125
Pieper, 1st Lieutenant Wilfred R. 216
Plan D 8
Pock, Lieutenant Hugh A. 134
Point of Embarkation (POE) 68
Porter, Capt. John L. "Blackie" 201
Pricer, Major Donald C. 202
Production Line Maintenance (PLM) 156, 157, 158, 159, 168
Project 7-A 12, 20, 23, 161, 205, 206, 207

Quadrant Conference 1, 5, 15, 16, 19, 20, 22, 23, 34, 73, 97, 106, 107, 110, 119
Quartermaster Corps 184, 198
Quebec 20, 34, 106
Quigley, Kenneth 2, 23

Radio Operator and Mechanic School 209
Rainbow 5, 8
Ramgarh Training Center 257
Rangoon 4, 106, 217, 229

Index

Raymer, Ralph, M. 212
Red Army 25
Red River Valley 37
Regular Army 183
Reynolds, Lt. Richard "Pop" 65, 68, 85, 90, 104
Robertson, Captain 228
Rock Pile 49
Rommel, Field Marshal Erwin 179
Roosevelt, Eleanor 184
Roosevelt, Franklin D. (FDR) 6, 8, 9, 11, 16, 17, 18, 19, 48, 72, 73, 74, 76, 77, 78, 119, 120, 167, 172, 176, 201
Roosevelt Air Field, Mineola 48
Roswell, New Mexico 211
R/OY.S.Liu 229
R/OY.W.Fie 229
Royal Air Force (RAF) 7, 11, 166, 190
Royal Canadian Air Force 48
Royal Engineers 174
Russians 26, 29
Ryukus 105, 133

Salina, Kansas 222
Salween River 197, 199
Satellite Test Center 61
Scholff 229
Scoones, Lt. General Geoffrey 78
Scott, Colonel Robert Lee 222
Scovell, Major Gen. W.E.R. 34
SCR-522 (VHF Radio) 239
Seedlock, Lieutenant Colonel Robert F. 134
Service of Supply (SOS) 13, 17, 34, 218
Sevareid, Eric 201
Sextant Conference 75, 97, 106, 107, 120
Shack Rat 68, 104
Sheng, T.J. 229
Sheridan, Ann 140
Shield-Desert Storm 62
Shull, Charles M. 212
Sigrist, Herman K. 221
Silva, Anthony 2, 23
Sino-Japanese conflict 7
Sioux City Falls, South Dakota 209
Slidell, Louisiana 142
Slim, Lt. General William J. 11, 15, 36, 64, 72, 86, 104, 211; 14th Army 11, 35, 133, 176, 189
Smith, Brigadier General Cyrus R. (C.R.) 95, 201, 215
Solomon Islands 133
Somervell, Lt. General Brehon B. 36
Sookerating 232
Soong, T.V. 11, 134, 136
SOS Transportation Service 34
Southeast Asia Command (SEAC) 5, 19, 64, 74, 134, 169, 188
Southwest Area 18
Southwest Pacific 163, 166
Southwest Pacific Area (SWPA) 182, 186, 189, 194, 196

Soviet Union 191
Stalin, Joseph 16
Stalingrad 26, 29
Stallings, 2nd Lieutenant John A. 216
Standard Oil of New Jersey 202
Staulcup, Harry 219
Sterlimg, Sergeant H.C. 173
Stimson, Henry 195
Stilwell, Lt. General Joseph W. "Vinegar Joe" 4, 5, 11, 13, 14, 16, 17, 18, 19, 22, 34, 63, 64, 71, 72, 73, 74, 76, 77, 79, 94, 110, 115, 117, 118, 119, 121, 125, 133, 134, 137, 139, 140, 147, 149, 176, 191, 193, 218, 249, 257; 30-Division Plan 19; Y Force 77
Stilwell Road 36, 135, 140, 192
Stratemeyer, General George E. 89, 176
Studebaker Diesels 29, 40
Stumpf, Robert A. "Stumpy" 225
Suez Canal 25, 147
Suifoo Sichuan Province 229
Sultan, General Daniel I. 134

Tanai River 123
Tarung River 118
Task Force 9156, 193
Tehran 25
Tengg, Tommy C.C. 228
Tongwa, John 244, 245, 246
Trans World Airlines 20
Transient Depot 145
Trident Conference 5, 6, 15, 16, 17, 19, 20, 23, 34, 71, 73, 85, 172, 176
Triest, Lt. Carl 48
Tunner, General William H. 14, 156, 157, 159, 176, 200, 201, 202
Turberville, Lt. 246

U.S. Air Force 203, 208
U.S. Army 29, 199
U.S. Army Air Corps 48
U.S. Army Air Forces (USAAF) 7, 12, 20, 42, 47, 48, 62, 71, 158, 198, 199, 203, 205; Air Transport Command (ATC) 12, 15, 17, 20, 21, 22, 51, 65, 72, 77, 78, 79, 86, 95, 97, 98, 99, 100, 104, 119, 122, 123, 137, 154, 157, 158, 159, 160, 162, 163, 171, 172, 173, 175, 176, 186, 189, 198, 200, 201, 205, 208, 211, 213, 217, 218, 221, 223, 224; Combat Cargo 35, 65, 67, 80, 217, 238; Combat Service Support Units (CSS) 182; Mechanic School 154
U.S. Army EE-5 Telephone 238
U.S. Army Quartermaster Corps 24, 29
U.S. Army Signal Corps 209, 237
U.S. Army Transport Command 200
U.S. Lend-Lease 25
U.S. Marines 133
U.S. Navy 45
U.S. Persian Gulf Command's Motor Transport Service (MTS) 25, 26, 29
U.S. Tenth Air Force 188

Vierling, Frank R. 209
Vietnam 23, 62
Vietnam War 193, 197
V-J Day 179, 197
Volga 26

Wainwright, General Jonathan 235, 259
Wallawbum 127
Wallen, Capt. 229
Wallson, Son 229
Wanaw, Sin 245, 246
War Department 20, 157, 183, 184, 196
Wavell, Field Marshall 16
Wavell, General Sir Archibald 7, 8, 11, 19, 166, 174
Wedemeyer, Lt. General Albert C. 21, 34, 89, 99, 176, 193
Welch, Lt. Colonel Dempsey W. 212
West Palm Beach, Florida 216
Wezzie 226
Wheeler, Major General Raymond A. 13, 17, 19, 20, 35, 63; Ferry Command 63; Service of Supply 13, 19
White, Lt. Colonel Robert B. "Bruce" 156, 201

Whitford, Joe 206
Wilbur, Colonel 216
Wilbur, Major Walter F. 216
Wilkinson, Lawrence, A. 212
Wilson, Field Marshall Henry 89
Wilson, Brigadier Gen. Thomas B. 34
Wingate, Brigadier Orde 15, 75, 78, 79, 142, 189; Chindits 35, 79, 81, 189; 16th Long-Range Penetration Group 78, 189
Woodham 246
World War I 194
World War II 197
Wright Patterson Air Force Base 61
Wu Zidan 224

Y Force 76
Y-Plan 13
Yellow Sea 233
Yoke (Y) Force 73
Yunnan (Providence) 75, 230
Yupang Ga 119, 121

Zedong, Mao 18, 36, 177
Zeros 207

www.ingramcontent.com/pod-product-compliance
Lightning Source LLC
Chambersburg PA
CBHW021341230426
43666CB00006B/367